Rites of Passage

Also by Judith Flanders

JUDITH FLANDERS

Rites of Passage

Death and Mourning in
Victorian Britain

PICADOR

First published 2024 by Picador
an imprint of Pan Macmillan
The Smithson, 6 Briset Street, London ECIM 5NR
EU representative: Macmillan Publishers Ireland Ltd, 1st Floor,
The Liffey Trust Centre, 117–126 Sheriff Street Upper,
Dublin 1, DOI YC43
Associated companies throughout the world
www.panmacmillan.com

ISBN 978-1-5098-1697-2

1 3 5 7 9 8 6 4 2

A CIP catalogue record for this book is available from the British Library.

Typeset by Palimpsest Book Production Limited, Falkirk, Stirlingshire
Printed and bound by CPI Group (UK) Ltd, Croydon, CRO 4YY

Visit **www.picador.com** to read more about all our books
and to buy them. You will also find features, author interviews and
news of any author events, and you can sign up for e-newsletters
so that you're always first to hear about our new releases.

For my sisters
Susan and Elle
and
in memory of my mother
Kappy Flanders –
a life force

Contents

List of Illustrations

PLATE SECTION

5. Fashion magazines illustrated what the well-dressed court mourner was wearing after the death of Princess Charlotte. (By courtesy of the author)

6. Manufacturers produced china tea-sets and other souvenirs to commemorate the dead princess. (© Victoria & Albert Museum, London)

7. In the House of Commons in 2022 MPs gather to pay their respects after the death of Queen Elizabeth II. (PA Images / Alamy Stock Photo)

8. Ring with hair insert. (© Victoria & Albert Museum, London)

9. A woman's long hair was frequently cut off, and then the entire length could be made into a watch-chain. (© Victoria & Albert Museum, London)

10. Richard Redgrave, *Preparing to Throw Off Her Weeds* (1845) (V&A, Given by John Sheepshanks, 1857)

11. The painter Henry Wallis found his first great success with *The Death of Chatterton* (1856). (Tate, London, 2011)

12. Louis-Édouard Fournier, *The Funeral of the Poet Shelley* (1889). (Louis-Édouard Fournier)

13. William Mumler was renowned for his spirit photographs, and in 1872 the ghost of Abraham Lincoln was said to have appeared in time to be photographed by him with the murdered president's widow, Mary Todd Lincoln. (William H. Mumler, Original CDV held by The Lincoln Financial Foundation Collection, Fort Wayne, IN)

14. The wedding of the Prince of Wales to Princess Alexandra of Denmark, held unusually in St George's Chapel, Windsor, to permit the Queen to continue to isolate herself three years after the death of Prince Albert. (William Powell Frith, Painted for Queen Victoria)

15. Queen Victoria, with her love of commemorative items, had the baby teeth of her youngest child, Princess Beatrice, made into a pendant and earrings shaped like fuchsia. (Royal Collection Trust / © His Majesty King Charles III 2023)

Introduction

One summer's day in 1836, so the story goes, a group of schoolboys went hunting for rabbits on Arthur's Seat, a hill to the east of Edinburgh Castle from which the walker can appreciate a panoramic view of the Scottish capital. The boys had little interest in the views, even less when they noticed a tiny opening in the rock face itself. Inside what appeared to be a small cave, they found a series of wooden boxes, piled up in two rows of eight, with one single box on top. The boys began to play with this new amusement, as boys will, tossing the boxes back and forth, before finally hurling them at each other with force.

These boxes were tiny, each less than 10.5 centimetres long, 3 centimetres across, and 2.5 centimetres deep, in shape very much like miniature coffins. Which comes as less of a surprise when they were opened to reveal that that is exactly what they were: inside each one was a small wooden figure dressed in knee breeches and boots, carved face with eyes wide open, staring blankly at, presumably, a group of unnerved boys. (See plate section.) The boys therewith abandoned the coffins, leaving them to be retrieved later by their tutor, to whom they had retailed their story. The man was an antiquary, and he took the coffins to the local archaeological society to be examined.

By now the newspapers were taking an interest, giving details of this bizarre find and informing readers that the coffins could be viewed at a local jeweller's shop in the city. A decade afterwards, the miniature boxes were reported to have been sold, and 'The celebrated Lilliputian coffins found on Arthur's Seat' were lost to history for half a century, until in 1901 they resurfaced as a donation to the Society of Antiquaries of Scotland, whence, ultimately, they were passed on to the National Museums of Scotland, where they can be seen today.

The story as it has been handed down to us has several gaping holes. The original newspaper articles state there were seventeen coffins, arranged in the three rows described, although the same stories go on to say, with no sense of contradiction, that 'a number [of the coffins] were destroyed by the boys pelting them at one another', making it clear that it is not possible to know how many coffins were originally in the little cave. The journalists also assumed that the boxes had been placed in the rock fissure at different times because one row of coffins was badly rotted, and thus, they concluded, must have been there for longer. Yet damp conditions were likely to have affected the coffins resting on the cave floor first, making it entirely possible that all the boxes had been placed there at once. And, while a set of miniature coffins was donated to the Society of Antiquaries in 1901, it cannot be known for certain that they were the same ones that had been found three-quarters of a century earlier.[1]

The questions that are raised by these dolls – can they be called dolls? – are far more numerous than the answers, for in truth there are no answers. Ultimately we do not, and most likely never will, know who put them there, and why. What we do know is that someone, or several someones, thought enough of some dead people, or maybe the idea of death more generally, to modify or carve at least seventeen dolls, sew miniature clothes for each one, carve at least seventeen coffins, decorate them with tiny strips of tin and close them with metal clasps. The person, or people, who did this had some heartfelt idea they wished to express. That this was the form they chose says something – something unintelligible to modern eyes, to be sure, but that is irrelevant. To those doing the carving, the dead mattered. Death mattered. The dead, through memory, lived on and were not quite dead, while the living were haunted by their ghostly presence.

In 1743, the Scottish poet Robert Blair described a world in which the living walk daily over the dead:

> What is this *World*?
> What? but a spacious *Burial-Field* unwall'd . . .
> The very Turf on which we tread, once liv'd;
> And we that live must lend our Carcases
> To cover our own Offspring: In their Turns
> They too must cover theirs.[2]

Life, he was saying, is contiguous with death. We live, we die and are buried, the living walk over us, going about their lives, and they will later be walked over in their turn. Many in the nineteenth century found this idea both terrifying and comforting, Thomas de Quincey coining for it the phrase 'the Parliament of ghosts', where the dead presided over the living.[3] Charles Dickens took this notion and spelt out its extraordinary breadth. It was, he wrote, 'a solemn consideration what enormous hosts of dead belong to one old great city, and how, if they were raised while the living slept . . . the vast armies of the dead would overflow the hills and valleys beyond the city, and would stretch away all round it, God knows how far.'[4] The living and the dead, in Dickens' view, cannot be separated, the dead spreading into the infinite distance like a ghostly army intermingled with those still alive.

This was not a bad description of a nineteenth-century town or city. Churchyards were not like our modern cemeteries, discreetly located in leafy suburbs, tucked away down side streets and further hidden behind high walls. Instead churchyards were sited in the middle of every village, town and city, walked through weekly to get to church, utilized daily as a playground for children and a meeting place for adults. Even aside from the churchyards, no one in the nineteenth century could go more than a few hundred metres without coming across some indicator of death: women in mourning dress, men wearing black armbands; sad, poor walking funerals; great, pompous expensive funerals; funeral mutes standing in front of houses with drawn blinds to indicate death was inside; and outside, ever and always, the poor and abandoned dying in the street: 'Dead . . . And dying thus around us every day.'[5]

Dy*ing*. In progress. For much of history, life was visibly the process that led to death, and major landmarks in life were therefore often marked with an indication of where they would end. In the 1560s, one couple commissioned a portrait to commemorate the start of their lives together by immortalizing them making their vows with their hands resting on a skull with, underneath, a corpse lying on its winding sheet, above a text reading 'Lyve to dye and dye to Lyve eternally'. (See plate section.)

This type of image was not so much a memento mori – a reminder that death comes to all – as it was a recognition of a continuum, that dying is a part of living. The imagery of death in the midst of life had been a commonplace of woodblocks and engravings from the Middle Ages onwards, with illustrations of a popular sequence, 'The Dance of Death', beginning to appear around the fourteenth century. Initially these folkloric vignettes showed a dancing skeleton approaching its victims, themselves almost always dancing with their friends, families or neighbours, a demonstration of the social hierarchy of the living that would be upended by death. In the middle of the sixteenth century, however, the painter Hans Holbein moved the figure of Death into people's homes, workshops, castles and fields. This new figure of cheerful annihilation was everywhere, gleefully snatching away the great and small, prince and pauper, bishop and bumpkin.[6] By the mid-eighteenth century in Britain, the artist William Hogarth had turned Death into a pugilist; half a century later, the caricaturist Thomas Rowlandson produced nearly two hundred drawings for his own 'English Dance of Death' series, published in monthly instalments so the subscriber could follow along as Death levelled all, whether picking off one of a group of genteel ladies playing cards, a huntsman falling off his horse or a drunkard wheeled away from the tavern, his tipsy companions watching aghast.

It is notable to a modern eye that all these deaths occured in public places, or among groups of people. Death in the past was public, in a way we have forgotten. In the nineteenth century there were the exceptional deaths, the ones that were not supposed to happen – the starving mother and child dead in the street, or the execution watched by crowds numbering in their thousands, and viewed at second-hand by still more through the sale of execution broadsides, or heard of in ballads and street songs. But even the most unexceptional, the most ordinary deaths were public in the sense that families nursed their dying at home, and then watched over their bodies after death until it was time for the burial. Today, in some ways, death is far more visible to us, on television and in films, in photo-journalism and video clips on social media, and yet it is far more distanced personally: in our own families, death tends to be outsourced to hospitals and hospices, and the reality of the dead body is rarely seen.

Then, the dead *were* dying around the living, openly and visibly. It made nineteenth-century attitudes to life, as well as death, entirely different to ours. By the twentieth, much less the twenty-first century, the idea of ever-present death had vanished with the dead themselves, now tucked away out of sight and out of mind, as strange to us as boys playing with miniature coffins. How those in the nineteenth century responded, how they thought, what they believed, how they behaved when faced with that vast army of the dead, is the subject of this book.

1

THE SICKROOM

In the modern world, the opposite of living is not dying, but death. Dying is a stage that is barely regarded, so brief is it. A person is alive, and then they are dead. Or a person is ill: they receive treatment, the treatment succeeds, in which case they go on living; or it fails – but only when that treatment is withdrawn does the patient enter a stage known as 'dying'.[1] So brief is it that a sociologist has described that period of dying in modern life as occurring simply between the time the patient and medical practitioners become aware of oncoming death and the death itself.[2] It could be said that in modern medicine death is a process – cessation of breath, organ failure, brain death, etc. In the nineteenth century, it was dying that was the process.

Because of the brevity of dying today, we rarely consider that being alive itself is a way station to being dead. Until the early twentieth century, there were many illnesses and diseases where death came slowly but with absolute certainty. Those afflicted with an illness such as consumption might have years ahead of them, but they were always obliged to live in the knowledge that death was relentlessly on its way. An invalid might head for Rome or Madeira in the hope that a warmer climate would prolong their lives, but that was all they could hope for – a little more time. So too with heart ailments, cancer and various types of fever. Before the developments in medicine in the twentieth century, sufferers and their friends and family knew that the invalid was alive, and was also dying. For example, rheumatic fever and scarlet fever, both streptococcal infections, frequently damaged the heart valves and tissue.

Even if the patient recovered from the fever, the possibility of dying of subsequent heart problems was high until the advent of antibiotic use in the mid-twentieth century.[3]

Then there were the unforeseen, overwhelming cases, turning the home into a field hospital, as families became nurses, struggling desperately against unwinnable odds. The series of sudden illness and deaths endured by the Tait family in the middle of the century are desperately shocking to our eyes, but they were typical of the period. Archibald Tait would be made Archbishop of Canterbury in 1869, but in 1856 he had been serving as Dean of Carlisle for only a matter of years, having previously been headmaster at Rugby School. He and his wife Catharine and their six small children had settled well into cathedral life. Their seventh child had been born just three weeks before five-year-old Charlotte, known as Chatty, was taken ill. She was feverish, thirsty and possibly delirious, saying prayers in the night that she could not remember in the morning. She was taken to her mother's room to be nursed and, after three days with no improvement, the doctor was summoned. On hearing that Chatty had already had measles, by default he thought it likely she had caught scarlet fever, a rampantly infectious illness. She therefore had to be isolated from her siblings, who were moved to 'the far end of the house'. Chatty was now febrile, and having seizures, and her hair was cut off. This was always a terrible moment in nineteenth-century illness. Shorter hair was thought to relieve pressure on the brain, but it was symbolically also understood to be an action that acknowledged the imminence of death. Catharine recorded that she felt 'as if by this act I was giving up my child'. She was. Chatty died less than twenty-four hours later.

Her parents hoped that, as she had shown none of the common symptoms of scarlet fever, she might perhaps have had brain fever instead. Brain fever was a catch-all term for a variety of illnesses, including the non-specific 'nervous' fever, which might be a break-down, but also encompassed typhus and rheumatic fever, which were contagious bacterial infections, and even the extremely contagious meningitis.[4] If it did turn out that Chatty had died of one of these communicable diseases, they hoped that, as the children had been 'separated so entirely and at once', they would be safe. How, quite, they could have deluded themselves about this separation is a mystery to the modern reader: the children had all been living in the same rooms until the third day of Chatty's illness, and on the day after her death, Catharine, who had slept in her bedroom with the little girl throughout, had joined her other six children, as well as the servants who had nursed the dying child, for the baptism of Lucy, the month-old baby.

The horrors continued. The day of Chatty's funeral, Susan, aged eighteen months, was taken ill. The children were again separated, and Susan was in turn moved into her mother's room, Catharine once more passing between the room with the sick toddler and those with her other children, even as she instructed that 'safe' beds, beds that had not previously been in the room with the infected children, be brought in for them. In the period before germ theory was understood, there was no sense that the infection might lurk in the bedding on those beds, or in their clothes, or even in the rooms themselves. It was only when Frances, the next child, fell ill that the remaining children were, finally, removed from the house to stay nearby.

It was too late. Susan and Frances both died, Frances after a long five days. Catharine, still weak from childbirth and nursing her newborn, was not strong enough to attend Chatty's funeral, and the family did without the usual funeral symbols – the carriages at the door, the tolling church bell (see pp. 107 and 88), so that the dying Susan would not know that her sister had gone. From her window, Catharine watched the small coffin being carried away, and watched, too, her remaining children peering out from a window of the house across the way. After Susan's death, which followed swiftly, Catharine put on mourning for the first time and stoically endured the funeral: 'I could not bear to see another carried out and wait in agony at home.' The three girls had died closely enough together that they were buried in the same grave.

Then young Catharine, known as Cattie, at ten the oldest, was struck down just as Catharine was churched following the birth of Lucy.* Mary, known as May, the next oldest, followed. It was gently explained to Cattie that her sisters had gone, and her parents prayed with her, telling her she would shortly be joining them. The child was too ill to speak, but pointed upwards, or so they interpreted the gesture, and Catharine clung to the belief that God had sent 'this blessed hour of triumph over death to comfort us'. But Cattie's small window of lucidity passed, and she again became delirious, crying out in pain, and, noted Catharine, 'How we passed through the next few hours I really do not know, so intense was the agony.' Finally, the servants were called to join the family in prayers, and Cattie died in the night, when Catharine was sleeping: Archibald had to wake her to tell her of this new 'unspeakable agony'.

The next day the devastated parents sat and read consolatory poems by the churchman John Keble, before the next funeral was held. Afterwards Archibald wrote that he had nothing more than 'a vague recollection' of the ceremony, or even of attending it. They returned to the sickbed of May, who was delirious and would shortly also die: their fifth child in just over four weeks. Of a family of seven children, only Lucy, the baby, and their son, Craufurd, aged seven, were left. After May's funeral, the four survivors fled. They went to recover in the Lake District, and never returned to that house of desolation. The Taits later had two more children, but every year on the anniversary of each dead child's birthday they started the day by reading the baptismal service together and ended it by reading the burial service.

Twenty-two years later, Craufurd also died, aged twenty-nine, and his mother followed a few months later, having never really recovered from that earlier slaughter. The following year, the now Archbishop Tait published a little book outlining the deaths, drawing on the journals both he and his wife had kept. It became one of the most

---

* Today in the Anglican church, churching is understood as a ceremony of thanksgiving for a safe birth, but historically it was a rite of purification after childbirth, before which post-parturient women did not go to church.

popular works of consolatory literature of its day, read by the many thousands who found themselves in similar situations.⁵ In the 1820s, a medical student named John Epps received a letter from his father telling him his sister Susan had died, and another sister, Mary, was 'in a very critical state'. But a second letter followed hard on its heels: 'O my dear son . . . Mary was taken from us very soon after death removed our dear Susan. It was too much to write of, too much for you to bear without preparation. O my dear child, surely you will not be taken too . . . she is gone to be with her mother and sister instead; and we must bow before the will of God . . . I cannot continue. Pardon me, for the present I must leave off.'*⁶

Not all sickroom episodes were as terrible as that of the Taits or the Epps. Sickness, or invalidism, could also be a separate state, an in-between but possibly semi-permanent condition, one of neither recovery, nor non-recovery – that is, death. The place that invalids held in the nineteenth century can be felt by the sheer number of novels in which they figure, from the 'valetudinarian' Mr Woodhouse, the father of Jane Austen's *Emma*, in 1815, to, eighty years later, Oscar Wilde's *The Importance of Being Earnest*, where theatre audiences met a protagonist who had an imaginary friend, the congenitally invalid Bunbury, whose frequent relapses enabled his creator to avoid tiresome social obligations. These fictional invalids were reproductions of real-world counterparts, people who endured long lives of ill health, some of whom perhaps even found refuge and strength in permanent invalidity. Alice James, sister of both the novelist Henry and the pioneer of psychology William James, was, by her twentieth birthday in 1868, well on her way to this state. She had no identifiable symptoms, and her mother thought her trouble was 'nervous', although also 'genuine'.⁷ In some ways, her illness

---

* Epps concluded his medical studies, and set himself up as a 'Homoeopathic Chemist', becoming well known in his field, and being among the first to sell cocoa powder in packets to be made up into a hot drink, advertising it as 'a delicately flavoured beverage which may save us many heavy doctors' bills'.

gave her a purpose: her 'tragic health was, in a manner, the only solution for her of the practical problem of life', wrote Henry.[8]

Others found a way of making the isolation and quiet of the sickroom operate in their favour. Charles Darwin (1809–1882) and Florence Nightingale (1820–1910) both worked prodigiously and innovatively while suffering from chronic illnesses, with Nightingale being bedbound for a quarter of a century. For many decades Nightingale's sickroom isolation was presented as the result of hypochondria, but today it is thought that she suffered from brucellosis, a bacterial infection which, like rheumatic and scarlet fever, causes subsequent heart problems. For her, the sickroom was a place where she could control the world, making it operate the way she wanted it to, rather than finding herself forced to function in the way society required of an upper-class woman. In her decades in bed, she managed to work because of her illness, not in spite of it. Her invalidism excused her from having to spend her days, as she wrote, in the 'frivolous little dut[ies]' required of the wives and daughters of prosperous men.[9] As two of her biographers point out, her illnesses, and the consequent benefits of the sickroom, enabled her 'to free herself from family commitments . . . She astutely exploited the isolation provided by her illness to further . . . reforms in the army, the promotion of sanitary science, the collection of statistics, the design of hospitals, and the reform of nursing and midwifery services.'[10] Invalidism also conferred authority, even power. In Elizabeth Gaskell's novel *Ruth* (1853), the daughter of a well-to-do merchant tells Ruth, who has refused to pay her a visit, 'I almost wish I were ill, that I might make you come.'[11] Illness enabled women to issue orders in a way that otherwise they could not.

A few invalids turned the sickroom itself into a business. In 1844 the writer and journalist Harriet Martineau (1802–1876), nearly a generation younger than Nightingale, summarized her thoughts in *Life in the Sickroom* after almost a decade as an invalid. At the other end of the century, Virginia Woolf's mother, Julia Stephen (1846–

1895), produced *Notes from Sick Rooms* (1883). Both these volumes were intended to instruct the families of invalids how best to serve and assist their sickroom residents. Some of the discussion concerned attitude: should one tell a dying person that they were dying? More covered the minutiae of daily care – Stephen devoted a full two pages to the importance of searching out crumbs in the sickbed.[12] Stephen's *Notes* were private, for the family only, but Martineau and others like Priscilla Maurice (1810–1854) saw their works as educational, intended for wider distribution.

Maurice was the sister of Christian socialist and theologian F.D. Maurice, and she produced a successful and long-lasting series of tracts on sickroom care that are a mixture of pragmatic nursing and religious advice: if the invalid is having trouble speaking, do not exacerbate their distress by asking questions; do not say anything you would not want them to hear if they were well; do not disturb them unnecessarily to give them 'comforts' they might not need or want, such as hot-water bottles; but also, if no clergyman is present, 'Speak to them of sin, of pardon, of "the blood of Christ which cleanest from all sin"'; encourage them to understand that their illness is 'sent to teach us charity and sympathy', and it is 'our duty' to learn humility and submission before God, to be cheerful under duress, because 'indulg[ing] in gloominess' is a sin.[13]

Maurice's stress on the religious life of the invalid, and the effects of illness on their spiritual obligations, was in a long tradition. In previous centuries, illness had not solely, nor even primarily, been the province of medicine and science, but of religion. Once a case was declared to be hopeless, the doctor was expected to give way to the clergyman. For with so few weapons in his medical arsenal, in many ways the doctor, too, was of psychological rather than scientific assistance. A character in Thackeray's novel *The History of Pendennis*, published between 1848 and 1850, thinks how the doctor's 'presence is often as good for [the patient's friends and family] as for the patient', bringing as he does new hope: 'what an emotion the thrill of his carriage-wheels in the street, and at length at the door, has made us feel! How we hang upon his words, and what a comfort we get from a smile or two . . . !'[14] The minor poet and novelist Menella Bute Smedley (1820–1877) was blunter, describing a fictional doctor who divided his patients into three groups: those who 'could possibly derive any benefit from his skill'; those he visited merely for the sake of form, being 'patients who could . . . have done perfectly well without him'; and those 'whom he could not help, but who were comforted by his presence'.[15] The comfort these medical men offered was not purely physical, nor even emotional. Frequently they also took on the mantle, as Maurice recommended, of spiritual guide. In Dickens' *Bleak House*, Jo, the poor crossing-sweeper, is found dying in the street. He is brought indoors, where the surgeon Allan Woodcourt does not do anything as medically prosaic as taking his pulse or attempting a diagnosis. Instead, recognizing the imminence of death, he helps the child stumble his way through the Lord's Prayer.

And yet in this 1852/3 novel Woodcourt is presented to the reader as an up-and-coming modern physician. The medical profession had not long been respected, and often still was not, with training being uneven, sometimes non-existent. As late as 1860, of the two dozen 'medical men' who gave evidence at inquests in Hastings, Sussex, a quarter had received no hospital training, while just two of the twenty-four were qualified as physicians at all, the rest being surgeon-apothecaries.[16] And while many surgeon-apothecaries did have credible levels of ability, public opinion of others was low, frequently with good reason. One reportedly advertised himself as 'I Popjay, Surgeon Apotecary [sic] and Midwife &c.; draws teeth and bleeds on lowest terms. Confectionary [sic] Tobacco Snuff Tea Coffee Sugar and all sorts of perfumery sold here. NB New laid eggs every morning by Mrs. Popjay.'[17] (My working assumption is that Mrs Popjay was selling the eggs, not laying them.) It was these practitioners people thought of when, in a penny-blood from the 1840s, a doctor's wife frets that in her husband's absence 'all his patients [are] getting well . . . and, when they find that out, do you think they will take any more filthy physic [that he sells]? No, to be sure not.'*[18]

It was frequently a doctor's mere presence, rather than his skill, that made or broke his reputation. In the 1840s, one woman whose child had typhus commended her doctors as '. . . two clever Physicians one very celebrated in fever cases . . . within the last four days they have seen [her child] 4 times each day & sometimes two & three times in the night', until [as the child recovered] they 'come but twice a day'.[19] Up to seven visits a day – attendance was a substitute for the ability to treat the illness.

The lack of treatment tools did not stop sickrooms filling up with the impedimenta of disease and cure, because the sickroom was, at its most basic level, a marketplace, not merely for medicines, but for the plenitude of items that were, in this new age of mass production, being created in specialized form to meet the needs of invalids, or the needs invalids were being taught they had. There were the medical and semi-medical items, such as 'scales, thermometers, sputum cups, paper handkerchiefs, rubber pocket liners, tents . . . awnings, and disinfectants'.[20] And then there were ordinary household items redesigned with invalid use in mind, such as cups with a rimmed edge, or a little spout like a teapot, to enable the patient to drink without sitting up. There were different mattresses to give comfort to those long bedridden – one invalid recorded having a 'hydrostatic bed' to relieve the pain caused by 'lying long' – as well as specially upholstered chairs, sofas, cots and even hammocks for the same purpose. There were invalid chairs, precursors to modern wheelchairs, which tilted or reclined, and could be wheeled into a patch of sun, or out of a draught.[21]

And of course there were the medicines, most of which were not

---

* Penny-bloods, later known as penny-dreadfuls, were published from the 1830s in weekly episodes of eight or sixteen pages, including a single, usually sanguineous or horrifying illustration. They were hugely popular and are useful to historians as they reflected many commonly accepted working-class views that failed to be recorded by middle-class observers.

expected to cure, but simply temporarily to alleviate suffering. Many were opium derivatives, whether in pill or liquid form, either compounded by individual apothecaries and doctors, or sold in shops and by itinerant sellers as patent medicines. 'Soothing syrups' might be made up of some kind of tincture or plant derivative like oil of sassafras, which was mixed with alcohol, a sweetener such as treacle, and then laudanum – opium dissolved in alcohol – with possibly the addition of more alcohol in the form of brandy, sherry or other fortified wine. The most famous, and universally available, patent medicines were Godfrey's Cordial, Daffy's Elixir, Battley's Sedative Solution and Darby's Carminative.* These and many others included the words 'soothing', 'quiet', or 'Nurse's' or 'Mother's Something' in their names and advertising copy, and were used for pain, as well as for babies' teething trouble, for coughs and colds, and as strengthening 'tonics' to 'bring on' weak or sickly infants. They were condemned by the middle classes when used by lower-class parents to keep their children quiet while they worked, but the same syrups were also stocked by middle-class shops such as the Civil Service Stores and the Army and Navy, indicating widespread use among those very middle-class disapprovers.[22]

These furnishings, this equipment, these drugs – even the advice in the sickroom treatises – all were built on an unspoken assumption that the invalid's family had a comfortable income. The *Lancet* medical journal, while campaigning strongly for public healthcare for the working classes, nevertheless had blind spots, arguing in 1861 that 'rich and poor alike had similar *simple* needs' (my italics): 'comparatively little' to be spent on drugs (comparative to what, it did not explore), plus a few basics such as 'a cushioned chair . . . a small quantity of varied and delicate food, a draught of some refreshing or effervescent drink', and nursing that came with 'a little

---

* 'Carminative' actually means 'having the quality of expelling flatulence', or creating wind, but here it was used to allude to the ancient theory of the four humours that were supposed to comprise the human system: blood, phlegm and the two biles, yellow and black. In this worldview, a carminative expelled bad humours, not gas.

sympathy and kind forbearance'.[23] Where any of these things were to be found, when men, women and children worked all day for bare subsistence, was left undiscussed.

As some invalids lingered for years, and doctors had few curative abilities, nursing was by default the main focus of the sickroom, around which families were reorganized, and lives altered. Margaret Emily Shore, known as Emily, was born in 1819 in Bury St Edmunds, a Suffolk town some fifty kilometres east of Cambridge. She was one of five children of a clergyman without a permanent appointment, who made his living tutoring students for Oxford. Emily began to keep a journal when she was eleven, and in it we can see her illness unfold. In March 1836, aged seventeen, she wrote that she had had a cough for a while, although she had not previously had one for years. Two months later, she had been 'so unwell for so many days with cold and rheumatism' and a persistent fever that she was rarely able to get out of bed before noon and was too weak to stay up for an entire day. By June the family planned to relocate to Hastings, hoping the sea air would help her, but a month later there was little enough improvement that she and her parents travelled to London to see a doctor, who 'taps me' – that is, listened to her lungs – which he thought were not 'yet' affected. The family moved to Tunbridge Wells, again in search of better air for her, before sending her on her own to stay with an aunt and uncle in the milder climate of Exeter. To no avail. By December 'I cannot read or write without a headache, and writing also gives me a pain in my chest.' Six months later walking upstairs was too much exertion, while holding a book exhausted her. She had been unable to go out for a walk in more than three months, and assumed that she would 'never . . . be strong again'. She made light of it, the following year mockingly referring to herself as having 'been addicted of late to growing faint after breakfast', even as she worried about the anxiety she was causing her parents. Her symptoms had developed into shortness of breath 'tinged with blood', a rapid pulse, a 'craving appetite' twinned with an inability to eat, night sweats, 'palpitations of the heart, and deep, circumscribed flushes'. It was only after listing all this that she dared to ask herself if 'consumption [had] really come at last', and admitted she knew the answer: 'I am not taken by surprise.' The family had discussed emigrating to Australia, a permanent invalid presumably pressing hard on the finances of a tutor, but ultimately they decided on Madeira. There, it was hoped, the climate would 'restore papa's health': care, money worries and nursing routinely affected more than just the invalid in the family. She and her mother travelled out first in the winter of 1838, and for a time the sunshine and warmth did bring about some improvement. But by the following April the death knell of consumption made its appearance: a broken blood vessel saw Emily coughing up blood. On 8 May 1839 she wrote, 'I . . . am now dying . . . in great suffering, and may not live many weeks. God be merciful to me as a sinner. God be praised for giving me such excellent parents.' On 27 May, as with Chatty Tait, her hair was cut off, and six weeks later, aged nineteen, she died.[24]

Henry Peach Robinson, 'Fading Away' (1858). This photographic composite image was one of Robinson's most successful works, capturing as it did the romantic image of the beautiful girl on her deathbed, but also, more realistically, the grieving family she was leaving behind.

Emily Shore wrote little of the mechanics of the sickroom, or who nursed her, and how, but these matters were ones about which people felt strongly, for they had important practical implications as well as moral ones. Just as bearing and raising children were assumed to be women's reasons for existence, so too was nursing a family member part of their biological nature; it derived from, and added to, their spiritual and moral values. But only if the labour remained unpaid. Nursing one's own family was 'an act of tenderness, sympathy and tact'; being paid to nurse someone else's family was 'menial, degrading and improper'.[25] The accepted image of that role was, for much of the century, not Florence Nightingale's ideal of the capable, highly trained professional, but instead a caricature of an alcoholic, argumentative mangler of the English language, someone who was not in fact a real person at all, but a character in Dickens' *The Life and Adventures of Martin Chuzzlewit* (1842/4). Sairey Gamp's wild popularity as a comic character also encouraged the general population to see her as the prototype of the paid nurse: drunken, slatternly, avaricious and entirely untrustworthy. Yet while the middle classes were routinely united in their disdain for the profession's practitioners, they also relied on the many real-life Mrs Gamps for the basics of nursing. Outwardly, the middle class was confident that it was not possible both to be paid for looking after a patient, and truly to care for that patient. Silently, however, they hired the Mrs Gamps for all the jobs that were too dirty or too undignified to be performed by those suppliers of what *The Lancet* had referred to as the essentials of care: 'sympathy and kind forbearance'. It is notable that while Julia Stephen dwells for pages in her *Notes from Sick Rooms* on the proper arrangement of sheets and pillows for a sickbed, and on the difficulties that arise when handkerchiefs are lost in the bedding, she dedicates just one single, very brief, paragraph to the management of bedpans. Stephen did acknowledge that her readers were likely to have a trained nurse on call, but quickly added that 'some member of the family' would be there in a supervisory capacity, 'watching and helping'.[26] That the paid carers took on the dirty and often dangerous chores commonly went unremarked, and possibly unconsidered. More frequently the focus was instead on the virtues of the unpaid, always female family member, whose love brought with it curative properties a commercial transaction did not, and indeed could not. Successful nursing required the 'quick eye, the soft hand, the light step' that were unique to women, but not any women: it was necessary that the labour was given freely, and for best results, by a relative, or at least a friend.[27]

Yet while treatises on illness and novels described the duties of nursing that mostly involved a 'bright manner and unfailing chatter' to keep the invalid amused, the fact was that nursing was a herculean and never-ending task as families were ripped apart by illness and death.[28] For the more prosperous, a veritable regiment of paid and unpaid carers might be available to (wo)man the sickroom. When Chatty Tait first fell ill, as well as the doctor visiting 'constantly', she was nursed by her mother and a Mrs Peach, possibly the nanny. As the other children followed her into the sickroom, the two women were aided by 'Cousin Nannie' and 'Aunt Lizzie', as well as the older children's governess, who slept on the floor beside May during her final days, all assisted by unnamed and unnumbered servants, including a housemaid, a nursery maid and others who were not even given a title.[29]

For while middle-class women of comfortable backgrounds took on the name and title of nurse, in reality the family's servants or outside hired women performed the lion's share of the work, particularly the least savoury, or physically heavy elements, such as washing the patients and dealing with their bedpans or other bodily fluids. Jeannette Marshall was the seventeen-year-old daughter of a fashionable London surgeon when in 1873 her brother, who had previously suffered from an unidentified gastric problem, was again taken ill. Sir William Jenner, later to become President of the Royal College of Physicians, was called in. Jenner had been the scientist who had distinguished typhoid from typhus, but it nevertheless took him five weeks to decide that young Reggie did have typhoid.* By this time he was already passing blood, and had developed peritonitis. Jeannette recorded in her diary that she, her mother and a professional nurse all cared for him, but as she described it, the family mostly helped him to bed, read to him, sat up at night with him and possibly gave him his medicine from time to time. (Reggie and Jeannette's fifteen-year-old brother John participated in none of these tasks, not even sitting up at night with his brother.)[30]

There was also an in-between form of paid-for care that did not quite count as a commercial transaction. In the 1820s, before the Courtauld family became financially comfortable, one member of the family wrote to an unmarried cousin to say that, as the cousin was thinking of 'enter[ing] some family as an instructor to the children . . . would you feel happy to take the care of our young ones? It would be my delight to receive you as my friend and [paid] companion', to look after the children when they were ill and care for them.† These blurred lines were probably far more routine than

---

* Typhus is transmitted via lice, and is very much a disease of crowded conditions and dirt. Typhoid is caused by bacteria which in the nineteenth century were regularly found in contaminated water or milk. By the time Reggie was taken ill, local government medical officers were employed to trace the sources of individual typhoid outbreaks to specific dairies. Seven months after Reggie's death, Dr Marshall also came down with a suspected case of typhoid, and the family immediately changed their milk supplier, passing the information on the old one to a doctor investigating the outbreak, and ultimately receiving what Jeannette called a 'sort of conscience-money' from someone 'at the top of the Dairy Reform Company'.

† The Courtauld family was of Huguenot descent, originally silversmiths before one son was apprenticed to a silk-weaver, a centuries-old Huguenot trade in London. From very uncertain beginnings, Samuel Courtauld and his brother George established Samuel Courtauld and Co. in the 1820s in Essex, striking gold when they began to produce a particular type of black, non-reflective silk known as crape, which became *the* fabric for mourning clothes for the next hundred years, for women's dresses, veils and ribbons, and also for men's mourning cloaks, armbands and hatbands. One of its chief merits to its manufacturer was undoubtedly that the dye used was extremely unstable: it ran and faded quickly, and was not water-resistant, meaning that mourning clothes had to be renewed regularly. (For more on mourning clothes, and crape, see Chapter 7.) Many of the Courtauld cousins intermarried, and their letters can give the inattentive reader the impression they were all named Samuel or George, so I will distinguish them as little as possible. The Courtauld family name retains its profile

we think today, with many families hiring their less prosperous relatives. In some households these lesser family members lived and worked as servants; in others, such as this one, the companion and nurse, who was paid, was nevertheless careful to clarify that 'I take all my meals with the family, you know; I am of course introduced, & am even encouraged, to mix more in conversation', adding proudly that visitors paid calls upon her, just as they did on the lady of the house. This was in stark contrast to her own family's attitudes to professional nurses when not of their own class. These women were, her brother complained, 'tipsy, pogey [slow], stupid, careless abominations'.[31]

It might be expected that paid nurses would be more commonly hired by the comfortably-off, but owing to the abundant leisure time of the women in these families, and their ability to call on the services of their household servants for nursing care as Catharine Tait had done, professional nurses were in reality more frequently found in the homes of the less well-to-do, usually in the families of either well-established labourers, or of those edging into the lower middle classes. The women in these families could not afford to leave their paid occupations to act as nurses, and they therefore hired neighbours or friends to perform that function.

Virtually all classes, whatever the financial or nursing situations, looked after their sick at home. Hospitals had very narrow remits as to which diseases they were willing to treat, and often excluded entire classes or groups – no children, for example, or women; no infectious diseases; no cancer patients. Some hospital physicians might recommend nurses to patients at home, but working-class nurses maintained their own networks, being recommended from family to family outside the influence of apothecaries or physicians – yet another reason for those professionals to denigrate and distrust

---

today owing to the art collection amassed by one of the twentieth-century Samuel Courtaulds, which formed the nucleus of what is now the Courtauld Institute, both a college of the University of London and its associated public art gallery.

them. Sairey Gamp, for one, is called on by the wealthy Chuzzlewit family in her role as layer-out of the dead (for more on laying out, see pp. 81–2); once in the house, however, 'with one eye on the future' she gives her card to Jonas Chuzzlewit's young wife against the day when she will need a midwife. Nurses were also less expensive, and did more or less the same thing. 'A sober creetur [is] to be got at eighteen pence a day for working people, and three and six for gentlefolks,' said Mrs Gamp, while a doctor charged a working-class family 5 shillings for the same visit, and as much as a guinea for 'gentlefolks'.[32]

Those charges mattered, even to the middle classes, as illness and death were regular visitors. Today we think of the Brontë family as particularly death-ridden. In 1821, Maria Brontë died of cancer; two of her daughters, Maria and Elizabeth, died of tuberculosis four years later; by 1849, their siblings Branwell, Emily and Anne were all dead, with Charlotte following in 1855, leaving their father the sole survivor of a nuclear family that had once numbered eight.[33] Yet to their contemporaries, the Brontës were not particularly out of the ordinary. The novelist Margaret Oliphant watched, nursed and sat by the deathbeds of her mother and father within four years of each other, followed by her husband, as well as all five of her children, her sister-in-law, her brother and her nephew.*[34] Mrs Oliphant read Archbishop Tait's volume on the death of his children after the death of her last surviving child: 'I have found a little, not comfort, but fellowship in reading about Archbishop Tait. I did not like his book. I thought it too personal, too sacred for publication, but now brought down to the very dust [myself], I turned to it with a sense of common suffering.'[35]

She was not alone. The mother of the economist and politician James Thorold Rogers had watched nine of her sixteen children die before, at the age of seventy-four, she nursed her eldest son, dying

---

* I have not itemized these deaths more fully because Mrs Oliphant's father, husband (who was also her cousin), son, brother and nephew were all named Francis and all known as Frank, while she, her mother and her daughter were all Margarets.

of alcoholism: 'George's long illness has almost worn me and [his sister] out, indeed I sometimes think it will be too much for her.' He needed feeding 'like a child', and had to be 'watched day and night' (although it is unclear if this was because he was so enfeebled, or if it was to keep him from finding more drink). That was not the end. Nearly ten years later, at the age of eighty-two, she cared for yet another dying child, this one a 'demanding and selfish daughter'.*[36] Even in a family not necessarily suffering from a series of deaths, illnesses could be prolonged. The poet Christina Rossetti (1830–1894) was diagnosed with Graves' disease in 1871, and then with cancer in 1891, for which she underwent surgery the following year. In 1893, the cancer was found to have returned, by which time a heart condition prevented further surgery. In 1894 she was confined to a sofa in the drawing room; developing dropsy later that summer, at which point she was kept stupefied by brandy and opiates, to prevent her cries of pain from disturbing the neighbours. Yet it took until November of that year before the family hired a professional nurse, relieving both family and servants in the final months before her death.[37]

Deaths were so common that children could not but be affected: they watched adults die, and they watched their brothers and sisters be born, and die, far more often than today. In the twenty-first century, it is generally the elderly who are at risk. In the nineteenth century, however, mortality was most common among children, in particular those under the age of five. These early deaths complicate life-expectancy figures. In 1800, life expectancy at birth was just under thirty-seven years; by the middle of the century, upper-middle-class professionals could expect to live to their mid-forties; while in the 1880s, that had risen to sixty-three. Their working-class brethren, however, were far behind: a labourer's life expectancy at birth at mid-century was twenty-two, rising to twenty-nine only in

* Pat Jalland, the historian who recorded her situation, adds that, of these eleven deaths, two of her children were alcoholic, 'one a vagrant, and one a sea-captain murdered by pirates', cruelly withholding further details.

the 1880s. However – and this is a crucial 'however' – these figures are heavily weighted by the deaths of the vast number of children who never saw their fifth birthday. Until 1877, babies who died before they were a year old were not even included in government statistics, so numerous were they, but were grouped with stillbirths and miscarriages, the latter two being considered indistinguishable.[38] Once children survived to the age of six, they could expect to reach adulthood, while those who lived to the age of forty were statistically likely to live into their late sixties or early seventies.[39] In general as the century progressed, infant mortality figures dropped, spurred by improved quality of housing; improved sanitation and access to clean drinking water; improved affordability of food, and thus better maternal health before birth; as well as decreased family sizes, which again improved nutrition of mothers and also the quality of their breastfeeding.[40] Until then, far more children than elderly died (in part for the very simple reason that there were far more children than there were elderly. In 1811, about 6 per cent of the population was aged over sixty, compared to nearly 25 per cent today).[41] In the first quarter of the nineteenth century, nearly one in three deaths were those of children under five; and the next third of deaths were from a wide range of causes, not specifically the diseases of old age.[42] The sickroom was an all-ages location, and no one remained unaffected.

In 1894 a passer-by in central London noticed a group of children playing a street game for which they had built 'a little arrangement like a cemetery' in the sand, with mounds heaped with flowers and surrounded by low walls. One mound, with the biggest bunch of flowers, was called 'Tubb's grave' by the children, who asked pedestrians, 'Please to remember Tommy on the tub's [sic] grave', just as in November they begged for 'A penny for the guy'. When questioned, they could not explain who, or what, Tubb was, nor what the game meant, except to say they had 'always' done it, meaning they had learned it from older children, who in turn had learned it from their elders. The game was played, they said, once a year, in

May. When this sighting was reported in a journal, others wrote in to say they had seen the same game played in other parts of London, and a few years later it was recorded that the children playing it had a little rhyme they chanted: 'Please to remember the grotto, / It is but once in a year, / Mother is dead, and father's gone to sea, / So will you please remember me.'*43 While there appear to be no reported sightings of this game outside London, children across the country played other singing games that related to death. In 'Jenny Jones', a group of girls formed a ring and sang a request to see Jenny Jones, to receive the response that Jenny could not come out to play because she was 'washing, washing, you can't see her now'. In the following verses Jenny was serially 'folding [the laundry]', then 'ill', 'dying' and finally 'dead!', whereupon the children ask if, instead of seeing Jenny, they might attend her funeral, before they carry one of the girls away, the others following behind as mourners.44

It might be said that these games were practice for the girls. They sang about death, and then, as adolescents and adults, they took on caring roles in their families, particularly if they did not marry. Unmarried daughters were expected to be nurses by virtue of their gender and by virtue of their single status which, as with widows, denoted they were to be at their families' disposal as a matter of course. They would have no shortage of patients, for the nineteenth century was the century of epidemics. Waves of cholera, smallpox, scarlet fever, typhus, typhoid, influenza and diphtheria broke over the population throughout the century. Only a bare half of the forty years between 1831 and 1871 were epidemic-free.

The first, and probably the most terrifying, of the epidemics was cholera. It initially emerged in South East Asia in 1817,

---

* 'Please to remember the grotto' shows signs of slippage from another day when children begged on the streets to fund a celebration, as with Guy Fawkes' day. The oyster season traditionally began on 5 August, which became the day when young working-class boys and girls built up small piles of empty oyster shells, lit by the stump of a candle, possibly with a bit of tinsel for decoration. They stood beside them and implored pedestrians to 'Please to remember the grotto' – the oyster-shell pile – via halfpenny donations.

spreading slowly to Russia before following the shipping routes to reach Britain in 1831. The first wave in the British Isles, lasting just under two years, killed approximately one in every 800 people, with the populations of towns and cities suffering far more acutely than those of rural districts. The disease returned in 1848/9, this time nearly doubling its kill rate to 53,000 in England and Wales; and again two years later, when another 23,000 died, before its final major outbreak, in 1866, produced another 14,000 deaths.[45] In between, separate epidemics of scarlet fever, typhus, diphtheria and typhoid roared through. Between 1837 and 1840, smallpox killed nearly 50,000 people, although that number was reduced by 90 per cent after the Vaccination Act of 1840, which made vaccines free to the working population; with the Vaccination Extension Act of 1853, which made them obligatory, infection rates slowed to a trickle.*

Cholera was terrifying not merely because it was so lethal – in the nineteenth century, between 40 and 60 per cent of those infected died – but because of the speed with which it acted. Of the 300 deaths reported in the first wave of the epidemic in Exeter alone, a third occurred within twenty-four hours of the first symptoms appearing, the rest within two days.[46] Initially, the infected person might just feel unwell, with perhaps some stomach upset, but this was rapidly followed by violent purging – vomiting and diarrhoea – that ended with 'rice water', when part of the intestine might be evacuated, and the resulting dehydration led to organ failure. At that point, pulse and temperature both dropped, the face collapsed inwards, severe muscle cramps drew the extremities up into clawlike shapes, nails turned blue and the skin appeared to be black.[47]

Today it is known that cholera is a waterborne bacterial infection, commonly spread by infected faecal matter. In the nineteenth

---

* It is impossible to read, or write, about these epidemics in the Covid-beleaguered 2020s without making comparisons. I will attempt not to belabour the point.

century, there were two competing general theories of disease: contagion and miasma. Contagion theory said that infection was passed from person to person in some unknown manner. If people in two neighbouring houses had water supplied by two different companies, a pattern was hard to discern; where whole cities drank from water in which raw sewage routinely ran, the pattern of contagion was almost impossibly obscure. Miasma theory understood illnesses to develop from some environmental point of origin, such as rotting animal or vegetable remains, which caused a smell to rise as a mist, or miasma, and spread across a district, poisoning all who lived there. Both beliefs required civic, and expensive, interventions for solutions. Contagion models demanded mass quarantine, with consequent disruption and loss of trade; miasma theory demanded civic reconstruction and reorganization of sewage, water and rubbish disposal on a vast scale – in effect, the alleviation of poverty and the reconstruction of all sociopolitical organizations. Neither was undertaken, although limited changes were made. The Board of Health in the first cholera wave recommended the immediate segregation of the sick from the healthy, although without any governmental support to enable the working poor to carry this out it remained societally impossible. The Board also recommended that the government improve the lives of the poor, a vague aspiration with no concrete suggestions as to how that aim was to be achieved. For good measure it also warned that 'those who have been addicted to the drinking of spirituous liquors, and indulgence of regular habits' were 'the greatest sufferers' from the epidemic, even though that was visibly not the case.[48]

Not that it mattered. The primary treatment for cholera today is oral rehydration therapy, which, if used promptly, cuts mortality from the disease from 60 per cent to 1 per cent of those affected. That was of course unavailable in the nineteenth century. Instead, mustard and linseed poultices were recommended, or the patient was kept warm with a hot bran bag, a precursor to the hot-water bottle.* One doctor working during the 1848 wave, who was a proponent of the miasma theory, thought the disease passed from patient to patient via a 'poisonous matter exhaled from their bodies' (this was true in a way, as expelled faecal matter was a prime vector for contagion). To counteract the diarrhoea, he recommended eating plenty of meat, 'light puddings, stale breads and good sound wine in moderate quantity', together with 'calomel combined with opium', or, for children, doses of calomel with laudanum, that diluted form of opium.† But then he threw up his hands. 'I scarcely know what to recommend. I have known every medicine relieve, and every medicine fail,' he wrote, and he ultimately opted for doing nothing, and the patient would live or die, as God or fate willed.[49]

The first two waves of cholera in London, in 1832 and in 1848/9, had initially affected the working classes, and thus reinforced for their social superiors the belief that the disease was linked to dirt, or weakness of character, or a predilection for alcohol, and therefore, in a leap, to immigrants. The syllogism ran something like: cholera is a filth disease, filthy people are immoral, the Irish are filthy and immoral, therefore the Irish suffer more from cholera. By 1854, however, this was clearly untrue, as the Cholera Inquiry Committee saw that 'the disease did not limit its attack to any one class, nor yet to the very poor'.[50] By the 1860s, the disease-equals-dirt-equals-poverty equation could be seen not to hold for cholera, and also for

---

* Poultices were traditional methods of treating many varieties of ailment, from inflammation to wounds, based on the principle of counter-irritant: an illness or infection was caused, it was thought, by an inflammation that could be alleviated by manufacturing a counter-inflammation. So an irritant such as mustard powder, or a soothing element like linseed, was mixed into a paste with bread, meal or similar and boiling water, the paste then being spread on a rag or bandage and laid on the specific area, which was supposed to draw the poison from the system.

† Calomel, or mercury chloride, is a purgative, just what a cholera patient did not need, but then, opium causes constipation. Given the speed of the disease, it is probable that neither drug had time to act. Nineteenth-century doctors and their patients had a passion for calomel for all manner of ailments, including, but not limited to, syphilis, cancer, tuberculosis, influenza and indigestion.

typhoid, especially following the 1861 death of Prince Albert, which was presumed at the time to be from typhoid. (Today it is thought more likely that he died of stomach cancer, having suffered from stomach problems for years. There had been no major typhoid outbreak at the time that tied in with Buckingham Palace, although the drains there were notoriously bad.) Contagion was now better understood in the general population than it had been earlier in the century. In 1870, the Reverend Francis Kilvert (1840–1879), who kept a diary of his daily life as a clergyman in the Welsh Marches, reported seeing a woman whose daughter had had scarlet fever. Neither woman 'apprehend[ed] any danger, infection or spreading of the disease, and had taken no pains to disinfect the clothes or house or anything', he marvelled, his views marking a notable change from the attitude of the Taits fifteen years earlier.[51] By now, the educated middle classes, at least, knew more.

The 1831 epidemic had seemed by many to be a visitation of God, and the government decreed a National Day of Fasting, Prayer and Humiliation for the population to pray for the alleviation of their suffering. Many of the working classes were finding themselves drawn to religion at this date, in particular to Nonconformism – the Primitive Methodists welcomed their largest number of converts in the 1840s as the epidemics raged.[52] Yet this interpretation of the epidemic laid the cause in the laps of the poor, not because they lived in substandard housing, nor ate a substandard diet, but because these poor were irreligious, or blasphemous, or drank, or were simply insufficiently respectable. One clergyman in a single sermon blamed cholera on 'our guilty country', and, more specifically, on sabbath-breakers and purchasers of 'infidel' texts, as well as the evils of alcohol, 'whoredom', Roman Catholicism and all those discontented with the station God had seen fit to place them in.[53] Reformers and the workers themselves, while acknowledging 'this awful visitation to be the direct interposition of a wide and all-seeing Providence', pointed to their 'acute and severe physical privation', the 'dwellings unfit for human habitation', the inadequate sanitary legislation and lack of sufficient food.[54] Yet others, on both the radical left and the Tory right, believed that contagion was a hoax, designed by parish employees to increase public funds in order to turn private profit.[55]

Between the first and second waves of the epidemic there was a marked shift from God to human causes. In 1832, Bishop Blomfield, the Bishop of London, had insisted that the word 'providence' be included in the parliamentary legislation that made up the Cholera Act; by 1849, the same man preached a sermon stressing the 'want of decent cleanly habitations' that had brought about this pestilence among the working population.[56] Many who saw that cholera did not distinguish between rich and poor nevertheless tried to determine God's reasons for the scourge: a Courtauld cousin noted 'upwards of *1000* deaths & many from amongst the higher classes', including 'three old Ladies *next door* to us' becoming ill, and one dying 'in the short space of 24 hours'. Even so, she added, 'I do trust & believe it has been *much blessed* in this place in leading people to think seriously [of religion] who never did before', and added that her family 'walked out . . . into the streets when business required', despite the risk of infection, as they were surely protected by attending church frequently.[57]

This believing and not believing at one and the same time was widespread. There *was* an epidemic; many *were* dying; yet 'we', whoever 'we' were, went on as normal, denying as much as possible. In 1837 Emily Shore referred to what 'they call an influenza', but while the newspapers were saying thousands were dying, 'I feel inclined to strike off a cypher from each number' – that is, if the papers reported six hundred deaths, she thought sixty was probably closer to the truth. Yet in the very next sentence she wrote that her cousins had told her of a family they shared a pew with in church, who had eight members of their family currently ill. Ten days later, 'There is scarce a family whom we know . . . which has escaped, and in most of them the greater part of the individuals in each family are ill . . . It is not,' she added stubbornly, 'infectious, but [it is] an epidemic.'[58]

She was not alone in this back and forth, even among the older, theoretically wiser intelligentsia. The historian and philosopher Thomas Carlyle (1795–1881), who made his living as a thinker, reflected this dichotomy. In January 1832 he wrote to his brother that, 'No Cholera, or other epidemic yet attacks us; nor except with very cowardly people is such greatly apprehended.' There were, he thought, 'far more frightful maladies which we look on with indifference', and in Sunderland, where cholera had first arisen in Britain, it had 'nearly burnt out'. A month later he was following a popular line in thinking that the disease 'seems to attack almost exclusively . . . the improvident, drunk and worthless: punishment follows hard on sin'. By December, he noted that 'the disease has been here for many weeks, but is in the highest degree insignificant', that the important thing was not to '*panic*' (those italics a definite sign of not panicking), adding, within four lines, both that 'Doctors . . . can do so very little towards defence against the malady' and that 'Our Doctors say, great things can be done, and the disease is *generally* curable' at an early stage, before adding that he was sending 'a dozen *cholera pills*' recommended by his friend Southwood Smith, which are 'at least entirely harmless, and must have a tendency in the right direction', since they were purgatives, before ending by saying that the politician Charles Buller had died 'suddenly; there have been many deaths in our circle here lately'.*[59]

A more realistic depiction of the ravages of epidemic came in Harriet Martineau's single foray into fiction, *Deerbrook*, published in 1839, which portrayed a market town in the grip of an unnamed epidemic. In it, Martineau, an economist and social reformer,

---

*   Thomas Southwood Smith (1788–1861) was a doctor and public health reformer. The pill that he recommended was made up of 'Hydrag creta gr ii, Quinin. sulph gr vi, Confect. Opiat. gr xxx; mix *optime*, and make 12 pills,—*pro re natâ*', which is essentially quinine, sulphur and opium, not greatly different from Carlyle's favourite 'blue pill', the above-mentioned mercury and opium combination, which he took for a variety of ailments over the years. The prescription uses roman numerals, while 'gr.' stands for grains, a commonly used pharmacological measurement of the day, equivalent to one-seven-thousandth of a pound avoirdupois.

focused on the need to 'clean, air and dry' the poor-quality workers' housing, and 'supply the indigent sick with warmth and food', but even that was 'of little avail', and she shows a town devastated. The village seamstress works through the nights to produce sufficient mourning clothes for all, 'having scarcely left her seat for the last fortnight, except to take orders' for more of the same, even as she cannot hire more workers, as they are all ill themselves. 'The churchyard was now the most frequented spot in the village', its grass worn away to bare earth owing to the number of funerals that had passed over it.[60]

Martineau gives her town a forward-thinking doctor, who joins forces with the vicar to work together to stem the endless parade of deathbeds that follow. The two men, between them, follow the path that history had long laid down in creating the 'good death', the essential end to the long story of the sickroom and what followed: the deathbed.

2

THE DEATHBED

The idea that a deathbed was the place from which the dying spoke words of wisdom, sharing profound and eternal truths worthy of being handed down to future generations, was not new. This 'good death' – dying well, whether nobly in battle, or virtuously, or piously, depending on the gender, values and social position of the person dying – had a history that went back to classical antiquity. In the British Isles after the Reformation, the Protestant ideal took the secular expression of the classical world, and combined it with new religious elements that concentrated on the community of believers. The dying were the focus of the prayers of family and friends, while in exchange the dying themselves offered 'godly exhortations' as they 'surrendered their souls willingly into God's hands'. In the seventeenth century, the clergyman Jeremy Taylor instructed his readers on the preparations that would lead to a good death, which was 'a great art', one that sensible and pious people did not leave until the last moment: 'he that prepares not for death, before his last sickness, is like him that begins to study Philosophy [only] when he is going to dispute publicly in the faculty.' Although it was never called that, a bad death, by contrast, was one that stole up on the living: it might be sudden, or even if the disease had progressed slowly, the sufferer might have failed – or refused – to prepare for death.* 'He that would die well must always look for

---

* It is worth considering that modern medicine continues to judge the ill. Cancer sufferers who do not respond to chemotherapy are frequently said by specialists to have 'failed chemo', instead of chemotherapy having failed the patient.

death, every day knocking at the gates of the grave', learning to accept death by living with it daily, whether by visiting churchyards, perhaps, or simply by meditating on last things.[1]

Taylor's volume, *The Rule and Exercise of Holy Dying*, was acclaimed in its day, and its popularity continued over the centuries, ensuring the book went through almost fifty editions by the end of the nineteenth century. The Victorians admired it greatly, with George Eliot making it one of the half-dozen books that her upright and moral hero Adam Bede owned in the 1859 novel of the same name. Bede was a Nonconformist, and his reading was very much in the tradition of Nonconformism, and the Evangelical movement, a tradition promoted especially by John Wesley and the Methodists. A good death benefited the dying, of course, but the final illness and death were also thought of as an educational experience for those present, 'an opportunity for God to work in the lives of all those at the deathbed' in the final days, or even hours.[2] Wesley's *Arminian Magazine* regularly featured deathbed narratives, stories of those who 'have lately finished their course with joy'. By the 1780s and 1790s, these biographical sketches were one of the magazine's most popular features, so much so that other publications followed suit. The *Evangelical Magazine*, published between 1793 and 1892, ran at least one deathbed story in every issue, and often far more, concentrating on the deaths of ordinary people, frequently women and children, encouraging readers to see themselves reflected in the pages. The pain and fear that came with death was not glossed over, although the core of each story was always the dying triumphing in their final hours, perhaps by receiving a vision of the afterlife, of angels (a favourite for the narratives of child deaths), or of family members who were already dead and, presumably, beckoning their loved ones onwards.

For the purposes of religion, a good death was a slow death, one that gave the dying time to make their peace with those whom they had wronged, to bid farewell to friends and family, as well as, importantly, to prepare spiritually. It also gave the family, children included, time to gather to witness 'the Christian's victory over death'.[3] Consolation was to be found not in quick or peaceful ends, but instead through painful struggles, as Christ had struggled at his own tormented death.[4] Those attending a deathbed took an active role: if the dying could not speak, the deathbed watchers might ask leading questions that could be answered by a single word, a nod or just a glance, through which the dying could be said to have shared words of repentance for their sins and hopes for future glory. If they were not strong enough even for that, family and friends might simply share the task of reading aloud, usually a mixture of prayers, tracts and Bible passages. For this purpose, publishers produced anthologies of extracts suitable to be read to the dying. Priscilla Maurice, who had written those tracts on the sickroom, also compiled books of verse with titles such as *Prayers for the Sick and Dying*. One of her chapters was entitled 'Suitable to be read to Persons in their Last Hours', and was interspersed with instructions: the poems should be read 'very slowly, distinctly, with intervals'. Most of the poems in these anthologies expressed religious consolation, but they also included what one literary critic has called 'self-elegies', poems in which the authors foretell in touching terms their own coming deaths, using details very like the ones their readers were living through, complete with a dying person, a deathbed gathering and a pending reunion in the afterlife.[5]

The good death had space for secular as well as spiritual resolutions. In 1848, when Archibald Tait was still headmaster of Rugby School, he was stricken with a bout of rheumatic fever so severe it was thought he might not survive. On hearing the diagnosis, he sent for his solicitor to dictate his will, after which he and his wife prayed and recited 'helpful texts and hymns', satisfied that both sacred and profane worlds had been taken care of.[6]

The conservative clergyman William Hett described an idealized deathbed in 1823, setting out what he said was a description for an engraving of this uplifting scene, one that today reads more like stage directions. The dying man was to be found

> sitting in the middle of the bed, his back supported. — His wife hanging over the bed side, his left hand grasped in her two hands, her eyes fixed upon his face in a silent agony of distress. — The children near the mother all in tears . . . The servants . . . standing in a group, at a small distance from the bottom of the bed, in mute and serious attention to the last good words of their dying master, which he is in the act of uttering. In the features of his countenance, the inward sentiments of hope and joy rising, as far as is possible, superior to the appearance of languor and debility. — his medical friend, at a small distance from the wife, in an attentive posture, his face full of thought, indicating this sentiment, 'How nobly a Christian can die!' — In the window an hourglass nearly run out. — Upon a small round table, near the bed . . . a Bible open at this passage of Job, which is legible, 'I know that my Redeemer liveth.' A prayer-book open at the Burial Service, with these words legible, 'I am the resurrection and the life.'[7]

Many at a deathbed did interpret those scenes in this positive manner, using words we do not today think of in connection to a deathbed, such as 'edifying', or even 'delightful'.[8]

These were considered to be commendable views, and were therefore written about, and we know of them. That does not mean, however, that they were universal. Others who remained silent at the time found no comfort in these last moments, indeed often finding instead that these religious views produced the opposite of comfort. The novelist Samuel Butler (1835–1902), the son and grandson of clergymen, wrote a lacerating satire of Christian deathbeds, excoriating those who oppressed the dying with such beliefs and behaviour. In his novel *The Way of All Flesh*, the Reverend Theobald Pontifex, a not-at-all disguised portrait of the author's own hated father, is placed at the deathbed of a parishioner to administer 'what he is pleased to call spiritual consolation'. The dying woman begs him to reassure her that she will not end up in hell, which shocks him deeply: 'If there is one thing more certain than another it is that . . . the wicked will be consumed in a lake of everlasting fire,' he pronounces, before returning home, 'conscious that he has . . . administered the comforts of religion'.

The novelist's depiction of the secular aspects of dying were no warmer. When Theobald's own wife is dying, his 'impatience became more and more transparent daily', and when she does die after a brief illness, he sums up their four decades of married life for his children: 'She has been the comfort and mainstay of my life . . . but one could not wish [her deathbed] prolonged,' he intones before burying his face in his handkerchief to conceal his want of emotion.[9] It is no surprise that this novel was published only after its author's own death.

Whether praising the virtues of the deathbed, using it as an educational tool or mocking it, it remained a very real presence in people's lives, an event that recurred and one on which therefore many held strong views. When William Gladstone's mother was dying in 1835, he expressed concern that the drugs she had been given for pain might cloud her mind and render her unable to prepare mentally and spiritually. The Gladstones were a deeply committed family of Evangelical Christians, although it became clear that Lady Gladstone was not quite as spiritually prepared as religious tracts would lead one to expect. 'You all give me the idea that this is my last hour,' she said to her grieving family gathered around her bed, 'but I have no such notion.' When her son offered to read prayers aloud, she demurred, saying she did not feel up to it, and she also headed him off when he tried to talk to her of her oncoming death and spiritual transformation. Gladstone comforted himself by deciding that this meant that death had been 'disarmed of its terrors', and that 'she was ready . . . to go forth and meet the bridegroom', that is, Christ.

Fifteen years later he was less phlegmatic at a far more traumatic deathbed, that of his four-year-old daughter Jessy, dying of tubercular meningitis. He wrestled with the injustice of this death, undergoing a 'spiritual struggle to accept God's will', his faith wavering as he watched his daughter's small body wracked by seizures. There was no talk now of triumph of the spirit, only desperate prayers that his daughter's sufferings might end quickly to spare her further pain. It was not to be, and the family was forced to watch the child convulse over and over until the end, with Gladstone struggling to find any redemptive grace in her suffering.

Almost as common, and as agonizing, as the death of a child was that of a mother in childbirth. Margaret Gladstone was the daughter of a clergyman; in 1869 she married John Hall Gladstone, a chemist later to become president of both the Physical and Chemical Societies, and no relation to the political family. The following year she gave birth, her mother recording both the birth and Margaret's subsequent death of puerperal fever (sepsis), which set in shortly after. It was, according to the tenets of religion, as good a death as anyone could have written in the pages of a novel. She had plenty of time, her mother wrote, and she was mentally alert enough to prepare: 'her husband said to her, "I think my love God is going to take you to Himself". She said, "Do you" and after a moment added, "When?" He replied, "I think today". After lying still a little, she said, "Bring baby[,] Mamma". When I came back with the little thing she looked to her husband and said, "John you dedicate our baby to God",' before asking to see her husband's children by his first wife. 'She took the hand of each and kissed each and said, "Goodbye".' Her husband then asked her if she would say farewell to their servants, and she agreed, but said she was not up to speaking to them. Nevertheless, when they appeared in the sickroom she rallied enough to address each one individually with her last words. The new baby's wet-nurse was crying, and 'When she heard this, she tried to raise herself a little and said with deep earnestness in broken accents "Do the best you can for baby – in God's name". Then she shook hands with all the servants and said as loudly as she could "Do the best you can for baby – in God's name – all of you."* As with many of these scenes, the pragmatic mixed in with the emotional: 'Once she said "There is nothing in [the] world that John would not get for me and there is nothing I want but a cup of pure cold water" . . . This was a very short time before her breath ceased . . . John stood at her pillow and I was beside her on the bed till almost the end. She motioned me off and crossed her hands on her breast and so passed very gently away.'[10]

Deathbeds which did not occur in as model a fashion might afterwards be rearranged in the retelling, either by those who had been present, or by those who would later claim that they had been present, to better conform to the ideal. Sometimes it was unconscious – what the living wished had taken place. At other times it might be more calculating. When the Duke of Wellington died in 1852, the artist Joseph Williams produced a widely admired engraving of an image of his final moments, with Lord and Lady Wellesley, his son and daughter-in-law, offering loving support on either side of the comfortable armchair in which the old duke was peacefully sleeping away his final moments. In reality, neither son nor daughter-in-law was present, and the duke's last hours were spent in violent convulsions, each fit worse than the last.[11]

Sometimes it was not who was present or absent, but what was said that was reconfigured to conform with expectations. The son-in-law of Walter Scott, the most renowned novelist of the early nineteenth century, produced a massive seven-volume memoir of his father-in-law after his death in 1832. In it he wrote movingly of how the dying man had said, urgently, 'I may have but a minute . . . My dear, be a good man – be virtuous – be religious.' It was only a century later that a letter was discovered, written by one of Scott's family and hinting heavily to the biographer, 'When you

* 'Baby', also named Margaret, grew up to become a prominent suffragette and socialist, and the wife of prime minister and co-founder of the Labour Party Ramsay MacDonald.

Joseph Williams, 'The Death of the Duke of Wellington' (1852),
engraved by John Gilbert.

write anything of the last very melancholy weeks . . . it will be
most valuable to many any of the few remarks he uttered . . . of a
religious tendency such as I heard he said occasionally . . . for
there *are* wicked people who will take a *pleasure* in saying that he
was not a religious man; and *proving the contrary will do much
good.*'[12]

While this was not discovered until after all involved were long
dead, other deathbed conventions were more openly understood
to be just that – conventions. A book entitled *Death-Bed Thoughts*
by a pseudonymous 'M.H.', published in 1838, soon after Scott's

death, consisted of a series of prayers written and offered up by the author who, 'when they were written, was in daily expectation of her final summons', as she explains in the third person in the preface, making it clear by the very fact of this publication that that final summons had not ultimately been issued. The prayers, she added, encompassed 'feelings [that] should not be too familiarly discussed', composed as they had been by her to be addressed solely to her Lord, which were too sacred to share with others, before going on to say that nevertheless, 'at the wish of some dear and intimate friends' who had asked for copies, she had decided in the event to publish. So the dying author of these private prayers had not been dying, the private prayers had first been shown to an unnamed number of friends, and so sacred were they that they were now being published for profit, all the while being presented, and accepted by readers, as non-commercial spiritual grace.[13]

At other deathbeds, the family helped to set the scene, as did, sometimes, the dying themselves. When Alfred, Lord Tennyson, the great poet of Victorian grief and mourning, was dying in 1892, his son Hallam wrote down the details of his final days. Father and son went out for a last drive, and Tennyson 'would point out his old accustomed haunts saying "I shall never walk there again."' Once bedridden, he asked Hallam to fetch the volume of Shakespeare that contained his three favourite plays, *King Lear*, *Cymbeline* and *Troilus and Cressida*, reading some lines from it to his doctor before telling him he would never recover. A few days later, he returned to the book before asking for the window blinds to be raised: 'I want to see the sky and the light,' he said, repeating, 'The sky and the light!' He soon became less aware of his surroundings, asking, 'Have I not been walking with Gladstone in the garden, and showing him my trees?' He talked to his doctors about death, and 'What a shadow this life is, and how men cling to what is after all but a small part of the great world's life.' Then, 'Suddenly he gathered himself together and spoke one word about himself to the doctor, "Death?" Dr Dabbs bowed his head, and he said, "That's well."'

When there was no context, families were often content to provide it. Tennyson said suddenly, 'I have opened it,' and Hallam wondered whether he was writing a new poem in his head, or perhaps referring to the volume of Shakespeare by his bed, although of course it could have been anything at all. When he was next conscious, he blessed his wife and Hallam, and

> For the next hours the full moon flooded the room and the great landscape outside with light; and we watched in solemn stillness . . . we felt thankful for the love and the utter peace of it all; and his own lines of comfort from 'In Memoriam' were strongly borne in upon us. He was quite restful, holding my wife's hand, and, as he was passing away, I spoke over him his own prayer, 'God accept him! Christ receive him!' because I knew that he would have wished it . . . Nothing could have been more striking than the scene during the last few hours. On the bed a figure of breathing marble, flooded and bathed in the light of the full moon streaming through the oriel window; his hand clasping the Shakespeare . . . the majestic figure as he lay there, 'drawing thicker breath'.[14]

Within those final few lines, Hallam painted what was virtually a theatrical picture, a dramatic scene complete with stage lighting and an architectural feature, the oriel window, a standard symbol for 'Olde England'. For text he drew on Tennyson's lifetime work, patching together lines from 'In Memoriam', a poem grieving the death of Tennyson's great friend Arthur Hallam, in whose memory Hallam Tennyson had been named, written between 1833 and 1850; from the 'Ode on the Death of the Duke of Wellington' of 1852; and from the 'Passing of Arthur' from his *Idylls of the King*, written between 1859 and 1885. With these, he carefully crafted a majestic deathbed that would be deemed appropriate to the century's great poet. It is hard not to compare this elaborately constructed scene to the bare description left by another literary son on his father's death. The poet Edward FitzGerald wrote, simply, of his father: 'He died . . . after an illness of three weeks, saying [only] "that engine works well".'[15] Of course, FitzGerald was writing a private letter; Hallam Tennyson's highly coloured deathbed scene was for public consumption, in a memoir of his father. It was not a deliberate deception, nor exactly false; instead it was an uplifting finale for his readers, similar to that supplied by W.E. Gladstone's daughter, who told his biographer that at her father's death in 1898, 'all that dreadful pain and suffering' was 'swallowed up in victory', a transformation that enabled her to feel not the horror of the medical details, but the moment where the 'beauty and the triumph' prevailed.'[16]

In reality, Gladstone's suffering had been prolonged. Earlier in the century, pain had routinely been controlled by the free usage of opium-based patent medicines, of laudanum and later of morphine and ether too, as well as copious amounts of alcohol, with fortified wines such as brandy, port and sherry all regularly recommended by doctors to stimulate their patients between doses of opiates. Sometimes chloroform was also used to keep the patient unconscious as much as possible, to 'assuage the torments of the parting hour'.[17] By the end of the century, however, anxiety about addiction was causing responsible doctors to question the quantity of opium products that were offered, restricting them, or refusing them altogether until the patient no longer had any chance of survival. It had taken many months before Gladstone's cancer was diagnosed, and until then he suffered. After the diagnosis, wrote his daughter, now 'the doctors can feel it right to do all they can to ease the pain'.[18]

The deathbeds here described were all among the comfortably off, among those who had the finances to pay for medical attendance, and for drugs and adequate food and drink, as well as enough leisure that their families could afford to dedicate their time to the dying.* Yet not only was this not the norm, it was extremely rare.

The mainstream middle class in Britain in the nineteenth century occupied a far smaller percentage of the population than it does today. In 1851, perhaps as few as 5 per cent of the population would have been defined as middle class; another 5 per cent might have been somewhat wealthier, in the upper middle classes, and then there were the gentry and upper classes, a yet smaller percentage. Well over 80 per cent of the population was working class.[19]

For this great mass of the population, a good death was a fast death, because delicate or nutritious food for the patient, or drugs that might ward off the worst pain, much less medical attendance, were all unaffordable. And if these items were purchased, and the patient died anyway, the money that had been swallowed up by these expensive foods and drugs was now unavailable to pay for the funeral, or for the daily expenses of a family who might well have lost its breadwinner. Following the death of his three-week-old child, a shoemaker had to purchase both the infant's coffin and grave on credit, which he then had to work extra time to pay off. Even in the more comfortable middle class, death, and sorrow, could imperil a family's finances. One small local newspaper proprietor wrote that 'Business was progressing satisfactorily when the greatest calamity of life befell me; I lost my only child, then in her nineteenth year. This was a blow that took me a long time to recover from . . . Humorous writing was out of the question for some time, indeed, any kind of writing, as I felt as if I had nothing further to live for . . . The circulation of the journal went down . . .

---

* The Gladstones were rather more than comfortable, their fortune having been founded by W.E. Gladstone's father, Sir John Gladstone (1764–1851), a merchant and plantation owner whose slave-holdings were so vast that after the abolition of slavery in 1833 he received the single largest payment of all those made by the British government to slave-holders as 'compensation' for the loss of their 'property'.[19]

My partner's health continued to decline, and we agreed to give up the business.'[20]

In the twentieth century some historians suggested that, since the great proportion of the population through history had seen their children die, they therefore invested little emotion in them. There is no evidence to back up this preposterous claim, while there is a great deal of evidence to show the opposite: that parents of every class were devastated by the deaths of their children. For example, some of these historians have interpreted the tradition of parents repeatedly giving their newborns the same name as their dead siblings as an indication of a stolid unconcern for the individuality of each infant, yet it is equally likely that these grieving parents were memorializing their lost children, whom they loved and mourned, the repeated names a testament to the affection that had been vested in each tiny being before their early deaths. In a world with few permanent graves for the masses, their names alone were their tombstones.[21] In the same way, parents who refused to talk about, or even mention, the names of their dead children had not necessarily forgotten them, nor did they not care about them – often, they cared so much they could not bear to hear their names.

The middle classes had the time, energy and leisure to devote to writing down their losses. Those without time, energy or leisure could do so far less, but they shared the emotions. The Reverend Francis Kilvert visited a working-class parishioner in 1875 following her child's death.

[T]he poor mother was . . . frantic with grief. Her face was wild and haggard, there was a hard, strong stare in her eyes . . . 'I think it will kill I,' she said, in a hard agony. 'I don't know whatever I shall do. The only comfort I have is thinking the Lord's time was come to take her. I was reading in the Book this morning and it said . . . "His hour was come" . . . so I hope Alice's time was come and that the Lord has taken her to heaven. But if the Lord would only take me too. Oh, if the Lord would only come to me in dreams or in some way and tell me that she was safe,' cried the poor heart-broken woman, with a burst of tears.[22]

Even those of a more stoical temperament could make their grief heart-rending by its sheer understatement, one woman saying of another, who had twins, 'But the children didn't stay . . . they went back again,' with Kilvert adding, 'as if they had just come into a room and gone out again' – so these children slipped away from their parents.[23] Almost three-quarters of a century earlier, another clergyman, Sydney Smith, otherwise known for his wit, concluded resignedly at his three-year-old son's deathbed, 'the life of a parent is the life of a gambler.'[24]

Others followed the route of Kilvert's parishioner, trying to accept their child's death as God's will, or even as a blessing, with their child now safely in a place where the struggles and pain of earthly life could not touch them. Some saw these deaths as punishment for their own sins: one woman wrote of her 'sore bereavement': '*I* made an idol of [my child] and so lost him and must travel my wilderness journey alone.'[25] Others tried to feel the loss as a reprieve. Catharine Tait, before the deaths of her own five children, commiserated with a close friend on the death of her baby. Her heart 'bleeds' in sympathy, she wrote, but 'that dear Saviour . . . has indeed heard your prayers and given early to your child that heavenly inheritance which he has purchased for him! O my darling, what a link you have with heaven [now]! . . . You will, I know, find comfort when you think your darling one will never now bring dishonour on that holy name'.[26]

These were mainstream attitudes, and there was a whole range of books, sometimes referred to as 'comfort literature', anthologies of religious extracts and consolatory verse available for bereaved parents. These books expressed for many the loss they could not put into words, but, more than that, they offered the hope that their children were in a better place. They also encouraged parents to practise submission to God's will, whose higher purpose was hidden from earthly eyes. The Reverend Edwin Davies, author of *Children in Heaven, or, Comfort for Bereaved Parents*, thought that some children died early to save them from becoming tainted by parents who were insufficiently pious; even as pious parents, he was quick to assure the sufficiently pious, had no need to berate themselves for their loss. Their children, he thought, had probably died young to enable them to avoid the temptations of the world as they grew up.[27] He interspersed these thoughts with poems and essays such as 'The Weeping Angel', with its lines: 'Some children belong to God and their mothers. But some seem to belong to God only. These die soon, and they like to die. Yet they love their mothers better than other children do.' Other volumes had doggerel ditties: 'Their wings were grown, / To Heaven they're flown.'[28]

For those without a bent for literature, there was a market in paintings and engravings that also offered comfort. Popular paintings were routinely reproduced in magazines and sold as prints, for those who neither went to art exhibitions nor had much money to spend. Thomas Brooks was a successful artist who in four years between 1859 and 1863 painted a trilogy: 'Consolation', depicting a dying girl with her mother and a clergyman, while on the mantelpiece a guardian angel can be seen shepherding a small figure protectively; 'Faith', where a girl reads from the Bible as her sister lies dying; and 'Resignation', once again a mother watching over her dying child, whose hand has fallen from her grasp. The genre-painter George Elgar Hicks' 1855 'The Peep of the Day' showed a small child sitting up in bed, gazing out of the window at a brightly lit scene beyond. The child was a portrait of Hicks' son Freddy, who died a month after the painting was exhibited, his death having been prefigured in the altar-like shape of the canvas, while the sunshine out of his reach symbolized the future glory awaiting him in heaven. Hicks lost another child ten years later, and as late as 1890 was still painting images of angels escorting dying children to heaven.[29]

Because of the legacy of these books and paintings, it has been easy to believe that people *were* resigned, were accepting of God's will. But that was not necessarily, or routinely, the case. The novelist Mrs Oliphant, who outlived all five of her children, tried her best. When her ten-year-old daughter died, she told herself first that the child was 'with God, she is in His hands'. But she could not maintain this, wondering, 'Can I trust her with Him? Can I trust Him that He has done what was best for her?' She admitted, 'I have not been resigned, I cannot feel resigned . . . I keep on always upbraiding and reproaching God.'[30]

For others, the rise of a more secular society concentrated people's minds on social conditions rather than on God's will. (By 1851, a religious census had revealed to the pious the shocking fact that more than half the adult population of the country probably did not attend religious services of any sort, increasing to possibly two-thirds of the population when children were included.)[31] Further change was driven by the increasing professionalization of the medical man, something that encouraged patients to transfer their faith from clergy to doctor, or at least to spread it equally between the two. This in turn promoted a change not merely in how the dying were expected to behave, but how others were expected to behave to them. Henry Halford (1766–1844) was a renowned physician with a long, distinguished career behind him as the official physician to four monarchs, George III, George IV, William IV and Victoria, as well as head of the Royal College of Physicians for a quarter of a century. He continued to follow the older path of telling his patients and their families when death was likely, so that they could prepare. The equally distinguished, pioneering medical ethicist Thomas Percival (1740–1804), although his elder by a generation, by contrast thought that a doctor's function was to prolong life by treatment where possible but also to offer the patient and family hope, which might well mean dissembling about a prognosis.[32] In this he was more in line with the new ideas filtering in from the Continent. C.W. Hufeland's *On the*

Relations of the Physician to the Sick was translated from German in 1846, and widely read. He too counselled that it was more important 'to preserve hope and courage', if necessary by 'conceal[ing] all danger'. His warning was stark: 'To announce death is to give death.'[33] While this obfuscation did not become standard practice, it does reveal a fissure in the previously widely held belief that complete knowledge of the medical situation was necessary for spiritual preparation.

How each family, and each family doctor, made the decision varied. Mrs Oliphant's views fluctuated depending on which end of the story she found herself. When her mother's doctor told her that her mother was terminally ill, she was dazed with shock, but she seemed never to have considered telling the dying woman, instead staying away because 'I never [kept] a secret' from her, and did not feel confident that she could keep this one. Less than thirty pages after writing this, she recorded how her husband was told 'his case was hopeless' by his doctor, but he in turn told Mrs Oliphant that 'the report was excellent', and he was just overworked. She was 'angry and wounded beyond measure' when she discovered that in truth he was dying, and 'would not believe that my Frank had deceived me'. Years later, she turned again, grateful and relieved that her son 'had no apprehensions' that his end was near.[34] In other cases, it could be the dying who knew their prognosis, while their families refused to hear it, or, having heard it, to understand it. Prince Albert was said to have known full well that he was dying, and wanted 'to speak openly of his condition' to the queen, as he 'had many wishes to express'. But 'she could not bear to listen, and shut her eyes to the danger' he was in until the very last moment, claimed at least one newspaper. Just days before his death, which was abundantly evident to medical men and family alike, she was still quite sure the doctors 'will save him for me'.[35]

Even as people were faced with the brutal truth of deathbeds on a regular basis, fiction in particular helped them to cope by presenting these ends not as they were, but as they would have liked them to be. In Taylor's *Holy Dying*, children on their deathbeds are presented as models from which to learn, 'murmur[ing] not' as they approach their last days, accepting their lot with meekness.[36] Dickens owned an anthology of Taylor's writings which included extracts from this volume, and it may well be, given its popularity, that he returned to it when drawing the character of Little Nell in *The Old Curiosity Shop* (1841). Her death was one of the most famous in the nineteenth century, and in all English literature, as was that of Paul Dombey, in *Dombey and Son*, written seven years later. Less remembered now, little Paul Dombey was in the nineteenth century the very model of the sickly, weak child, 'too good for this world', who just faded away out of life. Today these novelistic child deaths are mocked as sticky and sentimental, with the word sentimental used to describe those scenes of sadness from which all negative feelings have been removed, scenes of grief that, counter-intuitively, leave the reader with a warm glow where in real life sorrow would be. Oscar Wilde famously joked, 'One must have a heart of stone to read the death of Little Nell without laughing', which is very witty but overlooks the hundreds of thousands of parents who read that fictional death, and many others like it, and found comfort in the echo of their own losses.[37] Francis Jeffrey, an eminent judge as well as the co-founder and editor of the *Edinburgh Review*, and thus hardly a naive reader, wrote to Dickens that he had 'cried and sobbed' over the death of Paul Dombey, 'and felt my heart purified by those tears, and blessed and loved you for making me shed them'.[38] These deaths clearly possessed a power and meaning they no longer have, a sense of purpose in helping to ameliorate readers' suffering through the expression of grief.

For in sentimental fictional deaths, unlike the desperate struggles of real children like Jessy Gladstone, these imaginary golden-haired children are not in pain, not afraid. Little Nell actually looks forward to death: 'It would be no pain to sleep' among the dead in a pretty country churchyard, she muses; after her death, the narrator descants on how no real sleep had ever been 'so beautiful and calm, so free from trace of pain'. For the bereaved these fictional deaths could be a momentary break from the reality of the losses and trauma they lived with daily. Dickens' friend and biographer John Forster wrote afterwards that it was he who suggested Little Nell had to die: 'after taking so mere a child through such a tragedy of sorrow', he thought, it would be better to create a scenario in which 'the gentle pure little figure ... never change[s]'. Instead, as Wordsworth described in 'We are Seven', a hugely popular poem of the day, the 'simple Child' enumerates her six siblings: 'two of us at Conway dwell, / And two are gone to sea. // Two of us in the church-yard lie, / My sister and my brother'.[39] The dead live on in the churchyard, and on the page. And so Nell, who, as Taylor recommends, thinks regularly about death, visits churchyards, talks to gravediggers and finds comfort in the company of the dead. Her grandfather, a gambler whose actions put her in the path of the novel's villain, Quilp, could also be drawn from Taylor, who wrote of those who fail to lead model lives, as the type whom 'all the world say that it had been better this man had died sooner'.[40]

Yet while Dickens had read Taylor, he also subtly altered both Taylor's precepts and those of the Evangelical movement of his day. Nell does not die, as children in Evangelical tracts do, in front of the readers' eyes. Instead those final moments are discreetly moved offstage, and Nell is returned to readers only after death, when she has become, in effect, a beautiful waxwork, surrounded by flowers and winter berries. Again, this is a contrast to the realities of even the most religiously inclined. Margaret Gladstone spoke regularly of the happiness that awaited her after death, but also said she was 'so frightened': 'Some die so bravely – I die so stupidly,' her mother recorded her saying. In the 1880s, another pious woman dying in childbirth in her twenties, in a harrowing week of blood and vomit, had as her last words just a despairing 'God has forgotten me.'[41]

In fiction, this type of end was not for the young and the beautiful, but was allocated to the villains, who on their deathbeds were wracked with bodily pain, while mentally they were either tormented by fears of the afterlife, or died cavalierly protesting their disdain for future punishment. The good, particularly children, confessed their sins, prayed, or possibly were too weak to do so and asked those around them to do so. Frances Trollope's *Mabel's Progress* (1867) painted a model scene of this type:

'Don't be sorry, all of you. I think – I – hear mamma. It seems as if – as if – there was a voice calling me, ever so far away. It must be – mamma. Good-bye, papa. Kiss me, Alf, my own brother – my darling – be – good – God bless you, Alf. How dark it is!'. . . Suddenly she sat upright, as though struggling for breath; but in a moment the most lovely smile beamed over her sweet face, she stretched her arms out before her, crying, 'Yes, yes, it *is* mamma! She is calling me again. Oh, mamma, mamma, take Cora!' and fell back in Mabel's arms as softly as a little wave that melts upon the summer sea – dead.[42]

Fictional child deaths were equally welcomed in works for children. Especially among Evangelicals, a good deathbed was a useful lesson for young readers, a stern guidance onto the paths of righteousness. Children in children's fiction die like clockwork, keeling over from a range of common diseases, but more often from doing wrong, including minor childish infractions such as telling lies, or quarrelling, or failing to listen to adults, or even because they 'went to bathe instead of attending divine worship'.[43] *The History of the Fairchild Family*, by Mary Martha Southwood, was first published in 1818, as the Evangelical revival was reaching its height. It was so successful that a continuation of the adventures of these almost insanely pious children appeared in the 1840s, although by then popular religious fervour was somewhat muted. The Fairchild children, Lucy, Emily and Henry, are guided by their deeply religious parents to understand that they live in a world of mortal sin, and that every action – every minor squabble over a toy – is a reckless and weighty step on the path to damnation. Unrighteousness, and frequently righteousness too, leads inevitably to death. One of the neighbouring gentry family's children, Augusta Noble, has a 'custom' of playing with matches, and so she inevitably burns to death. Meanwhile, the children's grandmother tells them stories not of her own happy girlhood, but of the death of her childhood friend; a four-year-old is run over and killed by a carriage, whereupon another child present, being 'naturally delicate', is so traumatized that she too dies. The central death of the first volume, however, is that of the son of a local villager, a friend to the Fairchild children, who dies with his family grouped around the bed as he blesses his friends and family, accepts Christ as his redeemer and dies 'looking upwards'. After his funeral, the Fairchild children 'thought and talked much of little Charles and his happy death, all day'.*[44]

As the bereaved found comfort in these fictional recountings, so those dying also drew on novels to comfort themselves and others. On his deathbed, Julius Hare, a clergyman, was asked if he was comfortable, to which he replied by 'pointing with his finger as he spoke [the words], "Upwards, upwards."'[45] When his biographer reported this in 1855, there would be few among his readers who did not immediately think of *David Copperfield*, published five years earlier, when David commends the woman who will become his wife for her pious encouragement, 'ever directing me to higher things! . . . Until I die . . . I shall see you always before me, pointing

---

* The book's popularity did not mean it was not ripe for satire. Despite the prolonged dying of Paul Dombey in *Dombey and Son*, the author can't resist a sideswipe. When Paul is rebuked for inquisitiveness by being reminded of 'the story of the little boy who was gored to death by a mad bull for asking questions', he protests, 'Nobody can go and whisper secrets to a mad bull. I don't believe that story.' The success of soldier-turned-librettist Harry Graham's 1898 *Ruthless Rhymes for Heartless Homes* indicated *The Fairchild Family*'s continuing reach, even at the very end of the century: 'Billy, in one of his nice new sashes, / Fell in the fire and was burnt to ashes; / Now, although the room grows chilly, / I haven't the heart to poke poor Billy.'

upwards!' And he ends the novel, 'O Agnes, O my soul, so may thy face be by me when I close my life indeed; so may I, when realities are melting from me like the shadows . . . still find thee near me, pointing upwards!'[46] Whether the dying Mr Hare was therefore having thoughts of the afterlife, or whether he simply wanted to be propped up in bed, whether he was thinking of *David Copperfield* himself, or even whether the words and gesture were flourishes added by his biographer, we cannot know.

The interweaving of actual and fictional deathbeds found a further development among many of those who had the time, education and leisure to keep records of the illnesses, dying and deaths of their family and friends. Keeping a diary or journal had long been a recommended religious practice for those of Evangelical tendencies, a way of considering both thoughts and deeds, and accounting to God for them. At a deathbed, these memorials or memoranda (both words were used) were continuations of that practice, regularly encompassing medical records and social events as well as spiritual ones. The Taits had kept journals, although during the worst of their crisis Archibald had been unable to write in his; Catharine continued, and later left a letter for her children to be read after her death, in which she proposed they use her record of 'that time of trial' as 'a word of help and comfort to those upon whom a similar burden is laid'.[47] For most, however, these memorials were family documents, not for publication. The Gladstones and their cousins, the Lytteltons, kept memorials of the deaths of the members of their extended families, sharing them, copying out sections, adding to them and rereading them, finding comfort in following the details even of relatives they had not known, or could not remember. Similarly, the travel writer and memoirist Augustus Hare (1834–1903), who had been adopted as a child by his aunt, after her death found among her possessions 'a small parcel with a black edge . . . marked "Memorandums, Helas!"' containing the medical account of his sister's final illness, the newspaper notice of her death, and 'a little packet inscribed "Triste et Chere", enclosing the earliest primrose of that year's spring, on which

[she] had written, "The sweet angel brought me this little nosegay, Wednesday, 17th March. On Wednesday, 24th, she herself had faded, drooped, and ceased to breathe.""*48

The medical detail included in memorials can be astonishing, and disturbing, to modern eyes. The religious-tract writer Emily Gosse, the wife of naturalist Philip Gosse, had been treated by a quack who promised to cure her breast cancer, but instead ensured an agonizing and tormented death. Her husband's memorials of her final months were graphic, and were published by him in the hope that 'the Lord may possibly make use of this simple record of one of his servants, for the stirring up of the faith and love of those who knew her not, and thus to the extension of his own glory'.[49] The Gosses were Plymouth Brethren, a fundamentalist group of Nonconformist believers, but it is hard to comprehend today how the glory of God could be won by the details of an attempt to burn away Mrs Gosse's tumour with nitric acid.

The memorial tradition was not always a religious one, particularly later in the century. At Karl Marx's funeral in 1883, his colleague and partner Friedrich Engels detailed Marx's last days, including a description of his pus-filled pulmonary abscess.[50] The biographer Leslie Stephen (1832–1904), father of Virginia Woolf, grew up in an Evangelical family, and although as an adult he was a declared agnostic, the memorandum formula evidently spoke to him, if not in the way it would have to his family. When his first wife, Minny, died, and again after the death of Julia Stephen, his second wife and the author of *Notes from Sick Rooms*, he put together a record that was later referred to in the family as the 'Mausoleum Book'. He had initially intended it to be a letter 'for my darling Julia's children', but for him it was neither a religious testament nor a consolatory record. It was just that 'I do not

---

* Augustus Hare wrote in his autobiography that soon after his birth his aunt, who was also his godmother, had written to his parents, offering to adopt him. His mother responded at once: 'My dear Maria, how very kind of you! Yes, certainly, the baby shall be sent as soon as it is weaned; and if any one else would like one, would you kindly recollect that we have others.'

feel equal to taking up my old tasks again' right after her death, and so he spent the next days writing down 'some of the thoughts that have occurred to me'. Here there is no medical information, nor deathbed scene. Instead, for Minny, 'I remember only too clearly the details of what followed; but I will not set them down', while for Julia, 'I cannot venture to speak of the last terrible time'.[51]

More unusually, Alice James preferred to produce her own memorial. She had long kept a journal, and when she became too ill to continue writing she dictated her diary entries, and even a farewell telegraph: 'Tenderest love to all. Farewell. Am going soon.' Like Stephen, she included few medical details, but she focused instead on the process of dying. It was 'no doubt instructive, but it is disappointingly free from excitements . . . One sloughs off the activities one by one, and never knows that they're gone, until one suddenly finds that the months have slipped away and the sofa will never more be laid upon, the morning paper read, or the loss of the new book regretted.' Until, finally, 'I am being ground slowly on the grim grindstone of physical pain, and on two nights I had almost asked for [a] lethal dose, but one steps hesitantly along such unaccustomed ways and endures from second to second.'[52]

The Gladstones and the Lytteltons, the Stephens and Alice James, the mother of Margaret Gladstone who died in childbirth, all wrote for themselves, or for a limited circle. For the famous, dying was as detailed in public as these memoranda were in private. Royalty had long died publicly. In 1820 there had been complaints at the lack of details of the declining health of George III. When George IV was on his deathbed, therefore, first his medical details were disseminated, and after his death his post-mortem information, too, was published in *The Times*: 'The body exhibited but little sign of putrefaction . . . The stomach and intestines were . . . of a darker colour than natural, in consequence of their containing mucus tinged with blood, and in the stomach was found a clot of pure blood, weighing about six ounces . . . [the colon] had formed unnatural adhesions to the bladder, accompanied by a solid inflammatory deposit of the size of an orange . . .'[53] Politicians received the same treatment. When Sir Robert Peel fell from his horse and was crushed, he lingered for three days before he died, and the crowd that had gathered outside his house was given regular updates via bulletins posted on the railings, which were also reprinted in the newspapers. These moved from reports that described his injuries – a broken collarbone, but no head injuries – to assuring watchers that he was 'progressing as well as could be expected', although they became increasingly less sanguine: after the fall, he was 'completely insensible', 'pallid', and it had taken 'several moments' for him to be able to identify anyone, instead lapsing into 'a kind of stupor'. Then they grew more gloomy still: he was in pain, feverish, finally 'in a very precarious condition', with at least five updated bulletins on the day he died.[54] The same types of updates were made for Disraeli some thirty years later, in 1881; and for Tennyson, not a politician, but as the poet laureate a public figure.[55]

For some of these notables, the deaths were a beginning. It was what happened to them afterwards that created communities of grieving.

3

FROM CHURCHYARD TO CEMETERY

In the nineteenth century, before grieving could begin, families, communities, the church and the government were all faced with a new struggle: how best to dispose of the dead. For nearly a century, the idea of sun-dappled country churchyards – where wildflowers grew, children played, families gathered, a place of Romantic peace – had become deeply embedded. In *The Old Curiosity Shop*, Dickens drew on these tropes to create an enduring image, one which, given the great success of his book, in turn fixed the notion ever more firmly in place. He described just such a churchyard, where 'young children sported among the tombs, and hid from each other, with laughing faces. They had an infant with them, and had laid it down asleep upon a child's grave, in a little bed of leaves. It was a new grave – the resting place, perhaps, of some little creature, who, meek and patient in its illness, had often sat and watched them, and now seems to their minds scarcely changed.' One of the romping children tells Nell that it was not a grave at all, but 'a garden – his brother's. It is greener, he says, than all the other gardens . . . [and when] he had done speaking, he looked at her with a smile, and kneeling down and resting for a moment with his cheek against the turf, bounded merrily away.'[1]

This was written in 1841, and for decades afterwards, writers and artists painted similar pictures. The successful salon painter Henry Bowler's most famous work, *The Doubt: 'Can these Dry Bones Live?'*, showed a woman leaning on a gravestone. (See plate section.) She is not wearing black, so presumably the dead – given the symbolic name of John Faithful on his tombstone – has been gone for some years, yet she remains faithful too, even as his epigraph promises new life: 'I am the Resurrection and the Life', and also 'Resurgam' ('I will rise again'), as a butterfly, the symbol of the soul, flits across an uncovered skull.

Yet the bones visible in front of the tombstone give the modern viewer pause, indicating as they do the great shift in attitude, and in actuality, that was underway in the nineteenth century. In the classical Roman world, dead patricians had been buried with inscriptions in stone permanently marking their resting places. By the fifth century in Christian Europe, the dead were assumed to be in the care of the Church until the day of Resurrection, and no physical markers of identification were considered necessary.[2] Initially in Britain, the dead were buried in the fields without any markers, although by the seventh and eighth centuries chapels were frequently built nearby. The burial grounds, or churchyards as they became known, in fact came to be the element that defined a church, separating it from an abbey, a monastery or other place of prayer or contemplation – a church was a building that had a churchyard.*

Yet historically churchyards had by no means been the places of quiet, tomb-filled contemplation depicted by Dickens and Bowler. In the Middle Ages, churchyards, handily located in centres of population, were treated as commercial and civic venues where scribes set up their businesses, and booksellers, second-hand dealers and other merchants erected market stalls. In different parts of Europe between the thirteenth and the seventeenth centuries, multiple edicts banned dancing, gambling, mumming (pantomimes), juggling, sports of various types, music and theatrical performances from churchyards.[3] These repeated injunctions

---

* For clarity, the basic definition of a churchyard here is a burial site operating under the auspices of clergy of any denomination, usually but not always immediately adjacent to a church; a cemetery is run either by a private company or a civic, governmental body; graveyard and burial ground are generic terms that can mean either of the above.

make it clear that all of these activities were commonplace occurrences in these spaces: no one bothers to forbid things that are not occurring.

It was not only among the living in those vibrant, bustling churchyards that usage and custom had altered. Until the seventeenth century, bodies had routinely been buried directly in the ground, without coffins. There was no expectation that a body would remain in situ until the second coming of Christ, when the dead would rise – that is, in secular terms, for all eternity. Instead, as bodies decayed, older bones were removed to make room for the more recently dead. This is what was being depicted in Bowler's painting, and the passage of time is the reason the woman who continues to visit John Faithful's grave no longer wears mourning. Although, more generally, and in contrast to this image, because these graves were seen as temporary, they were rarely given any permanent marker such as a tombstone. As late as the end of the eighteenth and the first half of the nineteenth centuries in one churchyard in Leicestershire, fewer than 10 per cent of the graves had tombstones; in other districts where they were more numerous, even there, as many as half the graves were unmarked.[4] As tombstones came to be the norm, what was written on them began to alter. Between the sixteenth and the early eighteenth centuries, there had been a focus not on commemorating the people themselves, but on physical decay more generally, as a reminder and warning to the living. Images of skulls, bones and grave-digging tools were common, together with symbols indicating impermanence, such as snuffed-out candles or sundials. These were reminders, mementi mori: this will happen to you too.[5]

By the eighteenth century, more and more grave-markers were being erected, and the epitaphs and memorial images used on them also altered. Now they euphemized death as sleep, and even more they spoke not of the bodily decay that happened to everyone, but instead commemorated the specific person who had died, using set phrases such as 'in loving memory', 'dear sister/mother/brother/

father', mixed with words of emotion relating to the mourners, eternalizing in stone the 'deep anguish' and 'loving hearts' of those left behind.[6] Yet for some time this change was still not widespread. As late as 1809, in the political philosopher William Godwin's 'Essay on Sepulchres: or, A Proposal for Erecting Some Memorial of the Illustrious Dead in All Ages on the Spot Where their Remains Have been Interred', the idea of memorializing the dead permanently in stone was rare. 'Ordinary tombstones,' he wrote, 'are removed much after the manner, that the farmer removes the stubble of this year's crop that he may make room for the seed of the next. Go into any country church-yard. Three-fourths of the tombstones, you will find dated to within the last twenty or thirty years.' Even in St Paul's, where the great and good were majestically entombed, he noted that 'no thought occurred of marking the spot where the ashes of our ancestors reposed'.[7] Instead tombs were erected, only to be later swept away.

In reality, the situation of the dead was somewhat more compli-cated than Godwin suggested. Before 1852, the living were not purchasing space for the dead, but renting it for an unenumerated but finite period of time. However, the legal position regarding gravestones was in direct opposition to this, gravestones being the property of those who had paid for them. Thus, a body could osten-sibly be exhumed in order to make space for new burials, even as at the same time it was illegal to remove the gravestone that marked its spot. In practice, therefore, a grave with a tombstone was more likely to remain untouched than a grave without one.[8]

The only places where permanence, or just longevity, of burial was expected was inside the churches themselves, locations that were therefore more prestigious, and expensive, and so mostly reserved for the upper middle and upper classes. These sites long continued to be desirable. Many of the churches built in the seventeenth century had huge vaults designed to bury thousands, as in Nicholas Hawksmoor's design for Christ Church, in London's Spitalfields (built 1714–29). The vaults in this church were enlarged again in the eighteenth century to create private family burial sites containing up to forty-five bodies each, and once more in 1813. Ultimately nearly 70,000 people were buried inside the one church in just 130 years.[9] This overcrowding was at one and the same time regarded as entirely normal and something that people disapproved of. As early as 1664, the diarist Samuel Pepys was appalled when, following his request for his brother to be buried near to the family pew, he discovered how 'a man's tombes are at the mercy' of the employee known as the grave-marker, who 'for sixpence . . . would, (as his owne words were,) ". . . justle [the bodies already buried] together [to] . . . make room for him;" . . . and that he would, for my father's sake, do my brother that is dead all the civility he can; which was to disturb other corps that are not quite rotten, to make room for him . . .'[10]

In a similar vein, the narrator of a horror story published in 1831 passes through a churchyard, noting that, 'Some one had that day been buried, and less care than is usual had been taken in closing up the grave, for, as I went forward, my foot struck the fragment of a bone. I lifted it hastily, and was about to throw it away . . .' It is clear to a modern reader that the body had been buried without a coffin; that the narrator is not particularly shocked by this; and that he plans neither to rebury the bone, nor hand it over to be reburied, but simply tosses it aside.[11] All of this is incidental to the story, just used as local colour. For the overcrowding of churchyards by the 1830s had become a routine matter. In fact, it had come to be expected. To deal with the problem, in the first instance soil was simply added over past burial plots, in which more dead were interred above the earlier burials. Rising ground levels in burial plots were therefore the norm.* When more drastic action was needed, the older bodies were removed entirely, the bones, grave-clothes and coffin remains burned. When neither of these actions sufficed, every

---

* The results of this continue to be visible in London today. A children's playground rises at least one full storey above street level on the western side of Drury Lane. At the very back of this site, against the wall, rest a few of the gravestones that were removed when the churchyard was closed and the ground given over to civic use.

now and again an entire churchyard, or section of a churchyard, was completely dug up. In this manner, for example, Holy Trinity Church in the centre of Hull was able to accommodate the dead for half a millennium in just over half a hectare of ground.[12]

It was only in the 1820s and 1830s that people began to find these methods distasteful. This was a period of social and political agitation. A broader (although entirely male) population was winning the right to vote; factories and other workplaces were beginning to be regulated; and a new argument was being made: that the people's labour improved the value of the state, and thus their health should be considered the responsibility of the government. Discussions concerning the condition of churchyards were therefore subsumed into a discussion of public health, and of sanitation, with which it was inextricably entwined, all under the rubric of 'burial reform'.

Radical burial reform was enabled, in part, by a welcome innovation: the private cemetery. These garden cemeteries, as they quickly became known, were not affiliated with a specific church, nor even religion, nor were they any longer located in small, enclosed spaces in the middle of towns and cities. These new cemeteries were designed to be park-like, beautiful spaces for the dead and their mourners, and had evolved simultaneously in several parts of the world over the previous centuries. In Surat, in Gujarat, India, the Dutch had designed spacious areas for the dead far from both town centres and their churches. In 1767, a formal space with generous paths, carefully planted screens of trees and elegant vistas was laid out in Kolkata, creating a formula that was soon followed in Kanpur, and then further afield, in Malaya and in Sumatra. In Europe, the success of the Père Lachaise cemetery in Paris, which opened in 1804, with its paths and flowering plants and shrubs designed to showcase tombs and mausolea, made it a prototype.[13] Yet while it is often presented as a parent to the garden cemetery movement in Britain, Père Lachaise was as different from British cemeteries as French gardens were from British ones. Père Lachaise was designed on a grid pattern, with paths at right angles, graves set in straight lines and tightly packed together. By contrast, the British garden cemetery was more 'garden' than 'cemetery', intended to resemble the rolling parklands of aristocratic estates, a style heavily promoted by the Scottish garden writer and botanist John Claudius Loudon (1783–1843). In the eighteenth century, the word used to describe these parks was 'elysian', that is, a place a god would inhabit, referring to the Elysian Fields of Greek mythology, where heroes and those linked to the gods spent their afterlife.[14] In a some-what poetic reversal, then, in the nineteenth century these elysia of the elite were shaken about and turned into real-life gardens for the ordinary dead.

Loudon saw cemeteries as repositories of the dead, to be sure, but he and his fellow reformers understood these repositories to be permanent, which meant they required far more land than a city churchyard. More, he also saw them as places for the 'improvement of moral sentiments and general taste of all classes', as beautiful sites where every grave was 'a page, and every headstone or tomb a picture or engraving' that taught a moral lesson.[15] He popularized these views in a series of letters to the newspapers, a calculated campaign for public approval, before summing up his decades of plans in *On the Laying Out, Planting, and Managing of Cemeteries*, published in 1843, where he presented his ideal cemetery, how it should be designed, what it would cost and so on.* This ideal was not the French formula, of order and straight lines, but one of winding paths of differing sizes (in part for aesthetic reasons, and in part to allow for the distinctions of hierarchy and class, with the graves of the more socially prominent set on the grander, broader paths), bordered by trees and flowering plants, with carefully created vistas for the visitors, and with chapels and ancillary buildings in a range of architectural styles.

* The book began life as a series of articles in *Gardener's Magazine*. It is worth pausing on the idea of a modern gardening magazine running one article, much less a series, on cemetery design, which does indicate how vast the change in mentality between his day and ours is.

The earliest private cemeteries in the British Isles were not, however, focused on appearance, nor were they under the sway of Loudon. They were founded for more utilitarian purposes. Legally, Church of England parish churches were required to bury any parish resident of whatever faith or creed on payment of a set fee. Unofficially, some parish churches refused to bury non-Anglicans, whether they were Jews, Catholics (this was rare), or Dissenters and Nonconformists (far more frequent). And even when the clergy did accept non-Anglicans, their relatives found it repugnant to be obliged to pay church rates to have their dead buried, and distressing to see them buried with Anglican rites. The cost of the funeral was another obstacle. In a Church of England churchyard by the nineteenth century, everything apart from the burial was an extra: where the grave was, the choice of coffin, at what time of day the funeral was held, whether it was for a child or adult. St James' Chapel and Burial Ground in Westminster had so many add-ons to its burial charges, at so many different prices, that its list of fees was three pages long.[16]

There were burial grounds in Britain where non-Anglicans could find a resting place, but not many. The first Jewish cemetery had been established in Whitechapel, in east London, in 1697, and another four were opened in different parts of the country over the next century. The most famous cemetery for Dissenters, Bunhill (a corruption of bone-hill) Fields, was possibly functioning in the early seventeenth century, although the first concrete evidence we have of it as a graveyard dates from 1665, when it was used as a plague burial ground. By the eighteenth century, it was being run by private entrepreneurs.*

Bunhill Fields covers barely more than 1.5 hectares and is in the centre of London. Dissenters in other parts of Britain needed burial

---

* Today Bunhill Fields is owned by the Corporation of the City of London, which promotes it as holding the remains of the English language's first novelist, Daniel Defoe, the visionary poet William Blake, Thomas Bayes, for whom the Bayes theorem is named, several Cromwellian offspring, a few generals, and Susanna Wesley, mother of the founder of Methodism.

sites too, and ten of the first thirteen cemetery companies were established by Nonconformists, offering burials to the dead of any denomination. These companies were generally funded through joint-stock companies, public companies run by boards of directors, which raised operating capital by selling shares. The nineteenth century was the age of the joint-stock company, and as well as raising funds for new banks, or railways, or other speculative ventures, all of which were common, the method was also used to fund local amenities such as parks. The first Nonconformist cemetery of this type, the Rusholme Road Proprietary Cemetery, opened in Manchester in 1820, and soon there were similar cemeteries across the country.

The second element driving the shift from churchyard to cemetery, especially to garden cemetery, was not religion but hygiene. In the 1820s, religion had been the prime motivator for these companies. Then the 1830s saw the arrival of cholera, with its multiple swift deaths. The garden cemetery was promoted as a way of avoiding the old plague pits, or the temporary burial grounds of more recent epidemics. In 1836, the government passed an Act for Establishing Cemeteries for the Interment of the Dead, Northward, Southward and Eastward of the Metropolis by a Company to be Called 'The London Cemetery Company' – this mouthful generally referred to as the London Cemetery Act.[17] This enabled the London suburbs of Surrey, Kent and Middlesex to fund and create garden cemeteries to serve the capital, providing 'Paths, Walks, Avenues, Roads, Trees, Shrubs and Plantations as may be fitting and proper'. These cemeteries were desperately needed in this time of cholera. Thomas Carlyle, who it must be remembered discounted the epidemic, nevertheless reported in the year after the Act was passed: 'The funeral bell never ceased here, nothing but funerals whenever you stirred.'[18]

By now, emergency legislation had been passed that said the dead should be buried as quickly as possible, with as few people as possible in attendance. Over the next decades, recurrences of the cholera epidemic flared up, and more regulations ensued: that the bodies should not rest at home but be taken to cholera hospitals before burial, and that the dead were to be buried in mass graves, and in quicklime for sanitation, without any funeral service at all. These regulations caused not just protest, but riots.

Unfortunately for the government, the first wave of the epidemic reached Britain at exactly the date parliament was examining a change in the law on anatomization of the dead. Anatomization had been a historic post-mortem punishment that, until this period, had been inflicted only on the bodies of executed criminals. These bodies were sent to surgeons, who used them to teach anatomy to future generations of surgeons. There had never been very many of these criminal dead, but the decline of the bloody code, the harsh capital punishment laws for a vast array of offences, came just as the professionalization of medicine and medical education ensured the number of medical students was rising, causing the emergence of a new trade: the trade in dead bodies, carried out by what were known as resurrectionists, men who illicitly dug up the newly dead to sell their bodies to medical schools for the study of anatomy. To eradicate the practice, the government found itself considering permitting the sale of any body unclaimed by friends or family to hospitals and anatomy schools. To the poor, this sounded very like (and was) a licence to dissect the poor for the crime of being poor. (For more on resurrection men, see pp. 218–26.) Taken together with the simultaneous arrival of cholera, this new, foreign and incomprehensible disease overwhelming the country, it felt as if the government's additional sanitary regulations around funerals were just another way for the state to benefit the rich by harming the poor.

The poor, not unnaturally, objected, often violently. In Edinburgh, soon after cholera appeared, a crowd attacked a cholera van transporting a woman to hospital, in order to 'rescue' her from what the crowd feared would be medical experimentation by doctors. In Paisley, Glasgow, the magistrates had set aside a new burial ground for the poor – one they failed to have consecrated, and which was out of town and therefore difficult for mourners to visit. Riled up further by the rumours sweeping the country, groups of fearful and enraged working people exhumed a series of new graves there, only to find them empty, the bodies vanished. The obvious next step was to attack the cholera hospital itself, where they believed the exhumed dead had been taken for anatomization. Those who already thought that cholera was a plot by doctors to victimize the poor had these feelings reinforced by the hostility of the medical and scientific world towards them, many of whom believed that only 'Drunkards, Revellers, and . . . the thoughtless and imprudent' were struck down by cholera.[19] (This was the wording of placards erected by the Oxford Board of Health: the professionals were not keeping their views to themselves.)

Even where bodies were not being stolen by resurrectionists, churchyards were routinely desecrated and bodies dug up and disposed of for a far more basic reason: overcrowding. Cities had grown exponentially in the nineteenth century. In 1800, London had had just under 1 million residents in a population of 8.6 million in England and Wales; in 1850, there were nearly 2.4 million people living in London, and 16.5 million in England and Wales, with most of those people now living in urban environments. And where they lived, so they died and needed to be buried.

One of the fiercest popularizers of this problem, framing it as one of hygiene, was a London surgeon-apothecary named George Walker (1807–1884). Walker had set himself up in practice in Drury Lane, which was surrounded by almost a dozen church-yards of varying stages of pestilence owing to overcrowding, not even taking into account the 'several' (he does not quantify) local slaughterhouses for cattle that served the local markets. As well as working as a medical practitioner, Walker set out to examine and report on the conditions of London churchyards, publishing a series of pamphlets and books, from his first, *Gatherings from Graveyards*, through *Interment and Disinterment, Burial-Ground*

Incendiarism, A Series of Lectures on the Actual Conditions of Metropolitan Graveyards and, finally, *On the Past and Present State of Intramural Burying Practices.*

As these titles suggest, his books were not for the weak of stomach. Walker was a campaigner, and he was determined to appal his readers as much as he was appalled. In *Gatherings from Graveyards*, he described the Green Ground burial ground near his practice. It was 'saturated with human putrescence', he wrote, forcing pedestrians to walk by open graves, with bones lying any which way and exhumed coffins broken up for firewood as the gravediggers removed the coffin furniture (the handles and name-plates) to sell to second-hand dealers.[20] Then there was St Ann's, in Soho, where by his calculation 110,240 people had been buried over the past 160 years in just one half acre of ground – 1,000 bodies per acre, or 0.4 hectares, per year.[21]

A modern historian of death and dying has evaluated the infor-mation in Walker's books, and thinks that in actuality human remains probably made up 'easily less than 1 per cent of the foul-smelling organic dirt produced in London in 1840', the rest a combination of human excrement and urine, horse, cattle and sheep excrement and urine, animal matter from slaughterhouses, fish and oyster residue from merchants and sellers, as well as the by-products of the hundreds of tanning and dyeing workshops that were far more hazardous to city-dwellers.[22] This was not, however, Walker's view, nor that of his contemporaries, and by focusing on hygiene, on desecration and on the very worst cases, he made his point. He routinely described gravediggers pulling up just-buried bodies in order to make space for new ones, severing the limbs of barely disposed of corpses with their spades before burning them, or jumping on shallowly buried coffins to compress them in the ground so that new coffins could be dropped on top.[23] But he became famous for his dissemination of the details of a state of affairs that had begun before he moved to Drury Lane: the Enon Chapel scandal.

In 1822, a Baptist chapel had been opened in St Clement's Lane, off the Strand (now buried under the Aldwych, west of the Royal Courts of Justice), in one of a row of new houses, under the auspices of the Reverend Mr Howse, who held services and ran a Sunday school on the ground floor. Downstairs, he held funerals, with a burial ground in the cellar that mimicked the burials in vaults and crypts in churches. This was extremely popular, partly owing to the chapel's very low burial fees, a flat 15s., or a week's wages for many of the working poor. This compared favourably with the fees of the nearby church of St Clement Dane, which charged £1 17s. 2d. for a churchyard burial, rising to £2 15s. 10d. for non-parishioners. In addition, Enon Chapel had no requirement that the dead be Baptists. Those were the positives. The negatives were more pronounced. The basement was barely a basement, some describing it as being only five or six steps lower than the ground floor, with the barrier between the cellar and the floor above made of nothing more than the ground floor's floorboards, enabling both smells and vermin to travel upwards with ease. Here, in a cellar that measured approximately eighteen metres by nine metres, Mr Howse may have conducted as many as 12,000 funerals in seven years, earning nearly £1,000 in the process. Walker reported that congregants suffered numerous ailments from the stench, and the Sunday school children referred to the ever-present vermin as 'body-bugs'.

Walker publicized this in 1839, and the parish paused the burials for a year, but there was no formal ban before the chapel closed for good in 1842. In 1844, a reminder of the scandal flared up again when the building's new tenant found bones under his kitchen floor, and yet once more when, in the following decade, a teetotal group rented the building to hold dances, advertising them as 'Dancing Over the Dead'.*24

---

* In 1967, the London School of Economics, which owns the land on which St Clement's Lane once stood, laid the foundations for a new building. On excavation they found what they thought was a plague pit, but at least one historian thinks it is more likely to be the remains of the Enon Chapel cellar.

An 1850 print shows the defunct Enon Chapel turned into a dancing saloon, but still with its ominous cellar beneath.

In 1843 a report for parliament, 'A Supplementary Report on the Results of a Spiecal [sic] Inquiry into the Practice of Interment in Towns', appeared, written by Edwin Chadwick (1800–1890), a prickly, difficult and hugely influential social reformer who reinforced in governmental language the same message Walker was promoting to the population at large. By this time some of the country's newest and most forward-looking garden cemeteries had been open for years: Glasgow's Necropolis from 1832; Kensal Green Cemetery in north-west London from 1833; the twenty-hectare Norwood Cemetery from 1837; Highgate Cemetery from 1839; and more up and down the country. In popular culture, at any rate, these consciously beautiful sites were seen as a response to the horrors that Walker and Chadwick publicized. The most popular penny-blood of the century, G.W.M. Reynolds' *Mysteries of London* (1844), has a London gravedigger confess that, if a description of Enon Chapel, or his own churchyard, were to be published, 'you'd make the fortunes of them new cemetries [sic] that's opened all round

London, and the consekvence would be that the [burial] grounds *in* London would have to shut up shop.'[25]

The builders of these cemeteries had assimilated the ideas Chadwick focused on. Good surroundings, it was felt, promoted good behaviour and good morals: living beside the dead, whether next to city churchyards, or by being forced to keep one's dead at home until burials could be arranged, promoted 'vice and misery'. Extending this, cemetery-planners built chapels and outbuildings in a variety of historical and geographical styles: Egyptian obelisks and tombs, Gothic chapels, Romanesque cottages for groundskeepers, all 'teaching' history to visitors, who in addition would assimilate the benefits of the natural world and the virtues of the picturesque as they strolled in the landscaped grounds. Instead of religion, these cemeteries presented a social ideal, one that mirrored the new suburbs they were built in. Both valued bourgeois life in (semi-) rural quiet and tranquillity away from the thrum of big-city life, where middle-class families could rest together as a family unit, whether at home while alive, or in a garden cemetery for all eternity.

While today Glasgow's Necropolis, or Highgate Cemetery in London, or Brookwood in Surrey, which opened in 1852, might be more famous, and a part of a tourist visit, in the nineteenth century it was Kensal Green Cemetery that made the shift from churchyard to cemetery an acceptable, even fashionable, thing, both for the dead and for their mourners. Many literary figures of the day wrote about it. Dickens' *Household Words* magazine had an 1852 essayist boast that it was his 'fortune' to live nearby, 'within the range of the odours of the roses, the mignonette, and the other flowers', where 'the sacredness of death and burial' could be appreciated.[26] The journalist Samuel Blanchard first wrote an essay in praise of the place for a popular magazine in 1842, an essay so well received that it was then reissued as a guidebook to the new cemetery, its pages noting the cemetery's beauty, who was buried where, and then listing 'a long array of noble and honourable names', including Kensal Green's pride, the tomb of the Duke of Sussex, the first royal personage to choose to be buried in a civic cemetery.[27] The celebrated of the day followed him. Loudon himself was buried there, as were writers including Robert Browning, Leigh Hunt, Thackeray and Trollope, the engineer Isambard Kingdom Brunel, the publisher John Murray, and the artists Robert Smirke and Isaac Cruikshank.

So celebrated was Kensal Green that, by the 1880s, its very name stood as a synonym for death: 'we go to Paradise, by way of Kensal Green.'[28]

4

BEFORE THE FUNERAL

The long lead-up to 'Kensal Green', to death – sickness, deathbed, prayers and last words – was not a path to an end, but instead just the start of another lengthy process. In 1836, death had become a matter of governmental bureaucracy as well as a familial and religious event, when secular documentation supplanted parish registers and religious ceremonies as the means of formal certification of three major life events. Following that year's Birth, Deaths and Marriages Registration Act, and the consequent establishment of the General Register Office, it became obligatory within a set number of days after a death to supply the newly ensconced registrar of the district in which the death occurred with information regarding the date and time of death, and the person's name, sex, age and profession. After an expansion of the Act a few years later, the cause of death also became obligatory. While causes such as 'death by decline', 'long illness', 'cold' or 'old age' continued to be submitted, and accepted, these new requirements indicated a shift of both perception and expectation: everyone now had to have died of something, no matter how old they were.[1] A Certificate of Registration of Death (not yet what we know as a death certificate, which only became mandatory in 1874) was then issued, which had to be handed to the officiant before a funeral service could be conducted.[2]

In earlier centuries, what were known as Bills of Mortality had been attempts to create records of deaths through weekly mortality returns that were compiled from information supplied by local parish clerks. They recorded information supplied voluntarily by any parish that chose to participate, with no civil or ecclesiastical obligation or oversight. The individual causes of death reported in them were most commonly established by a searcher, a woman who, unusually, took on the role of the parish sexton: she seated congregants in church on Sundays and was in charge of the church keys. In her role as searcher, she also examined the bodies of the newly dead to ascertain the cause of death. Searchers had first been appointed in the sixteenth century, to account for plague victims, and these women continued to quantify and qualify deaths until the early decades of the nineteenth century, when the professionalization of both medicine and the civil service saw them written off as ignorant and uneducated. It is notable, however, that the men who in the nineteenth century made their careers from the dead – the statisticians, medical practitioners, registrars and coroners – all utilized the information that these supposedly ignorant women had amassed.[3]

London's Bills of Mortality had been kept, more or less continuously, from the seventeenth century, although geographically they never encompassed the entire city. Other urban areas began later or covered a limited number of districts. When the General Register Office was established for England and Wales in 1836, it was for the purpose of regularizing civic bureaucracy, not for medical or scientific reasons, and consequently registrars were typically legal professionals, either lawyers or clerks; fewer than 15 per cent were medically trained, even in the most minimal way. (One registrar listed himself as 'registrar, undertaker and comedian' when, perhaps inevitably, he went bankrupt in 1841.) Thus the records frequently continued to deploy the rather vague wording that the Bills of Mortality had used routinely, with causes of death including 'natural', 'bedridden', 'suddenly', 'grief' and even 'frightened'. Still other terms were descriptions rather than causes: 'nervous', 'decline', 'mortification' and the all-encompassing 'age'.[*][4]

* 'Mortification' had several meanings, from simply fading away to a technical term for gangrene or necrosis of some sort. It was also used to describe the state of unconsciousness that preceded death.

One of the many Bills of Mortality that preceded the establishment of the General Register Office in 1836, that newly centralized location for the registering of all births and marriages, as well as deaths.

Whatever the formal cause, in a world where virtually everyone died at home, what happened after death was generally dealt with by the family, not by professionals, and thus, just as there were books on how to look after the dying, so there were books on how the dead should be cared for. The Reverend W.H. Sewell's *On Christian Care of the Dying and the Dead: A Few Hints Designed for the Use of Friendly Readers* is a good example of the genre, mixing as it does religious precepts, prayers and biblical history with pragmatic, practical instructions. A prayer should be said following a death, the clergyman instructed his readers, but, more immediately, the eyes of the deceased should be closed, although never, he added, with 'pennies or half-crowns'. If the action were promptly taken it would be unnecessary to do something so disrespectful, indeed so 'frightful'. This should be immediately followed, he continued, by tying a cloth band around the head, from under the chin to the crown, to ensure the mouth stayed closed as rigor mortis set in, although rather than giving the technical scientific term, he referenced the biblical Lazarus.[5]

Early in the century folk belief held that until the actual burial, the deceased were not quite dead, although neither were they quite alive. Caring for the body of the newly deceased, therefore, was a way of helping to usher this half-and-half entity towards the afterlife. This was not any form of religious orthodoxy, and yet it was so widely believed that a number of traditions devolving from it were frequently practised, even among the many who had no idea why they were doing these things. The doors and windows of a house might be opened to let the soul out, said some, or to cleanse the sickroom of miasmatic airs, said others. Fires were extinguished, mirrors covered or turned to face the wall, blinds were drawn throughout the house (in some northern regions, the blinds were removed entirely, and white sheets, kept specifically for these occasions, were pinned up). A piece of cloth might be tied around the door knocker to muffle any sound from outdoors. Neighbours drew their own blinds on the day of the death, and again on the day of the funeral. For many, these were the normal conventions to be observed, ways of indicating respect and without any inherent meaning beyond that. Others, however, thought that the actions were more profound, for example preventing the not-quite-dead from seeing themselves reflected in the mirrors or glass and so becoming confused, possibly causing them to lose their way to the next world.[6]

At the same time, the body was to receive what were sometimes referred to as the 'last offices', the final services families could render to their dead: the laying out of the body, preparing it for the coffin. Whenever possible, said Sewell, these tasks should be done within two hours of death, for preference by a woman, or two women together. He assumed that they would be family members or their servants, thinking it 'heartless' to hand the task over to a stranger, although he simultaneously recommended calling in 'a Deaconess, or "Sister"', a laywoman connected to a religious institution.[7] Those were extremely uncommon in England, and it was far more usual, particularly for the working and middle classes, to call on the same women who were employed locally for nursing and midwifery. Julia Stephen, from an upper-middle-class background, assumed in her *Notes from Sick Rooms* that the laying out would be done by an employee, whether a household servant or a nurse, with supervision from the women of the family to ensure that the task was 'tenderly done'.[8]

A body was frequently laid out on the bed where that person had died, if the bedroom was not needed by other family members. If it were, then the body was moved to a table or a board. In preparation, the bedding was removed from the bed, or the table covered with a sheet, and then the body was washed, the hair, including beards and moustaches, tidied and trimmed. This washing served no medical or funereal function. Folklore held it was a form of after-death baptism, another custom to help usher the soul to the next world; others saw it as the final service, an act of love, that the living performed for the dead. The next instructions were, however, practical: the body's orifices were plugged, and the limbs straightened, with ankles tied together, before it was dressed in its grave-clothes.*

While many historical texts, and even modern studies, say that 'all' bodies were dressed in shrouds, or winding sheets, an archaeological analysis undertaken at Spitalfields in London shows that the majority of the dead examined there were buried wearing their own clothes, some with a shroud in addition, while only 40 per cent were dressed just in shrouds. Among the examples they found were a silk weaver wearing an old, darned cotton nightshirt that had clearly been his own in life; a man in uniform; another in clothes that had been fashionable sixty years before his burial; and a woman buried with a man's military uniform – two pairs of trousers, a coat, cap, gloves and shoes.[10] In other cases the dead were dressed in items specifically designed for the grave, items that resembled clothing in appearance but lacked functionality: they might have buttons, but with no corresponding buttonholes; or they had none of the finishing details such as linings or pockets; or the decorative elements were elaborate but without oversewing, which meant they could never be laundered.[11]

Nonetheless, shrouds, whether used alone or in conjunction with other clothes, made up a substantial proportion of grave-clothes. In the seventeenth century, to benefit the wool trade, an Act of Parliament had banned the use of any grave-clothes not made of wool, punishable by a £5 fine. This was repealed in 1814, after which cotton began to be used along with wool. Shrouds and winding sheets were now almost always one of those two fabrics, except for the tiny minority purchased by the ultra-wealthy, who might want luxury fabrics like silk.[12]

While the words 'winding sheet' and 'shroud' are often used interchangeably, they are not the same thing. A winding sheet was just that, a double-sized sheet that was wound around the body to

---

* In some areas, the tying was temporary, the cloth fastenings left until rigor mortis was complete, yet often still with folk beliefs attached: in Lincolnshire, for example, many thought that if the legs remained tied, the dead would be unable to rise at the Resurrection.[9]

wrap it, and then tied under the feet and at the top of the head, with the face left visible. In 1598, a tale by a minor Elizabethan writer named John Dickenson used the name of his then more famous coeval, Robert Greene (now best known for dismissing Shakespeare as an 'upstart Crow'), as its supposed narrator who, 'raised from the grave', sits at his desk in his winding sheet to write the story the reader is about to begin.[13]

This was a joke, but more soberly, the poet John Donne, who was Dean of St Paul's, had himself sculpted before his death in 1631 wrapped in his own winding sheet, with his feet resting on a funeral urn, supposedly ready for the Resurrection.

Robert Greene in his winding sheet, in John Dickenson's *Greene in Conceipt* (1598).

A shroud was more structured than the winding sheet. It had sleeves with, at the front, a collar and decoration at the neck or breast. The back, however, resembled a modern hospital gown, with nothing but ties to keep the sides in place. A visitor to Britain, who had evidently never seen anything like it, described one in 1719:

> the Dead shall be bury'd in a Woollen Stuff, which is a Kind of thin Bays [baize], which they call Flannel . . . This Shift is always white; but there are different Sorts of it as to Fineness, and consequently of different Prices. To make these Dresses is a particular Trade, and there are many that sell nothing else; so that these Habits for the Dead are always to be had ready made, of what Size and Price you please . . . After they have wash'd the Body thoroughly clean . . . they put it on a Flannel Shirt, which has commonly a Sleeve purfled [embroidered or decorated] about the Wrists, and the Slit of the Shirt down the Breast done in the same Manner. When these Ornaments are not of Woollen Lace, they are at least edg'd, and sometimes embroider'd with black Thread. The Shirt shou'd be at least half a Foot longer than the Body, that the Feet of the Deceas'd may be wrapped in it, as in a Bag. When they have thus folded the End of this Shirt close to the Feet, they tye the Part that is folded down with a Piece of Woollen Thread, as we do our Stockings; so that the End of the Shirt is done into a kind of Tuft.[14]

With this went a cap, differently styled for men and women, together with gloves and sometimes shoes and stockings. People whose work entailed professional or ceremonial dress, whether uniforms, robes or vestments, were frequently buried in them. The Reverend W.H. Sewell advised that, after the dead were dressed, their arms were to be crossed across the breast.* This was varied for

* This crossed-arm position was so common that one historian wonders if the children's expression of good faith, 'Cross my heart and hope to die', draws on the sight of the crossed arms of the dead.

the clergy, whose hands were placed in the prayer position while holding a chalice, Sewell adding pragmatically that, as the vessel would of course be buried, it could be made 'of inferior metal or [even] wax', directing his readers to a shop where these replicas could be purchased.[15]

After the bodies were laid out, the families who could afford it frequently surrounded them with fresh flowers, or, as in the case of the poet Hartley Coleridge, son of the more renowned Samuel Taylor Coleridge, others contributed their own floral offerings. After Hartley's death, Wordsworth and his wife paid a call: 'Mrs W kissed the cold face thrice, said it was beautiful, and decked the body with flowers,' recorded Hartley's sister Sara.[16] And, surrounded by these fresh flowers, or ferns or foliage, there the dead were left until the funeral. In the interim days, family and friends sat beside the dead, cherishing their last moments with their loved ones. For the bereaved, it was awful in the older sense – something that filled them with awe – and also a comfort.

Customs surrounding a death in the house frequently followed a similar pattern, whether for rich or poor, rural or urban.[17] There were other rituals that were less universal, found either in distinct areas of the country, or only among certain groups of people. The strength of belief in folklore depended on where people lived, their social and educational status and how embedded they were in the local community. But for many, ideas of death and the dead were foci of folkloric beliefs. For there were religious ideas associated with death; there were community ideas associated with death; and there were ideas that no one was quite sure where they came from.

The idea of death tokens, omens that foretold a death, was a popular one. With infant mortality so high, death tokens often clustered around the possibility that the life of a newborn would be cut short. A baby that failed to cry on baptism would die early, or it might if its first tooth broke through on the upper rather than lower jaw, or if anyone was foolish enough to set a cradle rocking before there was a baby to lay in it.* For a newly married couple, the first to turn from the altar after a wedding was solemnized would die first, or perhaps it would be the person who fell asleep first on their wedding night. If a dressmaker used a black pin when fitting a bride-to-be's wedding dress, the bride was doomed, as she and her new husband would be if they passed a funeral on their way to or from the church.

Birds were ominous. Death would follow a bird tapping at a window, or one flying down a chimney flue. So too would death come after seeing a magpie if the viewer were not quick enough to bow to it and recite a verse to keep it away. Other doom-warning wildlife included the deathwatch beetle, or rats that chewed the furniture, or a hare if it crossed one's path, or seeing a white rabbit anywhere, or bees settling on a hedge-stake. If a cock crowed before midnight, a death was sure to follow, as it would if an owl was heard hooting. An ox or cow breaking into a garden was a certain precursor of death.

Plants were ominous too. Digging up parsley would occasion an unnamed death, whereas if a child picked wild parsley, they were condemning their own mother. (The plant was therefore colloquially known as stepmother's blessing.) Bringing May blossom into the house would cause a death in the family. So too would many household accidents: breaking a glass or mirror; a clock stopping; the fire either sparking up or dying down unexpectedly; a picture falling off a wall; or a knocking sound, known as a death-knock. If the melted wax from a candle formed itself into a long curled piece,

---

* In a rare reversal portending life instead of death, babies born still surrounded by their cauls, or amniotic sacs, were said to be impervious to death by drowning. By extension owning a caul, no matter whose, was said to offer the same protection. This view was not confined to a rural or uneducated population. The catalogue of possessions of the poets Robert and Elizabeth Barrett Browning showed that they had a caul preserved among their papers, inscribed 'S.M. Barrett', which suggests it had surrounded Barrett Browning's brother at birth. By the end of the nineteenth century the belief was on the wane, only to flare up with the arrival of U-boats in World War I, when cauls once more became coveted objects around the docks.[18]

it was called a winding sheet and obviously foretold death. Even the humble tablecloth, if poorly folded so that the creases made a lozenge shape instead of a square, indicated a coming death.

Dreams could also portend death. Dreaming of an uprooted tree, or of broken eggs, was a bad sign, as was dreaming of a wedding. Seeing things that were not visible in a waking state was equally ominous. Most common was the phantom coach, known some-times as a deaf, rather than death, coach, supposedly because in the vision it made no sound. Or the death coach might drive up to the house where the death would later occur and instead of silence a hideous thud, as of a coffin being loaded onto it, would be heard.

While a vision of a coach was unexpected and distressing, at other times actions were actively taken to foresee if death were imminent. Those who wanted to know who was going to die, and when, stood on their church's porch on St Martin's Eve (24 April) and watched for a midnight procession made up of the ghosts of all those who were to die in the coming year. Watchers had to stay sharp, however. If they themselves fell asleep on the porch, they would never wake up, instead joining those passing spirits. The watchers also had to be committed. Once they watched for one year, they had to return and watch every year on that night: 'There is no escape.' Another onerous St Martin's Eve custom sent those anxious to know about future deaths to a barn, where they were to separate wheat from chaff at midnight, turn and turn about. The person left holding the riddle, or sieve, when a coffin passed by would die within the year. There was probably more than a little reliance here on metaphor: chaff was the husk around corn or other grain, separated when it was threshed or sieved, just as the living and dead would be separated, as the wheat from the chaff.

Then there were the beliefs concerning the dying. Slow, prolonged deathbeds were attributed to pigeon feathers being used in the bedding, which caused the dying to linger painfully. Kilvert reported that a Wiltshire parishioner went out to collect pheasant feathers for a dying family member, as 'folk do say that a person can't die on pigeons' feathers'. On the other hand, if a family member living at a distance was rushing back to see a dying person one last time, a bag of pigeon feathers under the bed would keep the invalid alive until their visitor could reach them.

After the death, lights, or corpse candles, might be seen 'leaving the house', dancing their way illusorily along the path the funeral procession would take a few days later. These were linked to will-o'-the-wisps, lights in the countryside that always stayed at a distance, and were thought to indicate the death of someone close, either in physical proximity or in terms of relationships. If the household had beehives, after a death someone had to go and formally notify the bees by tapping a house-key against each hive and announcing the death, or otherwise the bees would swarm and leave their hives. Sometimes a black crape ribbon was tied to each hive. (As late as the year this was written, 2022, on the death of Queen Elizabeth II, the queen's beekeepers were reported to have performed this ceremony.)

Across much of the country, especially in the first half of the century, deaths were marked with the tolling of the parish church's passing bell, sometimes also called a soul bell, or a death bell. Before the Reformation, the tolling had been a way of soliciting prayers for the dead; afterwards some maintained it rang to drive off any circling evil spirits. More prosaically, it was a way of conveying information to the community at large, announcing to all in hearing that a death had occurred. There was a code to the ringing, based on the tone, the number of strokes and how quickly or slowly the bell was rung. In general, a bell tolled a set number of times for a man, another, generally lesser, number for a woman, and even fewer for a child. Then came a pause before the age was counted out by a series of strikes. The hour that the bell was rung, or the number of peals, also permitted the dissemination of information about social class, with gentry being rung out at one hour, those of lesser caste another. The passing bell then rang once more at the funeral, 'to ring the dead home' as the procession walked to the churchyard, timed to finish as the funeral party reached the church gate. Each district had its own system, and in one area of Lincolnshire alone, antiquaries of the day counted eighty different ways of indicating who had died by the passing bell's strokes. It was also thought the passing bell could forewarn of future deaths. If it sounded different, perhaps owing to humidity or a storm, or if the bell was accidentally tolled at the wrong time, someone within hearing would die unexpectedly.

A dead body could also disseminate a warning. If rigor did not take hold in the normal time frame, another death in the family was imminent. Touching the body, or kissing it, could bring visitors long life, or good luck, or at least prevent the deceased from returning to haunt those who had paid it insufficient attention as a corpse. When the dead were removed from the bedroom and then the house for the funeral, they had to be carried out feet first, or bad luck would ensue. And that was if the householders had remembered to leave the front door open until the funeral guests returned from the churchyard: if not, bad luck inevitably followed.

More unusual, but regularly seen, especially in the border counties around Wales, was the practice of hiring a sin-eater. The main requirement was that food and drink be brought into contact with the dead, possibly by being left for a while on their coffin. In some areas, a dish of salt was put on the breast of the deceased, or beside or under the coffin. Sometimes the food or drink was left by the dead overnight before the arrival of the sin-eater, for the dead to consume in case they woke up and were hungry. The next day the sin-eater consumed the items, and in so doing relieved the dead of their sins, taking them on themselves instead. Unsurprisingly, the sin-eater tended to be some sort of social outcast, a person who at best lived on the edges of their community.

A large number of books, tracts and journalism expressed anxiety about the days between death and the funeral, an anxiety that living and working in close confinement with the dead was unwholesome, and unsavoury, and most of all unhealthy. Edwin Chadwick's 1843 report on the circumstances of the dead among the working poor was officially a discussion of health and hygiene in urban environments, but in actuality he was as much concerned with morality as he was with health. Chadwick was a proponent of the miasma theory of illness, believing that disease spread through rotten smells. He therefore thought the bodies of the dead acted as vectors, spreading disease in the working-class home in a way that did not appear to concern him, however, when speaking of laying out the dead in middle-class homes. In his report, he slid from stating that miasmas caused 'bodily injury' to his belief that living and working beside the dead emotionally desensitized the living and was therefore the cause of deviant, even criminal behaviour. (He also rather brutally noted that productivity would be negatively affected when the dead occupied the space where the living would otherwise be gainfully employed.)[19]

Although Chadwick had spoken to no one in the working classes while gathering his data, relying solely on those in supervisory roles over them – doctors, workhouse personnel, clergy – he was absolutely correct regarding the omnipresence of the dead in family accommodations in the days between death and the funeral. He simply failed to note that this was every bit as common among members of his own social class or higher. The extremely wealthy Gladstone family found they were 'much comforted by having Jessy near' before her funeral, and both her parents 'so deeply enjoyed the presence of her lifeless frame, with the now gentle traces of suffering, and the surpassing peace and purity, and even majesty that invested her countenance'.[20] Jeannette Marshall, the fashionable surgeon's daughter, felt the same knowing 'where [her brother] is, poor dear': in their parents' bedroom awaiting burial.[21]

For the wealthy or the merely prosperous like the Gladstones and the Marshalls, those days with the dead gave the families time to make funeral arrangements, perhaps allowing relatives to travel in from a distance. For the working poor, the same time was used to raise money for the burial. For all, however, at last the body was enclosed in its coffin after final farewells were said. By this time, decomposition had usually begun, a process that was euphemistically referred to as 'change', as when, in June 1858, a London widow sat beside her dead husband's body for a week, in one of the hottest summers ever known, when temperatures of 36°C in the shade were recorded, going up to 48°C in direct sunlight.*[22] After a week, she 'could not stay a moment [in the same room as his body], and it was no comfort, the whole was so changed.'[23] This 'change' was a problem. In winter, windows could be opened and fires left unlit. The funeral trade, however, needed solutions that worked year round, and one undertaker advertised 'Metallic Air-tight Shells', thinner inner coffins which were also said to be 'invaluable' for those who died of dropsy (now known as oedema, or fluid build-up), as they were perfectly watertight.[24]

The interior of a coffin was almost always lined with a mattress that, depending on the cost, was stuffed with wool, horsehair or straw, and was frequently decorated to match the coffin's lining and the shroud worn by the deceased. It was primarily a functional item however, helping to muffle any sound the jostled body might make when the coffin was lifted and, more importantly, there to soak up bodily fluids, while the coffin lining tacked to the sides also served to hide that reality from sight.[25]

Some families made the moment before the coffin was closed into a ceremony of farewell. 'I sat about an hour by him before the final moment came and covered his dear beautiful face with my handkerchief before I left him,' wrote Mrs Oliphant before her last child was buried.[26] The Marshall family created a far more elaborate ceremony. After her brother Reggie's death in 1873, Jeannette's father cut off a lock of his hair for each family member. They enclosed cuttings of their own hair in a piece of foil, on which Dr Marshall

* This was the summer that became known as the 'Great Stink', when the unusual heat in London saw the Thames reduced to a trickle, revealing the mass of festering sewage at its core. It was the precipitating event for the building of London's main sewer system, which ultimately reduced the number of epidemic outbreaks in the capital.

inscribed 'The hair of his Father, Mother, Sisters & Brother'. (The governess was permitted to include a clipping of her hair but was not named on the parcel.) The hair and a copy of Reggie's death announcement in *The Times*, also enclosed in foil, and inscribed 'The Little Soldier', were sealed in a bottle and placed in his hand. Mrs Marshall put a mourning ring she had been given on the death of her father on one of his fingers, just as she would two decades later on the death of Dr Marshall. The family encircled the coffin, placing their hands on it and asking forgiveness for any hurt or harm they had ever done their brother and son.[27]

Then came the funeral, a ceremony which increased, and then dramatically decreased, in elaboration and importance throughout the century, but a ceremony that long remained a subject of discussion, dispute and disagreement.

5

THE GREAT FUNERAL

Funeral customs and rites have changed over the centuries, even as those observing them continued to believe that their traditions were not merely the right, the real, traditions, but that they were hallowed by the ages, having been in place from time immemorial. As often happens with firm beliefs, there is little, if any, truth to this. Almost all nineteenth-century funeral conventions were fairly new creations, or reinterpretations of older ones.

Before the Reformation, a funeral was not the final ceremony for the dead. A second funeral service was frequently held a week after the first, and another at the end of the first month, called the month's mind. Still another might be held a year after the death, known variously as the twelve month's mind, the year-day or the obit, the word obit also being used to mean the prayers for the dead that were said at intervals following the death. The wealthy left money in their wills for these obits, with the formula that it was 'to be distributed for my soul', or even leaving it 'to me', that is, nominally to the testators to pay for prayers to be recited for their souls for ten, twenty or ninety-nine years after their death.[1]

The Reformation changed things greatly. No longer could prayers be offered to saints to intercede on behalf of the dead – in effect, it was no longer possible to pray the dead out of purgatory. By the 1540s the chantries where these prayers had been sung for the dead had been shut down. Thus, almost as a by-product, funerals changed from being a ceremony in which the living performed a vital function for the dead to being a ceremony that marked the secular life of the deceased retrospectively, commemorating how they had lived rather than showing concern for their future in the afterlife. In fact, by 1644 it was no longer necessary for a funeral service to be conducted by a minister of religion at all.

For the great, it was not the church that oversaw the details of a funeral, but the College of Heralds. Earlier the college had been in charge of royal ceremonies. Now they also began to lay down the rules for the funerals of aristocracy: who was to be appointed the official mourner; how many mourners were to follow the procession; in what order; how many bearers, horses, honours, flags and more. The minutely prescribed details were not about the dead as individuals, nor as souls to be prayed for, but were at their core about rank and hierarchy. Women could not be mourners, for example, because their rank and status derived from their husbands and fathers. Family relationships of all kinds were superseded by ties of status. Most importantly, the heraldic funeral was designed to stress continuity. It was about lineage and the status quo. The official mourner was usually the heir to the title or estates of the deceased, indicating that, while the individual had died, his rank and title continued.[2]

For the bulk of the population, however, even for the less exalted gentry, a heraldic funeral was a sideshow: something to see and admire, but nothing to do with them. Funerals for the population at large followed tradition, and in great measure they showed how the deceased, and the deceased's family, were enmeshed in a community.

It was not until the seventeenth century for some, and the eighteenth for the majority, that several of the elements we assume have always been present began to appear for the first time with any frequency. The Bayeux Tapestry, dating from around the late 1070s, includes a scene of the death of Edward the Confessor right next to a depiction of his funeral. The great king is taken to his grave wrapped in a winding sheet and carried on a bier by men who wear coloured clothes, as do the mourners behind, and two boys who are ringing handbells. There is no coffin as they bear their monarch to the priest waiting at the grave. More than half a

A woodcut from 'The Map of Mortalitie' shows a corpse in its winding sheet lying across a grave-digger's tools.

millennium later, a 1604 broadside, 'The Map of Mortalitie', shows this was still the custom.

Here the body in its winding sheet is ready to be interred directly into the ground, without a coffin. In practice, a body would rest for the service on a bier, a wooden frame with handles that was kept by the parish for communal use.* The bier was then carried to the

---

* As with the shroud and the winding sheet, there is more than a little confusion over terminology for the various funeral items, with the same words referring to different objects over the centuries. A bier was a wooden stretcher on which a body rested during the service, with a piece of fabric held up over it. This fabric was called a bier cloth or mortuary cloth. A hearse, meanwhile, was originally a wooden frame that went around the bier to hold decorations during the funeral service. Over time the word hearse began to be used for the bier and frame as it conveyed the dead to the churchyard. From the seventeenth century, the bier might be covered first with a white cloth and

grave, whereupon the body was lifted off and buried. A few parishes
owned communal coffins, in which the dead lay in church during
the funeral service. These were similarly carried to the grave, where
the bodies were lifted out before burial.[3]

By the mid-seventeenth century coffins were starting to be used
among the well-to-do; over the next hundred years, they became
the norm for everyone. Initially, this was seen as a religious change:
the coffin slowed down decomposition, preserving the body for its
ultimate resurrection on the Day of Judgement. These coffins at
first were formed in the rough shape of the bodies they encased:
narrower at the head, wider at the shoulders and then narrowing
again at the foot. A nameplate (or, for the impoverished, the
name chalked directly on the coffin's boards) added to the
sense that the coffin was a symbolic stand-in for the person it
contained. However, rectangular coffins soon became standard,
and shortly coffins came to represent not the body of the dead,
but their status: were the coffins covered in luxury fabrics, richly
decorated with nail-work studs? Did they have expensive metal
handles, or silver nameplates? By the 1770s, mourners could
pick out each element from a catalogue, making the funeral
a consumer moment.[4]

For the comfortably off, the singular 'coffin' was frequently a
misnomer, since it was not unusual to have one set inside another,
to deal with the decomposition that could be well underway by the
time of the funeral. If it could be afforded, the body was placed in
a lead interior shell, or coffin, and then another, or even two, outer
ones. The Reverend Mr Sewell, attempting to moderate the fashion
for expenditure at death, recommended a single wooden coffin,
preferably of elm, which had a nice finish, he stressed, without being

---

then, over it, a second black one, called a pall. These two cloths gradually became one,
a black cloth with a white border, which was now also called a pall. Theoretically each
church was assumed to have a bier, a pall and a hearse cloth for the use of its parishioners, but in reality many parishes lacked one or the other or all three.

showy. Polished wood, he added sternly, was 'more in keeping with the drawing-room than with the grave'.*⁵

Coffins were no longer communal and for temporary use to transport a shrouded body to the grave, but other funeral elements continued to be shared. Guilds, and later trades unions, kept ornamental palls, or hearse-cloths, to cover the coffins of their members. In Scotland, churches had their own mortcloths, which served the same purpose as palls, with different quality cloths rented out at different prices. In 1839, one church had twenty-six mortcloths in four different grades. The best one could be rented by mourners for £1 5s., the lowest grade for 3s., although the church also kept worn-out cloths that were no longer suitable for paying parishioners for the use of those families who could not otherwise afford funeral finery.[6] Not that reuse was unknown elsewhere. Kilvert recorded the scandal of a neighbouring vicar who draped his Good Friday communion table in an 'old filthy parish pall. Everyone was disgusted and shocked . . . It was the talk of the country.'[7] Other communal funerary items were lavish and flashy. One East Sussex village proudly owned an ornately decorated hearse, rather oddly made to commemorate Queen Victoria's Diamond Jubilee in 1897, which was pulled on ceremonial outings by the village milkman's pony.[8]

For funerals were often community events. There was private grief, for the loss of a child, a parent, a friend. And there was public grief, for the loss of a monarch, a statesman, a hero –

---

* While the shaped coffin fell out of fashion in Britain, it remained in use in the USA for longer, although by mid-century the link between the shape of the coffin and its contents was found disturbing by some. An advertisement for Patent Metallic Burial Cases and Caskets promised that the more modern rectangular shape 'will not promote . . . disagreeable sensations . . . So much that is repulsive has been discarded in its arrangement and shape that its name, "THE CASKET", is an involuntary suggestion.' This last reminds us that while in Britain the word casket retained its original meaning of a box containing something precious – jewels, or documents, or at most a preserved body part such as a heart – in the USA the idea of something valuable enclosed in a wooden box saw the word casket replacing, or at least becoming a synonym for, a coffin.

sometimes even a heroine. There were many gradations. State funerals were for monarchs, and were paid for by the government, as the name suggests; public funerals were also paid for by the government, but were for statesmen of particular renown, and required approval by parliament: the Duke of Wellington and Gladstone were the only two who were given this honour in the nineteenth century. (Gladstone's long-time professional rival, Disraeli, had pre-emptively stated he wished for a private funeral, so the question did not arise.) Other elaborate funerals of great men were an amalgam of public and private, organized and paid for by the families of the dead, but staged for outward display, and often utilizing the backdrop of Westminster Abbey or St Paul's Cathedral.

All of these were different from heraldic funerals. A state funeral could be heraldic, but a heraldic funeral did not have to be a state funeral. The College of Heralds had been founded under the Tudors in the sixteenth century as an official institution designed to guide and control the image of the monarchs and their courts through a vocabulary of visual display that reinforced the hierarchical status quo of aristocracy and monarchy. Funerals were a prime opportunity, here, not to glorify the deceased, but to re-inforce their position in a fixed world order, clarifying who their superiors were, who their inferiors and who their equals. Dress, fabrics, banners, escutcheons, gradations in numbers and partici-pants – all were elements designed to show what was known as the quality of the deceased: the part they played in society, not who they were as people.

The 1586 funeral of Sir Philip Sidney, an eminent Elizabethan courtier, was one of the great heraldic funerals, with a complex choreography of organization. First came thirty-two poor men, the number selected to indicate Sidney's age, their status to highlight his charitable nature. These were followed by, in order:

members of his regiment
his servants
his heraldic devices
60 'gentlemen and yeomen'
60 esquires from among his family and friends
10 knights
the horse he rode into battle
the horse he used for state ceremonies
banners
heralds carrying his spurs, sword and gauntlet
the body of Sidney, carried by his 'friends' (an older use,
meaning kin)
the mourners, a formal designation assigned by the College
of Heralds, starting with his heir as chief mourner, and
followed by male family members in order of societal
importance and inheritance
barons and earls
members of the Worshipful Company of Grocers, the livery
guild to which Sidney belonged.[9]

The mourners in the procession were not there to display grief
for the loss of Sidney the man, but to show that, despite his death,
his aristocratic rank and title had immediately been assumed by a
successor, and the power and status of the Sidney family continued.

By the seventeenth century, the College of Arms was losing
ground against the forces of commerce. While maintaining the
importance of their own symbols of mourning, they had begun to
farm out some of the more practical elements of the arrangements
to merchants who made, or sourced, the necessary goods, such as
palls, items of funeral dress, biers, hearses and so on. This was a
grave error of judgement, as the merchants, who would soon begin
to refer to themselves as undertakers, saw no reason not to take on
all the organization, as well as the labour and of course the profit.
In the eighteenth century, therefore, the College found itself so

regularly overlooked for funerals that it took to the newspapers to complain that – dreadful to relate – one recent merchant's funeral procession had included the wrong number of heralds for the rank of the deceased.[10] But to the horror of the College, they found that no one much cared, even the great aristocrats now preferring to deal directly with the undertakers, who obsequiously received instructions on what the families wanted, rather than imperiously instructing the families on what they must do. Even worse, this newspaper report unwittingly announced to the wealthy middle classes that there was nothing to stop them from taking on the trappings that had previously been jealously confined to the gentry. All those glamorous display elements – the heralds, the flags, the hatchments* – that were used to indicate rank and status could simply be purchased, or even rented, by those with no formal claim on them, to make their own lavish display of grief.

The last great heraldic funeral was, suitably, orchestrated at the very start of the nineteenth century, the century when the formal dictates of heraldry would forever be replaced by private customs and private desires. That final outburst of the old style was the funeral of Lord Nelson, the great naval tactician of the French Revolutionary Wars, the hero of the Battle of the Nile who was killed at the height of his success as he was leading the navy at the Battle of Trafalgar in 1805.

The aims of government – a display of power – and the populace – a spectacle – coincided, and a London newspaper laid out their desire for a hierarchical set piece:

> Let the whole Cavalcade be ordered and regulated by the College
> of Heralds, in their appropriate habiliments, assisted by the City
> Marshals and their men. Let the children on board the Marine

---

* Hatchments were confined to those families with a heraldic coat of arms. They were wooden or canvas panels painted with the family coat of arms that were suspended on the facade of the house of the deceased, and then carried in the funeral procession before they were hung in the family's parish church.

Society's Ships, and as many Sea-boys as can be spared from the vessels in the river, walk first . . . with a piece of crape round their left arms; then let a large body of Seamen and Marines . . . follow, and let the Veteran Inmates of Greenwich Hospital immediately precede the Body. Let the Pall-bearers be Admirals; let the Chief Mourner be one of his Lordship's own Family. Let the Lords of the Admiralty and the Commissioners of the Navy walk next. Then let the Lord Mayor of the City of London, the Aldermen, and the Common Council, in their Gowns of Ceremony succeed. The whole Procession to be headed and closed by large detachments of Dragoons . . . Soldiers, Militia, and Volunteers . . . intermixed . . .[11]

There were also forty-eight crew members from HMS *Victory*, as well as the ship's colours, unfurled, carried at the end of the procession, some said marked not just by battle, but with Nelson's own blood.*

As with Sidney, the poor who were to head the procession numbered the age of the dead hero; the Greenwich pensioners were, one historian thinks, wounded sailors, whose own lost limbs referred sympathetically to 'the body of the most famous amputee of the day'. But against initial expectations, the chief mourner was not Nelson's brother, the new Lord Nelson, heir to his titles and estate, an omission that was likely made owing to the dead man's unconventional living arrangements with Emma Hamilton. Instead that honour was divided. At the lying-in-state the chief mourner was the brother of Nelson's private secretary, who had died in action with Nelson; at the funeral the position was given to Sir Peter Parker, Admiral of the Fleet, the two men thus representative heirs to Nelson's naval wartime command.[12]

While the College of Heralds had so far been in charge of this event, the City of London, as keepers of St Paul's Cathedral, Nelson's

* At the interment at St Paul's, those bearing the colours were supposed to throw them into Nelson's grave, but instead they tore them to pieces to keep as souvenirs.

final resting place, began to interfere with protocol, another indication of the College's waning powers. The Lord Mayor even demanded
that he be given a more prominent position than the Prince of Wales,
who himself had demanded to be designated the chief mourner. (It
was understood that monarchs did not attend the funerals of their
subjects. George III watched the procession from a balcony at St
James's Palace.) Refused that request, once at the cathedral the
prince insisted the *Victory*'s crew members be moved up closer to
the grave and to himself; his brother, the Duke of Clarence, also
repositioned himself near the head of the procession under the guise
of greeting each sailor. It was abundantly clear that these royal
personages were using the funeral of this commoner as a venue to
display their own importance.

Nelson's body, and the funeral car which carried it,* both looked
back to heraldic funerals, and also forward to more personal, and
more theatrical, displays. In style the car had been designed to
mimic the hull of the *Victory*, with the coffin, made from the main-
mast of a ship lost at the Battle of the Nile, sitting on what would
have been the quarterdeck. The notion of the funeral car originated
in the classical world, but more than anything, Nelson's resembled
the popular entertainments in public gardens like Vauxhall, and
Sadler's Wells Theatre, where mock sea battles were performed to
the accompaniment of fireworks. The coffin itself was emblazoned
with the names of the four great battleships Nelson had defeated –
the *San Josef*, *L'Orient*, *Trinidad* and *Bucentaure* – with the word
'Trafalgar' running along the side of the car, all under a naval jack
flying at half-mast. In a heraldic funeral Nelson's coronet would
have rested on a cushion on his coffin, but here it was placed in a
separate carriage entirely; pragmatically, so that spectators along the

---

* A funeral car was a temporary platform or superstructure, usually elaborately
painted or otherwise decorated, on which a coffin was placed before a funeral. It could
either be erected in the church where a funeral was to be performed (in which case it
was often called a catafalque), or it could be mobile, set on wheels and pulled by horses,
as was Nelson's, and, later, the Duke of Wellington's (p. 114).

route could see the coffin better, and also symbolically, serving to indicate the lesser importance of his social position when compared to his renown as a wartime leader.

All this was a far cry from the funerals of those who considered themselves to be socially superior to Nelson, who had died a viscount but was by birth merely the son of a country clergyman. Royal funerals were most often held at St George's Chapel, inside the grounds of Windsor Castle, and therefore were not visible to the public. They were also commonly held at night, further reducing the number of people in attendance, as those present would then be obliged to stay overnight in what was at the time nothing more than a small market town. Unlike Nelson's lying-in-state at Greenwich, where thousands came to pay their respects, royal deceased lay in state in semi-private, St George's accommodating no more than three or four hundred people.

Certainly at this stage royal funerals were short on pomp, with little to attract by way of spectacle, notwithstanding a cascade of royal deaths at the beginning of the century.* The end of the long reign of George III (1760–1820) was barely marked. The king had been living in seclusion for years, blind, deaf and demented. His funeral cost just £26,000, half the amount spent on the funeral of Mary II, who had died more than a century previously.[13] Even when the Duke of York and Albany died in 1827, one observer condemned his funeral as 'very badly managed, the service ill performed, the decorations shabby & the procession all huddled together'.[14] Things were still worse when his brother, William IV, died in 1837 after a seven-year reign. First the coffin had to be punctured to let a build-up of gases escape, for fear that it might explode. That was followed by a service so poorly organized that the heralds were

* The pre-eminent deaths were: Princess Charlotte (1817), the Duke of Kent (1820), George III (1820), Queen Caroline (1821), the Duke of York (1827), George IV (1830) and William IV (1837), followed by the long, long reign of Victoria, with no funeral of a monarch between 1837 and 1901.

described as 'scampering about' to find their places.[15] These funerals left the greater population entirely unmoved. It was, instead, the funerals of two royal women that were to arouse the most public interest and emotional investment.

In 1817, Princess Charlotte, the only child of the future George IV, was second in line to the throne. She was also young and newly married when, like thousands of women of far less privilege, she died suddenly in childbirth. A wave of mourning swept the country. In part this was an expression of political anxiety. Charlotte had not been just *an* heir to the throne; after her father she was *the* heir to the throne, the sole legitimate grandchild of George III.* In part, too, it was the ordinariness of her death: a happy marriage swiftly followed by a dead child, a dead mother and a grieving husband. So many knew this pain. One woman wrote to her sister-in-law: 'But a few days since, she was well . . . The uncertainty of life was never so *realized* to my mind as at present.'[16] Within weeks of Charlotte's death, therefore, hundreds of pamphlets, sermons, songs, elegies, epitaphs, poems, dirges and more were published, mourning what was termed the 'nation's' loss.[17]

The silver-trimmed, crimson-covered coffins of Charlotte and her baby were driven from her home in Surrey to Windsor, each hearse drawn by eight horses, the procession arriving at two o'clock in the morning. The baby, as a stillbirth, had not been christened, as he had not lived, and he was therefore buried immediately, without any service being read. Charlotte's coffin lay in state in the

---

* Her death therefore set off a breeding race among some of the surviving sons of George III, encouraged by an actual financial bounty offered by parliament. Several of the royal siblings were disqualified: the women were all past childbearing age; Charlotte's father, the Prince Regent, and the Duke of York and Albany were both estranged from their wives, ruling out further offspring; the Duke of Cumberland was married and had no children; the Duke of Sussex had married without permission, and any progeny were therefore barred from the succession. This left the Dukes of Clarence (who already had ten illegitimate children), Cambridge and Kent, who all quickly married. The Duke of Kent won the race in 1819, with the birth of Alexandrina Victoria, later to be known as Queen Victoria.

chapel for twenty-four hours, allowing those who had acquired tickets to file past. The following evening, the Royal Horse Guards lined the route, every fifth man holding a torch aloft, as liveried royal servants wearing black hatbands and gloves, and themselves carrying torches, led the funeral procession to the accompaniment of tolling bells and muffled drums. This procession was headed by the chief mourner, Charlotte's widower, Prince Leopold, with his two supporters, her uncles the Dukes of Clarence and York. (Her father, the Prince Regent, was represented by his carriage.)*[18]

The nation was said to be in mourning, and on the day of her funeral, churches found themselves with filled pews. But even more did it appear to be a commercial opportunity. The innkeepers along the route from Charlotte's house to Windsor all raised their prices; at the chapel, tickets were available for 10 guineas for a seat in the organ loft, or as much as 7 guineas simply to stand in an aisle.[19] More money was to be made in the ensuing weeks and months. All those poems and sermons and songs were after all being sold commercially. So too were commemorative medals, and cups and saucers bearing Charlotte's portrait, and engravings in magazines showing what the well-dressed matron was wearing to express her feelings of loss. (See plate section.) As one woman wrote to her friend on her new mourning clothes: 'very fine [and] interesting . . . you will be in a crape body [that is, a bodice] and short sleeves . . . dash[ing] about in . . . style.'[20]

Mourning jewellery had long been customary for the prosperous. After a death, the families of the dead ordered rings to give to family and friends. At their simplest, they carried the initials and dates and were valued as tokens of remembrance. For the princess, more expensive memorial jewels were created for sale rather than necessarily for gifts of remembrance.

---

*   How this is to be read is an interesting question. Sending an empty carriage to represent oneself and one's family was a customary form of polite condolence among the upper echelons of society. For a father mourning his daughter, it was more unusual. The claim that monarchs did not attend funerals is countered by the undeniable reality that the Prince Regent was just that – a regent – and not yet a monarch.

For those who had less to spend, an engraving was a suitable gift for a friend. 'Passing through London,' wrote one woman to a relative in the country, 'I stoped [sic] to look at the portraits of the late Princess & his Royal Highness, engraved by Wedgewood [sic]. I resolved to present them to you . . . that you might receive the gift with the association fresh upon it, and cherish both together.'[21]

The public at large found Charlotte easy to love. Her character was relatively unknown, and she had no public political positions that could affront anyone. The same could not be said in 1821 on the death of her mother, Queen Caroline, the acrimoniously estranged wife of George IV. (It was claimed that when the king was notified that his 'bitterest enemy', meaning Napoleon, was dead, he replied, 'Is she, by God!')[22] With her marriage irretrievably broken down, Caroline had left Britain for Italy in 1814, but on the accession of her husband as George IV in 1820, she returned, causing riots even as she was physically barred from the coronation service at Westminster Abbey. For many Radicals, she had become a symbol of the country's urgent need for reform, and as such the government feared that her funeral would pose a risk of further rioting, demonstrations or other anti-government, anti-monarchical displays.

Caroline had died in west London, leaving a will that requested her body be returned to her birthplace in Brunswick, in Lower Saxony. The direct route to accomplish this was to have her body leave England via Harwich, in Essex, with her funeral procession traversing central London before travelling the nearly 130 kilometres to the coast. The king had at first refused to order the court to wear mourning dress. (For more on mourning dress, see Chapter 7.) While the risk of riots was destabilizing, the government equally knew that such a gesture of contempt would be seen as a political provocation, and thus suggested both modified court mourning and a route that would see the procession avoid the main roads. But, as one woman in domestic service in the West End of London recalled with satisfaction, 'the people blocked up the back streets with carriages, carts and coaches and forced the procession to go by the great streets'. The military escort had been given orders to march straight through to Harwich without stopping, but by four o'clock in the morning it became evident that the attendants could go no further without rest, and a message was sent to the prime minister requesting permission for an overnight stop, and another the following night. At each place, sympathetic crowds gathered, and in one a plate was covertly attached to the coffin, announcing that here lay 'Caroline of Brunswick, the injured Queen of England'.[23]

Unlike Nelson, who had been accorded all the power and display of a state funeral, Caroline's was a private, barely royal funeral. Yet both made evident the appetite the public had for funerals of the famous, or notorious, an appetite for joining in as participants rather than just as spectators. This was manifested in a variety of ways. At the most sober, the crowds might attend special church services, as they had done for Princess Charlotte; or they might gather in public spaces, as they did for Queen Caroline; they could produce, or purchase, memorabilia; and they could close their businesses and watch a procession, as they did for many, both public and private. Because no longer did one have to be one of the great and good to have a public-facing funeral. There were numerous funerals that were of interest to the general populace, who played a substantial role as spectators.

The display elements, and funeral accoutrements as a whole, harked back to the heraldic funerals of previous centuries, despite the modern participants rarely having any idea of these objects' original meanings. In a funeral of any size, it was expected that there would be a featherman carrying a tray of black ostrich plumes in the procession; in more expensive ones, he was followed by feather pages, these men representing the feudal esquire and his followers in their feathered casques. After them came the pall-bearers, carrying batons, formerly symbols that they were the deceased nobleman's fellow-soldiers. Then came the mourning coaches, the number and ownership of which, regardless of their occupants, indicated the prestige of the person being buried. Before a procession set out, two funeral mutes stood on either side of the front door of the deceased's house, the modern-day equivalent of the porters who had kept watch at a castle's gates. These men were entirely dressed in black, with black sashes across their chests, black weepers – long pieces of veil-like fabric – hanging from their hats, and, in their hands, wands, or sticks, around which were wrapped what were called love ribbons, also in black, with white for the funerals of young girls. When the coffin left the house, the mutes fell in and led off the procession.

By the time this photograph was taken in 1901, funeral mutes were almost a symbol of a past age, here captured for posterity by the MP and photographer Benjamin Stone, who recorded many customs and traditions he feared were becoming obsolete.

One did not have to be a politician, nor even an elected officer, to have an elaborate public funeral. From the 1830s onwards, trades unions began to adopt the iconography and symbols of the old heraldic-style funerals, using them to create an image of an aristocracy of work, and of fraternal and class bonding. A funeral of a humble labourer in a trades union therefore could have the same appurtenances as the funeral of a prosperous middle-class person as supplied by an under-taker, incorporating these archaic elements and adding modern ones. There was likely to be a band or a choir (or a band *and* a choir), with fellow union members and the union's officers wearing rosettes and official insignia on sashes across their chests. Different union lodges sent their own members, and quite ordinary members could well be accompanied by more than a thousand people, which in turn brought out many more spectators. These funerals were expressly designed to make political statements. One man, who had been jailed after the Chartist uprisings of 1848, was accompanied to his grave by four mutes selected specifically because they had been present at the Peterloo Massacre of 1819; among his twelve coffin- and pall-bearers were fellow Chartists who had been arrested with him and also those more recently prominent in the movement, all watched by a crowd numbering in the 'tens of thousands'.*[24]

These funerals were considered very suspect by the ruling caste, who saw them as 'a first step towards a general strike' – that was the warning given before the funeral of a shoemaker in Northampton, where the Grand National Consolidated Trades Union led off with a hundred women workers, followed by 800 union members.[25] Because of this, trades-union funerals were regarded not as marks of respect to the dead, but as forms of collective action, and the proces-sions were frequently banned.[26] That is not to say these beliefs were

---

* The Peterloo Massacre had itself produced some unusual funerals. When the horse owned by Henry 'Orator' Hunt, who had been arrested and jailed after the events of 1819, died, thousands were said to have attended the animal's funeral. Later on, a grave-stone was erected that read, 'Alas, Poor Bob'. Less heroically, Bob's skeleton was exhumed in 1826 and turned into snuffboxes, one of which was given to Hunt.

wrong. One of the largest funerals of the century was that of Feargus O'Connor in 1855. O'Connor, a one-time MP and charismatic Radical and Chartist speaker, had, by the time of his death, fallen on hard times – indeed, he might have been insane. But an outpouring of public sentiment saw money raised for a funeral procession that was, said some, the largest ever seen apart from the funerals of the triumvirate of Nelson, Queen Caroline and the Duke of Wellington, drawing as it did ever more followers as it processed through working-class areas of London and wended its way to Kensal Green. There, frightened administrators closed the gates to keep the forty thousand 'rabble' out, but they tore down the fencing and followed their hero to his final resting place.[27]

There were plenty of funerals that did not require a political element to draw spectators. Funerals were entertainment, or, at least, entertainment included funerals, real or imagined. Playbills in the first half of the nineteenth century often highlighted the funeral scenes in an evening's entertainment, which suggests they were a particular selling point for the public. A playbill for a production of *Romeo and Juliet* mentioned two scenes, 'A Masquerade and Dance, incidental to the play' and 'The Funeral Procession of Juliet'. Another playbill, for *Antony and Cleopatra*, highlighted the scene 'The grand FUNERAL of ANTONY and CLEOPATRA', which Shakespeare himself had perhaps foolishly forgotten to write, and which must therefore have been added in this production in the knowledge that it would be popular.[28] Real funerals were also theatrical fodder. Two years after the death of the Duke of Wellington, a panorama – an illustrated depiction of the event displayed in 360 degrees – was exhibited complete with lighting and musical effects in a specially designed venue. The life of the explorer David Livingstone received the same treatment. Kilvert took a group of schoolchildren to this one. Their favourite moment, he recorded, was Livingstone's funeral: 'The Abbey was first shown empty. Then by slight . . . effect or dissolving view the open space in the Nave gradually melted into the forms of the funeral party', after which

they watched the service being read as the mourners grouped themselves picturesquely around the coffin.[29]

The year after Kensal Green tried to bar the working-class crowds
from their nice middle-class cemetery, Highgate Cemetery, the final
destination of many upper-class patrons, welcomed not just Tom
Sayers (1826–1865), perhaps the century's most famous pugilist, but
the crowds who accompanied him on his final journey. Bare-
knuckle fighting had attracted both high and low in the louche
period under George IV, but now, nearing the midpoint of Victoria's
reign, it was barely respectable, and continued to be at best semi-
legal. Sayers, however, was the much-loved 'Champion of England',
and five years before his death his last fight had played out in front
of a crowd possibly numbering a hundred thousand, supposedly
with Dickens, Thackeray, Palmerston and even the Prince of Wales
in attendance at a location described as 'secret', even if it had been
a secret known to a hundred thousand people. On his death, the
newspaper reports were a curious mixture of condemnation for the
sport and a sometimes unwilling affection for Sayers.

On the day of his funeral, all the shops in Sayers' neighbourhood
in Camden, north London, closed for business, drawing their blinds
or shutters and putting out flags and banners, one, on a pub,
reading 'Peace to England's champion'. Before the procession set off,
funeral mutes stood outside the door of Sayers' house, as was traditional, while a band entertained the crowd, which was not. A police
escort was needed to accompany the procession as it covered the
three and a half kilometres to the cemetery, followed all the way by
a music-hall band playing the Dead March from Handel's oratorio
Saul, which had become the nineteenth century's great go-to for
death. The procession was made up of sixteen black-plumed horses,
a featherman, then the hearse, followed by Sayers' own pony and
phaeton (a small carriage), in the manner of an officer being
attended to the grave by his warhorse. 'Tom's leopard skin' was
draped over the pony's back, and his dog, Lion, occupied the phaeton's passenger seat. (Lion was later immortalized in stone, lying

before Sayers' grave for all eternity. (See plate section.) After that
came the customary mourning coaches of family and friends.

While local businesses closed out of respect, that did not extend
to those serving the observers, such as the pubs along the route. In
the streets nearby, acrobats and other street performers tumbled and
sang for pennies. A photographer's studio offered portraits of Sayers
with a banner inscribed 'Peace to his Ashes' superimposed (6*d.*
plain, 9*d.* hand-coloured). A cookshop, mournfully draped in black,
nevertheless promised its patrons 'superior brisket' on the funeral
day. Ballad-sellers gathered outside the cemetery gates to sell sheet
music printed with popular songs about the fighter.[30]

More respectably middle class, but no less celebrity-driven,
was the funeral of David Livingstone. After he died in 1873 in what
is today Zambia, his body was carried to the coast and then
sent by ship to England, a journey that altogether took two weeks
short of a year. While his body was still being carried overland in
Africa, the Royal Geographic Society petitioned the government
for a funeral in Westminster Abbey, with the government to cover
the costs. The government said yes to the Abbey, no to the bill, in
part because they worried that it might not be Livingstone's body
that was being returned. *The Times* then put them in a difficult
position by reporting that the government had after all agreed
to pay, which embarrassed ministers enough that they offered
£250 towards the costs, later raising that to a little under £500.*

---

* Fees for burials at Westminster Abbey were no small consideration. For the burial
of a man of status below that of a duke, the Dean of Westminster received £18; the
sub-dean £6 10*s.*; the chanter £5; the two vergers £8 between them; the porter £2; twelve
almoners £4 16*s.* in total; and then descending amounts ending with 5*s.* for the man
who blew the bellows for the organist. The final bill was never less than £100, and that
was before additional fees, called 'fines', were added to cover potential damage to the
fabric of the building when the grave or monument was installed. Each of the individual fees, too, was subject to increase depending on the status of the deceased. The
£4 16*s.* for the almoners went up to £14 8*s.* if a duke was being interred. A monument
for an earl or bishop cost £40; for a duke or archbishop it was £50. After all of this,
there remained charges for the choir and the lighting, payable even if there was, said
some disgruntled observers, no singing, and the funeral took place in broad daylight.[31]

(Happily, the body was after all Livingstone's, being identified by the Royal Geographic Society fellows on its arrival by the marks of an old injury.)[32]

Livingstone's funeral took place more than two decades after the largest public funeral of all, one so elaborate, so expensive and so extreme that it sickened many and was said to have been one of the factors that ushered in the vogue for quieter, more modest funeral practices in the second half of the century. That was the funeral of the Duke of Wellington.[33] In the days immediately following his death, there was little sign of what an event it was to become. The news arrived in Doncaster the morning the famous St Leger horse race was scheduled to run and, recorded the diarist Charles Greville, 'most people were too much occupied with their own concerns to bestow much thought or lamentation on this great national loss'. At the Three Choirs Festival in Hereford, the Dead March was added to the scheduled programme, but no further notice was taken. In his journal Gladstone merely wrote that that he was 'astounded' by the news before he passed on to other matters.[34] Instead, it was in the two-month interval between death and funeral that the event grew from sad but not unexpected to one that was considered to encapsulate national pride and national mourning.

It also became a commercial bonanza. There were many hundreds, if not thousands, of advertisements in the months leading up to the funeral, selling everything from tickets for seats in houses along the route the procession would take, to food and drink named for the duke, mementoes both real – items he had owned, or had touched, or had written on – or imagined, reprints of what were said to be his favourite books, or sheet music of his supposed favourite songs. Those who disapproved of the commercial activity were nevertheless part of the process as they wrote articles for the press about how wrong it was to use the event as a basis for commerce. The *Illustrated London News* published a special issue in which it criticized the souvenirs on sale even as that very issue included engravings of supposedly private moments such as the duke's deathbed, to be 'framed and preserved as lasting Records of this solemn Spectacle'. And in a later issue, the journal boasted of the 'extreme and unprecedented' sales figures that special edition had achieved.[35]

The funeral itself was overwhelming: the procession was made up of some ten thousand men, preceding and following a funeral car more than eight metres in length and seven and a half metres wide and so tall it needed special hinges in the canopy in order for it to be able to pass under Temple Bar, the stone arch that marked the entry to the City of London. Cumbersome and top-heavy, it nevertheless managed to be somehow still heavier than it looked – over ten imperial tons (more than 10,000 kilograms) – and required twelve horses to pull it and a special team of men behind to act as a brake on the downhill sections of the route as the procession wound its way to St Paul's.

Many agreed that all this had taken the event out of the realm of respectful homage and far into that of grotesque theatricality.[36] Even those who were not condemnatory somehow unconsciously fell into the language of theatre to describe the event. *The Times* referred to the sight of the soldiers accompanying the hearse as an 'imposing effect', the standard term for special effects at the theatre; others called the procession 'the sight', as in sightseeing. And the cathedral where the duke was to rest participated enthusiastically in the staging, installing new gas lighting for the occasion, and making a plan to cover the windows with black fabric to heighten the drama. (In the event, the workmen did not finish in time, and the funeral was held in daylight.) Spectators also ventured to St Paul's the day before, one visitor again using the word 'effect' to describe the setting, adding 'it was like a great rout [party].' Another wrote that he watched the service in the cathedral 'with artistic eyes', commenting on the '*chiaroscuro*' as if reviewing an art exhibition.[37] And then there was the cathedral's newly installed pulley system, which lowered the duke's coffin from the nave to the crypt just like a stage trapdoor, known as a vampire-trap, impressing many but shocking others. *Household Words* magazine called it 'a palpably got up theatrical trick'.*[38]

Those who attended probably enjoyed the ceremony, for few appeared to feel it was a time for solemn reflection, with numerous comments on 'the loud hum of ceaseless conversation' in the cathedral. One newspaper described the order of service pamphlets being distributed by 'choristers [flinging] them up in handfuls', followed by 'a general scramble . . . amidst cries of "Up here – higher, higher"'. Those on the lower benches within reach of the booklets screwed them up into balls before 'casting them at the occupants of the back benches'.[39] The bulk of the population, however, watched from the streets, and it truly was the bulk. Historians have estimated that up to 5 per cent of the population of England and Wales was present for some portion of the funeral, possibly a million people, or 40 per cent of the inhabitants of London.[40]

The funeral was far more commercially focused, or at least more visibly commercially focused, than most. The funeral car's cost, said to have been £11,000, completely overwhelmed its symbolism, despite it being made out of the cannon used in the Battle of Waterloo.[41] Buildings along the route sold viewing spots to the populace, sometimes with great promotional ingenuity. One seller offered cheaper seats to clergymen as long as they wore their surplices, with Dickens mockingly highlighting this 'shop-window of four-and-twenty clergymen', as if they had become the item that was on sale. After the funeral, the governmental Office of Works auctioned off items used in the procession, including the pall that had covered the coffin, while St Paul's displayed the funeral car, now pulled by wicker horses for paying tourists.[42]

---

* This new pulley system had some unintended consequences. The coffin dropped down into the crypt below, as planned, getting caught and falling on top of the tomb of Nelson, unplanned. There it sat for four and a half years while letters went back and forth between the Ministry of Works, the Chapter Clerk of St Paul's, the Office of Woods and Forests and the Office of the Commissioner of Works, all of them disclaiming responsibility for interring the coffin and building the tomb.

The funeral car itself was passed back and forth. The Office of Works handed it to St Paul's, who after its initial display sent it back to Wellington's family. (It has since been on display at their family home, Stratfield Saye, as part of an all-inclusive timed ticket tour of the house and gardens for £15.) Thomas Carlyle failed to be impressed by it: 'a monstrous bronze mass, which broke through the pavement in various places' owing to its weight. It was 'of all the objects I ever saw the abominably ugliest . . . An incoherent huddle of expensive palls, flags, sheets, and gilt emblems and cross poles, more like one of the street carts that hawk door-mats than the bier for a hero', he growled in his journal.[43]

Ultimately the funeral, he lamented, was 'all hypocrisy, noise, and expensive upholstery; from which a serious mind turns away with sorrow and abhorrence'. The lying-in-state before the funeral, he added, had had 'all the empty fools of creation running' (this before admitting that he too had gone to see the duke). And the procession and its crowds, which he watched from the Piccadilly house of his great friend and patron Lady Ashburton, was more of a mockery, the 'canaille', as he called them, the rabble, being so numerous that 'it strikes me there ought to be no more Public Funerals transacted'.[44]

He was not the only one to think this way.

6

THE FAMILY FUNERAL

The funerals of state, and the funerals of the renowned, were at best loosely connected to the funerals of ordinary people. There were, of course, as many types of funeral as there were people, and financial outlay played a part, but only a part. Two examples, held within three years of each other, in 1867 and 1870, both from the middle classes, show the range of possibility.

The funeral of John Rutter Chorley, a wealthy but socially reticent literary man, was attended by seven people: his two brothers, his doctor, his three servants, and just one person who was neither related to, nor paid by, the deceased. There was a simple, brief service, with a gravestone that stated the man's name and dates with the bare epitaph, 'An upright man, and an excellent scholar'.[1]

By contrast, the funeral of Maria Kilvert, a wealthy clergyman's daughter who lived in Worcester's cathedral close, left 'simple' far behind, and in the hands of her distant, and estranged, relative, the Reverend Francis Kilvert, the retelling of events is a comic masterpiece.[2] First, Kilvert makes clear before he leaves home that, by her having bequeathed £15,000 to charitable causes and just some rose bushes, lace and furs 'worth a few shillings' to his mother and father, Miss Kilvert had wronged his side of the family by this 'most unprincipled unnatural act and piece of ostentation'. It was, he added for good measure, 'a most erroneous injustice'. Nevertheless, he and his aggrieved parents, having been invited, travelled to Worcester for the funeral. At Miss Kilvert's house they paid their respects with a formal viewing of the deceased as she lay in her oak coffin, a lead shell fitted inside and lined with white satin, and with a brass nameplate on the lid. This was immediately followed by Miss Kilvert's 'charwoman saying she could get no fowls for the funeral breakfast tomorrow. "Should she get a small turkey?" – "Yes, she should get a small turkey".'

The next morning the clergy who were serving as pall-bearers assembled in the dining room with the other mourners, where a funeral breakfast was served, and mourning scarves and hatbands were passed out as the coffin sat in the hall, covered with a luxurious black velvet pall with a white velvet border.

> Boom went the great bell of the Cathedral. Church was over, and someone said they ought to have used the tenor bell, but they were using the bell and no mistake. Boom went the bell again. The coffin went out immediately and the pall bearers filed out in pairs after it, taking their places and holding each his pall tassel on either side. My Father and I followed as Chief mourners in crape scarves and hatbands. All the rest in silk. The bearers had been selected not at all with reference to their fitness for the task, but with reference to the friendship entertained for them by the servants of the house. One of the bearers on the right side was very short, so short he could not properly support the coffin level. The coffin seemed very heavy. As the procession moved across College Green to the Cloister arch, the men staggered under the weight and the coffin lurched and tilted to one side over the short bearer. One very fat man had constituted himself chiefest mourner of all and walked next the coffin before my Father and myself. The bearers, blinded by the sweeping pall, could not see where they were going and nearly missed the Cloister arch, but at length we got safe into the narrow dark passage and into the Cloisters.

At the cathedral door, they were met by choir and clergy, who preceded them in procession down the nave.

'I am the Resurrection and the Life saith the Lord.' But meanwhile there was a dreadful struggle at the steps leading up from the Cloisters to the door. The bearers were quite unequal to the task and the coffin seemed crushingly heavy. There was a stamping and a scuffling, a mass of struggling men swaying to and fro, pushing and writhing and wrestling while the coffin sank and rose and sank again. Once or twice I thought the whole mass of men must have been down together with the coffin atop them and someone killed or maimed at least. But now came the time of the fat chief mourner. Seizing his opportunity he rushed into the strife by an opening large and the rescued coffin rose. At last by a wild effort and tremendous heave the ponderous coffin was borne up the steps and through the door in to the Cathedral where the choristers, quite unconscious of the scene and the fearful struggle going on behind, were singing up the nave like a company of angels. In the Choir there was another dreadful struggle to let the coffin down. The bearers were completely overweighted, they bowed and bent and nearly fell and threw the coffin down on the floor. When it was safely deposited we all retired to seats right and left and a verger or beadle, in a black gown and holding a mace, took up his position at the head of the coffin, standing.

Kilvert then adds some shocked remarks about what he presumes to be the cost of the ceremony before going home with the executor to be formally told the contents of the will, which turned out to be more generous than they had thought.

Apart from the sheer pleasure of the telling, this account covers many of the elements the Victorians felt were essential at funerals: invitations, mourning wear, the coffin and accoutrements, the funeral meal, the tolling bell, the fees and other financial obligations of the day.

By the nineteenth century, a number of these elements came under the purview of the undertaker. The word 'undertaker' itself, to mean a person whose profession it is to arrange funerals, first began to be

used in this way only at the very end of the seventeenth century –
before that an undertaker was simply someone who undertook
something, often a contracted-out job like tax-collecting. As time
progressed, undertaking as a trade subsumed the previously disparate
independent tradesmen and women who had supplied the items
required by funerals – coffin-makers, metal-workers, dressmakers,
milliners, livery-stable hands, upholsterers and more – subcontracting
from them to present the family of the dead with a single tradesman,
himself. This became more important as inner-city or country
churchyards were replaced by suburban cemeteries. Now families no
longer lived near the burial location, and would not know how to find
the necessary tradesmen. If they happened to know a coffin-maker
locally, they would not know from whom to order a gravestone in an
entirely different neighbourhood nearer the cemetery. And thus
undertakers' advertisements stressed that they supplied everything:
'Mourning costume of every description ... Horses, Coaches,
Hearses, Shillibeers, Palls, Cloaks, Feathers, &c.'*3

Even if the mourners knew how to locate all these suppliers,
there was so much choice available that it was easier for one person
to narrow the goods down to what customers were assured were
'fashionable', or 'select'. Did the family want a single-break coffin,
the old-fashioned kind shaped like a person? Or did they prefer the
newer, rectangular style? Until the 1820s, coffins had been covered
with velvet, tacked in place by decorative nailwork. Should the
velvet be made of wool? In black or red? Or should it be a silk velvet,
where the colour possibilities had broadened out from the traditional red and black to include 'midnight blue, holly green and
turquoise'. Should the nails be brass, gilt, silvered brass, iron or
enamel? And then there was the coffin furniture. Did the family
want the nameplate in lead, brass, tin, pewter, iron or enamel? In

---

*   In daily life, a shillibeer was a synonym for an omnibus, as the idea for the public
transport bus had been brought from Paris to London by an enterprising coach-builder
named George Shillibeer (1797–1866). Mr Shillibeer also patented a mourning carriage
and hearse combined into a single vehicle, which is what is being referred to here.

what shape? Rectangles, shields, lozenges and diamond shapes were all fashionable. The same choice about the metals had to be made for the handles, with the addition of decorative elements. Were cherubs, flowers or angels with trumpets the right addition?[4]

While they were undoubtedly performing a useful function, that did not make undertakers universally liked, nor even accepted. The connection between grief and commerce seemed irreconcilable to many. The playwright Richard Steele (1672–1729), more famous as the co-founder of the *Spectator* magazine, as early as 1701 had prefaced his play, *The Funeral, or, Grief A-la-mode*, with the hope that it would be 'acceptable to all Lovers of Mankind' since it mocked 'a Sett of People who live in impatient Hopes to see us out of the World, a Flock of Ravens that attend this numerous City for their Carkases' – that is, the undertakers who preyed on the desire of the living to honour the dead. Worse, according to Steele, all undertakers were hypocrites who would present a mournful countenance for cash. Mr Sable, the play's undertaker, instructs his employees to 'put on your sad Looks', before berating them: 'Did not I give you . . . Twenty Shillings a Week, to be Sorrowful?'[5]

By the nineteenth century, writers were condemning undertakers not just for hypocrisy, but for theatrical hypocrisy, with the undertaker acting as a 'master of ceremonies' to the dead, the 'grandmarshal' of the funeral.[6] Today we use words like 'performing' and 'conducting' a funeral without a second thought, but in the nineteenth century those words were tightly linked to the theatre, and newspapers could be scathing. Did undertakers and their employees adjust their levels of sorrow according to price, they asked rhetorically? 'They have different qualities of grief, you may be sure, according to the price you pay', just as one had better or worse seats in a theatre depending on the price of the ticket. For a lesser sum, the undertaker's 'regard is very small'; as the price rose, 'the sighs are deep and audible'; for a little more, 'the woe is profound', until 'for £10 the despair bursts through all restraint'. In the end, thundered the journalist, undertakers were nothing but 'funeral pantomimists'.[7]

Just as one could not trust the authenticity of an undertaker's emotions, so too customers had to beware of their ethics. In the 1840s, a parliamentary commission recorded the case of an ex-shoemaker-turned-undertaker in the east of London, who arranged funerals before he also turned up at the local cemetery dressed as a clergyman to perform the funeral service – and pocket another fee.[8] In the penny-blood *The Mysteries of London*, the undertaker is not merely a hypocrite but is actively in cahoots with the local resurrection man, a connection that is treated as a matter of course.[9]

Families therefore kept some elements of the funeral in their own hands. After a death, the first thing was to send out invitations, to ensure that those whom one wanted were present at the funeral. In the countryside among the working people, a 'bidder', often the church's sexton or the parish clerk, called on those the mourners wanted to attend, announcing in a series of set phrases, 'You are expected to join So-and-so's burying tomorrow, at such-and-such an hour. We bury at thus-and-so churchyard.' The parish's clergyman would be bidden first, followed by the more prominent members of the community and finally guests further down the social scale. To attend a funeral without being bidden was a social solecism.[10] In Scotland, after people were notified that they were expected, the response was, 'When do you lift?', meaning, at what time would the procession set out.

For the middle classes, as always, there were conflicting views on correct behaviour, each choice unfailingly presented as the one correct way to do things. *Cassell's Household Guide*, a very popular work, instructed its readers that it was 'advisable' to contact those who might wish to attend (note the difference: not those whom you wished would attend), by asking a friend who was not in mourning to call on them, or by writing, either a letter in one's own hand, or a pre-printed black-edged memorial card, which could be purchased from stationers, and which read: 'The favour of your company is requested on [insert day] next, the [date] of [the month], to attend the funeral of the late [name]. The mourners will assemble at [repeat name]'s late residence, [address], at [hour] o'clock, to proceed to [name of cemetery].' But the purchaser of these cards, while grateful not to have to write many individual letters, might have been disconcerted to find that *Etiquette for Ladies and Gentlemen* was equally certain: 'Memorial cards are never sent by people in good society,' it stated, with no further discussion. One clergyman author tried to find a halfway house, advising his readers that, 'as a rule', the pre-printed, purchased memorial cards were 'incorrectly designed, if not positively grotesque', but that one could find cards 'of good design' from a religious guild he names. He did not, however, inform his readers what good design consisted of, nor what it was that made one set of cards good, the other 'grotesque', so that they could purchase them elsewhere.[11]

Many simply wrote letters requesting the presence of their friends and family. Carlyle and three of his relatives sat and wrote 'about 150 letters' on the death of his mother in 1853. In that case, the mourners were to gather directly at the churchyard. The following year Carlyle took on the same task for his brother after the death of his wife, and the letters have that same peremptory tone as the bidders' instructions: 'The hour of Starting from this House (No 21 Westbourne Place) is 10 a.m. Wednesday 30th; so that you have to be here sharp by that hour, – sooner than the hour is not necessary.'[12] An invitation to a funeral, in whatever form, was an honour if extended by a social superior. The Kilverts had presumably received their letter or card from Miss Kilvert's executors and felt obliged to attend, as their deceased relative was far more socially prominent than they. When the mother of Carlyle's friend Lady Ashburton died, 'L[or]d Sandwich . . . distinguished me by an invitation to the Funeral,' Carlyle wrote, adding with some pride that he was 'the only person not of kin who was there'.[13]

Those invited gathered at the location where the body lay, which was almost always the deceased's own home or lodgings. In the countryside, among the prosperous working classes, these visitors would be welcomed with some form of food and drink, according to their financial abilities, by those who had been waking, or watching over the dead. If it could be afforded, a full meal was offered: beef and ham, or bacon, with 'the necessary "wet"', or alcohol.[14] Frequently a collection to cover these costs was carried out, either at home, where a relative might be designated as being in charge of receiving the donations during the viewing, or a receptacle might be left out in which visitors deposited their offering. In some places the money was handed to the clergyman at the church before the service, who would keep his fee and give the rest to the family.

A more stately way of marking the occasion was by passing trays of wine and 'small round cakes of the crisp sponge description', wrote a vicar in 1891, talking of his country parish in the past, adding he had 'heard' these were called funeral biscuits, as though this were not a term he knew, or at least was not a genteel one. This is more than a little surprising, as different varieties of funeral biscuit had been customary among all classes of society from at least the seventeenth century. After Pepys' brother's funeral in 1663/4, those whom he had bid (and he too used the term, although he added crossly that far more people attended than had been bidden) were served six biscuits each, and 'what they pleased' of wine.[15] In the early part of the nineteenth century, one recipe for funeral biscuits was for an enriched shortbread, listing as ingredients twenty-four eggs and three pounds each of flour and sugar. Later recipes were often for sponge finger-biscuits, but the advantage of the old-fashioned shortbread was that timely mottoes could be impressed into them: *dies mortis aeternae vitae*, the day of death is the birth of eternal life, for example. As always, different places had different traditions. In some parts of Shropshire, the biscuits were notably small, and each one was individually wrapped in black-edged writing paper and sealed with black wax. Unusually, these particular biscuits were not for the funeral-goers, but were sent to friends and family members who could not be present on the day. In parts of Wales, the tradition was to have two cakes, one plum, one seed, also wrapped in black-edged paper. For those who could not afford cakes, there were biscuits 'about the size of an ordinary tea saucer', which were served with a hot spiced ale. In Whitby, the style was 'a round, flat, and rather sweet, sort of cake biscuit . . . white, slightly sprinkled with sugar'; in Lincolnshire it was sponge fingers; in Cumberland, each mourner at the funeral received a small piece of cake wrapped in white paper, which was to be taken home unsealed. The advantage of the biscuit wrappers was that, like the shortbread, they could have a motto or even a funeral poem, illustrated with little mementi mori such as skulls, crossbones and coffins. For a slightly higher price, the family could order personalized labels that included the name and dates of the deceased.[16]

By the early nineteenth century, undertakers were responsible for all funerals above the level of the most modest. Charles Dickens, a furious opponent of elaborate funerals, mocked their pretensions in both his fiction and his reportage, fulminating against the cost and quantity of the commodities people were being assured were essential in order to be 'respectable'. Respectability was assumed to be

JOSEPH HOWELL,
PASTRY-COOK AND CONFECTIONER,
FANCY BREAD AND BISCUIT BAKER,
No. 34, VICTORIA PLACE, HAYES,
CARDIFF.

RICH WEDDING CAKES AND FUNERAL BISCUITS.
TEA PARTIES, FESTIVALS, & SCHOOL ANNIVERSARIES
CONTRACTED FOR ON REASONABLE TERMS.
JELLIES, PRESERVES, BRITISH WINES, ETC., ETC.

A Cardiff pastry-cook advertises his range, from weddings to funerals, in an 1863 gazetteer, or local directory.

neither class- nor cash-based, although in truth it was both. The middle and working classes were repeatedly told that respectability was demonstrated by the qualities of thrift, cleanliness, hard work, religious belief and a 'decent' family life. A funeral was an occasion on which many of those qualities could be displayed: the family had worked hard and been thrifty enough to be able to afford all of the elements; the family was devout; the family was loving. All of these, said the moral and spiritual guides, could be achieved by anyone at any income level. In truth it was much harder, if not impossible, to be respectable without money, and the reverse was also true: having money was what made you respectable.

Dickens saw through this confusion as it related to funerals. In one article highlighting the commercial interests lining their pockets by promoting ever-more ritualized mourning forms, he imagined a scenario where the mourner is shamed out of the simple funeral he had planned. 'Hearse and four?' he is asked by the undertaker.

'No, a pair will be sufficient.' 'I beg your pardon, Sir, but when we buried Mr. Grundy at number twenty, there was four on 'em, Sir; I think it right to mention it.' 'Well, perhaps there had better be four.' 'Thank you, Sir. Two coaches and four, Sir, shall we say?'

'No, Coaches and pair.' 'You'll excuse my mentioning it, Sir, but pairs to the coaches, and four to the hearse, would have a singular appearance to the neighbours. When we put four to anything, we always carry four right through.' 'Well! Say four!' 'Thank you, Sir. Feathers of course?' 'No. No feathers. They're absurd.' 'Very good, sir. *No* feathers?' 'No.' '*Very* good, sir. We *can* do fours without feathers, Sir, but it's what we never do. When we buried Mr. Grundy, there was feathers, and — I only throw it out, Sir — Mrs. Grundy might think it strange.' 'Very well! Feathers!' 'Thank you, Sir,' — and so on.[17]

That this was very close to reality can be seen in the journal of Jeannette Marshall. Following the death of her wealthy grandmother, 'In order that people shd. not think it was meanness', the family ordered four horses to pull the hearse, rather than the two they had first considered.[18]

At a middle-class funeral the family, via the undertaker, expected to supply, at a minimum, gloves, scarves and hatbands to all the attendants and mourners present. These items were almost always black, and they came in different fabrics, at different prices, graded for the social standing of the mourners and how close they were to the deceased.* An undertaker in Derby distributed a sixteen-page pamphlet outlining the goods he had available and their prices. His most inexpensive funeral for an adult was £2 14s., and included a polished coffin (whatever the Reverend Mr Sewell, p. 97, said about

---

* Funerals for very young unmarried women as well as adolescent girls often gave prominence to white symbols. Through the first half of the century, girls might be carried to the grave by their female friends wearing white hoods, scarves and gloves. Garlands of white flowers were displayed, and after the funeral were hung in the deceased's parish church. In Portsmouth in 1881, a young woman who died just before her wedding was buried in her wedding dress. At the church, her coffin was stood up on end so the groom could 'marry' his dead bride before the funeral service followed and her coffin, covered in orange blossom, was carried out by the women who would have been her bridesmaids, wearing their bridesmaids' dresses. But this event was far enough out of the ordinary that it appeared in the newspapers.[19]

polished coffins being worldly and vulgar, they had long been the norm, as they remain today), lined; a flannel shroud; a pall; a hearse and one black horse with a single plume, the driver wearing a black cloak, hatband and gloves; as well as the use of eight hatbands, four in silk and four made of crape that were to be returned at the end of the funeral; four pairs of gloves, fabric unstated. The type of fabric was an indication of status, and every undertaker carried a wide range. This supplier had wool gloves for as little as 8*d*. a pair, silk at 1*s*. 4*d*. and kid at nearly 4*s*. a pair. The humble cotton glove was, apparently, too commonplace for him to bother with. As each of his funeral plans increased in price, the items supplied went from silk and crape to 'best silk' and 'best crape', the numbers of gloves and hatbands rose and scarves and armbands were added. The highest priced funeral, at £15, included the attendance of four bearers in black, and the undertaker himself dignified the funeral with his presence.[20] Getting each of these details right was important. Kilvert made much of his dismay when in 1872 he presided at a child's funeral that he had 'thought . . . would be a white glove funeral', 'but the mourners were in black gloves'.[21]

The Derby undertaker went no higher than £15 for his funerals, but *Cassell's Household Guide* presented a £53 funeral as standard for the middle classes. (It was not. A doctor might earn as little as £100 or £150 a year, or as much as £1,000, which would surpass the income of many of the gentry. Even at the upper end of that range, £53, or 5 per cent of a year's income, was a fabulous amount to spend on a funeral.) For £53, the undertaker supplied four horses to pull the hearse, two mourning coaches for the family, each also pulled by four horses, with two dozen ostrich feathers and velvet coverings for the horses and coaches, a featherman, a double coffin lined with 'superfine cambric' and with brass coffin furniture, the use of a silk pall, two mutes wearing hats with black streamers, black sashes across their chests, and with staffs tied with black ribbons, silk gloves and hatbands for the mourners, fourteen pages, all attendants dressed in full mourning.[22]

Male mourners wore scarves of mourning crape swathed around

their hats. For the first half of the century, they also wore cloaks, again supplied by the undertaker, but gradually these became old-fashioned and then disappeared for the mourners, although the undertaker and his men continued to appear in them. The chief mourner had been accustomed to wear a black sash across his chest (white for a child), although this too was becoming increasingly rare as the century progressed. And there was a long-standing custom whereby the family of the deceased had mourning rings made, with the deceased's name or initials engraved, or incised, or picked out in different coloured enamels. These had been given to friends and family for centuries, but, possibly owing to the expense, this tradition faded more rapidly than the funeral wear.

After the mourners had gathered, had their meal, or their wine and biscuits, and the undertakers' men had passed out the scarves, hatbands, armbands and gloves, the procession set off. For walking funerals in the countryside, folklore said that the act of carrying a coffin from house to church created a de facto legal and perpetual right of way over the ground the procession covered. As such, local landlords frequently barred the paths on their land, specifically forbidding funeral processions. The equally folkloric solution was for a designated person in the procession to stop and stick pins in every gatepost they passed en route, these pins being a formal acknowledgement to the landowner that no claim to a right of way was being made.[23]

In towns, and for funerals with coaches, the two mutes who had been standing outside the door of the house led the procession, followed by the feathermen, then the hearse, the chief mourner and finally the other attendees in mourning coaches. More mourning coaches might be sent by family and friends wishing to show their respects but unable, or unwilling, to attend themselves: these therefore had a driver on the box, but were otherwise empty of passengers.* During the recurrence of cholera in the 1850s, one

---

* Dickens savaged this too. In *Bleak House*, a funeral had 'strictly speaking' just three 'human followers', but that sad little number was made up for by 'the amount of inconsolable carriages' and 'four-wheeled affliction' in attendance. Back in the real

funeral-goer noted that the rising number of deaths meant a general shortage of mourning coaches, with mourners finding themselves forced to hire cabs instead.[25] Mourning coaches were a very public, outward form of display, adding gravitas by lengthening the procession in tribute to the deceased. One 1843 funeral 'conducted in the most private manner' had a full complement of mutes, pages and feathermen, as well as the attendance of 'the most respectable inhabitants of the neighbourhood'.[26] The sole element that made it a private rather than public funeral was the absence of mourning coaches.

When churchyards were still customary, and the parish church the likely destination, a 'walking pace procession' was the norm, one where carriages were used, but with the pace geared to the pedestrians of the mourning party. Once the large garden cemeteries, habitually sited in suburbs or outside cities, became the destination, changes had to be made to cover the increased distance in a reasonable amount of time. The procession was therefore 'paged' at a walking pace from the house of the deceased up to the nearest main road or junction. There it was halted, the horses' decorations and plumes were stripped off, the undertaker's men jumped into one of the coaches and everyone set off at a normal trot until the gates of the cemetery came into view. There was another pause as the horses' plumage was fixed back into place, the undertaker's men tumbled out of their coach and the slow walking pace was resumed, allowing the funeral party to arrive at the cemetery with sober, grief-stricken dignity.[27]

For many outside of cities, whatever their social rank or financial status, a funeral procession was much less formal. The coffin was

---

world, for a fee undertakers would arrange for a mourning coach to collect individual mourners to transport them to the deceased's house, and then on to the cemetery, usually notifying them that this service was available by adding to the card of invitation normally sent for funerals: 'The friends of the late [name], of [address], request the favour of your company on [day] next, to unite with them in paying the last tribute of respect to the deceased, [name], and for which purpose a mourning coach will call for [name] at [address] to convey [name] to [name's] late residence. An early answer to [name] undertaker, will oblige.'[24]

'lifted' – carried out of the house – and placed on a wheeled bier that each parish kept for the purpose, to be pushed along the lanes to the churchyard. In some regions, the mourners carried the coffin on their shoulders; in parts of Scotland they used 'spokes', or poles that were passed under the coffin; in the Yorkshire Dales, towels were used in the same manner.[28] There was no lack of dignity, nor any class diminution in this mode of conveyance. When the former prime minister Benjamin Disraeli died in 1881, leaving instructions for a private funeral at his Buckinghamshire home, his coffin was taken to the grave on a wheeled bier. When Gladstone died in the following decade, and was given a great funeral in Westminster Abbey, his coffin was nevertheless taken from his house to the railway station on a wheeled bier pulled by the men employed on his estate.[29] Greater simplicity had become more common, with display decreasing imperceptibly but consistently from the 1840s onwards, picking up speed after the excesses of the Duke of Wellington's funeral in 1852. In 1876, that Derby undertaker was advertising 'a Hearse built on the Funeral Reform principle', 'reform' in this case meaning the procession had no feathers or feathermen. If mourners were willing to forgo hatbands and scarves too, his prices dropped further.[30] By 1892, one upper-class woman, in requesting the bare minimum, wrote that she was rejecting any pretensions of 'undertakerism at all', the phrase a sign of the serious loss in funeral prestige.[31]

In part this was exacerbated by an increased reliance on public transport. When carriages were used, it was possible to close one's eyes to the undignified trot between the walking pace start and finish. Trains were a different story. In 1842, when plans were initially being made for Brookwood Cemetery in Surrey, to be reached primarily by rail, the Bishop of London dismissed the mode of transport as 'improper' for the 'solemnity of a Christian funeral'. The haphazard mixing of social classes that occurred in railway carriages meant that the body of a 'respectable member of the church' might end up travelling with a 'profligate spendthrift', which would naturally 'shock the feelings of his friends'.[32] But this desire for segregation could not hold out against the need of cemeteries for more, and cheaper, land. As they moved further and further out of towns, transport by train became routine, even for the most devout. By the time the Reverend Alexander Mackonochie froze to death in a blizzard in Scotland in 1887, the connection between trains and funerals was entirely normal. Mackonochie, a mission priest who had worked in the docks, and had been prosecuted for his adherence to Anglo-Catholic, High Church ceremonial, was given a pointedly lavish funeral by his old church. The procession included a choir and fifty clergymen, followed by nearly four hundred congregants and mourners who walked all the way through central London, from Holborn to Waterloo Bridge and across it to the station, where mourners and the body were taken to Woking for the interment.[33]

All these funeral processions conformed to a greater or lesser degree to the long-standing traditions outlined above, but the detail could vary by district or class, with norms in one location being found contentious in another. A surgeon living in a market town recorded with approval that in the early part of the century mourners in a funeral procession would leave the house of the deceased 'singing appropriate hymns with great . . . devoutness'.[34] In other places, hymns raised clerical hackles. The Order for the Burial of the Dead in the Book of Common Prayer makes no mention of hymns, rather it states specifically that the appropriate Psalms 'shall be read', not sung. In the eighteenth century, Dissenters in particular had begun to include hymns in their funerals. Some Church of England clergy accepted that Psalms that had been set to music could be sung, although it was mostly a country tradition, and the practice remained contested. In 1850, a vicar in Ditchling, Sussex, refused to allow the mourners at one funeral to sing a funeral anthem at the grave, while in Alfriston, thirty kilometres away, his colleague made no attempt to prevent a choir and mourners singing together.[35] One Lancashire clergyman remembered mourners singing at wakes, again on lifting the body, and finally during the procession to the churchyard – so much singing, in fact, that he worried that music was overtaking the burial service itself, and he made a move to end the custom.[36]

Quaker funerals were known for their silence; at least, most of them were. They were also much plainer than Church of England funerals, with no pall, no funeral wear such as scarves or hatbands. But at times the prevailing tastes of the majority population could not help but seep in. A young Quaker in London in 1829 thought his cousin's coffin had been 'handsome', with 'a beautiful sermon' given by two men, while a third eulogized the deceased's fine character. The procession had included 'twelve glass coaches, and two hackney coaches'. At another funeral, he gave the coffin the Quaker commendation of being 'plain' and 'neat', before adding that it also had fine brass handles.[37]

After a burial, there was usually another gathering of mourners, where food and drink was again offered. In the country, or where there was not much money, mourners might go from the church-yard to a nearby tavern or inn. The market-town surgeon reported that in his district these meals were called 'arvils', which he said was an old tradition, but not one he had previously encountered. The word arval, or arvel, however, dates back to Old Norse, and meant a funeral feast, very similar to or the same as a wake. Until the nineteenth century a wake had referred to the watching over the dead before the funeral, but now it was used to mean the post-funeral event. The idea aroused a great deal of distrust among the middle-class English in particular, who regarded wakes as an Irish custom and thus an excuse for drinking and unruly behaviour. In actuality, the word is entirely Old English in origin and the custom was wide-spread: the post-funeral event could be anything from bread and cheese and ale to a full meal. One student of local traditions in Scotland recorded that funerals routinely paused on the way to a churchyard at the 'stage hoos', where whisky, bread, cheese and oatcakes were consumed, with funeral biscuits distributed for the mourners to take home to their children.[38] Sometimes funeral guests were divided up by class: the prosperous in one room, receiving wine and cake, the less well-off in the kitchen given beer, while the labourers were relegated to the scullery with ale and portions of bread and cheese.[39] The meals could be substantial. One family in 1884 purchased twenty pounds of ham, twenty-four pounds of beef, spiced bread, white bread, cheese, gingerbread, tea, sugar and tobacco for what looks like it might have been a hundred guests.[40] In almost all regions, the provision of food, alcohol and, often, tobacco, were standard, considered to reflect credit on the deceased and also to be a way of helping mourners alleviate their grief through conversation and praise of the dead.[41]

Of course, there were many funerals, possibly the majority, where none of this was possible. Working-class people had to scrape together the money to purchase the bare necessities for burial, and little else could be afforded. Yet the importance of what today appear to be extraneous elements is demonstrated when we see that where the money could be found, working-class funerals included at least a gesture towards those items the middle classes declared necessary for respectability. One memoirist told of the death of his baby brother. His father was in full-time work, and his mother did piecework at home. In addition, they had a little bit of insurance, and so his mother bought him mourning clothes – the first new suit of clothes he had ever worn. The mourners were, in addition, supplied with black-bordered handkerchiefs, and a carriage conveyed the family to the churchyard, with a half-hour stop at the pub on the way home to offer hospitality to those who had attended the service.[42]

But many other funerals were more like the one seen in the middle of London in 1832, where 'a yellow faced, weaver-looking man, with a child's coffin on his shoulder, covered over instead of by a Pall by what seemed to be an old brown woollen shawl with the bordering jagged off; and at his heels a sickly looking youngish woman, with a little girl of 7 or 8 at her side. And thus they passed along, apparently unobservant and unobserved.'[43] No procession, no friends nor family, just a young couple carrying their dead child to the churchyard themselves. It is hard to think of anything more spare, yet it is notable that even here there was an attempt to have at least some of the display elements the middle-class world had decided indicated respectability, even if it were only a ragged shawl doing tragic double duty as a pall.

For the brutal truth was, death was expensive. Even those who died in hospital – at this time, hospital patients were the least well-off, unable to afford the costs of being nursed at home – even they had to face fees, as hospitals charged a deposit on admission to cover the cost of burial if the patient died. At St Bartholomew's, in the City of London, if the patients had insufficient funds, they were required to produce a 'respectable' guarantor 'for . . . THEIR BURIAL when they die in Hospital', refundable if they left under their own steam. It was no small sum either: 1s. for the certificate of death; 1s. for the porter to take that piece of paper to the deceased's home parish; 2s. to have the body carried to the hospital gate; 1s. for the use of a pall. If the family then collected the body, then they owed only (only) this 6s. If the patient had no family, it cost another 19s. 6d. for the coffin, shroud, burial plot, minister, bearers and pall, together with an extra fee for the ominously named 'Sisters of the Cutting Ward'.[44]

Most could not begin to afford this, nor could they pay the funeral costs. The New Poor Laws of 1834 had reduced the amount of cash assistance given to those in need, forcing the very poorest to become inmates of the workhouse instead, the aim of the law being to make poverty as grinding and desperate as possible, as if the poor were not already ground down and desperate. After this, what little assistance was supplied by the parish to the indigent on the death of a family member was reduced further, and for this segment of the population the pauper funeral was the final ignominy.

Yet even here, there was a hierarchy of despair. In the 1830s, in Hulme, near Manchester, an individual grave cost between 5s. and 6s., while at the edge of the churchyard a grave that contained

multiple burials cost 1s. or 2s.[45] These out-of-the-way graves were the
final resting places for the impoverished, and also for stillborn
babies, and for this reason, it was not unusual to ask a local midwife
to declare that a child who had died after birth had been stillborn,
since a child's grave was far more expensive.[46] After the New Poor
Laws were passed, many district Poor Law Guardians initially
attempted where possible to give the dead, and their survivors, some
of the funeral elements that others took for granted. In Hulme
again, in 1836, the local Guardians received this letter: 'Gentlemen,
I must again begge youre pardon for writeing to you for some help
from the payers. My wife has been layinge dead for this past week
and we have not the means to burye her in proper fashion. The
coffing we have got upon credit on your regular allowance to us and
my mother has givein the cloth but we have not the money to pay
the buryal dues nor to intertane the mourners. I begge of yu that yu
will help us to do this at yure earliest oportunitie.' And the
Guardians did, giving the man the money he requested, including,
it is notable, money to enable him to 'intertane' the mourners – to
give them food and drink.[47]

But gradually the enthusiasts of grinding the poor won out over
the would-be compassionate. The 'decent' accoutrements of a
funeral disappeared first in large cities. Then the quality of what
remained deteriorated. Families of those to be buried in paupers'
graves were required to use coffins provided by the parish, made of
plain deal (pine), without nameplate or anything more than a chalk
scrawl to identify their loved one. The cheapness of the coffin wood
was said to be selected because it decayed more quickly, and thus
new paupers could be added to the communal graves in a shorter
period of time. However, the refusal to use any permanent identification seemed to contemporaries, as it does today, cruelty for
cruelty's sake. There were other indignities heaped upon this one:
coffins that were so poorly constructed that bodily fluids leaked
from them before burial; worse, coffins so poorly constructed that
bodies fell out on the way to the grave. Some clergy refused to hold

burial services for paupers; others would conduct the service, but would not allow the families to enter the church to hear it.[48] The poor, claimed a Spitalfields, London, clergyman, were an 'intrusion of a squalid and irreverent mob' into 'this sacred and beautiful structure', a space 'desecrated and disfigured' by their very presence.[49] As the sad little jingle ran:

> Rattle his bones over the stones;
> He's only a pauper whom nobody owns . . .
> Not a tear in the eye of a child, woman or man:
> To the grave with his carcass as fast as you can.

There are reports of the working poor doing everything they could to avoid this fate: paying a penny a week into small, locally run insurance clubs; borrowing from neighbours, friends and family as indigent as they; pawning household goods or clothes to come up with the burial fees. And when all else failed, there was a pattern of giving their loved ones a pauper's funeral but, once having managed to put together enough money, petitioning for the body to be moved from its mass grave into a more permanent individual one. This was treated as fairly routine both by those who wanted to move their dead, and by the burial boards that received and granted these requests.[50] Tidied up in fiction, the situation could even become a 'happily ever after' for middle-class audiences. In Dickens' first novel, *The Pickwick Papers*, there is a story about a debtor in the Marshalsea prison, whose wife and child die of hunger and despair, the wife, with her last breath, requesting, 'promise me, that if you ever . . . grow rich, you will have us removed to some quiet country churchyard . . . where we can rest in peace.' The man does indeed leave prison and grow rich, and so 'Beneath a plain grave-stone, in one of the most peaceful and secluded church-yards in Kent . . . lie the bones of the young mother and her gentle child'.[51] An exhumation and reburial presented as a satisfying, virtually romantic, ending to a tale.

The working classes expected men, women and children to attend funerals. For the middle classes, the presence of women was more fraught. In Jeremy Taylor's *Holy Dying*, that seventeenth-century work still so admired two centuries later, crying at a death was 'an ill expression', suggesting as it did a lack of submission to God's will. Thus, wrote manuals to middle-class mores, women, 'unable' as they were 'to restrain their emotions', would 'interrupt and destroy the solemnity of the ceremony with their sobs, and even by fainting'. This would, in turn, distress their normally stoic menfolk so much that they too might break down. Women were therefore advised to stay away.[52] That became the standard for the upper classes too, with one 1849 court etiquette manual warning that only 'eccentric' women were to be seen at funerals. Certainly the good women of fiction stayed home. In one novel of 1861, by the devout, High Church Charlotte M. Yonge, when a young man dies of wounds heroically sustained in the Crimean War, his beloved stepmother watches from the window of her lodgings as his coffin is carried by his regiment, kneeling to read the burial service all alone as his father and brother attend the funeral.[53]

As always, though, the rules were never fixed. By the 1880s, *Manners and Rules of Good Society* thought it was 'customary' for women to attend family funerals 'if disposed'.[54] In 1894, Mrs Oliphant wrote about the funeral of her last surviving child: 'I thought at first I could not go, but then bethought me that I could not let him be laid in his grave only by those who loved him in a secondary degree. They were all fond of him . . . but only I and Denny [her niece, whom she brought up] were his very own. So I went and laid my boy in his last rest. I can feel at least that I have never left him until the moment when no one earthly would be with him any more.'[55]

Jeannette Marshall's diary, by contrast, headed in the opposite direction. When her brother Reggie died in 1873, her sixteen-year-old sister went to the funeral with their father and uncle, while Jeannette and her aunt stayed home with Jeannette's mother. Twenty years later, when Jeannette's father died, her uncle was already dead, and her mother was 'so hysterical', recorded Jeannette, that she was not able, or willing, to attend the funeral, and neither would she allow her daughters to do so, nor even accompany the coffin as far as the station. Ultimately, it went alone, as the doctor, the sole mourner to leave from the house, was late and had to follow afterwards. Jeannette was sent details of the burial, but it does not erase the fact that her father's funeral was attended by none of his immediate family. Nevertheless, she wrote, '*our* wreath was put *in* the grave, & the others on it', which she thought highly appropriate. 'We have not,' she added, 'that foolish prejudice against flowers.'[56]

That 'foolish prejudice' against flowers and wreaths was worth commenting on, because cut flowers at a grave were a novelty in the 1890s. There had been a much older tradition of lining a grave with greenery, and sometimes with flowers, but even as late as 1881, people were remarking on the oddity of the primroses laid on Disraeli's grave.[57] Yet a mere two years later, the clergyman Mr Sewell was writing omnisciently that 'some [sort of] floral offering' was 'an ancient English custom' that had '[o]f late years . . . [been] revived'. He hastily added that there was 'no need to quote precedents', presumably because there were no precedents to quote, but he did note that the custom had 'always been prevalent in Wales'.[58] While laying bouquets or wreaths on graves had not been the practice in Wales either, Sewell may have been thinking of the custom of 'dressing' the graves of family and friends at Easter, which Kilvert had recorded over the years. As he described it, wooden crosses were made, and children in particular added them to the graves beside bunches of primroses, daffodils and greenery, which they dug into the ground to make it look as if they were growing.[59]

This was a small change. The great change over the nineteenth century was the shift from public to private, from a funeral that was a communal display of mourning to one that was a mark of personal loss. Dickens himself was clear about which side of the argument he was on, in giving instructions for his own end. 'I emphatically direct that I be buried in an inexpensive, unostentatious, and strictly private manner; that no public announcement be made of the time or place of my burial; that at the utmost not more than three plain mourning coaches be employed; and that those who attend my funeral wear no scarf, cloak, black bow, long hat-band, or other such revolting absurdity.'[60] He felt no differently, either, about other people's funerals, in 1868 refusing to attend the funeral of his own nephew: 'just as I should expressly prohibit the summoning to my own burial of anybody who was not very near or dear to me, so I revolt from myself appearing at that solemn rite unless the deceased was very near or dear to me.'[61] To Dickens a funeral was a communion between the dead and each mourner specifically. It was not a demonstration of community solidarity, nor did individual mourners attend as a mark of support for those to whom the deceased was 'very near and dear'.

Yet community engagement, embedding mourners and mourning rituals tightly into the fabric of society, was an essential part of facing death.

7

MOURNING DRESS

Mourning, and the mourning wear that came to be understood as grief's outward, public face, were important elements in the death process. Mourning correctly, or appropriately, whatever that might mean to different social classes and those of different income levels, was an endless source of discussion and dissent. The new print culture – magazines, newspapers, journals and novels – disseminated both the idea that mourning dress was the sole socially appropriate way to express grief, and that the mourning fashions worn by the higher classes were the sole socially appropriate form of clothing for it.

Today we understand 'mourning' to refer to the clothes worn by, mostly, women, and at the time writing on the subject did centre around what women wore. But there were other elements of mourning that encompassed many parts of daily life. As there were rules for society as to when, and on whom, one should pay a call, so too there were rules as to when to pay a condolence call, although the magazine and advice-writers all had different views on what was correct.

After a death in the family it was considered polite among the middle and upper classes to pay one's respects through a condolence call as soon as the family had made a public appearance at a Sunday church service. (Given that we have seen that half the population did not attend church regularly, this was a bourgeois ideal, not reality.) It was likely that the family was not yet receiving visitors, or, in the parlance of the day, were 'Not at home', that is, they had given instructions that visitors were to be politely refused entrance. In that case, the visitor would leave a card – a mourning card, naturally, which it was expected that all women of a certain social level would possess for these circumstances. Mourning cards were the same as regular visiting cards, with the woman's name – Mrs John Smith – printed on it, with the addition of a black border around the edge. On this card, Mrs Smith then wrote at the top, 'To inquire after Mrs A—.' For the call, even though she knew she would be told the mourning family was 'not at home', she was expected to wear, if not black, then a dark-coloured dress without too much decoration on it. In a sort of society round-robin, the family then returned her call by sending their own card, marked 'Returning thanks for kind inquiries'. On receipt, Mrs Smith visited once again, at which time the family was 'At home' to her. After all that, the ladies then sat for a regulation fifteen-minute chat that was designed to be light and superficial. While some were like Jane Carlyle, the wife of Thomas Carlyle, who grumbled at 'The letters and calls of inquiry and condolence . . . [that eat] up my days', this social dance mattered a great deal for those who thought of themselves as genteel. Taking part in these formalities was not simply for close friends and family. One popular novel portrays a woman's umbrage that her neighbour had neglected to send a card on the occasion of her husband's sister's husband's death.[1]

As well as mourning visiting cards, households that could afford it also kept mourning stationery on hand. This was not as simple as having a stock of regular writing paper with a printed black border added, as with the cards. In 1880, *Queen* magazine gave readers detailed instructions. There were, it warned, three kinds of black-bordered writing paper, with borders that could be broad, extra broad or double broad. Double-broad borders were only to be used by a widow mourning her husband; for any other level of grief, it said dismissively, they were vulgar. Extra-broad borders were for a parent mourning a child, or vice versa, while narrow borders were for mourning a sibling. For correspondents who were not in mourning, but were instead writing to those in mourning, there was a yet smaller width, called a 'slight' mourning border, which was, *Queen* assured its readers, entirely appropriate for this situation.[2] Other nuances could not be purchased, only understood, internalized and practised. In Mrs Wood's sensation novel *East Lynne*, the daughter of a recently deceased earl receives a letter from the wife of the heir, the new earl, who has the temerity, or perhaps it is the ill-breeding, to sign it with her only recently acquired title instead of, more modestly, the title she had borne until a few days previously.[3] Most of the world was not likely to need to know how much time to leave after a death before a newly inherited title could genteelly be used in correspondence, but it is notable that Mrs Wood's middle-class audience was expected to understand the disrespect implicit in such a signature at such a time.

It was dress, however, and in particular women's dress, that bore the weight of conveying the nuances of mourning, and the degree of loss. The main fabric used in mourning clothes was crape. Crape had historically been made of silk, or later of a silk and wool mix known as bombazine, or a wool and cotton mix known as paramatta. The key element, whatever its constituent parts, was that the material had been heat-treated in the manufacturing process to produce a stiff finish and a non-reflective surface, shininess being equated with cheerfulness. Women's mourning dresses were made of crape, and it was also the standard fabric for mourning veils, cloaks, armbands, hatbands, scarves and ribbons. Pure wool, or cashmere, being naturally non-reflective, could also be used for mourning dresses, although if that were the case in the initial stages of mourning, particularly by new widows, then bands of crape were added to the skirt horizontally in layers of one, two or three, frequently covering the skirt from hem to waist.

Crape did not wear well, its surface quickly discolouring, making it look as if it had been attacked by rust. If a single drop of water touched the fabric, it marked indelibly, which meant widows were confined indoors on wet days, or on days that looked like they might later be wet, or days that were now dry but the pavements

This woman is wearing deep mourning, with two wide crape bands at the bottom of her skirt. It may be that some time has passed since her bereavement, as a small white collar is visible, and she wears a brooch. It and the locket on the chain around her neck are likely to contain portraits or locks of hair of the deceased.

and streets were still wet. It also meant that those of lesser means were doomed to wear crape that looked dowdier than crape normally did, at least until the late 1860s, when a fabric known as Albert crape began to be manufactured. This was a silk and cotton mix that was suitably flat and lustreless, but it cost less, and did not age as poorly.[4] A method for waterproofing crape was invented in 1897, by which time full mourning was already reduced, but no doubt the new fabric was nonetheless welcome.

Historically mourning dress had not followed the fashions, but by the nineteenth century as long as the fabric was crape and the colour black, any cut or style could be considered to be mourning wear. This shift greatly suited the fashion industries, whether the textile industry, shopkeepers, dressmakers or fashion journalism: as new fashions were disseminated, so mourning dresses now became démodé, and thus, for the prosperous at least, had to be replaced for every new loss. For the less prosperous, this was a desire if not a requirement, and so after a mourning period was completed, they sold their soon-to-be unfashionable dresses to those with less money still, who in their turn were selling their coloured day dresses, which they could not wear while in mourning, and which would be out of fashion by the time mourning was over, a long chain of mourning and commerce.[5]

Of course many could not, or would not, buy new outfits for each death to be mourned, and others just arranged to have their own clothes dyed black. Local dyers routinely advertised that clothes could be dyed and returned to their grieving customers within twenty-four hours. (These tradesmen were the forefathers of modern-day dry-cleaners, as they were also performing chemical services.) Dark-dyed clothes generated their own problems, however, and women's magazines found it lucrative to carry advice on how to remove the black dye that inevitably transferred itself from clothes to skin.[6] The recipes for these home-made dye-removing solutions included ingredients such as cream of tartar and oxalic acid, the latter of which is a skin irritant, dangerous if inhaled, and is today used to remove rust from metal objects. Other dyed items required different, and laboriously time-consuming procedures to keep them looking fresh: 'To Restore Rusty Black Lace. — Half cup rain water, one teaspoonful borax, one teaspoonful alcohol; squeeze the lace through this four times; then rinse in a cup of hot water in which a black kid glove has been boiled. Pull out the edges of lace until almost dry, then press for two days between the leaves of a heavy book.'[7]

As this suggests, there was mourning as the commercial, advice-

book, magazine-selling world set it out, and then there was
mourning as it was carried out by real people in real life. The two
things were not always, or not even often, the same. And the 'rules'
of mourning were, equally, not rules, but socially accepted norms,
and therefore different for virtually everyone. If readers turned to
advice books to tell them how to behave, as the middle classes in
particular did, especially if they found themselves in a class they had
not been born to, they might be forgiven for throwing up their
hands and doing as they liked, for each author advised something
different, while all of them invariably asserted that their own prefer-
ences were the 'rules of good society'.

It was generally accepted that a new widow of the middle classes
or upward would wear deepest mourning, known as first mourning,
for her husband for a year, or a year and a day, that extra day indicating that she was not too eager to divest herself of her crape
burden. This was followed by what was called second mourning,
where less crape was worn, which lasted anything from another six
to twelve months, depending on which guide one read, after which
came several more months in half-mourning, when, to the mourning
colours of black and white, other acceptable colours were added:
'delicate shades of slate-colour, grey, mauve, and purple . . . [as well
as] the palest violet' (which could be translated more prosaically to
greys and mauves/lavenders).[8] The *Englishwoman's Domestic
Magazine*, published by the husband of Mrs Beeton, was firm on
the subject: a widow's dress was

> always of paramatta entirely covered with crape to within an inch
> or two of the waist, the crape being in one piece, not in separate
> tucks, for the first nine months. If after this period it requires
> renewing, it may be put on in two deep tucks . . . The [widow's]
> cap [which was worn indoors] was formerly constructed so as
> almost entirely to cancel the hair and to fasten under the chin;
> but this severe style is now considerably mitigated, and many
> different shapes are worn . . . for a year and a day. The outdoor

dress has a jacket or mantle of paramatta very heavily trimmed with crape: neither fur nor velvet can be worn. The bonnet [for outdoor wear] is entirely crape, with a widow's cap tacked inside it, and with a crape veil with a deep hem. This constitutes the dress for the first twelve months. After that . . . silk heavily trimmed with crape may be worn for six months, after which the crape can be considerably lessened . . . After nine months, plain black . . . is permissible; and after two years mourning may be laid aside, though it is in much better taste to wear half-mourning for at least six months more.[9]

The widow's cap was a white crape confection with long streamers hanging from it, the Marie Stuart being a variant that had an indent at the top and fitted less closely to the head around the ears, to form a heart shape around the face. While the Marie Stuart was considered to be slightly more fashionable, many women hated the caps, whatever style they came in. In a novel of 1854, the widowed heroine is encouraged to stop wearing her cap by two friends: 'A horrid thing it is. She would look four years younger without it — yes, five . . . A widow's cap . . . is a species of suttee,' says one. The other agrees. 'I'd rather have "sacred to the memory" printed on my forehead in capital letters' than wear one, she proclaims. The widow herself, however, is more careful. 'I believe I should be more comfortable without it . . . but what would the world say?'[10]

She had a point. The world, made up of essayists, novelists, journalists, politicians, friends, family and neighbours, all had plenty to say about widows. Mourning dress was, it seemed, the best way to tell women they were in the wrong: they were not mourning enough, or they were mourning too ostentatiously, or too quietly, they were wearing too much black, or too little, or for an insufficient or excessive period of time. One advice writer of the 1890s managed to condemn women who wore too much black, women who wore too little, women who thought too much about their mourning dress, women whose mourning was too fashionable, or who mourned for those who were too distantly related, all in five pages.[11] And she was writing at a time when mourning had become less important.

At the beginning of Victoria's reign, a comic journal had already published a satire on the commercialization of mourning, the advice books and of course the women who mourned. Here Squire Hamper and his wife, up from the country to 'see the sights', go to 'that black shop' as part of their tourist routine. The shop assistant shows them a variety of mourning wear, from goods suitable for 'matrimonial bereavements', to those moving from 'a grief *prononcé* to the slightest *nuance* of regret', including the goods in the 'Intermediate Sorrow Department', 'to suit a woe moderated by time', and a fabric called 'a Gleam of Comfort', which 'harmonises beautifully with the monuments and epitaphs' at Kensal Green.[12] Some contemporary readers might be excused from recognizing this as comedy: in the real world the famous Oxford Street department store, Peter Robinson, had an even more famed next-door venue that sold nothing but mourning wear and was known to everyone as Black Peter Robinson; within that shop, the space given to half-mourning was called the Mitigated Affliction Department.

Mourning was for the most part a female activity, and a female responsibility. In the first twelve months after the death of their husbands, widows were supposed to leave their houses only for church, or to see their closest family, with visits to a somewhat wider circle being postponed until the second year. Men, meanwhile, were not merely expected to return to work within days, or at the most weeks, of their wives' deaths, with no other constraints on their movements, they were morally obliged to do so: 'I know [it] is my duty,' said one doctor.[13] Advice writers rarely mentioned men at all when it came to mourning. By the middle of the century, men's mourning wear consisted of little more than a crape hatband after the first few weeks: seven inches wide for a widower, five for a father

In this photograph from the 1850s, only a tiny
section of the shiny top hat remains visible above
the wide crape mourning band.

mourning his child or, for lesser grief, anything from two and a half
to four inches, said one manual.[14] Later, the hatband vanished, to be
replaced by a black armband. Court mourning, the dress regulations
laid down for those who attended the monarch, had the most elaborate rules. So complicated were they for women that they were
advised to check for the full requirements of any period of royal
mourning in the *London Gazette*, the government newspaper. Men,
by contrast, did not even have to possess their own armband in the
1880s, but could pick one up 'in the cloak-room of the Palace' as
needed.[15]

Customer. "A SLIGHT MOURNING HAT-BAND, IF YOU PLEASE."
Hatter. "WHAT RELATION, SIR?"
Customer. "WIFE'S UNCLE."
Hatter. "FAVOURITE UNCLE, SIR?"
Customer. "'UM—WELL, YES."
Hatter. "MAY I ASK, SIR, ARE YOU MENTIONED IN THE WILL?"
Customer. "NO SUCH LUCK."
Hatter (to his Assistant, briskly). "COUPLE O' INCHES, JOHN!"

Punch magazine in 1864 was happy to satirize the minute distinctions in mourning dress that many observed.

When Jeannette Marshall's brother died in 1873, her father and schoolboy brother returned to work and school the day after the funeral. Jeannette, by contrast, together with her sister and mother, spent the next weeks replying to condolence letters and making more mourning dresses. Jeannette and her sister could have left off mourning for their brother the following year, but it was considered to be in poor taste for women to wear colours when anyone else in their household was still in black, and so the two girls continued to wear mourning with their mother for a full eighteen months.

These requirements became ever more elaborate as the availability of commodity goods increased in the nineteenth century, driving the establishment of shops that catered *only* to those in mourning. Frequently known as Mourning Warehouses (warehouse, as well as meaning a place to keep stock, was used to mean a large shop), the fashionable emporia dignified themselves further by naming themselves 'Magasins de Deuil', which was simply French for 'mourning shops', but sounded fancy. In 1841, Jay's Mourning Warehouse opened across three buildings in London's fashionable shopping street, Regent Street, in advertisements often dubbing itself 'Maison Jay', to emphasize its connection to Paris and the home of fashion rather than death. So successful was it that it was shortly joined by Pugh's Mourning Warehouse, the Argyll General Mourning and Mantle Warehouse, and of course Black Peter Robinson.

In the early part of the century, women were expected to first put on mourning dress a week after a death, which gave them time to be fitted and have the clothes made. By the 1860s, mourning warehouses everywhere boasted that they were able to provide all the requisites in as little as a day, a trend greatly helped by the increasing adoption of ready-to-wear by the middle classes. The arrival of sewing machines did the same for those who made their clothes at home. In a novel of 1861, a woman is setting off to see her dying stepson. As she hurriedly packs, her stepdaughter removes 'the bright border of a travelling-cloak' in order to tack on a crape border instead.[16] It is notable both that she is dressing in black even before the boy's death, and that the family keeps crape in the house, presumably for situations like this one.

By mid-century, in almost all circumstances, if the newly ordered black clothes were not ready, the mourner was expected to stay at home entirely. When a man was too ill in 1853 to attend his mother's funeral, his wife could not go in his place, she wrote, 'not having a bonnet I could wear – the one I have ordered not having made its appearance'.[17] Even the very poorest felt these requirements. Francis Kilvert met a labourer on the road who was tramping the countryside looking for work. 'My mother was buried to-day,' he cried to the clergyman. 'I would have stayed to follow my mother to the grave but I had no black clothes except a jacket and couldn't get any', and so going to her funeral was unthinkable.[18] These requirements could also encompass the deaths of the great whom one did not know. Jane Carlyle wrote crossly that watching the Duke of Wellington's funeral procession from a house along the route 'cost me a new black bonnet'.[19]

For many, mourning was a sign not merely of respectability, but of morality. Some interpreted the desire for simpler funeral wear as so radical it must presage political uprising: to overthrow mourning customs was to overthrow society. The conservative and middle-class *Englishwoman's Domestic Magazine* drew a direct parallel between those who were hesitant to convert their wardrobes to black owing to the cost, and the 'often quoted fact' that the upper classes in France had begun to wear less ostentatious and less obligatory mourning before the Revolution. ('Fact' here does not appear to mean what we take it to mean.) 'With a shudder', the journalist therefore wondered if the funeral reforms mooted in Britain would 'be followed by as awful a retribution' – the guillotine apparently an appropriately severe punishment for wanting to wear less crape.[20] Yet for many at that time, this might not have seemed extreme, at least rhetorically. Mourning had long been a way for the rich and titled to affirm caste and the status quo as much as to indicate grief.

In the seventeenth century it was not just the dress of mourning gentry that was black: black hangings were pinned to the walls and beds, while horses mourned via black harnesses and saddles. Lower down the social scale, the middle classes emulated their effects. When Pepys' brother died, he had the soles of his shoes blackened, so that when he knelt in church no unseemly light colour would show itself.[21] On the other hand, the mourning period was then much shorter for all than it would be two centuries later. Pepys' wife wore full mourning for a brief six weeks after her mother-in-law's death before moving on to half-mourning. This did infuriate Pepys, who thought it 'too soon', and although he ordered her to change, 'she would not', and there were no social consequences that he recorded.[22] In general, mourning was more a matter of navigating the day-to-day difficulties caused by the dress: in 1770, the diplomat and writer Horace Walpole wrote to a friend asking if he could stay the night before an early morning meeting he had planned nearby the next day. He was in mourning for his brother-in-law, he explained, and 'it would be extremely inconvenient' to have to be 'dressed up in weepers and hatbands by six o'clock in the morning'.[23]

This type of pragmatism was routine. While mourning was theoretically all-important, in reality it mutated as necessary, being abbreviated, or lifted entirely, for a day or two to mark some event of public significance, or with acceptable fabrics and decorative elements added to suit the needs of tradesmen and merchants. The *London Gazette*, for example, set out the detail for mourning wear for the wider public on the death of a member of the royal family as though the rules were inviolable, even as they changed over time. The mourning period for the Duke of Kent (the father of Queen Victoria) was set at three months, but when the duke's father, George III, died a week later, mourning was attenuated to six weeks by order of the new king. (The Hanoverians had notoriously terrible father–son relationships.) In 1830, when George IV died in turn, it was decided to return the mourning period to three months; in 1861, on the death of Prince Albert, it contracted to two, indicative of the trend to briefer mourning periods, although the queen herself was never happier than when ostentatiously wrapped in black. (For Queen Victoria and mourning, see Chapter 12.) The letters of Lady Stanley of Alderley demonstrate this diminution. In 1844, she advises her daughter-in-law that, even though court mourning was in abeyance, she should wear mourning for her (Lady Stanley's) first cousin, despite it being a most distant connection to her daughter-in-law (her mother-in-law's sibling's child). There were, Lady Stanley wrote, 'several of the family in town who might observe and be hurt if you did not'. A couple of years later, advising once more on what was appropriate after another family death, this time she thinks that 'a little black may be necessary', but not full mourning, while she herself is planning to do less, mourning only 'in *black wax*', that is, by using black sealing wax instead of red on her letters.* Four years later, even that was too much for her. The first cousin who had recently died had lived such a quiet life, she wrote, 'that I never thought of your mourning for her, or doing so myself, though I did seal with black'.[25] Quite an alteration in less than a decade.

It was Princess Alexandra of Denmark, the wife of the future Edward VII, who quietly reduced the royal emphasis on mourning. When she arrived in Britain in 1863, fifteen months after the death of Prince Albert, she accommodated her new mother-in-law's penchant for long-term mourning by wearing a grey dress with a violet cloak, half-mourning colours. But when her own son died in 1892, while she discarded the brightly coloured clothes she had previously worn to great effect, she nonetheless never wore black, instead again adopting half-mourning colours: silvers, greys and lavenders. And when Queen Victoria died in 1901, she refused entirely to dictate what court mourning should be: 'such questions bore me intensely.'[26]

This had been some time coming. By the final quarter of the nineteenth century, for many in the middle classes as well as the

* Black sealing wax had long been recognized as a sign of a death in the family. In the 1880s, one of the Courtaulds wrote to her cousin, 'You will judge by my wax that we have lost the dear girl, she died about a fortnight [ago].'[24]

upper, 'excessive grief' was beginning to be seen not as an appropriate display of feeling, but as 'wicked'.[27] And to many observers at the time, it seemed as if the reluctance to change was not owing to grief itself, but to how society perceived their expressions of grief. The upper-class Lady Charlotte Schreiber, as the first publisher of the Welsh medieval stories that comprise the Mabinogion, and, after her first husband's death, the administrator of a large ironworks, had long flouted norms for women. Even she, however, worried about being seen attending the opera a year and a half after she was widowed. It was not the attendance at the opera itself that troubled her, but what other people would think, and so she went, but told herself that she was unlikely to be noticed all 'muffled up going and coming and . . . [sitting] in the back of the box'.*[28]

The more middle-class Carlyles were exactly the kind of people who had opinions on the mourning behaviour of others. Jane Carlyle's usual staccato phrasing became even more abrupt in her indignation at the perceived lack of respect among the Wedgwood family on the death of Josiah Wedgwood, an MP and the son of the famous potter. 'The Wedgwoods were to have gone to Mair [Maer Hall, Staffordshire, where Wedgwood died] at the beginning of the week – "Oh what a pity I said that they had not gone the week before – that they might have been in time to see their Father" – "Why no, said he it was much better as it is – for it is much more convenient for them being all here to get their mournings before going – there are such a quantity needed so many children – servants and all that – they are quite spending their life in Jay's in Regent Street! –". It made me quite sick to hear of a Father gone out of the world and no other care felt about the matter except that of getting mournings . . .'[29]

---

* Mourning dress remained a serious matter to her. Even in 1852, when she had been widowed for a full four years, she was nevertheless careful to wear a white dress with a red scarf to her son's wedding, white being a mourning colour, and red then considered to be the best colour for women in mourning to wear when attending weddings as it was, curiously, classed as 'no colour'.

The Wedgwoods could afford to buy an all-new mourning ward-robe for everyone in their household, including their servants. Most people, even the comfortably off middle classes, could not. Mourning was expensive, inconvenient and tiresome. Reformers stressed that it was the symbol of loss that was the important part, not that a three-year-old was dressed in the appropriate colours to express toddler grief at the death of her mother's half-sister's husband.*[30] All too often, however, the advice was given by those with little real sense of the economics of people's lives. The Reverend Mr Sewell imagined that men ordered six suits at a time, women twenty dresses; in reality, many relatively financially secure middle-class women were content with one new dress a year for best, while the previous year's best dress was demoted to serve as their sole day dress.[31] Others, including the wealthy, simply accepted that not all their clothes would say 'mourning' to outsiders. In 1803 the future Lady Wharncliffe listed her bombazine dresses, black crape bands and black gloves, together with a 'coloured pelisse as one cannot be expected to make up such ruinous[ly expensive] articles for every mourning'.[32] A clothing diary kept by an Anne Sykes, the wife of a Midlands textile merchant, preserves snippets of the mourning fabrics she purchased on the death of her mother: two patterned black-on-black cotton gauzes and a plain black satin.[33] She, at least, did not feel it necessary to purchase fabrics created solely for mourning. And Jeannette Marshall, on a similar social level, both women far below the aristocratic Lady Wharncliffe, followed the same pattern, buying a single crape dress following her brother's death for best, and otherwise making do with a dark day dress she already owned.†[34] And a late vestige of this solemnity-mixed-with-pragmatism

---

*   This was the fate of Princess Beatrice, Victoria's youngest child, who was put into black crape when the queen's half-sister's husband died in Baden-Baden. The queen on another occasion wrote to check that her five-month-old grandchild would be appro-priately dressed following the death of the baby's great-grandmother. By the 1870s, however, advice books for the middle classes were dismissing children dressed in mourning as 'absurd', although seemingly without intentional reference to the queen.
†   The Marshalls had some difficult moments with mourning. When Jeannette's grand-

was visible on British television in 2022, on the day the death of Elizabeth II was announced, with MPs pouring into the House of Commons dressed theoretically in black, although it could be seen that many did the best they could by wearing navy. (See plate section.)

In a similar fashion, the dictates of advice books that all decent people of any status put their servants into mourning on the death of a family member was a polite fiction. Some, such as the Wedgwoods, did. Other, much grander, families did not. When the Duke of Sussex lay in state in 1843, the visitors wore mourning but were directed to their places by his servants dressed in crimson livery 'blazing with gold lace'.[35] Much more common were the middle-class households with single servants, or maids of all work, who might add nothing more than a black ribbon or other token to their regular dress, to gesture towards mourning. When Prince Albert died, the *Illustrated London News* noted approvingly that 'schoolchildren, hucksters [pedlars or street hawkers], flymen [drivers of a type of hired carriage known as a fly], old pauper women . . . had put on "decent mourning"', if only represented by 'a ribbon or a crape bow'.[36] 'Decent mourning' was frequently nothing more than this.

On Jane Carlyle's death her widower sent a favoured servant £25 to buy a mourning dress, which was considered by reformers to be the right thing to do for a valued ex-servant.[37] Yet two things are notable here. Carlyle sent his sister the same amount for the same purpose; and the price of a dress at a fashionable Regent Street shop at the time was less than an eighth of this amount. Either Carlyle was unaware of the cost of women's clothes, or he was using this form of words to send his sister and his ex-servant a sort of bequest

---

mother was ill, they received a telegram saying, 'Morituro est Mrs. Williams' – Mrs Williams is dying. They mistranslated it as 'Mrs Williams is dead', and had bought mourning fabric and hired a dressmaker before they discovered their mistake. As the goods had already been paid for, they had the dresses made up (and Mrs Williams did die shortly afterwards). It is unclear from the diary entry whether Latin had been used as a way of euphemizing the harsh news, or if the sender just thought it was more elegant.

from his wife.[38] Others in the middle class might give a new dress or a cast-off one of their own to working women who would themselves have no possibility of purchasing a new, or even second-hand, mourning dress.[39]

For the working classes, like the middle classes, felt that wearing mourning was a sign of respect, and more, of respectability. Whether they borrowed a black dress, received a cast-off or bought one at a second-hand market, reselling it or pawning it afterwards, the symbol was important. If a new outfit could not be managed, sometimes the money could be scraped together to dye some garments, or a few pennies found to purchase a black ribbon, tie or hatband to indicate that the wearer honoured the dead, and, more importantly, felt part of society and wanted to participate in its mores. The well-to-do could afford to mock the excesses of mourning; the working class could not afford to not take part, for their own self-respect.

8

MOURNING CUSTOMS

In 1759, Adam Smith, the father of economic theory, wrote that the way we sympathize with the dead, and with their survivors, is by putting ourselves in the place of the dead. He saw the tribute that we pay to the dead, the payment of feeling, as a debt that was due. He used these words of commerce – tribute, payment, debt – to express a circulation not of money, but of emotion. So too, in the nineteenth century, were the dead a part of the commercial world, a commodity in themselves, in their funeral requirements, and also as a generator of a larger industry. Mourning required the manufacture and sale of a vast number of material objects that indicated the status of the dead, and the living, as well as the emotions felt by the latter. This was spoken of openly. While, obviously, Prince Albert did not die on purpose in order to come to the aid of the British economy, the *Illustrated London News*, a great booster of the monarchy, made his death sound like nothing short of providence. The loss of the prince consort had 'plunged the nation' into mourning, but his death had 'created an almost incalculable demand for mourning' at a time when, owing to earlier unusually low prices in France, many British textile merchants had over-purchased and had recently begun to fear they would never manage to sell their stocks. Suddenly, the royal death 'brought about an extraordinary change'.[1] One feels that it was only with great effort that the journal refrained from referring to the prince's end as 'that happy event'.

Many tradesmen might have thought the same. The choices of souvenir items created for the death of royalty were endless: jewellery, medals, china, dried flowers and wreaths, sheet music, hymns and sermons, poems, photographs, prints and paintings, ribbons, gloves and handkerchiefs, pamphlets, magazine and newspaper articles.

For non-royal deaths, there were also mourning accoutrements to suit every pocket. In the seventeenth and eighteenth centuries, pall-bearers, the clergy who officiated at the funeral, the doctor who treated the deceased, close friends and relatives all expected to receive mourning scarves and gloves at the funeral, together with ribbons for the women, hatbands for the men, and, for many, a mourning ring. Among the well-to-do, these items might make up as much as half the cost of the funeral: at one in 1723, 147 rings, 238 scarves and 1,886 pairs of gloves were distributed.[2]

By the nineteenth century, the rings in particular were far less common, although they survived among some levels of society in the first half of the century. But not everyone left the choice of gifts to the family. In 1852, as the mathematician and proto-computer pioneer Ada Lovelace lay dying she ordered the rings herself. While the mottoes engraved on those for her husband and daughter were unexceptionable – 'in token of my earnest and humble hopes of our eternal union!' and 'with earnest exhortation to unvarying sincerity and truth!' – there must have been some small satisfaction in the motto selected for her bullying, hectoring mother. 'Malgré Tout', it said: Despite Everything.[3]

As the century progressed this custom was replaced by one where rings were bought, or commissioned, by the living to memorialize the dead. Mourning jewellery was expected to conform to the same rules as for dress fabrics. The metal must neither shine, nor be reflective. Thus, enamelled pieces were acceptable, especially in black and white, and pieces were made containing the initials, or miniatures, of the deceased, or with classical motifs that were understood to express mourning: tombstones, urns, weeping willows, broken columns. As well as these, some jewellery included emblems that did not overtly reference death but were considered memorial pieces because of the symbolism read into them: an anchor, a cross and a heart together represented faith, hope and charity; a hand with a wreath stood for the loss of a loved one; an ouroboros, or serpent biting its tail, symbolized eternity, and thus life after death. (Or in some instances just life: Queen Victoria's engagement ring, with a design commissioned by Albert, was an ouroboros.) Pearls were also acceptable as mourning jewellery, as they were understood to symbolize tears.

It was jet, however, that became the most common material for mourning pieces. Jet is fossilized wood that has been washed up from reefs or is excavated on land. The hardest jet could be carved into cameos, or decorative pendants for necklaces, or bracelets and earrings. It was impossible to get sharp edges or delicate detailing using second-rank jet, and so the softer pieces were used for beads. Jet from Whitby, in Yorkshire, was a particularly dark, deep, dense black, and was considered to be the best, and over the century the Whitby jet trade rose, and then fell, with the prevalence of formal mourning. In 1832, the local manufacturing and retail jet trade employed a scant two dozen workers; by 1870, a hundred local shops and manufactories kept 1,500 people in employment. Such was the popularity of jet that those with less money could purchase imitation jet jewellery, often glass backed with metal (it was known hopefully as French jet, although it tended to come from Bohemia), or horn that had been dyed black, or bog oak from Ireland, steam-moulded to resemble the finest carved jet. By the end of the century, vulcanite, or hardened rubber, was also being used, although by then the decline in the popularity of mourning dress meant that mourning jewellery was seen less often.[4]

While these mourning pieces were highly valued, they were also generic. Even if they were engraved with initials or dates, they were commercial products, commercially acquired. Far more personal was something that could only be given, or taken, from a specific individual: hair. Snippets of hair had circulated for centuries as tokens of affection. So too had hair that had been taken from the head of the newly dead. These cuttings could be connected with celebrity, such as locks of the hair of the executed Charles I. They were shared in the same manner as other morbid souvenirs of famous deaths: handkerchiefs said to have been dipped in the blood of the king on the scaffold, or pieces from the clothes he was said to have worn that day, small flasks of blood-soaked sand from beneath the execution block, or the block itself, cut up and sold in matchstick-sized pieces.

More mementoes and celebrity souvenirs were to be found among the relics of writers and poets, and their pedigrees were enhanced not merely by the items themselves and with whom they originated, but also by those people who were handing them along. Leigh Hunt, a literary critic, had been given a lock of Milton's hair, which he in turn presented to the poet Robert Browning, and the names of both men were carefully recorded and kept with it. What was not recorded was how Hunt came to have the hair. It is unlikely that it came directly from Milton's descendants, or Hunt would have said so. More possible is an unsavoury episode, although it is extremely unlikely that Hunt himself knew of it. In 1790, over a century after the poet's death, Milton's grave at St Giles, Cripplegate, in London, was dug up, ostensibly for the purpose of locating it precisely so that a monument could be erected. A local antiquarian said both that the body had initially appeared 'perfect', and also that the ribcage soon collapsed, even as one of those present 'pulled hard at the teeth, which resisted, until some one hit them a knock with a stone, when they easily came out'. Another said that 'he had at one time a mind to bring away the whole under-jaw with the teeth in it; he had it in his hand, but tossed it back again'. Contemporaries added that the dead poet's hair was pulled out in clumps from the skull, a leg bone was also removed, as were unnamed 'other body parts', as well as secondary relics like wood from the coffin. The body was then exhibited for a day and a half, first at 6*d.* a viewing, then dropping to 3*d.*, and finally 2*d.*, while pieces of the shroud, hair and bones were sold off when they were not pilfered.[5]

While the Romantic poets collected these kinds of relics, all unknowing of their origins, and venerated them – Keats wrote 'Lines on Seeing a Lock of Milton's Hair' – they also created many of their own, and cuttings of the hair of Shelley, Mary Shelley and Keats can be found in contemporary archives, together with dried flowers or tufts of grass picked from their graves and the graves of their contemporaries. The novelist Nathaniel Hawthorne made a special trip to Wordsworth's grave in the Lake District where he 'plucked some grass and weeds from it', which he believed that, since it had been 'so few years' since the poet's death, 'may fairly be thought to have drawn their nutriment from Wordsworth's mortal remains – and I gathered them from just above his head'.[6] In the same way, a close friend of Browning, after helping to organize his funeral, took some laurel leaves from the wreath on his coffin and had them framed with a label saying what they were and when and where acquired.[7] This form of collecting was prevalent enough that Dickens parodied it in *David Copperfield*, where he created a hair-dresser who keeps the nail clippings – 'fingers *and* toes!' – of a Russian prince, in order to promote herself via the elegance of her clientele.[8]

As well as preserving the hair of the dead, there was also a trad-ition of placing hair cuttings of the living in the grave of a loved one, as the Marshall family had done when Jeannette's brother died. Keats, too, was buried with a lock of the hair of Fanny Brawne, his great love, as well as her letters to him. In *Wuthering Heights*, Emily Brontë set a scene where Cathy is dying. Heathcliff removes her husband Linton's hair from the locket around her neck and replaces it with his own. The servant later finds the discarded hair and returns it to the locket without removing what is already there, ensuring that the two men who love her will symbolically accom-pany her to the grave. Heathcliff also bribes the church sexton and gravedigger to loosen the side of Cathy's coffin, planning to be buried in the next plot so that he will, literally, lie with her for all eternity. This type of virtually sexual physicality linked to hair was repeated in the real world. A brief six months after meeting the then Elizabeth Barrett, Robert Browning asked her for a lock of her hair: 'I will live and die with it, and with the memory of you.' She replied: 'I never gave away what you ask me to give you, to a human being, except my nearest relatives . . . never, though reproached for it; and it is just three weeks since I last said no to an asker that I was "too great a prude for such a thing"!', although she did relent and later give him a snippet. After their marriage she wore – 'day and night' – jewellery that contained the hair of Browning, and of her sisters, 'among other most precious hair'.*[9]

As well as these clippings of hair, there was also a great vogue for hair jewellery as a mourning token. For this, human hair, ideally cut by the giver, or by their loved ones on their death, was stiffened with glue and then plaited, arranged in decorative curls and affixed against a backing. Or the cutting was used as thread to sew, or as it was then termed, 'paint' an image, frequently those same classical motifs of urns, or women in classical robes weeping by a tomb and so on. These hair pieces were then placed behind glass in a locket or pendant, or in what was called a box, a hidden compartment behind an outwardly standard piece of commercial jewellery. Queen Victoria, naturally, had dozens of pieces made that included the hair of her much-mourned husband, including lockets, brooches and bracelets which she wore, and others that she gave as gifts to friends and family. For men, the hair was treated in the same way, plaited to the required thickness, and then, with

---

* If anyone doubts the erotic nature of hair cuttings, and the Victorians' own awareness of it, a look at Wilkie Collins' 1862 novel *No Name* makes the subtext plain. The heroine, Magdalen, keeps her lost young lover's hair in a silk bag around her neck, sometimes taking it out and speaking to it: '"You are better than nothing . . . I can sit and look at you sometimes, till I almost think I am looking at Frank. Oh, my darling! my darling!" Her voice faltered softly, and she put the lock of hair, with a languid gentleness, to her lips. It fell from her fingers into her bosom. A lovely tinge of colour rose on her cheeks, and spread downward to her neck, as if it followed the falling hair. She closed her eyes, and let her fair head droop softly. The world passed from her; and, for one enchanted moment, Love opened the gates of Paradise to the daughter of Eve.'

metal clasps on the ends, made into watch chains. (See plate section.) In 1839, the young Emily Shore, dying of tuberculosis, wrote in her journal two weeks before her death: 'I have had my long back hair cut off. Dear Papa wears a chain of it.'[10]

Theoretically, hair could be treated at home and turned into jewellery by women who were skilled at craftwork, as many middle-class women were. Ladies' magazines and manuals gave instructions for those who wanted to try their hand. It was a tricky job and required skills, and many preferred to rely on the hair jewellers who advertised their work as a speciality subset of the jewellery trade. A multitude of catalogues displayed the variety of hair items that could be purchased, including ready-made pieces that had already been engraved with 'In Memory of', with an area left blank for a name or initials to be inserted after the hair was put in place, although there were frequent concerns that the hair that came back was not necessarily the same hair that had been despatched. Further anxiety was caused by imagining what the source of that new hair might be. One ladies' magazine felt the need to assure its readers in one article that while hair was sold for a variety of reasons such as poverty or 'vice', the particular company it was profiling never bought from those sellers; nor, it added, was any of the hair they were using taken from corpses.[11] Perhaps the idea of a stranger's hair being used in place of a loved one's was similar to the horror of burial in a pauper's grave: the annihilation of the physical object represented the fear of an annihilation of memory.[12]

The number of mourning pieces a person owned could mount up over a lifetime. In *Great Expectations*, Dickens portrays a lawyer's clerk who 'appeared to have sustained a good many bereavements, for he wore at least four mourning rings, besides a brooch repre-senting a lady and a weeping willow at a tomb with an urn on it'.[13] This was no fictional exaggeration. The number of hair and other mourning tokens possessed by Robert and Elizabeth Barrett Browning was not unusual, and included, among nearly fifty locks of hair and other mourning jewellery:

a death mask of Keats, with two lots of flowers, pressed and mounted, from the graves of Keats and Shelley, as well as another framed display of leaves from Shelley's grave; a leaf taken from the garden of Byron's residence in Pisa some two decades after his death

a gold and enamel mourning ring commemorating Browning's grandfather; two brooches with his hair

Barrett Browning's great-grandfather's hair

two locks of hair from Barrett Browning's father, one cut off when he was a baby; more belonging to Barrett Browning and her five siblings

several pieces of Barrett Browning's hair, cut at various stages of her life and given to friends; more cut after her death, variously mounted under glass, preserved in slips of paper, made into a bracelet and set together with what was said to be a lock of Milton's hair in a silver reliquary with a glazed case

a gold ring with an oval bezel engraved 'Ba.' (Barrett Browning's nickname), 'God bless you, June 29, 1861' (the date she died), with a lock of her hair behind the stone under glass

Browning's hair, in lockets, in paper, under glass, in paper wrappers or envelopes, in a reliquary, in a leather case

locks of hair from Pen, the Brownings' son; from Browning's sister and mother 'which Robert cut off and always carried with him'

a lock of hair from the widow of an acquaintance, who had sent it as a token of her appreciation of the verses Barrett Browning had written about her husband.[14]

Many arranged their affairs so that items like these could be handed on to those who would care about them. The philosopher William Godwin wrote in 1809: 'every thing which practically has been associated with my friend, acquires a value from that consideration; his ring, his watch, his books, and his habitation.'[15]

The miniature coffins found in a cave at Arthur's Seat, Edinburgh in 1836.

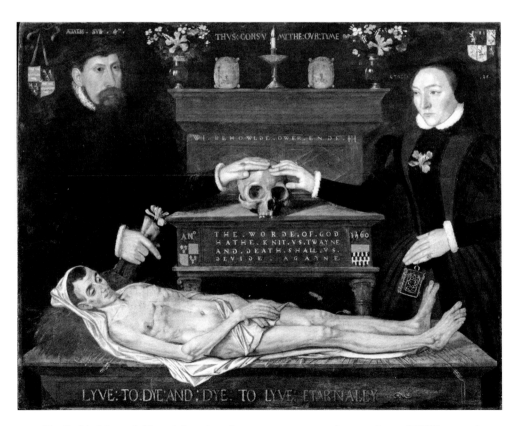

The Judde Memorial (*c.*1560), painted to commemorate the marriage of William and Joan Judde, reminds the happy couple of the transience of human life – the flowers will wither, the candle extinguish and, of course, the corpse is the end for all.

Henry Alexander Bowler, *The Doubt: 'Can these Dry Bones Live?'* (1855), shows a woman, many years after a death (she no longer wears mourning), continuing to visit a grave where the bones of the dead are in the process of being exhumed, presumably to make room in the churchyard for more newly deceased.

The Highgate Cemetery grave of the celebrated prize-fighter Tom Sayers (1826–65), where he is still accompanied by his faithful dog Lion.

The 1817 death in childbirth of Princess Charlotte, expected to succeed her grandfather and father to the throne, created a political as well as an emotional storm, and mourning memorabilia abounded. Fashion magazines illustrated what the well-dressed court-mourner was wearing; manufacturers produced china tea-sets and other souvenirs to commemorate the dead princess.

In the House of Commons in 2022, MPs gather to pay their respects after the death of Queen Elizabeth II. Even in the twenty-first century most try to wear, if not black, then the darkest colours they own as a sign of respect.

Gifts of hair cuttings between friends, family and lovers were common, whether to put in lockets or set into jewellery as tokens of affection, or after death as a memorial piece. On serious illness, a woman's long hair was frequently cut off, and then the entire length could be made into a watch-chain.

Richard Redgrave's *Preparing to Throw Off Her Weeds* (1845) was one of this successful genre painter's rare misses. Here a widow prepares to remarry (see the orange blossom on the table behind her), admiring her brightly coloured new clothes even as she still wears mourning. So shocking was this picture considered to be that Redgrave painted out her new lover, previously standing in the doorway on the left.

The painter Henry Wallis found his first great success with *The Death of Chatterton* (1856), a reimagining of the final hour of seventeen-year-old Thomas Chatterton, the poet and forger who died in 1770, said to be a suicide.

Louis Edouard Fournier, *The Funeral of Shelley* (1889), similarly reimagines the 1822 cremation of the poet Percy Bysshe Shelley on a beach in Italy where his body was found after his boat foundered at sea.

William Mumler was renowned for his spirit photographs, and in 1872 the ghost of Abraham Lincoln was said to have appeared in time to be photographed with his widow, Mary Todd Lincoln. Mumler insisted that Mrs Lincoln had not identified herself, and he had no idea who she was until she saw the finished photograph.

William Powell Frith was renowned for his large genre scenes, and in 1863 he commemorated the wedding of the Prince of Wales and Princess Alexandra of Denmark, held unusually in St George's Chapel, Windsor, to permit the Queen to continue to isolate herself three years after the death of Prince Albert. Refusing to join the wedding party, she can be seen looking down from the gallery, top right.

While hair jewellery to remember a loved one was not unusual, somewhat rarer was jewellery with baby teeth. Queen Victoria, with her love of commemorative items, had the baby teeth of her youngest child, Princess Beatrice, made into a pendant and earrings shaped like fuchsia.

Married women, in particular, who before the 1870 and 1882 Married Women's Property Acts could not legally own anything (according to the law, it belonged to their husbands), and could therefore not formally bequeath anything, often arranged for small items to be given to people as mementoes. Even women who possessed little of value listed out their dishes, dresses, petticoats or fireplace tools. Sometimes these items had sentimental meaning – things that had belonged to dead relatives. Other times there were more idiosyncratic reasons. Mary Drew, Gladstone's daughter, on her deathbed left one friend 'An ugly black enamel locket'. She said she had had it made up for a loved one, but 'as he had left off being my great friend', she had kept it.[16] This method of distribution was expected to keep the memory of the previous owner in people's minds, and the givers and recipients noted those relationships in the way they described the items: a watch 'given to me by Helen my dear departed wife', or 'Grandma's bookcase', or 'Mama's dessert service'.[17]

Thus mass-produced, factory-made items gained personal resonance through usage and memory. Even more did mourning jewellery when it was made with the addition of the hair of a loved one. Hair was special. It was a gift of friendship, a memorial token or a symbol of love, or all three. It also removed the commercial taint of purchased goods, since the addition of the hair meant the piece had no resale value – no one would want to purchase a watch chain, say, made out of a stranger's hair.

By mid-century, a new technology enabled the melding of the commercial and the personal: photography. For the wealthy or the famous, there was a long history of commemorative images. Death masks went back at least to the classical world. By the nineteenth century they were most often made by forming a plaster of Paris cast of the newly deceased's face, as well as, sometimes, casts of their hands and even feet. These masks might be replicated for sale, or distributed among friends, or used by an artist as the basis for a statue or bust of the celebrated dead. The process was, however, expensive, and therefore rare. More common was a drawing of the dead, either by a professional, again for the wealthy or famous, or an amateur production by a family member. Now, with the arrival of photography, a memorial photograph not only became the norm for the great, but for many others as well.

From the earliest days of the technology, professional photographers advertised their services by advising families to have images made of loved ones in preparation for the day when they were no longer there, souvenirs 'which you can look upon with pleasure, when the grave covers the original'. If the living had failed to heed this warning, photographers could also be hired at the final moment, or even after the final moment, to come to the deathbed to capture that last image of the ill, the dying or the dead. The naturalist Philip Gosse arranged such a visit when his wife Emily was near death. The resulting photograph, he wrote, was 'somewhat undefined', as she was by then unconscious and breathing stertorously, unable to remain immobile for the requisite period of time. (Gosse and his son had also had to push the couch she lay on across the room in order to get sufficient light for the image.)*[18]

Professional studio photographers carefully filed their records of portrait sessions they had had with the living so that, when called upon, they could reprint the images for newly bereaved friends and family, frequently adding a birth and death date, together with a black border or other death motifs, perhaps with the words 'In Memoriam'. Families purchased these to send to those who could not attend the funeral, and also to put in scrapbooks, or frame and mount on the wall. Photographs of the famous were given similar treatment on their deaths and displayed in shop windows for sale.

---

* Advances in photography quickly changed what was possible. Daguerreotypes in the 1840s and the wet collodion process of the late 1850s required extremely careful handling of the plates, and with the wet collodion process they also had to be prepared just moments before exposure. Lighting, as here, was a chronic problem before the 1880s, although that could be partly overcome by longer exposure times for the dead, if not for those like Mrs Gosse.

There was always a good market for images that could be advertised as 'the final photograph'.

The famous were also photographed after death, lying on their deathbed. For the less celebrated, these images were taken for private contemplation for family and friends. When the politician Lord Frederick Cavendish was murdered in Dublin in 1882, in what were known as the Phoenix Park killings, friends in Ireland sent his widow a cutting of his 'dear hair' and also 'the dear beautiful photograph of sleeping Freddy'. 'Such a deep comfort,' she wrote, and sent copies of it to her friends.[19]

Cavendish was photographed with the sheets pulled up around his face, to cover his wounds (he was shot in the chest and neck and had also sustained a broken arm). But without the sheets quite so tightly drawn, this pose was the standard one for adults. In the USA and in parts of Europe photographs were taken of the deceased in their coffin, although this was unknown in Britain, which is perhaps why the photographs Sarah Bernhardt had taken of herself in her coffin – in preparation, as it were, although she

Lord Frederick Cavendish after death.

would not in fact die for another half-century – were viewed with such appalled fascination.

Children were the age group most photographed for post-mortem commemoration, especially if they had died in the first days or weeks of their life, when it was likely that there were no other images of them. This was their parents' single opportunity for a tangible representation, as the poet Matthew Arnold recognized when he commissioned a portrait of his son Basil, dead at sixteen months: 'we should else have had no picture of him whatever.'[20] The custom was to show the child lying on a bed, or on a sofa, or their mother's lap, as if they were asleep. For the middle classes, the photographer came to the house; the working poor carried their dead babies and smaller children to the photographer's studio. Where the prosperous might then have these images set into jewellery, or elaborate frames, one option for those with less disposable income was to have the photographs of their lost children mounted, often with a lock of hair, onto a card to hang on the wall, or even 'onto a matchbox with "lovely little scrolls"', enticed one photographic studio.[21]

Sarah Bernhardt boldly anticipating her own death.

The most frequent use of memorial photographs was to enclose the images in a locket together with a snippet of hair. The locket that held both also resolved another problem, one that few liked to mention. Hair, if not carefully preserved and labelled, all too easily becomes unidentifiable. The Brontë Parsonage Museum, for example, today holds nineteen hair cuttings or hair jewellery, of which only ten can with confidence be attributed to their original owner.[22]

Photographs resolved this problem, and where no image was available, people found other ways to memorialize their loss. In the 1860s, one family arranged to have their child's straw hat photographed, with an inscription pinned around its brim: 'In affectionate remembrance Richard Nicholls Milliken Born Feb 11 1857 Died Dec 23 1861'. On the back of the photo was written: '. . . dead when 5 years old. Having no photo A[unt] Anne had his hat photographed . . .'[23] This was rare, of course. More common, when photographs were available, was to indicate the depth of grief throughout the entire family by creating a Russian-doll effect: photographing the living staring longingly at a photograph of those who had died or holding the image out for a second person to look at, or prominently wearing a locket with the image of the deceased set in it.

From the 1870s, there was another trend, less popular but not uncommon, to have the grave of a lost friend or family member photographed. Some people used them for memorial cards, to send to friends at a distance, or to notify them of the death. When the death itself occurred at a distance, these photographs were a way for family and friends to visualize where their loved ones rested – a type of virtual cemetery visit.

The one place where the dead were entirely absent in photographs was in war photography. Roger Fenton (1819–1869), a pioneering photographer who in 1855 was commissioned by a print-seller to cover the Crimean War, produced images of soldiers in camp as well as set-ups of batteries and outposts, and a great many landscapes, but he carefully avoided – and indeed the British army banned – any photographs of the dead and wounded. (Technology at this date did not yet permit photographs of action.) One biographer has described Fenton's Crimean photographs as 'represent[ing] the war as a series of heroic portraits, tableaux, and expansive battlefields that implied a nobility of spirit and sense of moral purpose profoundly at odds with the reality of the Crimean campaign'.[24]

The same cannot be said of the Venetian-British Felice Beato (c.1832–1909), who used a secret dry-plate process that enabled him to capture far more immediate images. He arrived in Lucknow, India, half a year after the Sepoy Revolt of 1857 had been suppressed and savagely punished. Acting as a sort of semi-official adjunct of the British army, he photographed the ongoing devastation through images of ruined and destroyed buildings, occasionally with soldiers in front of them. One image, however, is different, that of the Sikandarbagh, a Lucknow villa with a walled garden where up to 2,000 sepoys had been killed.

This photograph was taken in 1858, some six months after the massacre, and to capture the feelings of horror and outrage, Beato literally set the scene, ordering that 'hundreds of skeletal corpses of Indians [be] exhumed' to create this grisly vision of imperial retribution and power. Beato's images were widely disseminated, printed in journals where they were mis-captioned to state that they had been taken the day after the British stormed the building. Individuals also purchased prints of this photograph and others to interleave in albums and scrapbooks between portraits of military relatives, or other images commemorating the event, like Robert and Harriet Tytler's 'The Slaughter Ghat in Cawnpore, 1858', which showed the riverside where the besieged British had been massacred, its emptiness giving eerie acknowledgement of those who were no longer there.[25]

On a personal rather than imperial scale, death brought emptiness to no one more than widows. The situation of widows was

Felice Beato's grisly restaging of the Sikandarbagh massacre in Lucknow.

twofold, one of actuality, one of assumption. Rising life expectancy meant that while couples had longer marriages than in previous centuries, that increased longevity, when combined with a rapidly expanding population, ensured that the real numbers of men and women who survived their partners, and thus lived as widows or widowers, also rose. The majority of these were widows: women lived longer and remarried less; men who remarried were older, and thus more likely to die before their second wives. By the end of the century, there were more widowed women over sixty-five than there were married women altogether.[26]

The notion of the mildly financially distressed elderly widow, living in a country town perhaps, keeping up appearances with the help of a single servant, is one regularly presented in nineteenth-century novels such as Elizabeth Gaskell's *Cranford*, but in real life these women were the exception. Most widows were in financial difficulty. The household income they might have shared as part of a couple was, for the middle classes as well as for the working class, consistently low across the century, even when the male breadwinner was alive. Bookkeepers earned as little as £60 a year, much less than skilled labourers; a cashier in an office or bank, a more prestigious occupation, was paid around £100, barely tipping the family into the ranks of the middle classes, despite their white-collar status. While men knew that they should be paying into life insurance policies to protect their wives and children in case of their early deaths, this was rarely achievable. Still less possible was the frequently cited advice for breadwinners to set aside a third of their income annually for the potential widowhood of their wives, yet another fiscally prudent pipe dream presented by the wealthy as a moral imperative for their poorer brethren.

It is difficult to judge how many widows worked after their husbands' deaths. Even when they were in paid employment, it was not uncommon to omit that socially embarrassing fact on the census return. Other widows worked with their families, whether in agricultural labour, or by taking on partwork such as sewing or boot-making, and again recorded themselves as 'not in employment'. Where the information is given, it suggests that as few as two in every ten widows managed to live on their income without additional paid employment. And for the remaining eight in ten, work was always uncertain. Age greatly reduced women's earning potential: more than a third of women over sixty-five required some form of charitable or state support, a far larger proportion than widowers of the same age.

Even for widows from more prosperous walks of life, the law was not kind. Early in the century, common law laid out that widows were to receive what was known as the widow's third: one-third of their husband's real property (land or property). If he were to die intestate with children, she received another third, or half if there were no children. This was absolute and was calculated before the eldest son's portion was allocated. Or at least that was the situation in theory. In practice, dower rights had been hedged about and chipped away throughout the previous century. Furthermore, few women had any knowledge of their right to this widow's third, and when they did, they were societally prevented from acting on that knowledge. In 1833, the Act for the Amendment of the Law Relating to Dower, known as the 1833 Dower Act, took those rights away, giving husbands the power to order the distribution of their entire estate as they desired after death, with no obligation to provide for any specific family members.* With this change, a man who had married a wealthy wife, and had enriched himself by becoming the legal possessor of all her money and property, as the law dictated on marriage, was now able to bequeath that money and property away from the very person who had given him what the law enabled him to consider 'his' wealth. He could also tie up any inheritance with conditions. A widow could enjoy a set income until their children were grown, he might decide, or until (or if) she remarried. Essentially, the new Act was designed to ensure that a dead husband continued to control his living widow.[27]

The idea that most, or even many, widows remarried rapidly is one that has been created by fiction, occurring in novels far more than in actuality. In the sixteenth century, about a third of all marriages were second marriages for one or both partners; by 1851, it was one in ten, and that was the way it remained.[28] One cultural contributor to the change was the

---

* This sounds perfectly normal to those in the Anglo-American world, but it remains an anomaly in Europe, where many countries have legislation that makes it obligatory that much of the estate is shared out between, at least, spouse and children, and often other family connections. In France, for example, a single child must receive 50 per cent of a parent's estate; two children share 66.6 per cent; three, 75 per cent; if there are no children the spouse must receive at least 25 per cent. In Italy, the spouse receives half, the spouse and a single child one-third each, etc.

nineteenth-century perception of women who remarried, which followed the precept that a widow's place was in the wrong. *The Whole Duty of Women*, an advice book from the early part of the century, unintentionally outlined the lose-lose position of widows. A widow's first duty, it instructed, was to arrange her husband's funeral 'according to the quality he had lived in', in order to preserve his reputation and posthumous social status. At the same time, the expenditure should not be so great that it risked damaging his children's futures. And while the new widow was undertaking this delicate balancing act, it went on, she should be mourning sufficiently to demonstrate her loss, without displaying a 'frantic excess' of sorrow.[29]

Anthony Trollope's novel *Can You Forgive Her* (1864/5) shows exactly how impossible these demands were, as Arabella Greenow's nieces discuss her new widowhood. One weakly protests the criticism that has been levelled at her:

'Aunt Greenow always seems to me to be a very good sort of woman.'

'She may be a good woman, but I must say I think she's of a bad sort. You've never heard her talk about her husband?'

'No, never; I think she did cry a little the first day she came to Queen Anne Street, but that wasn't unnatural.'

'He was thirty years older than herself.'

'But still he was her husband. And even if her tears are assumed, what of that? What's a woman to do? Of course she was wrong to marry him. She was thirty-five, and had nothing, while he was sixty-five, and was very rich. According to all accounts she made him a very good wife, and now that she's got all his money, you wouldn't have her go about laughing within three months of his death.'

'No; I wouldn't have her laugh; but neither would I have her cry. And she's quite right to wear weeds;* but she needn't be so very outrageous in the depth of her hems, or so very careful that her caps are becoming.'[30]

So Aunt Greenow does not talk about her late husband enough, and she does not cry enough, except when she cries too much; she is to blame for being too young for her husband, although it is notable that he was not to blame for being too old for her; she was too poor before and is now too rich; she wears too much mourning, but has failed to wear it appropriately as it does not make her look dowdy. Elsewhere, Trollope uses the word 'uncontrolled' to describe her and her actions: she is in 'uncontrolled possession' of £40,000; she also grieves 'uncontrollably'. What 'uncontrolled' appears to mean to Trollope is that she is a woman who is not controlled by a man, for we learn that she *is* in control – very much so. Mental self-control allows her to tell her story the way she wants, while her financial control allows her not to care what others think. And when she does remarry, she prudently structures things so that her husband cannot touch her money, and equally prudently stores her mourning dresses for 'future possible occasions'.[31] Second husbands beware, was the final disapproving message for the reader, who probably did not need to hear it yet again.

Second marriages for women were frowned upon by society, although men who remarried, particularly men with young children, were another thing entirely. It was understandable, thought contemporaries, that men would need a housekeeper for their homes and a substitute mother for their children. Widowers were expected to be stoic and to set grief aside as quickly as possible. They must 'get [their] wounds healed as quickly as [they] can'.[32] By contrast, women were not merely expected to grieve, it was their duty to do so, and to remain perpetually faithful to the deceased's memory. If a widow was

---

* Widow's weeds was a standard term for mourning dress, deriving from the Old Saxon word *wād* for clothing more generally.

older, her desire to remarry made her a figure of fun; if she was young,
it was likely, said the gossips, that she was over-sexed, and therefore
also likely to make odious comparisons. 'To step, not merely into a
dead man's shoes, but to put your head in his very nightcap – to have
a ghost for a rival – to have base comparisons drawn between yourself
and an apparition' was a terrifying notion for many men.[33] The objec-
tions to women remarrying went on and on. If the widow had no
children, then she probably was infertile, so why would anyone marry
her? If she already had children, the new husband would have to

Dickens satirized the fear of remarried widows in *Bleak House*, where Mr Bayham
Badger lives with the prestige – and portraits – of Mrs Badger's two previous husbands,
Captain Swosser of the Royal Navy and Professor Dingo 'of European reputation'.

spend his hard-earned money and care on another man's offspring, who would also require an inheritance, taking away from the children of his blood.

Furthermore, there was a generally accepted view that a second marriage was a form of adultery, a betrayal of the first husband, who was after all waiting for his wife in the afterlife. How would one introduce Husband Two to Husband One was the unspoken query, a query that never seems to have been posed to the men who remarried. Marriage, said Queen Victoria's chaplain, was 'a union which shall be perfect', and 'once solemnized' could never be broken, even by death. (The queen, a firm adherent to this view, left instructions that she was to be buried in her wedding veil.)[34] Trollope had his characters live this out. In *The Small House in Allington*, Lily Dale refuses a suitor because 'In my heart I am married' already, even if her 'marriage' was to a man who had jilted her, and she was not married at all. 'I gave myself to him', she says stubbornly, and so, despite the fact that he left her for a richer woman before they ever reached the altar, 'I am as you are, mamma – widowed'.[35] Back in the real world, the public's disapproval of second marriages was plain, as witness a tablet in a church in Suffolk:

In memory of Charles Ward who died May 1770, aged 63 years; a dutiful son, a loving brother and an affectionate husband. N.B. This stone was not erected by Susan his wife. She erected a stone to John Salter, her second husband, forgetting the affection of Charles Ward, her first husband.[36]

Instead of finding a second husband, widows were supposed to consider themselves under the protection of God, who would look after them and their fatherless children. There was an entire genre of paintings of widows in church, or at their husbands' graves, bearing titles like 'Faithful'.

Far more unusual was to see this subject treated frivolously. Richard Redgrave, a successful genre painter of domestic life, had a rare failure with 'Preparing to Throw Off Her Weeds' in 1846. (See plate section.) In the original painting, the young woman at the end of her mourning period unfastens her dress preparatory to changing into the light-coloured frock being held out to her, with yet more highly coloured textiles on her lap and at her feet, while her soon-to-be new husband comes in the door at the left. This was a step too far – 'toned with vulgarity', sniffed one reviewer – and Redgrave painted the man out, although he left a sprig of orange blossom on the dressing table, indicating the merry widow's forthcoming wedding.[37]

In a less prominent manner, widows featured in genre paintings as ordinary participants in daily life: as mothers of brides, walking on the beach, at railway stations, collecting dividends at the bank.[38] And from 1861 photographs of the mourning queen became familiar to everyone, in journals and for sale, in shop windows and on mantelpieces and walls. These omnipresent women in their black dresses, whether the queen or the middle-class women in art, are useful correctives to the etiquette manuals and magazines that state firmly that women *never* went out in the first year of heavy mourning, a reminder too that etiquette manuals are, more frequently than not, in the business of telling people what society thought they should be doing, rather than describing what actually occurs. Their heavy emphasis on the seclusion of widows might, counter-intuitively, indicate that the public sphere was exactly where these women were to be found. As such, in their ostentatious widows' weeds, they would have been a constant reminder of ever-present death.

In Catholic, pre-Reformation theology, death was a voyage, and the dead, assisted by the prayers of the living and the care of the saints, journeyed from their 'last home' in the churchyard through purgatory, where sins were repented and purged, finally to stand before God. After the Reformation, the Bible offered a more complicated story about the afterlife, various chapters and verses containing a range of possibilities: the dead sleep until the trumpet sounds; the dead go straight to heaven; the dead are in hell until the Resurrection and a personal judgement for each; or there is a communal Last Judgement at the end of time, when all are resurrected.

In civil society, however, it was customary to think, and talk, of death as sleep, the newly dead often described as 'resting in Abraham's bosom'. In the Methodist *Arminian* magazine, a full third of features on deathbeds use 'sleep' as a synonym for death, especially for women, who were said to have fallen 'asleep in the arms of her Beloved', only the capital letter making it clear that this was their Eternal Bridegroom, not their temporal one.[39]

If the dead were sleeping, it was not much of a leap to think, and speak, as if the same dead returned to visit those they had left behind. A civil engineer named Alexander Beazeley wrote after his mother's sudden death: 'as I lay in bed, I fancied . . . that she was arranging my pillow and that I felt her breath on my face. Oh, that she *were* near me and would visit me in my sleep!' After his much-loved stepsister died shortly after, 'I did not shed a tear . . . I don't feel as if she were so separated from us . . . and I sincerely hope she will come to us in dreams as she promised to do if permitted.'[40]

'If permitted' by whom, is the obvious question, and here the views of the afterlife become complex. Mrs Oliphant was one of many who attributed to the dead the same feelings, wants and desires they had had in life. When her daughter died, she asked herself if the dead slept until Judgement Day, but unlike Beazeley she hoped that they did *not* return: 'It would not be happiness but pain' to have the dead near her, but unable to communicate, she thought. She did, however, worry that when her Maggie reached heaven, did she ask, '"Where is Mamma?" . . . Do they dwell in families [there]? . . . Was my mother called to receive the child who was her baby as well as mine?' If only, Mrs Oliphant continued, she could but see her daughter with her deceased family all gathered together in heaven, 'even in a dream'.[41]

From the middle of the century, the idea of the dead passing time in heaven with their dead friends and families, as if in a replica of their life on earth, was perhaps the standard view of the afterlife, and was entirely part of mainstream religion. The clergyman William Branks, in *Heaven Our Home* (1861), described heaven as the place where we would end up surrounded by friends and family. The very title of the Bishop of Ripon's book, *The Recognition of Friends in Heaven* (1866), spelt out this generally accepted view. And another clergyman, the Reverend Norman Macleod, concurred: 'Since man is a social being, so in Heaven there will be society.'[42] The clergy was preaching to an already converted choir. Even the deeply devout Christina Rossetti seemed to think of heaven as a place where social niceties continued to be observed, on her deathbed asking her brother, 'If I meet mamma in the other world, shall I give her your love?'[43]

The dead also liked to be kept *au courant* with current events. Tennyson, in his 'Ode on the Death of the Duke of Wellington', imagines Admiral Nelson being updated on Wellington's achievements so that he will know what the duke had been up to since Nelson's own death half a century earlier and they can catch up as equals. In a similar vein, in 1829 the *Morning Herald* printed a story of a woman in Nottinghamshire who had asked a friend to ensure that when she died a specific packet of letters from her son be enclosed in her coffin. Her friend unfortunately forgot, but soon afterwards the village postman died, and so she arranged for the letters to be buried with him instead, thinking he could deliver them in the next world as he had in this.[44] This was primarily middle-class urban mockery of rural working-class folk, who were presumed to be naive and unable to differentiate between actions appropriate to this world and the next. Yet this story was really no different from Tennyson's more poetic version of the afterlife.

For while the dead were routinely imagined as living placid after-lives, at the same time their still-alive families continued without discomfort in a world where the dead were commodities, whether as content for newspaper pieces, or actual physical items for sale. When the diarist Henry Crabb Robinson (1775–1867) lost a tooth, he was offered a replacement proudly advertised as having been taken from the battlefield at Waterloo – that is, from the mouth of a soldier killed in action.[45] This was perhaps more overtly commercial an activity than others concerning the dead, but not by much. From at least 1850, the Paris morgue was a regular stop on the tourist trail for British visitors. This was the place where the unidentified dead of the city were laid out on display, in the hope that friends or family would recognize and claim them. But many others also visited. The bestselling guidebooks of the period included entries for it; Dickens was fascinated, and went several times; the poet Thomas Hardy took his new wife there on his honeymoon, joining the less famous tourists and locals who did the same.[46]

Even more than bodies, it was the grave that became a commercial object of attention. Matthew Arnold was one of many poets who wrote about Wordsworth's funeral in 1850, concentrating on the image of the grave. Even when the graves themselves were not in Britain, they could still be sold as an idea: prints of the graves of Shelley and Keats in Rome were a popular item. More than evocations or images of graves, however, it was the graves themselves, the physical items, that were the draw. There were handbooks to the new cemeteries, which detailed where the famous, the infamous and the simply rich or well-born were buried. William Howitt's *Homes and Haunts of the Most Eminent British Poets* (1847) focused on both homes of the living and 'last homes', or graves, of the dead. These final homes had an enthusiastic following, with the richly designed tombstone of the poet and artist Dante Gabriel Rossetti in Birchington, Kent, requiring a railing to be added a decade after his death, so great was the number of admirers chipping away at the stone piece by piece.[47] The ultimate in grave tourism, however, was the century's elaboration and celebration of Poets' Corner in Westminster Abbey, a way of efficiently viewing multiple graves in a single half-hour.

The idea of Poets' Corner, like so much in nineteenth-century Britain, is a carefully constructed myth, this one created, or at least embellished and burnished, by one man, Arthur Stanley, Dean of Westminster from 1864 to 1881. The Abbey had been used to bury the famous for centuries, but it had also been used as the burial place of those who were of no great importance. In the fourteenth century, Chaucer had been buried in the Abbey, not because he was celebrated, or in recognition of his poetry, but because he had lived and died nearby, and the Abbey was his local church. We do not know where in the building he was buried, for it was not until 1556 that a monument was erected, possibly over his grave, but also possibly not. In 1599 the poet Edmund Spenser was buried there, and these two interments were the foundation on which Stanley built. In his telling, Spenser's hearse 'was attended by poets, and mournful elegies, and poems, with the pens that wrote them, thrown into his tomb. What a funeral was that at which Beaumont, Fletcher, Jonson, and in all probability, Shakespeare attended! – what a grave in which the pen of Shakespeare may be mouldering away!' This is, of course, almost entirely fabricated, for the event he claimed to be describing had occurred more than a quarter of a millennium in the past, with little information having survived. Note how Stanley moved from the possibility (which he calls 'probability') that Shakespeare had been present at this funeral, to somehow stating first as possibility ('may be') that the potentially present Shakespeare had not merely been there, to a situation where the poet was not only there, but had left one of his very own pens in the grave. Thus he neatly centres Shakespeare in this scene of the final resting place of Britain's greatest poets, lightly skimming over the annoyingly stubborn reality that Shakespeare had no known connection to the Abbey and was buried in Warwickshire, 160 kilometres away.

Stanley was building on the eighteenth century's love of antiquarian literary lore, where the happenstance that Chaucer and Spenser had been buried in the same approximate area of the Abbey had been boosted by the contemporary burial in the same church of Abraham Cowley, a poet famous in his lifetime and since virtually forgotten. It seemed like a good place to create a national pantheon of dead poets, and throughout the century a raft of literary men followed Cowley. Others, such as Shakespeare and Milton, were given commemorative monuments. By 1868, when Stanley wrote his paean to Poets' Corner, he gaily swept in other poets who had had the misfortune to have been buried elsewhere, as if only mentioning the names of Wordsworth, Burns, Scott, Byron and Coleridge were enough to give them a mystical presence in the Abbey. The renown of Browning, a Dissenter, happily overcame religious scruples, and he was proudly given an Abbey burial, although it was a full twenty years after his death before Elizabeth Barrett Browning received a token 'His wife' mention at the foot of his grave: her fame as a poet, in their lifetimes far eclipsing her husband's, was presumably sunk by her unfortunate gender.[48]

Other acclaimed poets of the day were left out, Byron owing to his scandalous life, Shelley and Keats presumably on account of their well-recorded atheism. Reputation mattered as much after death as in life. And, as in life, after-death reputations were no more stable than they were when the living could actively make a choice and change their paths. For the dead, the paths could be changed for them.

The poet Thomas Chatterton was just such a one. Chatterton (1752–1770), the boy poet, dead at seventeen, was a profound influence on the Romantics. (See plate section). Born and raised in Bristol, the posthumous son of a schoolmaster and church sexton, Chatterton was influenced by antiquarian works and, using a hoard of old manuscripts, he created the works and persona of Thomas Rowley, a supposed fifteenth-century monk. These 'medieval' works found a ready audience, and Chatterton moved to London to make his – or Rowley's – fortune in the literary world, lodging in the garret above a brothel. Until, that is, he died of an overdose of laudanum and arsenic, possibly taken as a cure for a venereal infection. Or was it suicide? Certainly this was the commonly accepted view – the genius boy poet (which he was), rejected by the literary world (which he was not), starving in his garret (the brothel below tactfully omitted), dead of despair (not of a quack cure for a sexually transmitted disease).

For suicide was the most wildly Romantic thing of all, placing Chatterton not only outside the pale of the church, but of much of society too.

9

UNNATURAL DEATH

A good death was part of life, and theoretically not to be feared. A bad death, however, set those involved outside society.

Infant death is one of the hardest deaths to analyse retrospectively, even in basic ways. Had the mother miscarried? Had her child been stillborn? Died after birth? At the time it was not possible to tell the first from the second, and difficult to tell the second from the third. Throw into the mix that the mother might have been unmarried, and societal questions began to override medico-legal ones. There was a long tradition of believing that unmarried women were prone to murdering their babies, either out of shame at bearing them at all, or because they could not care for them. As early as 1624, an Act to Prevent the Destroying and Murthering of Bastard Children was placed on the statute books, establishing a legal concept called 'concealment of birth': if an unmarried woman gave birth alone, without having told anyone she was pregnant, there was a legal presumption that she hoped the child would die. From this, many extrapolated that, if that were the case, a woman would not simply leave her child to die of neglect but was likely to have helped it out of this world.

By the eighteenth century, positive actions by the mother before the birth, such as buying swaddling clothes or in other ways preparing for the arrival of her child, were used to defend against a charge of concealment. In reality, few prosecutions against these sad, terrified women were ever brought when contrasted with the vast number of infants who died shortly after birth. And even then,

when charges were brought, convictions were rare. In the eighty
years before 1800, just 200 women were charged with concealment
in one judicial circuit in the north of England. Of the 200, six were
convicted, and of those six, two were executed. This is a conviction
rate of 3 per cent, with just 1 per cent of women charged being
executed, and leaving uncounted the thousands of women who had
given birth out of wedlock to children who did not survive and who
never entered the legal system. Of course, one was too many, and in
1803, the Act was replaced by another law that modified the nearly
two-century-old legislation. Now both married as well as unmarried
women were covered under the Act, and the concealment of a birth
was not considered to be a predisposing assumption of murder. The
rarity of the crime and the lack of any ability to assess it could be
seen in the changed penalty for those found guilty, reducing the
older death penalty to a maximum sentence of two years in jail.[1]

And yet throughout the 1830s and the economically dire 1840s,
popular fears that many women murdered their babies ran
rampant. Some anti-Poor Law campaigners claimed to see a rise in
infanticide, owing to the shift from 'outdoor relief' (cash payments
made directly to the impoverished to help them survive in their
own homes and communities) to the workhouse, those quasi-
prisons where conditions were made intentionally harsh in order
to 'encourage' the poor to turn to them only when in abject need.
This belief in the prevalence of murderous women was further
helped along once a group of campaigning medical men entered
into a power struggle with the legal fraternity over the control of
inquests. The medical professionals argued that they alone could
tame this terrible scourge sweeping the country – a belief that had
become so widespread that in 1865 the *Telegraph* reported that
'infanticide is an absolute custom among English society of the
present day . . . [and] is frightfully increasing', while a clergyman
wildly described seeing 'bundles . . . left lying about in the streets,
which people will not touch, lest the too often familiar objects – a
dead body – should be revealed, perchance with a pitch plaster over

its mouth [to smother it], or a woman's garter [to strangle it] around its neck'.[2] Even more hysterical in tone was the London coroner who asserted that as many as 12,000 women a year murdered their babies in London alone. (According to the 1861 census, there were 93,600 deaths per annum in the capital; if 12,000 of those were babies murdered by their mothers, a staggering 8 per cent of all deaths was attributable to infanticide, and an even more staggering one in every sixty-two women of child-bearing age was a murderer.) Yet even as people genuinely feared that tens of thousands of babies were being murdered annually across the country, when faced with the broken, agonized women who gave birth alone and ashamed, the conviction rates for concealment of birth gave evidence that without any firm proof of intent to murder, rather than neglect, or ignorance, or simply being paralysed by fear, juries were less condemnatory than might have been expected. By the second half of the nineteenth century, of those women found guilty of this crime, half received a sentence of less than one month, and another one in ten were released on conviction with no further time to be served.[3]

There was one other type of death condemned even more brutally by the law than these supposed infanticides, and over the course of the century society came to accept it too, with far more tolerance than the legislation would suggest. According to both religion and the courts, taking one's own life, suicide, was criminal, an act that set the suicides' desires against those of their superiors, whether those superiors were God or the state. The suicide was therefore a *felo de se*, or self-felon, who 'deliberately puts an end to his own existence, or commits an unlawful malicious act', as defined by the jurist Sir William Blackstone, the eighteenth-century author of *Commentaries on the Laws of England*. As criminals, therefore, these dead were punished even after their deaths: from the thirteenth century onwards a suicide's goods and estates were forfeited to the Crown, and their bodies frequently buried in unconsecrated ground, at night. While the non-criminal unbaptized were interred in an unconsecrated section of the churchyard, for these state-created felons, more extreme action might be taken. In some parts of England this burial took place at a crossroads, the suicides being placed prone in the grave, and a stake driven through them, a posthumous disgrace heaped on the body as retribution for an act for which no other punishment was possible.

A variety of folkloric reasons were given: the stakes kept the ghosts of the dead from wandering; or the constant footfall at crossroads ensured the ghosts could not rise. Other explanations focused on the cross element of the crossroads, seeing it as a Christian symbol that restrained the dead; still others presented these locations as pagan sites of sacrifice. None of these suggestions has any more weight than another, and all, or none, were possible. The stakes driven through the bodies were long enough that a large portion remained visible above ground, and they may have been nothing more than a way to mark a burial site in default of a churchyard burial and, later, a tombstone.[4]

These post-mortem punishments for suicide were neither civilly nor ecclesiastically ordained, but were instead a response of the people, although neither church nor state made any effort to prevent them from occurring. Yet what the law and what religion said, and what people thought and how they acted, were not in these cases in harmony. Inquest juries were presented with a choice. They could find those charged with suicide guilty as *felo de se*, or they could find them *non compos mentis*, of unsound mind and therefore not criminally responsible. By the end of the eighteenth century, juries were finding for *felo de se* in a bare 3 per cent of cases. For the rest, wherever possible, and grasping at whatever excuse they could find, they were showing themselves sympathetic if not to those who took their own lives, then to their families, on whom the punishment of extramural burial and forfeiture of their estate would fall. The injustice of seizing property from the living to punish the dead was manifest to the juries, if not to legislators.

This often held good even when deliberate intention was plain to see. The diplomat and politician Viscount Castlereagh, after being heralded as one of the leaders of the post-Napoleonic carve-up of Europe, had found himself deeply unpopular with the country at large for his anti-democratic rejection of political reform, and in particular for his part as one of the prime movers in the Peterloo Massacre of 1819, later immortalized by Shelley in *The Masque of Anarchy*:

> I met Murder on the way –
> He had a mask like Castlereagh –
> Very smooth he looked, yet grim;
> Seven bloodhounds followed him:
>
> All were fat; and well they might
> Be in admirable plight,
> For one by one, and two by two,
> He tossed them human hearts to chew . . .[5]

Castlereagh had become overwhelmed on the death of his father, by pressures of work and by a general instability of mind. He was beset by paranoid delusions that concentrated on an episode that had occurred years earlier, when he had been blackmailed after going 'with a woman to an improper house'. Now, in his paranoid state, this incident had been transformed into being accused of a 'crime not to be named' – that is, homosexuality. No one in his circle was under any illusions about his fragile mental state. His wife had hidden his pistols and his razors, the king had warned the prime minister, and the Duke of Wellington had written to Castlereagh's doctor concerning his obvious delusions. Despite the care of all around him, in 1822 he managed to find a set of razors and cut his throat. This was no secret. His friend Mrs Arbuthnot recorded he 'has died by his own hand!' in her diary. In the wider world too it was known that the troubled politician had taken his own life, and the caricaturist Isaac Cruikshank even produced engravings of the likely scene, while the Radical publisher and polemicist Richard Carlile (1790–1843), who had been present at the 1819 massacre, dedicated a work 'To the Memory of Robert Stewart, Marquis of Londonderry, Viscount Castlereagh, &c., who eventually did that for himself which millions wished some noble mind would do for him – *cut his throat*'.[6] Yet with all this, and despite the law, Castlereagh was never found to be *felo de se*, and was instead buried at Westminster Abbey with full honours.

In part owing to Castlereagh's end, in the following year an Act to Alter and Amend the Law relating to the Interment of the Remains of Any Person Found *Felo de Se* made it a requirement that the dead must be established to have been of sound mind before they could be convicted of this crime. Even if they were, they could now be buried in a churchyard, although still at night and with no funeral service. Their estates and property continued to be liable to forfeit to the Crown, although this was usually ignored unless the suicide had been prosecuted for another crime and had killed himself to avoid it. One such example was the case of Abel Griffiths, a law student, who in the same year the Act became law killed his father and then himself. While there was no shortage of witnesses to testify at Griffiths' inquest as to his mental instability, the jury nevertheless found him *felo de se*. Even here, however, it can be seen how the law and the public's own views diverged. One journal referred to his crossroads burial as a 'disgusting' practice; constables had to be posted all along the route to prevent the public from disrupting the event; and later Griffiths' body was quietly exhumed and reburied near his father.[7]

This more compassionate view seems to have held consistently across the country: it was rare that more than one or two out of every two dozen or so suicides were buried at a crossroads, and these were most often people who had been convicted of another crime. For the rest, many suicides' bodies were treated in exactly the same way as any other dead, the newly deceased resting at home, being waked, and then carried to the churchyard, although they were then buried on the north side of the churchyard, where the unbaptized were laid. There were sometimes reports, too, of rural 'rough music' or public community shaming occurring, but that was for those who were held responsible for their deaths: excessively harsh parents, or unfaithful spouses, or unfair employers. Doctors, meanwhile, were unwilling to upset the families of the more prosperous dead, who were after all the ones who would be paying their bills. And they were often in sympathy: 'It does not seem to me to be any part of my duty to act as a private detective,' snapped one doctor when asked to determine whether a death was suicide or not. Insurance companies would not pay out on a verdict of suicide, and inquest juries once more acted to show they were on the side of the ordinary citizen, protecting the families of the dead against the church, the state and now the banks and the insurers.[8]

In 1840, a surgeon named Forbes Winslow published *The Anatomy of Suicide*, a mishmash of ideas lifted, or directly copied, from other writers, which nonetheless made a popular case for suicide as an illness rather than as a crime against state and religion. Winslow was one of the doctors who examined Daniel M'Naghten, a man who had killed a civil servant while in the grip of a paranoid delusion that he was the prime minister, Robert Peel. M'Naghten was sentenced to an asylum rather than death, leading to the creating of the M'Naghten rules, which said the accused had to understand at the time of the crime that what they were doing was wrong. Suicide thus became inextricably linked to mental instability. As early as 1788, one member of the Royal College of Physicians had stated baldly: 'No man in his senses will burn, drown, or stab himself . . . everyone who commits suicide is indubitably *non compos mentis*.'[9] No *man*. In popular culture, women who killed themselves, by contrast, were almost always assumed to have been sane, and to have been driven to that extremity out of despair at stepping outside their natural sphere. The hundreds of women in art and literature who killed themselves as a result of extramarital relations, illegitimate children or abandonment by a lover became the paradigm of the suicidal female. In fiction, however, the men who killed themselves did so primarily for financial reasons (they were usually more than a little criminal, too): bankrupted speculators and ruined financial titans who take their own lives occur through the decades in the works of Trollope, Dickens, Charles Reade and others.[10]

In middle-class fiction suicide was a 'tortured, shameful death'; in the penny-bloods of the working classes, it was a fact of life, and rather than the euphemisms their social superiors used – doing away with oneself, putting an end to things – it was referred to plainly as suicide.[11] G.M.W. Reynolds' multi-part *The Mysteries of London* has characters who almost automatically assume that suicide is their final option when all other routes are closed: Lady Georgiana Hatfield, one of the book's heroines, 'would have [been] driven' to it if her rape by a highwayman had become known; her lover meanwhile imagines his own 'grave . . . stained' by his suicide's blood if he cannot marry her; a remorseful female character has 'an invincible idea of suicide' after she commits theft – and these are only a few of the would-be suicides in the novel's several thousand pages.[12] There is little sense of condemnation, nor any religious discussion either, in another great working-class success of the 1840s, *Varney the Vampyre*. In this narrative, the father of the novel's hero has killed himself before the story begins, but throughout he is described in pitying terms, as simply 'misguided'.[13]

By the 1840s, middle-class social reformers recognized that suicide was caused by none of these more romantic reasons, being instead commonly driven by poverty and hunger. And, once more contrary to depictions in art, statistics routinely demonstrated that men killed themselves with far more frequency than women did. One typical suicide was a millwright named Charlie Sudds, from south London, who had been dismissed by the engineering firm where he had worked for a quarter of a century, replaced by someone less experienced and on a smaller wage.[14] But that truthful view of the oppressed little man never captured the public imagination. Instead, by the 1860s, the popular narrative of suicide no longer presented these desperate people as victims of an uncaring, even iniquitous, system, but instead viewed them as active perpetrators in their own fate, usually exacerbated by alcohol.[15]

The change over the decades is most easily seen in Dickens. In *Oliver Twist* (1837/9), Nancy is a victim. Friendless, beaten (and later murdered) by her lover, Bill Sikes, she looks at the Thames and says, 'I shall come to that at last', 'leav[ing] no living thing to care for or bewail' her. Twenty years later, in a magazine piece entitled 'Wapping Workhouse', Dickens has a young boy callously refer to the women who drown themselves in the river as 'jumpers', removing their gender, and virtually their humanity. They have become no more than their actions, for which we are given no rationale: they 'ketches off their bonnets or shorls, takes a run, and headers down here, they does. Always a headerin' down here, they is. Like one o'clock.'[16] The desperate are desperate no longer, having become nothing more than a joke, a cuckoo clock of death, leaping out into the void on the hour, every hour.

The leap was perceived as a particularly female act, whether the women were throwing themselves into the Thames or off the Monument. The Monument had been erected in the 1670s in the City of London to mark the location where the Great Fire of London was said to have started. Being very high (sixty-two metres) and with unrestricted access to the viewing platform at the top, by the end of the eighteenth century it was said to be the favourite spot for suicides, especially suicidal women. Several men had thrown themselves from the Monument, but it was Margaret Moyes in 1839 who captured the public imagination. She left a note and then went to the Monument, where she ended her life. She was possibly the daughter of a baker, who might perhaps have been dying – the details are vague. The lack of information, however, did not prevent massive newspaper coverage, nor the sale of broadsides, with poems and song lyrics to old tunes, most including a generic image of the act.

The very different attitudes to male suicide were on view

COPY OF VERSES

ON THE MELANCHOLY DEATH OF

Margaret Moyes

committed Suicide by throwing herself off the Monument on Wednesday,
September 11, 1839.

Scarce twenty minutes had elaps'd,
  Before she reached the top,
When many persons in the yard,
  To see her they did stop ;
Upon the cornice she did stand,
  Outside the iron rails,
In that dreadful situation,
  Many did her fate bewail.

From strangers oh ! what awful shrieks,
  When she let go her hold,
Like lightning she decended,
  'Twas dreadful to behold ;
With a heavy crash upon the rail,
  The shock was most severe,
Which cut off her arm, & it was found,
  Near the centre of the square

This maiden's mother has been dead,
  Two years, we have been told,
Her father with sickness long confin'd,
  Beside he's very old ;
Which plung'd the family in distress,
  That to service she must go,
That so afflicted her youthful mind,
  Cans'd this dreadful scene of woe.

Now may God in his great mercy,
  This maid's rash act forgive,
And her dreadful fate a warning be,
  To others while they live ;
In their station for to be content,
  Tho' reduc'd to poverty,
And not while in the prime of life,
  Plunge themselves into eternity.

You heedless youths of either sex,
  I pray you will attend,
And to this melancholy tale,
  A serious ear now lend ;
Of Margaret Moyes a blooming maid,
  Her death I will unfold,
And when the same you come to hear,
  Will make your blood run cold.

On Wednesday last in the prime of life,
  To the Monument did go
She said her friends had not arriv'd,
  So she asked to sit below ;
Soon after for admission paid,
  To the top she did ascend,
But little did the keeper think,
  Her life was so near its end.

*BIRT, Printer, 39, Great St. Andrew Street,
Seven Dials.*

A broadside marking the death of Margaret Moyes, complete with doggerel verse
and stereotypical woodcut image.

following the death of the historical painter Benjamin Robert Haydon.[17] Haydon had been a painter of some fame, although little financial success. He was always in debt – he had been arrested for it over and over – and had had some truly spectacular failures at exhibitions. He protested that 'In such humours Men shoot themselves – but not me', even as he recorded in his voluminous diaries examples of suicide among great men, being obsessed with the deaths of, among others, both Castlereagh and Margaret Moyes. By 1846 he was recording the relief he imagined he would feel as his head smashed against paving stones. He wrote to one of his patrons, the prime minister Sir Robert Peel: 'Life is unsupportable. Accept my gratitude for *always* feeling for me in adversity. I hope I have earned for my dear wife security from want. God bless you.' He purchased a pistol, wrote letters to his wife and children, as well as a will, and a final diary entry:

God forgive – me – Amen.
Finis
of
B.R. Haydon.
'Stretch me no longer on this rough world' – Lear.
End –

He placed his wife's portrait on an easel facing the picture he had been working on, and set out his diary, open at this final page, together with the letters, his watch and a prayer book open at Matthew 24:24: 'For there shall arise false Christs, and false prophets, and shall shew great signs and wonders; insomuch that, if it were possible, they shall deceive the very elect.' After recording his last thoughts, he stood by his canvas and shot himself. Still alive, he attempted to reload before cutting his throat with a razor.

The Times reported obliquely, allowing the act of suicide to be understood without using the word: 'We regret to state that Mr. B.R. Haydon, the historical painter, died suddenly at his residence in Burwood-place, yesterday morning. The unfortunate gentleman was in his usual health on the previous evening, and it is believed that his decease was hastened by pecuniary embarrassment.' Elizabeth Barrett Browning responded with the circular logic that suicide often produced: 'That such a man should go mad for a few paltry pounds! For he was *mad* if he killed himself! of that I am as sure as if I knew it. If he killed himself, he was mad first.' Peel sent £200 (two years' income for a clerk, and probably more than Haydon had ever averaged annually) to help the family. The Duke of Wellington, known for neither kindness nor generosity of spirit, dispatched a servant to demand the return of his hat, which Haydon had borrowed while he was painting the duke's portrait.

At the inquest, the coroner worked hard to ensure a verdict of unsound mind was returned, asking leading questions of Haydon's children – had their father complained of pains in the head, had he given indications of being disturbed, had there been any behaviour that could be regarded as out of the ordinary? – before having his stepson read entries from Haydon's diary to reinforce his view. The jury did find 'the said Benjamin Robert Haydon was in an unsound state of mind when he committed the act', and his tombstone reminded passers-by not of his death, but of the circumstances that led him to it:

HE DEVOTED FORTY TWO YEARS
TO THE IMPROVEMENT OF THE TASTE
OF THE ENGLISH PEOPLE
IN HIGH ART
AND DIED BROKEN HEARTED
FROM PECUNIARY DISTRESS.

Haydon, and Castlereagh before him, had had powerful patrons, or been powerful themselves, and their treatment followed their status, in the pattern Shakespeare had recognized centuries before, when the gravediggers in *Hamlet* say of Ophelia, 'If this had not been a gentlewoman, she should have been buried out o' Christian burial.'[18] In the nineteenth century, even when a jury ruled that the dead had been *non compos mentis*, it was all too commonplace to find that the local clergy refused to bury a suicide who was not socially prominent, nor wealthy, nor protected by the prominent or wealthy. Some churchmen might agree to conduct the funeral, but in the unconsecrated section of the churchyard, where the unbaptized lay. To put a stop to this, an 1865 court ruling reiterated the clergy's legal obligation to bury in consecrated ground those who had died by their own hand while of unsound mind. Even so, many refused into the 1880s, when the sole right to burial was finally removed from the clergy.[19]

This secularization of burial had been long delayed. After the English Civil War, clergy who refused to conform to the use of the 1662 Book of Common Prayer had been barred from governmental and clerical positions, creating that prominent assemblage of Nonconformists and Dissenters – Methodists, Baptists, Congregationalists, Presbyterians and Quakers. The 1851 religious census suggested that a full half of the churchgoing population were Nonconformists or Dissenters. Yet in spite of their numbers, throughout their lives these non-Church of England adherents of the early nineteenth century were faced with endless hurdles and obstructions. They were obliged to pay parish rates to the Church of England; they could not attend university without being a communicant in the Church of England; marriages could only be solemnized by the Church of England; and while theoretically churchyards accepted all who lived and died in their parish, in actuality this remained very much at the whim of the presiding cleric. If he felt strongly about Nonconformists, the dead could be banished to the north side of the churchyard; or he could refuse to perform the burial service over them; or, in pettier form, he could refuse to allow the mourners to enter the church, or carry their dead via the main churchyard gate, or allow the coffin to rest in the church.

By this point the Methodists in particular were finding themselves increasingly buffeted. In the eighteenth century the founders
of Methodism had been ordained Church of England clergymen,
but as the Wesleyans began to ordain their own clergy, Anglican
churchmen refused to accept their legitimacy, treating the dead they
had ministered to as if they had died unbaptized. Time and again
the courts found for the Dissenters and against the clergy. Time and
again, the clergy ignored the rulings and carried on doing exactly as
they liked.

The new government system of registering births in 1836 had
marked a shift in societal expectations. It was no longer the baptism,
or spiritual birth, that was being recorded, as they had been in the
old parish registers, but the physical birth itself. Death, too, was
beginning to be seen as a bureaucratic and emotional familial event,
not a religious translation. Combined with the London Cemetery
Act of the same year, which permitted the establishment of new
civic cemeteries, with their areas for Nonconformists, those outside
the Church of England were beginning to hope that the practices
they faced would soon begin to align with what the law ordained.

Ostensibly the Burial Acts of the 1850s privileged the civic over
the religious, but behind the scenes the clergy worked furiously to
maintain their vice-like grip on these final life ceremonies. The new
Acts established parish boards to purchase land and either extend
current cemeteries or open their own new ones in the suburbs, and
churches rushed to do the same, worried that their lucrative
monopoly would be blown apart. One anonymous pamphlet
written by a proponent of the Necropolis Company and its cemetery in Woking, Surrey, laid out three proposals to comply with the
new Acts while enabling the clergy to maintain their privileges. The
first proposal, which it says was the view of the 'London clergy', has
a preamble noting their happiness at the flourishing suburban cemeteries, 'provided such [cemeteries] . . . be parochial burial grounds,
with a reservation . . . by law . . . of all the same rights, privileges,
and duties' to those who currently hold them – that is, provided the

clergy continued to receive their fees. The pamphlet then sets out their current rights, and every single one of these rights is followed by the phrase 'subject to the payment of certain fees'.[20] Parishioners had rights only if those rights could be paid for. The pamphlet tucked away the fact that the poor also had the legal right to be buried by their own parish, instead asserting that increased population and lack of space meant that new grounds had had to be purchased, and thus the poor also had to contribute via payment of fees, in a single subclause doing away with centuries of custom: up to half a city clergyman's income came from these fees, it reminded its readers.

Everything came to a head with what became known as the Akenham burial case of 1878. A clergyman named George Drury told Mr and Mrs Ramsay, both Baptists, and labourers in a small village outside Ipswich, in Suffolk, that as their toddler had not been baptized, he would have to be buried in the unconsecrated area of the churchyard kept for stillbirths, and that furthermore no funeral service could be read. The local newspaper, the *East Anglian Daily Times*, furiously raged at this offer to bury a child 'like a dog', and it was arranged that a Congregationalist minister would perform the service. When the funeral procession and the coffin neared the churchyard, however, the sexton blocked them from entering, saying the service would have to be read outside, because it was a sin to bury an unbaptized child with Christian rites. Wickham Tozer, the Congregationalist minister, therefore began to read the service for the dead on the road outside the gates. Although he was following the instructions he had been given, Drury rushed out in a rage, shouting that the baby was 'not a Christian, and I object to its being buried as such'. Nonetheless, Tozer completed the service, the child was buried and that was that.

Or, that was that until the *East Anglian Daily Times* published its version of the episode (later revealed to have been written by Tozer himself). Drury sued for libel and won, but he was awarded a derisory £2 in damages, indicating that the jury accepted that while he might have been right in law, in humanity, and even in Christian charity, he had behaved shamefully. Drury was, however, represent-ative of a substantial proportion of the clergy who, fearful of a loss of income, and the sense that in sheer numbers the Church of England was losing its pre-eminence, seemed 'to go out of their way to antagonize or insult the families of the dead'. In another equally ugly case, where one newborn twin had been baptized before he died, but his brother had died before the ceremony could be completed, the local vicar insisted on separating the children in death, one relegated to unconsecrated ground, one consecrated.[21]

One puzzling element of the Akenham case is who promoted it, and why. It was a village affair that should have garnered no local, much less national, notice. Ultimately it was revealed that the legal costs, which amounted to nearly £1,000, as well as the fine and a tombstone for the Ramsays' child, had been paid for by a group of MPs, magistrates, clergy and newspaper owners, presumably to create momentum for the continuing campaign for burial reform.[22] Whether or not that was the intent, it was in fact what occurred. In 1880 the Burial Amendment Act finally gave everyone, of every, or no, religion the legal right to be buried in a churchyard, and to have a service of any denomination read over them.

While this battle – the right to be buried, regardless of creed or reli-gion – was being fought, the right *not* to be buried was being discussed for the first time, as a new idea, burning the dead, was beginning to get a hearing.

The most famous early cremation in Britain did not take place in Britain, nor was it desired by the family of the dead. This was the burning of the body of the poet Percy Bysshe Shelley on a beach in Italy. On 8 July 1822, Shelley, his friend Edward Williams and a local boy were caught in a storm as they sailed from Livorno to Lerici. They never arrived. Instead, first a coracle that had been onboard washed up on shore; then three bodies, in three locations. Shelley's body, severely decayed after ten days in the water, was identified by his jacket and the book in his pocket. Italian maritime quarantine law dictated that, to prevent the spread of infection, bodies had to be burned where they were found, and so Shelley's body was cremated on the beach.

What was done as a legal requirement was, by Shelley's friends, turned into a myth, an apotheosis. Shelley's friend and hagiographer, Edward Trelawny, attended the cremation together with Byron and the critic Leigh Hunt, neither of whom could bear to watch: Hunt stayed in Byron's carriage, Byron went down to the sea.* In Trelawny's accounts, he noted that the cremation was legally enforced, with dragoons watching to ensure that regulations were observed, but after that he created a scene of the heroic immolation of a poetic god, with Trelawny himself as the acolyte throwing 'incense, honey, wine, salt, and sugar' onto the pyre, even if to modern eyes that looks more like a recipe than a libation. Shelley's heart, it was reported, was not entirely consumed by the flames. Trelawny illicitly snatched it from the fire, and there followed a round robin of recriminations as he, Hunt and Mary Shelley all claimed it as their own. Mary Shelley, the widow, won. After much wrangling with the Italian authorities, she arranged to have Shelley's ashes exhumed from the unconsecrated plot where they had been laid, and sent to the Protestant cemetery at Rome, to be buried beside their son. The tragi-comic squabble over ownership of the dead did not stop there. Trelawny later paid a gravedigger to move Shelley's ashes to a more picturesque location in the cemetery, only informing Mary after the fact, magnanimously, or perhaps with a polyamorous subtext, offering: 'You may lay on the other side, or I will share my narrow bed with you if you like.' (The resemblance to the situation in *Wuthering Heights*, p. 163, not to be written for another two decades, is remarkable.) Trelawny's ashes were buried nearby in 1881, but he never did share his 'narrow bed' with Mary.

* The greater part of the story of Shelley's cremation was recounted a number of times by Trelawny, the details changing with each telling. The one constant was that Trelawny was his greatest friend, and that he was present while the others were not.

She later changed her mind, asking to be buried instead at St Pancras Old Churchyard near her mother and father, Mary Wollstonecraft and William Godwin. However, the cemetery had become foul and rank, and so her parents' remains were exhumed and reburied in Bournemouth, where the author of *Frankenstein* was herself buried in 1851. The following year her daughter-in-law opened a locked box that had been Mary's, to find what she thought were probably some of Shelley's ashes, and what was left of his half-burnt heart. These were finally buried with Mary and Shelley's surviving son when he died in 1889.[23]

In that very same year, the campaign for cremation and Shelley's death had become one in Louis-Édouard Fournier's painting 'The Funeral of the Poet Shelley', a panoramic imagining of heroic immolation. (See plate section.) This campaign had developed out of what had been decades of discussion, opposition and argument about cremation. The hygiene arguments around burials and the horrors of the state of churchyards in the 1840s, as well as the burial reform campaigns of the 1850s, had moved the responsibility of the disposal of the dead from the church to the government. This in turn made the idea of cremation seem at least possible to some. The two-month period between the death of the Duke of Wellington and his funeral had contravened everything that burial reformers had been working towards for two decades, a period so long that the duke had to be interred in four coffins, one inside the other. It may well be that this very public situation subliminally pushed many towards an acceptance of quick, hygienic end-of-life arrangements. In 1857, *The Lancet* medical journal had opined that cremation was 'decent, speedy, and effectual'.[24] But the church gathered its forces in opposition: cremation was barbarous, a heathen import from the classical world and, worst of all, it would mean that at the Resurrection the bodies that should be lying ready to rise up for judgement would be no more. With no fear of final punishment or reward, the church argued, society would feel no constraints on its behaviour, producing a world of sin. The actual, corporeal presence of the dead was a moral necessity for the living.

For many this was a persuasive argument. The idea that it was necessary for a physical body to be present before the otherworldly final judge was widespread, both in religion and also folk belief. For others, cremation felt too close to the Hindu practice of sati, where a new widow joined her husband in the afterworld by dying on his funeral pyre. The practice had been banned by the British colonial rulers in 1829, even as the popular press kept it at the forefront of popular imagination, especially after the Sepoy Revolt of 1857, when the press presented it as just another way in which the colonized population of the subcontinent were 'savage'. With all these converging threads, *The Lancet* saw which way popular opinion was leaning, or thought it did, and in 1870 reversed itself. Cremation, it re-pronounced, was 'antagonistic to the genius of Christianity', and there was 'nothing so imbecile as an adoption of the heathen practice of burning the dead'.[25]

The journal was soon to reverse itself once more. In 1873, Sir Henry Thompson, an eminent London surgeon and the main promoter of cremation in Britain, attended an exhibition in Vienna at which a cremated body was displayed with the caption, in Latin, 'Saved from the worms, we are consumed by the flames'. He began to conduct his own experiments, and the following year he received word that a Lady Dilke, who had died in childbirth, had left a request that her body be cremated. This was impossible in Britain, so he had her embalmed and transported to Dresden to be cremated in a modified factory furnace. This was, trumpeted the Secretary to the newly formed Cremation Society, not destruction, but a way to 'protect the living from corruption' by circumventing the process of decay after death. Cremation, added Sir Henry in an essay in the *Contemporary Review*, was also a sound 'economic system [for] a crowded country'. While his political economy arguments (the ashes from bones could bring in half a million pounds annually if sold for fertilizer, he estimated) were condemned by horrified critics,

Thompson's clever interweaving of scientific terms and a vocabulary of emotional resonance – 'mother earth', 'nature' – created a far more soothing picture. So too did his plans, ultimately followed, of building crematoria in suburban and rural districts.[26] Cremation thus found a following among the intelligentsia and the arts communities, the Cremation Society being promoted by, among others, Shirley Brooks, the editor of *Punch* magazine, the novelists Anthony Trollope and George du Maurier, and artists John Everett Millais and John Tenniel, illustrator of *Alice in Wonderland*.[27] The Cremation Society purchased land outside London and began to build Britain's first crematorium.

While there was establishment opposition, however, and while the act itself was not yet possible in Britain, the concept of cremation had become part of the culture. In 1882, the Australian cricket team won a series at the Oval cricket ground in London, and *The Times* carried a mock obituary written by the son of Shirley Brooks: 'In affectionate remembrance of English Cricket, which died at the Oval on 29 August 1882. Deeply lamented by a large circle of sorrowing friends and acquaintances. R.I.P. N.B. – The body will be cremated and the ashes taken to Australia.' A bail was said to have been ceremonially burnt, and, on England winning the next series, the Australian team returned the consequent ashes encased in an urn. (The competition continues today, still officially known as The Ashes.)

As the Akenham burial case had changed people's perceptions by highlighting how unfairly burial law was applied, so too did a more bizarre set of events in Wales in 1844 promote a change in the law regarding cremation. William Price of Pontypridd had been a prominent Chartist in his youth; he later became a surgeon and, somewhat more unusually, a Druid who worshipped publicly in his local park. (His green trousers and fox-skin headdress drew particular comment.) In 1884, his young son, the remarkably named Iesu Grist, died. By this date Price was eighty-three years old, and Iesu Grist was said to be one of a dozen or so of his illegitimate offspring, although other reports put the number at a more modest three. Price placed the child's body in a barrel filled with paraffin, said some prayers he claimed were Celtic, and set it alight in a field. Outraged bystanders put out the fire before the body could be consumed, and Price was arrested, but once the inquest determined the child's death had been natural, it was not immediately obvious that Price had broken any laws. He therefore set out to cremate the body once more, this time on a pyre, and was again arrested. This case went to court, where the judge, the eminent James Fitzjames Stephen, ruled that 'a person who burns instead of burying a body, does not commit a criminal act'.

While the trial had determined that cremation was not illegal, it was less clear that it was actually legal, an evidently ludicrous position. The House of Commons therefore quickly presented the Disposal of the Dead Regulation Bill, to bring cremation under government control. It failed to pass, but it showed that the concept of cremation had enough popular support that the Cremation Society felt able to open the crematorium they had built in Woking that, under an earlier threat of prosecution from the Home Secretary, had never operated. The following year, the first official cremation in Britain was performed, on the body of the painter Jeannette Pickersgill. At this date, the process was very overt. There was no chapel, nothing that in theatrical parlance would be called 'front of house': just the bare bones of a furnace hidden behind some screens. (Shortly afterwards the now-routine facilities for mourners were added, all Gothic in style, which the British in the nineteenth century had learned to read as symbolizing religion more generally, and Christianity more specifically.)

As a coda, William Price was not beguiled by these establishment institutions, although by the time he died at the age of ninety-two there were crematoria in Woking, in Manchester and in Glasgow. Instead he arranged that after his death his body was to be encased in metal sheeting within a stone structure, designed to retain heat and reach high temperatures, in which he was publicly cremated in a field in front of what were estimated to have been 20,000 people.[28]

The 1893 cremation of William Price, described by the *Oxford Dictionary of National Biography* as a 'physician, self-styled archdruid, and advocate of cremation.'

There was one further reason for opposition to both cremation *and* to burial: the fear of premature burial. Today the conceits and arrangements made to prevent this, such as tying a string attached to a bell around the corpse's hand, so they could ring from the tomb, seem like elaborate jokes from comic books. Yet perfectly ordinary, perfectly well-read and well-educated people were beset by these anxieties. Jeannette Pickersgill, for example, had left detailed instructions that a medical attendant had to be present to certify her death, and then, to make doubly sure, she ordered that her arteries be severed before cremation.[29]

The fear was not unreasonable. Throughout much of the century, there were only the most basic methods to confirm death, and everyone knew it. In the eighteenth century, successive editions of *The Uncertainty of the Signs of Death, and the Evil of Premature Burial and Embalming* had reached 800 pages, such was the anxiety among the population at large. Stories regularly appeared in the newspapers of people saved from premature burial when they recovered from a coma or a trance in the nick of time. Humane Societies taught resuscitation techniques for victims of drowning, and a large part of their remit was to distinguish the seemingly dead from the actually dead. Their claim, that they managed to revive up to two-thirds of those accident victims who were initially reported to have perished, exacerbated rather than calmed fears. The Reverend W.H. Sewell, in his book on funeral reform, expressed in print what many thought: premature burial was 'a not unusual form of murder'.[30] The 1836 legislation for the registration of deaths had not required that those deaths be certified by a trained medical attendant. And to receive a certificate, a witness did not even have to have seen the person they were registering, but merely declare that they had been told So-and-so had died.

The arrival of cholera just a few years before this legislation was enacted had only increased these worries, as some of the symptoms of that disease – extreme dehydration, physical shrinking and muscle cramps that relaxed after death – made the dead seem alive, while others – extremely lowered heart and breathing rates – made the living appear dead: 'We thought her dying when she slept, / And sleeping when she died', wrote the poet Thomas Hood, and it is notable that accounts of the living being mistakenly buried were far more common in this decade than in the one preceding it. Fiction reinforced it. James Hogg's 'Some Terrible Letters from Scotland' was published during the first wave of the epidemic, with a narrator whose mother and sweetheart conceal his death although it turns out he is – surprise! – alive literally to tell the tale. In the following decade Edgar Allan Poe's 'The Premature Burial' has as a narrator a man who suffers from cataleptic fits and fears being buried alive. As late as 1864, Dickens' fiction was a precursor to Jeannette Pickersgill's fact, when in *Our Mutual Friend* the dead Harmon includes a clause in his will with 'certain eccentric ceremonies and precautions against him coming to life'.[31]

It is, however, in *The Mysteries of London* that the ultimate fear is named. It was not merely the exhumation of a coffin that contained a 'body [that] had turned [itself] completely round' – that is, the 'dead' person had recovered consciousness after burial and struggled to escape their living tomb – but that discovery was made by one of the century's bogeymen: a resurrection man.[32]

10

CRIMINAL DEATH

Just as a court of law had declared cremation neither to be illegal nor legal, so, in a similar vein, who owned the dead, or whether anyone *could* own the dead, were even more vexed questions. In the seventeenth century, the jurist Edward Coke had written that a 'corpse subsisted outside both civil and criminal law': the dead could not be owned, nor could they own anything. Stealing a shroud was larceny, punishable by law; stealing the body that had been wrapped in that shroud could not be a crime because that body belonged to no one. At least, that was the law, although by 1800, 'It has been determined', intoned *The Commentaries on the Laws of England*, that stealing dead bodies was a felony.* In 1822, a trial verdict created the precedent that, while stealing a body from a grave was not illegal, selling it afterwards was a misdemeanour. As Dickens has Gaffer Hexam, a man who makes his living dredging corpses out of the Thames for the reward money, say: 'Has a dead man any use for money . . . How can money

---

* This was more than a little bit of legal sleight of hand. In 1788, a London surgeon was charged with taking a body from a churchyard. The judge cited as precedent a 1744 case in which some grave-robbers had been found guilty. However, in reality they had been found guilty of stealing the coffin, not the body it contained. Nevertheless, from 1788 onwards there was an understanding that those found stealing bodies could be charged, although with a misdemeanour, not a felony. The legal sharp practice did not stop there. While it was laid down that stealing grave-clothes was a felony, from whom they were being stolen was never stated. Depriving someone of something is the essence of property theft. It may be that it was the all-encompassing state, 'the Crown', although no case appears to establish this. Otherwise, as Ruth Richardson, the expert on the 1832 Anatomy Act has suggested, it looks very likely that the law was there more to protect doctors 'in flagrante dissecto'.[1]

be a corpse's? Can a corpse own it, want it, spend it, claim it, miss it?'*² The dead have no value, and are not themselves valuable. Except that, as everyone was aware in the nineteenth century, they absolutely were.

Burial had through much of history been impermanent for ordinary people, who were routinely exhumed after decomposition had done its work in order to make room for the newly dead. Before the Reformation, Catholic saints had been exhumed and translated, their body parts divided and disseminated as relics. There were exhumations too for fame. When the poet Robert Burns died in 1796, he was buried modestly. In 1815, his admirers arranged for a grander location and a monument to honour Scotland's poet, and his remains were exhumed and transferred (against his widow's wishes). Two decades after that, his widow safely dead, there was yet another exhumation, and Burns' skull was uplifted in order for a cast to be made. Still the poor man was not allowed to rest. Twenty years later his grave was opened once more on the death of one of his children, and his skull again removed for examination. By the centenary of Burns' death, in 1896, a commemorative volume darkly noted, 'Pity that the Poet did not, like his great Predecessor, Shakespeare, invoke a curse on those who should disturb his bones.'³

Even exhumation for fame was a more peaceful afterlife than exhumation for revenge or hatred, as happened to Oliver Cromwell, Lord Protector from 1653. On his death in 1658, Cromwell's body had been embalmed, but it was poorly done and his body was buried 'hurriedly and privately' two months before his state funeral, which had to make do with an effigy. In 1660, after the restoration of the monarchy, the still-living regicides who had overseen the execution of the current king's father were hanged and disembow-

---

* Scottish law had, in 1742, made exactly this point, and had therefore made exhuming a body for profit an offence not as theft, but as injury to the memory of the dead. While the dead had no property, obligations towards them continued, the law said, finding a neat workaround for the problem of who exactly was being deprived of property that had been deposited in a grave.

elled, 'their members cut off' before their bodies were quartered, the pieces displayed in different parts of the city. That Cromwell and three other regicides were already dead was not seen as sufficient excuse for a lack of punishment, and it was decreed that their 'Carcases' were to be exhumed 'and drawn upon a Hurdle to *Tyburne*, and there hanged up in their Coffins for some time; and after that buried under the said Gallows'.

The exhumed coffins of the three London regicides (the body of the fourth, who had been buried outside London, was left in peace, presumably because logistics made it complicated) were drawn on 'sledges' to the gallows on the anniversary of the death of Charles I. There their enshrouded bodies were hung for a day, facing in the direction of Whitehall, the site of the king's execution, before being cut down and decapitated, their heads held up to the crowd as was the custom for traitors, and then driven onto spikes and mounted on a pole 'over the High Court of Justice [at Westminster Hall] where the old King was sentenced to dy [sic]'. The bodies were buried at Tyburn in a mass grave for criminals.

The pole with its grisly remains stayed in place for a couple of decades. Eventually a storm brought down the pole together with its skeletal remains, at which point Cromwell's head began its travels. It vanished until 1710, when a collector displayed it in his private museum. It then passed to a failed actor named Samuel Russell, who may have been a distant descendant of the Cromwell family. In 1775, one of this family took the relic to the British Museum, where it was compared to Cromwell's head as it appeared on medals and coins struck during his rule, and it was proclaimed genuine. By 1799, the head was to be found in a 'curiosity museum' in Old Bond Street, London's fashionable shopping street, advertised as 'The Real Embalmed Head of the Powerful and Renowned Usurper', on display 'where the Rattle-snake was shown last year'. Its authenticity was adduced by the signs it showed of both embalming and decapitation, its owners claiming that Cromwell's had been the sole body to have undergone both. (This was not correct even among the small group of regicides: Henry Ireton, who had been exhumed and decapitated along with Cromwell, had also been embalmed.) Finally, in 1957, the well-travelled head's last owner arranged with Sidney Sussex College, Cromwell's Cambridge college, to see to its burial, which was done privately in 1960, in an unnamed location and with the entire matter kept quiet for another two years. The college has since erected a plaque to mark the event, although it makes no mention of the head's centuries-long voyage, nor of its therefore more than unreliable provenance.[4]

Such was the treatment of a criminal head by a vengeful reinstated ruler, a voyage that was turned into popular entertainment ('where the Rattle-snake was shown last year'). A more rarefied, and belatedly publicized, literary exhumation arranged for a more pragmatic reason was that of the artist Lizzie Siddal, the wife of the painter and poet Dante Gabriel Rossetti. In 1862, Siddal had died of a laudanum overdose; whether intentionally or not is unknown. Rossetti, in a move of distraught artistic renunciation, arranged for the sole manuscript copy of his new poems to be buried with her in her coffin, killing them before their birth in print as his and Siddal's child, stillborn, had died the year before. 'The sacrifice was a grave one,' wrote his brother years later, apparently not intending the pun.

Seven years after Siddal's death, her loss no longer fresh, Rossetti wanted to publish the poems, and he asked the Home Secretary, whose formal approval was necessary, to agree to an exhumation so that he could 'recover . . . my lost MSS', he said, sounding as if the task were similar to recovering an umbrella left behind at the theatre.[5] The Home Secretary agreed to the exhumation, despite Rossetti's mother being the legal owner of the grave, purchased on the death of her husband in 1854. The exhumation was to be conducted privately, at night, and Rossetti's acolyte Charles Augustus Howell and a lawyer were in attendance. According to Howell, when the coffin was opened, Siddal's body was undecayed – 'perfect' was his word, just as Milton's exhumed body had been said to have been three-quarters of a century earlier – and the coffin entirely filled with her famously beautiful red-gold hair, which he seemed to be suggesting had grown after her death. (No doubt this was taken with a pinch of salt at the time. Even Howell's friends called him a chronic liar and fantasist.) The manuscript was found to be worm-eaten, and required disinfecting before it could be handled, and Rossetti acknowledged that the public would sooner or later learn of its origins. The truth, he said, would ultimately 'ooze out', a word choice that suggests that he for one did not believe Howell's report of a lack of decomposition.

Rossetti's later actions indicate that, unlike those earlier romanticized exhumations to move the dead to better surroundings, the poet found the episode traumatic. At least until 1868, he had been attempting spiritual communication with his dead wife.[6] He died two decades later, in Kent, and was buried there, but right to the end he evinced a hysterical fear of Siddal's grave, begging his friends and family to ensure he was not buried there, fearing that vengeful spirits – Siddal's own? – would beset his corpse. And if they did not, he said, grave-robbers, which after all he himself had been by proxy, would.* By the time of his death in 1882, grave-robbers, or resurrection men, had become nothing more than a story to scare children, but in Rossetti's youth they had been very real.

At the beginning of the eighteenth century, about sixty crimes carried a death sentence. By 1800, this had ballooned to more than two hundred. To set murder apart from other capital crimes such as stealing goods worth more than a shilling, or trapping rabbits, or being out on the highway with a blackened face, the Murder Act was passed in 1752, heaping further punishment on those convicted of 'the horrid Crime

---

*   The vengeful woman returning from the grave comes into her own in the following decade in Bram Stoker's *Dracula* (see pp. 249–50). Here it is simply worth noting that John Polidori, the 1819 author of *The Vampire*, the first vampire fiction in English, was Rossetti's uncle; while Rossetti's close friend Hall Caine, the author of *The Recollections of Dante Gabriel Rossetti*, the volume which told the world of Siddal's exhumation, was one of Stoker's closest friends. In 1892, Stoker's 'The Secret of Growing Gold' in turn parallels elements of Siddal's life in this story of a woman killed by her husband and buried under the hearth, only for him to see 'with growing horror . . . [her] golden hair' rising through the cracks in the floor. It 'grew and grew' until 'his feet . . . [were] twined with tresses of golden hair'.[7]

of Murder', in order to create 'some further Terror and peculiar Mark of Infamy'.[8] Those extra marks of infamy could include hanging the body in chains after death, also known as gibbeting (pp. 231–3), or having the body of the executed criminal dissected or anatomized.* A royal grant in the sixteenth century had ensured a set, small number of criminal bodies were annually sent to the Edinburgh Guild of Surgeons and Barbers in Scotland, and the Company of Barbers and Surgeons in England (extended later to the College of Physicians and Gonville Hall, Cambridge) for the same purpose. By the eighteenth century, each institution received six bodies a year.

The formal procedure in England following the Murder Act was for the body of the executed criminal to be handed over to the College of Surgeons for anatomization and dissection. The body was given what was entitled a 'proper' examination, meaning that a single incision was made to indicate the college's right to anatomization and dissection, as per their legal monopoly. This incision also performed a secondary, more terrible function. In the days of execution via the short drop, the person to be hanged stood on a chair, box or cart, which was then pulled away, the resultant fall causing death by slow strangulation. If the executioner was merciful, he permitted the victim's friends or family to stand below and pull on the legs of the most likely still struggling person at the end of the rope. Even with this extra help, the executed person was frequently still alive on reaching Surgeon's Hall, hours after being cut down from the gallows. Thus the concept of legal death and medical death developed: at the scaffold, the executed was declared legally dead; later, at the College of Surgeons, they were anatomized and thus became medically dead. William Clift, who was charged with receiving the bodies of executed criminals at Surgeon's Hall, kept notes over a period of twenty years,

* The words overlap, but dissection and anatomization were historically different procedures. An autopsy or post-mortem is today performed to determine a cause of death. In the nineteenth century anatomization was an action taken after an execution, to ensure that the person was actually dead; dissection was the post-mortem punishment by which a body was cut open and examined, frequently in public.[9]

and they show that a quarter of those pronounced legally dead at the scaffold were medically alive on arrival.[10]

After the proper anatomization, the bodies of the executed were distributed by the College to private surgeons or anatomy schools, or to hospitals. Many criminals were then dissected in anatomy theatres or other public spaces, particularly if their crimes had been in some way remarkable or notorious. These events were open to the public at large, and were 'constantly crowded, and the applause excessive' as the dissection proceeded, said one surgeon.[11]

In William Hogarth's moral cycle, 'The Four Stages of Cruelty' (1751), the antihero Tom Nero spirals from hurting a dog, to theft and then to murder, before ending on the gallows and, ultimately, anatomized in front of a raucous crowd with, in a neat artistic twist, a dog sniffing at his entrails.

By the eighteenth century, when anatomy began to be taught more widely both in private medical schools and in universities and teaching hospitals, this tiny number of legally available bodies became untenable, and to supply the lack, bodies were clandestinely exhumed from churchyards. As early as 1721, apprentices registering at the Edinburgh College of Surgeons were required to swear that they would not use exhumed bodies, which almost certainly means that that was exactly what their fellow students were doing. In other places, rumours circulated that students could have their fees waived if they were willing to supply the rest of the class with bodies. By the nineteenth century, the shortage was more extreme than could be alleviated even by willing students: in London alone, a dozen legally acquired bodies were meant to serve up to a thousand medical students, a number that more realistically required a minimum of six hundred bodies.[12] In addition, there were places for 750 medical students every year in Edinburgh; Liverpool had two medical schools of its own, and its docks were a well-known jumping-off point to supply the medical schools of Dublin and Edinburgh.[13] The Murder Act was woefully out of date.

Thus the appearance of resurrection men, so called because they 'resurrected' the newly dead, digging them up clandestinely by night to sell to surgeons and their students, as well as to physicians, dentists, articulators and artists' model-makers.*[14] The trade had been quietly carried on from at least the 1760s. The term resurrection man seems to have come into use sometime in the 1770s, although the men were also known as 'sack-'em-up men', or, more genteelly, they were 'in the body business'. The medical men referred to the bodies they purchased as 'subjects'; the resurrection men, or

---

* An articulator was a person who put together bones to make skeletons, either zoological or human, for teaching purposes. Dentists used real teeth to supply their patients who had lost their own, and thus also had an interest in the dead. During the Peninsular Wars (1809–14), it was taken for granted that men followed the Duke of Wellington's army across Spain to collect teeth from dead soldiers on the battlefields. It was even claimed that the administrators of St Thomas' Hospital in London had sent their own porter out for that purpose.

at least according to one of them, bluntly referred to them as 'things'.[15] In 1768 Laurence Sterne, the author of *Tristram Shandy*, had been buried in central London only a short time before, according to rumour, his body turned up in a dissecting room in Cambridge. It was recognized, the story went, by the university's professor of anatomy, who had been a friend, and who had the body removed and quietly reinterred.

Whether or not this particular episode occurred, it makes clear that resurrection men were already active, and a range of processes and commodities were developed and marketed to try to foil them. To have any value to an anatomist, a body had to be fairly recently dead. Thus, if it could be kept safe until decomposition was well underway, the resurrectionists would leave it, knowing it could not be sold. The establishment of 'dead houses', buildings where bodies were kept under guard for several days before burial, was one possibility. There were also patent coffins with special keys, or iron straps, or reinforced lids guaranteed not to break under the pressure of a crowbar. A mort-safe was an iron cage that either surrounded the coffin before it was buried, or could be dug into the ground after burial, then set in mortar so it could not be removed. A less expensive version was the portable mort-safe, a heavy cage that had to be winched into place. After a week or so, once it was too late for the resurrectionists, the cage could be winched away to be used on a new grave.[16] Interring a body in multiple coffins was another attempt to foil the resurrectionists. One burial in Spitalfields, London, was that of an undertaker himself. His family had his body encased in three coffins, the outermost protected by iron straps; the middle one made of lead; the innermost coffin strengthened with two iron bars and more iron straps before being inserted upside down, so that the soldered edges were inaccessible to a resurrectionist's tools.[17] It was natural that an undertaker was this careful: those in the trade knew exactly how vulnerable the dead were. Sir Astley Cooper, one of London's pre-eminent surgeons, teachers and anatomists in the early part of the century, told parliament: 'There is no person, let his situation in life be what it may, whom, if I were disposed to dissect, I could not obtain [after their death]. The law only enhances the price, it does not prevent exhumation.'[18]

Cooper's views carried weight, for he was one of the resurrection men's best customers. To offer a single exculpation of Cooper's behaviour, he was not alone. A surgeon at St Bartholomew's Hospital in 1829 said that there was only one way to learn to be a good surgeon: 'we must be companions with the dead.' In that pre-anaesthetic age, if a surgeon was slow, or clumsy, it was more than likely that their patient would go into shock before the surgery was completed.[19] A thorough knowledge of anatomy and a mastery of knife skills separated the competent surgeon from the surgeon whose patients were dead.

Because of Cooper's eminence, because he gave evidence to a House of Commons select committee on anatomy, and because he made as many enemies as he did friends, we know a great deal about his interactions with the resurrectionists, and his story can be representative. The first two decades of the nineteenth century saw the transformation of the 'body business' from an amateur requirement of students and those only intermittently involved, to a fully fledged network linking criminals who did just this one job to the professionals of the medical, governmental and clerical worlds: surgeons, hospital administrators, porters, dressers, medical students, undertakers, workhouse supervisors, nurses and doctors, church sextons, watchmen and gravediggers.

Cooper had set up his own private dissecting room in 1791, working with Daniel Butler, the superintendent of the dissecting rooms at St Thomas' Hospital and himself the son of an articulator and dealer in teeth. Butler liaised with a resurrectionist named Bill Harnett, acting as go-between for surgeon and body-man. But after more than a decade of this mutually satisfactory business arrangement, Harnett was arrested for receiving stolen goods (grave-clothes), and Cooper moved on to deal with Ben Crouch, who was possibly the most successful, definitely the most notorious, resurrection man in the country. Crouch, by virtue of both his organizational abilities and his domineering, frequently violent, personality, had become the main supplier to at least two of London's largest hospitals, setting up what were effectively monopolies with their dissecting rooms, negotiating a set price per body at the beginning of each 'season' (after the hot weather), plus additional 'opening money' – down payments on future bodies, supposedly used to bribe the necessary people, but more truthfully a supplement he demanded because as a monopolist he could. Harnett charged Cooper about 2 guineas (£2 2s.) for each adult, half that for a child; in 1810, it had doubled; and by 1828 the price had risen to 8 or 9 guineas per body. Yet the anatomists had little choice. Crouch bribed, bullied or cajoled any resurrectionist who was good at his work to join his men. If they refused, Crouch informed on them to the police, so they would be caught in the act; or he paid the gravediggers in the churchyards they frequented to spoil the burial grounds, digging up coffins, throwing around body parts, doing enough to ensure the residents would set a watch on the grounds and make it impossible for resurrectionists to operate there. If a surgeon or anatomist refused to fall into line, Crouch and his men raided their rooms, wrecking the furniture and damaging the bodies so that their students would have nothing to work on. Such was the resurrectionists' hold on the medical profession that those resurrectionists who were caught expected to have their fines paid by the men they supplied, with additional funds sent to support their families if they were jailed. When one of Astley Cooper's regular suppliers was arrested, for example, the surgeon paid more than £14 towards his bail and the expenses of an intermediary to travel to the country to arrange it; after the resurrectionist was jailed, he continued to pay 6s. a week to his wife, and 10s. a week to the prisoner.[20]

In 1843, Cooper's much less distinguished and successful nephew Bransby Cooper wrote a two-volume hagiography of his celebrated uncle. Yet while setting out to raise him to posthumous eminence, Bransby showed that both the medical profession and the government knew what was going on, approved what was going on, and just wanted no one to discuss it publicly. He tells a story, for instance, of Bill Harnett supplying three bodies to Daniel Butler, who collected them in a hired coach. The coachmen became uneasy, telling a passer-by on the street that he had 'a load inside, that he didn't much like the looks of'. Butler, overhearing, quietly opened the door and slid away when the coach was stopped in traffic. Butler being his employee, Cooper was questioned by the watch the next day. He didn't know what the coachman was talking about, he expostulated, before rushing off to warn the Lord Mayor that he would have to suppress the watch's inquiries.[21] Bransby shows he was not the sharpest knife in the drawer in repeating this story to boost Cooper's reputation. He also quoted the governors of an unnamed hospital who worked hard, he said, to ensure that their own burial grounds were 'inviolate', a place where their patients' families could be reassured they would rest undisturbed. So much so, added Bransby, that many patients asked to be 'examined after death', apparently expecting readers to believe that the patients demanded to be anatomized in order to ensure that they would be buried without being anatomized.[22]

Bransby was truthful, if inadvertently. Most hospital managements *were* involved in the clandestine supply of bodies to their institutions. So were undertakers, who sold the dead after they had been placed in their coffins, using bricks or other heavy weights as a substitute so the pall-bearers would not notice. Others stole bodies awaiting inquests, which was relatively easy, as inquests sat wherever a person had died, their bodies left in situ until a verdict was returned. Still others posed as the family of recently deceased workhouse inmates, come to take them home for burial. Servants were said to be bribed to tip off resurrectionists of deaths in the family, afterwards arranging for a door or window to be carelessly left open.[23] In retailing these stratagems, Bransby Cooper is entirely unconscious of the feelings of the families involved. Resurrectionists' exploits are 'most ingenious and amusing', although the story of a resurrectionist holding a hospital demonstrator at pistol-point is merely 'amusing', but apparently not ingenious. The only people he shows sympathy for are the anatomists who cannot get their hands on a sufficient number of subjects, which can be a 'harassing situation'.[24]

Until 1828, no one except the working-class resurrection men paid any penalty for these acts. At worst, a hospital porter, also working class, might be sacked for selling his dissecting rooms' subjects to another hospital. But there was no risk to anyone in the professional class until, in that year in Liverpool, a surgeon named William Gill was prosecuted for receiving a body he knew to be exhumed. He was found guilty and fined. At his trial, Gill outlined the surgeons' dilemma: the law punished doctors who practised without qualifications; the law also made it impossible to qualify without breaking the law.[25] With this succinct summary, and with one of their colleagues in the dock for a crime that previously only those of lower social status had been punished for, surgeons and anatomists began to agitate for a change in the law. The House of Commons set up a select committee on 'the manner of obtaining Subjects for Dissection in the Schools of Anatomy, and into the State of the Law affecting the Persons employed in obtaining and dissecting Bodies'.

The select committee heard from distinguished men such as Astley Cooper, but, very unusually, it also took direct testimony from three resurrection men. Their identities were disguised by initials, but they gave, for the sole time on record, a first-hand, realistic picture of the trade as it was conducted, instead of the fevered imaginings of newspapers and Gothic novelists hypothesized. The only other first-person account that is known is a brief series of diary entries made by one resurrectionist in 1811–12, a man who is thought to have also been one of the men who gave evidence before the committee. From these two accounts, it appears that, instead of the couple of hundred London gangs that the press, and thus the population at large, believed existed, gangs who between them raised thousands of bodies a year, it seemed that there were as few as ten gangs, and, said one, he himself raised around a hundred bodies a year, which earned him a decent living. This figure was backed up by John Bishop, another London resurrectionist, who between 1821 and his execution for murder in 1831, said that he and his partner between them had lifted on average fifty to a hundred bodies a year.[26]

As early as 1819, a surgeon had suggested that the bodies of paupers might be used to benefit society by being made available for dissection. The idea was revived during the hearings of this parliamentary commission, and although the final report made a woolly attempt to disguise its meaning, it nevertheless promoted the plan that those paupers whose bodies were not claimed by their friends or family were to be made available to the anatomists. The committee report did not, however, clarify what 'claimed' meant. How quickly did it have to happen? Did the family simply have to say they were family, or did they have to be able to afford to pay for a funeral? The vagueness was intentional, designed to blur the brutal reality that poverty was to become the sole criterion for the separation of those who were to be handed over for dissection from those who could be laid to rest in a grave undisturbed.

The committee's findings were influential, although the bill itself failed to pass. Still more influential on the public was the outcry after the crimes of Burke and Hare had been revealed in Edinburgh in 1828. Burke and Hare were two men who, failing to find a resurrection gang willing to work with them, had discovered a more direct route to the cash paid by anatomists. The pair invited indigents to their lodgings, offered them a drink and then smothered or strangled them before selling their bodies to the anatomy school of the ultra-respectable Dr Knox. The complicity of the professional world was notable. The institution's porter and instructors were under no illusion as to the condition of the bodies they were buying, which had very obviously died within days, or possibly hours, and had just as obviously never been laid out, much less buried. Hare, in exchange for immunity, admitted to sixteen murders over ten months; Burke was found guilty and hanged; and no charges were ever laid against anyone at Dr Knox's school.*

In 1831, the same thing happened again, this time in London, where John Bishop and Thomas Williams murdered at least three, possibly more, homeless people in order to sell their bodies to the anatomists. (Bishop and Williams were convicted and executed; a third man, James May, although a well-known resurrectionist, was acquitted.) These two sets of murders created the impetus for the subject to return to parliament. A second Anatomy Bill was introduced two weeks after the executions of Bishop and Williams, highlighting these 'late enormities', as did the final Anatomy Act when it passed in the following year.[27]

There is no question that those presenting the bill knew how shocking it was to propose using the poor as anatomy subjects without their consent, and how outrageously unfair the public would consider it were they to learn the details. The bill was hustled through parliament with as little exposure as possible, and with many of the debates held in the middle of the night. How the Act was to be enforced was left vague, which meant it was not debated at all, and it was even said – an outright lie – that workhouses and hospitals would not be able to sell unclaimed bodies to anatomists. The bill, were it to become law, was an assault on the poor for the crime of being poor. Riots erupted across the country. A petition was presented to parliament noting that while the petitioners had 'a great horror of burking', they had 'a still greater horror at the provisions of the Anatomy Bill which would . . . be the means of opening the door for a new and refined

---

* Some historians have suggested that the Edinburgh miniature coffins mentioned in the Introduction might represent Burke and Hare's victims. Yet the two men's death tally was generally put at sixteen people, most of whom were women. Two of the very few things we know for sure about the dolls is that, at a minimum, there were at least seventeen figurines, and they were all male.

species of Burking'.* And in a moment of timing that could not have been anticipated, the bill came up for a vote just as the first wave of cholera reached Britain. Bishop and Williams, Burke and Hare, cholera and the Anatomy Bill (soon, Anatomy Act) merged in people's minds. While it was not true that cholera was an illness fabricated by a government anxious to push healthy people into hospitals in order to have them murdered for the use of their corpses, it was true that corruption, dishonesty and poor administration saw the bodies of working-class people sent for dissection before their families knew they were dead, much less had gathered enough money to pay for burial. Over the first hundred years of the Act, just under 57,000 bodies were dissected in London alone; 99.5 per cent came from workhouses and hospitals – that is, none but the poor were dissected post-mortem.[28]

While grave-robbing was an act of desecration, whether religious or familial, it had also been oddly democratic: resurrection men stole the bodies of both rich and poor alike. As the poet Robert Southey wrote in his comic poem 'The Surgeon's Warning' (1799), in the voice of a dying surgeon to his apprentices:

> All kinds of carcases I have cut up,
> And the judgement now must be –
> But brothers I took care of you,
> So, pray take care of me![29]

(They did not, instead quickly selling him to his fellow anatomists for 3 guineas.) Two months after the Reform Bill became law, the Anatomy Act received royal assent, ensuring the opposite of reform: that the rich would no longer be required to share post-mortem indignity with their poor coevals. Societal hierarchy after death was restored.

*

* To burk originally meant to murder for dissection, as Burke and Hare had done, but it came to be used to refer to all those who had died whose bodies were subsequently sold by resurrectionists.

While the resurrection trade was something that people knew about, but virtually never saw, the presence of the criminal dead more generally was far more widespread and ordinary than in our own times. Sometimes it was art, sometimes dressed up as science, sometimes it was in the newspapers or children's books.

Early in the century, the bodies of the executed were used on occasion to produce academic casts for art schools. A member of the Royal Academy took delivery of a body fresh from Tyburn so that he could pose it the way he wanted before rigor mortis set in, afterwards having the skin flayed to display the musculature underneath as the basis for a plaster cast to be used by art students. (The piece, known as The Dying Gladiator, survives and is owned and intermittently displayed by the Edinburgh College of Art.) Another cast, today belonging to the Royal Academy in London, was created for the artists Benjamin West and Richard Cosway, who used the body of an elderly Chelsea pensioner, executed for murdering a fellow pensioner. They were both working on pieces depicting the crucifixion, and they commissioned an anatomist to purchase the body and crucify it before turning it into a cast.[30] In the 1860s, Jeannette Marshall's surgeon father helped the artist Ford Madox Ford with the 'obtainment' of a 'dead boddy' for study.[31]

There were anatomical museums, where bodies, or body parts, were displayed to the public. Lectures and quasi-scientific demonstrations also used the recently dead. Some of these audiences were limited to 'scientific gentlemen', but many more were open to the public at large. Early in the century a Professor Giovanni Aldini performed a series of experiments designed to 'excite' the bodies of the recently dead via an electric current, a vogue known as galvanism. The current stimulated the nerves and muscles in the dead body, making it twitch in a way that resembled animation. While in 1812 regulations were established to prevent this type of display, there was no method of enforcement, and the demonstrations continued through the 1820s.[32]

Mary Shelley's novel *Frankenstein* (1818), a classic of the resurrection, Gothic body genre, was therefore in some ways replicating and elaborating in fiction what was transpiring in the real world. Victor Frankenstein's described methods and sources could have been those of any of these lecturers:

> To examine the causes of life, we must first have recourse to death. I became acquainted with the science of anatomy . . . I must also observe the natural decay and corruption of the human body . . . [T]he churchyard to me was merely the receptacle of bodies deprived of life . . . I dabbled among the unhallowed damps of the grave or tortured the living to animate the lifeless clay . . . I collected bones from charnel-houses and disturbed, with profane fingers, the tremendous secrets of the human frame . . . The dissecting-room and the slaughter-house furnished many of my materials.[33]

But Victor Frankenstein was just the most famous of a number of medical students who created the monsters that densely populated early Victorian literature. In 1847, in *Varney the Vampyre*, Varney is brought back to active vampire-dom by a young medical student who, like Aldini and Frankenstein, galvanizes the body of an executed criminal. In Reynolds' *Mysteries of London*, a villain-turned-hero is cut down from the scaffold and galloped off to a private laboratory where he is returned to life via hartshorn (smelling salts), a mysterious 'silver tube' that he had inserted into his throat prior to his execution, as well as, of course, a galvanic current.[34]

Newspapers, even the most respectable of them, published physical details of death in a way that today is inconceivable, as seen with the post-mortem of George IV, or of murder victims in criminal trials. The journals also reported on the multiple execution-adjacent souvenirs that were available: pieces of skin from executed criminals, including Burke, were advertised, tanned and turned into leather goods such as wallets, book-bindings or, in one case, overprinted with a portrait of the skin's original wearer.[35]

A stranger case was the self-determined post-mortem fate of Jeremy Bentham, the social reformer, founder of the philosophical school of utilitarianism and one of the prime movers of the Anatomy Act. Bentham stage-managed his post-death existence in order to promote his utilitarian belief that even dead bodies could serve society. In many ways, his death in 1832 followed a conventional path, at his own request. He had ordered mourning rings to be distributed to his friends and family, complete with cuttings of his hair. But instead of his friends receiving printed invitations to his funeral, Bentham instead arranged for them to receive invitations to the public dissection of his body. After that, as he explained himself in a letter:

My body I give to my dear friend Dr Southwood Smith . . .

The skeleton he will cause to be put together in such a manner that the whole figure may be seated in a chair usually occupied by me when living, in the attitude in which I am sitting while engaged in thought in the course of time occupied in writing.

I direct that the body thus prepared shall be transferred to my executor. He will cause the skeleton to be clad in one of the suits of black occasionally worn by me. The body so clothed, together with the chair and the staff in my later years borne by me, he will take charge of, and for containing the whole apparatus he will cause to be prepared an appropriate box or case, and will cause to be engraved in conspicuous characters on a plate to be affixed thereon and also on the labels on the glass case in which the preparations of the soft parts of my body shall be contained . . . my name at length with the letters ob: [from Latin, 'obiit', he died] followed by the day of my decease.

If it should so happen that my personal friends and other disciples should be disposed to meet together on some day or days of the year for the purpose of commemorating the founder of the greatest happiness system of morals and legislation, my executor will from time to time cause to be conveyed in the room in which they meet the said box or case with the contents therein, to be stationed in such part of the room as to the assembled company shall seem meet.[36]

And that is exactly what happened. Southwood Smith kept his friend's 'Auto-Icon' on display in his consulting rooms until his retirement, after which by a circuitous route it ended up at University College London, where it remains on display.

While a dead body sitting fully dressed in a college is considered unusual today, in the nineteenth century, as we have seen, viewing the dead, especially the criminal dead, was far more routine. Even children were exposed. Many memoirs included recollections of being taken to watch executions in childhood.[37] While she was not taken to executions, when she was seven Marjory Fleming, daughter of a middle-class Kirkaldy accountant, recorded in her precocious diary almost in passing that 'Many people are hanged for Highway robbery Housebreking Murder &c &c [her cousin] Isabella teaches me everything I know and I am much indebted to her she is learnen witty & sensible.' And the following year, 'We are reading a book about a man went into a house & he saw a sack & he went & look into it & he saw a dead body in it.'[38]

Entertainment, whether at a remove, via reading as Marjory did, or at the gallows itself, was a prime motive. But others attended executions owing to the folkloric beliefs associated with dead bodies, particularly the bodies of those executed, or the rope with which they were hanged: touching them would cure scrofula, ague, epilepsy, tumours, ulcers, asthma and other chronic ailments. Warts could be reduced by rubbing the dead hand of the criminal a set number of times against the afflicted area; a growth elsewhere on the body, after being touched, would fade away as the body decomposed. Teeth from the dead were traded as amulets, a prophylactic against the wearer getting toothache in the future.[39]

It has been suggested that those miniature coffins described in the Introduction were in some way representative of either folkloric or magic beliefs, that they were possibly witchcraft tokens, the figurines standing in for people who had been cursed; or that they were symbolic burials of family or friends who had died at sea, or far from home; or that they were good luck charms. Others, however, have countered that witchcraft tokens were generally destroyed after a curse was uttered, and if not, the curse figures generally bore signs of violence, such as sharp objects stuck through them, which was not the case here; there was no tradition of symbolic burials in Scotland, and no other examples of the practice are known; the same holds true for good luck tokens. Yet while those dolls were clearly linked somehow to death beliefs, they fit somewhat uncomfortably into the folklore pattern.

More traditional folklore revolved around the gibbet, that post-execution punishment sometimes called hanging in chains, or in irons, that had faded out by the time of the Anatomy Act, although its legend lingered. Because the gibbet had always been overshadowed by the horrors of dissection, this form of punishment is often overlooked today. Gibbeting was another 'Mark of Infamy' laid down in the Murder Act of 1752 as a deterrent and an ongoing punishment to make the public feel justice was being done. It was a more local punishment than executions were, executions almost always being held in larger towns. By contrast, the body to be gibbeted was frequently returned to the site of the crime, where it was left hanging sometimes for decades to serve as a warning, either in a local gathering spot for the community (beside a main road, at a crossing), or somewhere easily visible (a hill, or a flat moor, or by a local landmark).[40] For crimes committed at sea, gibbets were erected along the Thames estuary and in Portsmouth, the main criterion being that they were on major shipping lanes to ensure the widest possible audience.[41]

Once the criminal was executed, they were taken to the location where they were to be hung in chains. Depending on the distance, the body might be coated in some form of preservative, although not dipped entirely in pitch or tar, which appears was a fictional invention.* It was then inserted into what was known as a cage. The term is misleading, creating an image of an oversized birdcage in which the dead body sat. More accurately, this cage was a set of iron bands in the shape of the person it was to enclose, bands that fitted so tightly the prisoner had to be measured for them before his execution. Once locked, they held the body stiffly: in 'A Shropshire Lad', A.E. Houseman accurately described how a gibbeted body looked as if it 'stood on air'. The caged body then was attached to a post by an iron chain that hooked onto a loop soldered at the top of the bands surrounding the head. The posts were nine or ten metres high, to ensure the figure could be seen at a great distance, and the chain was designed to make a terrible clanking sound as it swung in the breeze. Some posts had nails studded around the base, or an iron sheath, to prevent families from climbing up to remove their dead. (Pieces of the post were touted as cures for toothache, so it is possible that the nails or iron also protected the wood from casual vandalism.) Erected in the community where the criminal had lived, the gibbets were often near the family's home, which meant a mother, say, would daily see (and smell) the decomposing body of her son.† Gradually, as the body disintegrated, birds pecked away at the flesh, and the bones fell to the ground beneath, with nothing but the head left behind, encased tightly in its cage.[43] The Irish writer William Carleton (1794–1869) described the horror of the gibbet with its 'decom-

---

* This idea was prevalent as early as the 1890s. In a supposed history of gibbeting, one author claimed that the bodies to be hung in chains were taken after execution to 'the Kitchen', where 'a caldron [sic] of boiling pitch' was kept ready for them to be dipped into. The premise has, however, been debunked by the foremost scholar of gibbeting, Sarah Tarlow, who notes the complete absence of charges for the pitch and the fees paid to people to carry out the process, despite the survival of very detailed lists of execution expenses. She also notes that covering the body with pitch or tar hides the identity of the deceased, which was contrary to the aim of punishment, as the body was displayed at the scene of the crime, where the criminal had lived or was at least known.[42]

† I say son because, while women were also executed, it was in far smaller numbers than men. That relative rarity made them more valuable to anatomists, and it was therefore atypical for an executed woman to be gibbeted rather than dissected.

posed masses' dropping away, 'ooz[ing] out . . . in slimy ropes', with everything 'literally covered in flies'.[44]

As with Cromwell's head, gibbeted bodies were left up until they rotted away completely, or winds or a storm brought the pole, or at least its burden, down. So although the last prisoner to be gibbeted was hung in chains in 1834, gibbets were part of the landscape until late in the century, and they remained a presence as landmarks long after, locations routinely taking their name from the act (Gibbet Hill, Gibbet's Field) or from the murderer whose body had hung there for so long.[45] Even when 'Mouldered was the gibbet-mast; The bones were gone', and 'Only a long green ridge of turf remained', the spot where a gibbet had once stood seemed to Wordsworth to have retained a 'shape . . . like a grave'.[46] In folklore and legend they remained for even longer, being an understandably favourite site for revenants in ghost stories, although it tended to be the ghost of the murdered person rather than the murderer who haunted the area. Ghosts, and the undead, were to many even more omnipresent than the dead.

11

THE NON-DEAD AND THE UNDEAD

In the Gothic novels of the early part of the century, murderers were supervillains, often foreign, living in alpine castles, debauching maidens and murdering profligately. Or they were thugs, street louts who lived in hovels but otherwise acted as the supervillains did in the debauching and murdering line. In *The Mysteries of London*, published in the early 1840s, villainy was brought home from Europe to the heart of London when the lovely Eliza escapes death at the hands of a resurrectionist and his gang by dropping through a secret trapdoor that opened into the Fleet Ditch, the part-covered river that had become a byword for filth and, by extension, crime.[1] Forty years later, in Robert Louis Stevenson's *The Strange Case of Dr Jekyll and Mr Hyde*, the supervillain had transformed into a medical man, a professional just like his readers. But the violence, while hidden, was no longer in castles, or in thugs' secret lairs, but in sitting rooms and bedrooms of the middle classes that exactly resembled those of their readers.

What was transpiring in these ordinary homes was as wild as the events that had previously been imagined in romances of mysterious doings in Italian convents. Even when the characters were entirely phantasmagorical, the same shift towards domesticity was evident. In the past, ghostly aristocratic apparitions had returned to the site of their murders, or to haunted churchyards, or they had walked the lonely crossroads to tell future generations how they had been killed for their property or cheated out of an inheritance. Modern middle-class spectres, by contrast, like their living counterparts, mostly stayed at home. By the late 1770s, one novel of ghostly haunting prosaically ended with a chapter-long back and forth about who owned which house and who was going to live where, a spectral musical chairs of inheritance and property law.[2] At the other end of the century, the father of psychoanalysis, Sigmund Freud, examined the possible meanings of the word *heimlich*, which in German means intimate, comfortable, quietly content, and yet also concealed, secret and withheld. *Unheimlich*, literally un-homelike in a direct translation into English, in German means occult. Something that was homelike to Freud, and many people, by this time, was also something separate, private and concealed – something where, possibly, danger lurked.[3]

With the ravages of epidemics through the century, with high mortality rates, especially among young children, with the visibility of the dead in daily life, it is unsurprising that the living and the dead did not merely coexist, but perhaps could be considered to have mixed. With the lightest of touches, easily overlooked, Dickens encapsulated that sense of in-between, of people who were not dead, and yet who were not alive either. In his most famous opening, of what might be his most famous piece of writing, *A Christmas Carol*, the narrator begins: 'Marley was dead: to begin with. There is no doubt whatever about that.'[4] But those first sentences are two-faced. The literal meaning is, 'Let me begin my tale by stating that there was no question that Marley was dead.' It can, however, also be read to mean that Marley was dead to begin with, but only to begin with, and later on he was not. Whichever way that opening sentence is read, there is the additional emphasis. Death, which is normally considered to be the end, here becomes 'to begin with': this story will deal with what happens *after* death. Twenty years later, Dickens repeated his dead/alive double vision, this time as comedy. In *Our Mutual Friend*, Mr Boffin, who mangles his words, refers to his late employer and benefactor as his 'diseased' (deceased) governor. He is questioned, '[Is the] Gentleman dead, sir?' and he explodes, 'Man alive, don't I tell you? A deceased governor.' The deceased here is both living and dead through the grammatical and idiomatic juxta-position: Man alive, he's dead![5]

Were ghosts real, or were they figments of the imagination? The troubled times, the many dead in the French wars, and then later the waves of epidemics, increased uncertainty, or at least increased the desire to be uncertain. In the ten years following the storming of the Bastille in 1789, in London alone there were nearly three dozen public lectures on the existence or otherwise of ghosts.[6] In *A Christmas Carol*, Scrooge takes the rationalist view at first, happier to believe that the apparition he is faced with is a bad dream brought on by a bout of indigestion: 'There's more of gravy than of grave about you,' he tells the ghost who is attempting to haunt him.[7] But others felt that something otherworldly did exist, even if they did not know what it might be. Romanticism and its adherents drew on a kind of non-ghostly aura, using the word 'haunted' to refer not to actual or imagined spiritual activity, but for the first time giving it the meaning we do today, to be haunted by memories, or by the past more generally.[8] One did not necessarily have to be haunted by an actual, or imagined, spiritual presence. It could be some form of intangible spiritual communication, as in Charlotte Brontë's *Jane Eyre*, where 'presentiments', 'sympathies' and 'signs' all 'combined to make one mystery', a kind of ethereal connection where 'far-distant, long-absent, wholly estranged relatives' were all tuned in to a form of mystic sympathetic communication.[9]

It was in the 1850s that ghosts, or revenants, or spirit beings – whatever people understood them to be – really came into their own. Previously ghosts had appeared as they willed, and seemed to have little agency apart from their ability to be seen by some, usually outdoors, or at a window, or in a churchyard. Later nineteenth-century spirits or apparitions, by contrast, came when called by someone who had a foot in both worlds, someone who from this date became known as a medium, and who tended to operate in an intimate domestic setting such as a dining or drawing room, where those who longed to hear from the dead gathered.

The origin of spiritualism was to be found in a small town in New York State, where three sisters named Fox claimed to have received, via 'rappings', messages from the spirit of a pedlar who told them that he had been murdered years before, and buried in their cellar. In 1849, the sisters began publicly to act as mediums between the spirits and the living world, and spiritualism became a topic of fascination. In Britain, a Mrs Hayden arrived from the USA in 1852, giving sittings for upwards of half a guinea to the prosperous; in the Midlands and the north, spiritualism spread rapidly among the Nonconformists and Dissenters, who had long traditions of interactions with the ghostly. John Wesley's father had believed he had met an 'invisible power' three times in his life, and Wesley himself believed in ghosts, even though he had never seen one: after all, he said, he also believed in murder even though he had never met a murderer.[10] In the great majority of cases for those attending seances, from whatever background or social class, the driving force was to connect with one's loved ones who had 'gone before'. William Cowper-Temple, Lord Mount Temple, for example, wrote of his dead wife, 'It is not till death do us part, but till death do us join', as he participated in seances with a medium.[11] The spirit world became a place from which death could be understood, the place where those who had been lost waited for the living to join them.

One of the common denominators among spiritualists, ghost stories and mediumship was children. Children and death were tightly linked, and thus, as spiritualism spread, children in the afterlife became a well-trodden route into the practice. This may have been the source of one of the strangest cases of spiritual connection in the nineteenth century, that of Morell Theobald and his family, alive and dead, in the London suburbs of 1860.[12] Morell was an accountant, born in 1828, the son of a bookseller. He and his wife and children were devout, not just regularly attending Nonconformist services, but also holding daily family prayers. Ellen Theobald had seen seven of her eleven pregnancies end in stillbirth or infant death through the 1860s and 1870s, although she would ultimately have six children who lived to adulthood. These tragedies had under-standably taken a toll, until one day, Morell wrote, he and his wife 'sat wondering if these three [dead babies] . . . were lonely'. All of a sudden, 'our little ones stood at the door and knocked!'

Spiritualism had not come out of nowhere for the Theobalds. Morell's sister, a semi-invalid who lived with them for long periods, had spent time communing with their dead uncle before being introduced more formally to the subject of the afterlife by their neighbours, Mary and William Howitt. The Howitts were deeply enmeshed in the literary world: she a translator of fairy tales and also a poet (her most famous children's poem begins, 'Will you walk into my parlour, said the spider to the fly'); Howitt was primarily a historian, but was also known for having written on the 'last homes', or graves, of the poets. Ellen joined her sister-in-law and the Howitts in sessions, first via table-turning, then seances, where they attempted to reach her dead children. With the help of her living children, who were found to have great mediumistic powers, their siblings in the afterworld responded, giving reassurances of the 'bright cord of light' that was God's love that protected them, and recounting their daily doings. The oldest dead child assured her mother that the younger ones with her on the 'other side' were happy and growing well. (Children appeared routinely to grow at a this-world pace in the afterlife: the author Florence Marryat reported that her own dead baby had turned seventeen by the time they began to communicate.)[13] The Theobald children's daily lives in the afterworld were more detailed than most, as they updated their parents on their doings in a place that was remarkably like the middle-class suburban life their living siblings enjoyed: the dead children went to school, had a garden to play in and even a pony to ride. And as various family members died, the living Theobalds were comforted to hear that they had joined the children and passed on messages of their own.

Over time, as the living children grew up and lost interest in talking to the dead (the senior Theobalds did not possess mediumistic abilities), it was discovered that their cook, Mary, could also reach family members in the next world. She gradually moved from 'downstairs' to 'upstairs', and became a virtual sister to Nellie Theobald, even as the rest of the servants, offended and overworked, handed in their notice after Mary gave up her share of the kitchen work. (There is an unintentionally comic series of asides in Morell's recounting of this, where he explains how the 'social difficulty' of their servant becoming quasi-family 'distressed some of [his] friends' because they had failed to understand that Mary had always been 'superior to the servant class in many ways', and thus the change was not the social and caste upheaval that others might think.)* In any case, Nellie and Mary announced that it would be unnecessary to hire new servants as the spirits would undertake all the household chores, making up the fires and cooking the meals. Mr and Mrs Theobald tried in vain to catch the spirits performing these tasks, but never quite managed, although both Nellie and Mary, by remarkable coincidence, frequently found themselves 'alone' with the spirits at work. (Theobald himself used these inverted commas around 'alone', as he knew they were not alone, but in the company of the housekeeping spirits.)

At first glance the Theobalds' story exemplifies the desperate thread of loss and longing that promoted spiritualism to so many: where were their dead children? Were they afraid, or sad, or lonely? Spiritualism reassured. It also attracted the credulous, and what today would be called the conspiracy-minded. Morell and his two brothers sat on the committee of the Bacon Society, founded to

---

* Robert Browning had foreseen just such an episode in his poem 'Mr Sludge, "The Medium"' (1864), narrated by a medium who as a young servant had listened at doors, pretending that what he had overheard were messages from the afterworld and thus won praise, status and finally a living as a medium. The poet was perhaps understandably deeply cynical about spiritualism. In the previous decade he and Elizabeth Barrett Browning had attended a seance where they were shown an apparition that was said to be their infant who had died at birth. Unfortunately for the medium, the Brownings had not had a child who had died in infancy. Browning made a grab for the object, and found that he was holding the medium's bare foot.

prove that Francis Bacon, not Shakespeare, had written the works of Shakespeare. And Morell, together with his wife and brother, belonged to a number of spiritualist societies, including the British National Association of Spiritualists, which in the 1870s was formally prosecuted for 'trickery'. He was also the auditor for the Society for Psychical Research, which took a more detached stance to spiritualism, claiming to be searching for proof for or against the existence of psychic phenomena. But when the founder of the society, Frank Podmore, asked to send an independent observer to see the Theobald spirits at home, Morell refused on the grounds that he would be 'a skeleton at the feast and frighten away the invisible guests'.

Soon it was a moot point, as Morell was revealed to have long been involved in the largest City financial scandal of the century, led by the politician and fraudster Jabez Balfour, who for years had run a proto-Ponzi scheme, ostensibly raising capital for building projects, but instead using the funds paid in by new investors to produce his profits. At first the Theobald brothers' firm was simply one of many caught up in the scandal, but eventually it was revealed that Morell had himself been a director or auditor for at least four of the companies Balfour was using to shuffle the money around, producing paperwork at Balfour's demand and signing cheques for payment of false invoices. Was Morell a puppet, unconsciously manipulated by Balfour, as he had been manipulated by his children and Mary? Or was he complicit, aware of the fraud but not wanting to lose his lucrative business connection, just as unmasking the mediums would have left him without the consolation of the voices of his lost children? In the 1890s, when a recession brought Balfour's schemes tumbling down, Morell's remarkably feeble defence for the falsification of the accounts was that he was 'ignorant of both matters of business and accounts', despite working for three decades as a City accountant. The line between knowing, not knowing and not wanting to know was porous in matters of belief as well as business.

Other situations called for other types of spiritual interchange between the dead and the living. In the past, ghosts had appeared wrapped in white sheets, representing the grave-clothes they had been buried in. Now apparitions tended to be more modern. The Fox sisters' rappings began four years after the invention of the telegraph, and spirit knocks moved from the simple 'one for yes, two for no' that had been used to communicate in the eighteenth century to rapping at the appropriate letter when the alphabet was recited, just a decade after the creation of Morse code. Commentators even initially dubbed messages received from the afterworld as the 'spiritual telegraph'.[14] By the 1890s a survey suggested that possibly one in ten of the population had had some kind of supernatural experience, most often at a moment of crisis. The classic example was the wife who heard her husband calling to her when he was half a world away, only to learn later that he had died at that precise moment. It was notable that this type of death-telepathy had become widespread in a period where, owing to immigration and the vast stretch of empire, families and friends were physically further apart than ever, even as telegraphs, railways and steamships had collapsed the time it took for news to travel.[15] Although rare, telephones did by now exist, and the idea that voices could speak to each other across extreme distances was current. More astonishing was the phonograph, which produced recordings of voices that could still be heard years after the person speaking was dead. 'This,' wrote a vicar of a recording of Robert Browning reciting a few lines of one of his poems, 'is the first time that . . . [a] voice has been heard from beyond the grave.'* Another journal called a phonograph recording a 'seance': technology seemed to prove that death was not the end.[16] And if technology proved that, then who could doubt the reality of spirits themselves?

---

* The Edison recording, all fifty seconds of crackling glory, can be found on YouTube, where Browning recites the first few lines of his 'How They Brought the Good News from Ghent to Aix', before stopping to confess, 'I'm terribly sorry but I can't remember me [sic] own verses.'

Spirits and technology were entwined. Mediums who presided at seances frequently availed themselves of lighting to heighten the theatricality. In the 1870s one spectator at a seance led by the teenaged Mary Rosina Showers described a room so dimly lit they could not see people's features, even as Showers' own face was lit up 'to present a corpse-like appearance'. Showers' very successful sessions used other technology as well, one participant noting a 'charnel-house smell about her, as if she'd been buried a few weeks and dug up again'.[17] More often, some sort of automatic or distancing tool was held out as proof of the veracity of the presence of spirits. A planchette, or small board fitted with a pencil or pen that produced 'automatic writing' without any discernible input from the medium, had been quickly replaced by a 'spiritual telegraph dial', where an automatic pointer ticked over to the required letters of the alphabet.[18] Other seances highlighted musical instruments that played themselves, or objects that floated in the air.

And then there was spirit photography. In the eighteenth century, there had been a minor genre of paintings where portraits of the living had included a lost member of the family, portrayed as if they were alive, or with perhaps some indication that they were keeping watch in the afterlife. Hogarth's 1732 conversation piece 'The Cholmondeley Family', complete with romping children, looks like a standard family image until one notices a pair of putti hovering over the woman on the far left, literally drawing back a curtain to tell the viewer that the reason the woman is not looking at her children is that she cannot – she had died the year before Hogarth began work.[19]

These paintings were memorials. They were not attempting to persuade the viewer that the dead person was in some way visible to the living. This was not the case with spirit photography. There were two basic types of spirit photographs, both used as evidence by believers that there was life after death, that spirits did actually manifest themselves in this world. It is easy for us to forget how magical photographs themselves had been when the technology was first developed, and how closely linked to the spirit world contemporaries viewed them. In 1843, Elizabeth Barrett Browning saw her first daguerreotype and compared it directly to mesmerism, that precursor of spiritualist trances, seeing the sitter as 'a disembodied spirit'. The French novelist Balzac did the same a few years later, wondering if, as people or things were photographed, they somehow were themselves dematerialized and turned into 'a kind of *spectre*'.[20]

Spirit photography took the connection between technology and the other world one step further. In 1861, in Boston, Massachusetts, a jewellery-engraver-turned-photographer named William Mumler began to produce photographic portraits of the living that included what he referred to as 'extras', spirits that hovered behind or beside his sitters. These photos of the living and the dead together were on a different level entirely from the photographs taken of the newly dead, whose purpose was to fix their image firmly in the minds of those who had been left behind. Spirit photographs, by contrast, centred on the living, usually a figure dressed in deep mourning, who was being comforted by the presence of one who had returned from the dead for that purpose. These new photographs were so popular that Mumler was able to charge a staggering $10 per spirit photograph, in contrast to a photograph only of the living, which might cost as little as 25 cents. Mrs Mumler, who conveniently enough was a practising medium, assisted her husband in his studio, entering into trance states as needed, while Mumler's camera was said to dance about if the spirits were willing.

All went well, with numerous successful sittings of living and dead, including Mumler's pinnacle of spirit visitation when the widow of Abraham Lincoln, apparently incognito, came for a sitting in 1872 and her dead husband made an appearance on the plate as it was developed. (See plate section.) All went well, that is, until a spiritualist lecturer happened to recognize the spirit in one of Mumler's prints as someone they knew, someone who was very much alive. Mumler moved to New York and opened another studio, but there too doubts mounted, until he was arrested for fraud. At his trial, Mumler defended himself by using the analogy of the tele-graph. If there had been no response when Morse sent his first message in code, he said, today we would say there had been a tech-nical problem, not that he was perpetrating a fraud. So too Mumler claimed he was simply working with new technology, and if someone failed to recognize the spirit who had manifested in their photo-graph, or recognized a spirit as a person who was alive, not dead, well, those kinds of problems were to be expected with such advanced systems.[21] Mumler was acquitted, not because the jury accepted his argument, but because the prosecution could not say how his images had been produced. Professional photographers at the time offered several possibilities, but the inability to point to one with any certainty was fatal to the case. The most likely way was that before a sitting Mumler briefly exposed a plate. Once he had the living sitter in front of him, he used the same plate for the full time period, creating a double exposure, with one faint image and one strong. Another possibility was that paper or tissue cut-outs were superim-posed on the image afterwards; or that a second figure moved out of shot halfway through the exposure; or the spirit sitter might have been photographed behind glass, the living sitter in front. (The last two would have meant the living sitters were aware that the spirits were not real, and there appears to be no evidence that they partici-pated knowingly in the imposture.)

Notwithstanding the publicity of Mumler's trial and a similar fraud prosecution of a photographer in France in 1875, spirit photography thrived in Europe.[22] By this time, photographers and mediums were accustomed to joining forces, the photographers finding new and inventive ways to produce images of the medium's own new and inventive projections such as ectoplasm. These prints were then sold by both parties for mutual profit. For many, this additional revenue stream became part of the spiritualist narrative. Georgiana Houghton, who had mounted an unsuccessful exhib-ition of spirit drawings, was told by her 'spirit counsellors' to go instead to the studio of the photographer Frederick Hudson, who was already in business with a medium named Mrs Guppy, where, she marvelled, they were able to produce a number of spirit photographs that 'many of [her] friends' asked to buy, and 'which Mr. Hudson let [her] have on professional terms'. She also later published them in a book. The spirits were remarkably commercially minded, too, in one case relaying new technical methods of processing photographs to Hudson via Mrs Guppy, accompanied by a warning that the spirit would spoil all the plates if the secret formula were to be revealed.[23]

Not all spirit photography was publicized, or for sale. Florence Cook (1856–1904) was one of the most successful mediums of the mid-1870s. By this date, it was common for mediums to operate with a single spirit guide, known as a control, who participated regularly at their seances. These were not the spirits of the dead whom those attending the seance wanted to contact, but rather tutelary spirits who acted as conduits to transmit messages in both directions. A medium named Frank Herne had had a successful career with his spirit guide John King, supposedly in life the pirate-turned-Governor of Jamaica, Henry Morgan. (Why the spirit had a different afterlife name is not clear.) When Florence Cook, the daughter of a prosperous middle-class Church-of-England-attending suburban London family, began to channel the spirits in her teens, her spirit guide was Katie King, the spirit daughter of John King/ Henry Morgan. Soon Cook's mediumistic powers gained much public interest owing to her connection to Sir William Crookes, a distinguished man of science who had discovered the element thallium and produced foundational work on vacuum tubes, essential to both chemistry and physics. He also discovered Florence Cook and promoted her career, arranging a number of seances for her in 1873 and 1874.

The standard format for Cook's seances was for her to have one of those present tie her to a chair in her spirit cabinet, a small enclosed space with partition walls but no ceiling that sat in the room selected for the seance. She then fell into a trance, at which

'Katie King', the control of medium Florence Cook, as photographed by Sir William Crookes.

point her control, Katie King, emerged, dressed in white with a white turban on her head, to walk around the room and interact with the evening's participants. Sir William claimed that he had proof of the veracity of Cook and King, having connected Cook to 'a mild galvanic current' with an attached galvanometer, which he said would have sounded an alarm if the medium had left the spirit cabinet. The reports of these seances are contradictory, some saying the galvanized King frequently failed to appear, or that if she did, she was visibly Cook, just wearing a turban. The popular clergyman H.W. Haweis, however, preached of his belief in this 'materialized form that appeared apart from the medium, and moved about the room freely while a continuous current of electricity was being passed through the entranced medium'. It was only 'scientific bigotry' that encouraged doubters, he added bitterly. That, and perhaps what Haweis referred to as Crookes' 'abnormal photos'. Crookes had taken dozens of photographs of King as she promenaded at the seance, but he described just two, and none was published in his lifetime. After his death his family, worrying about his posthumous reputation, destroyed as many as they could. A few have survived, and the strong resemblance between the medium and the spirit gives a good guess as to why Crookes kept them to himself.[24]

About a century before the processes that led to portrait photography had been invented, the eighteenth-century essayist, critic and lexicographer Samuel Johnson attempted to explain what he saw as the function of portraits. For him they were 'employed in diffusing friendship, in reviving tenderness, in quickening the affections of the absent, and *in continuing the presence of the dead*' (my italics).[25] Pictures last far longer than people, and have more constancy. In pictures no one goes grey, nor bald, nor gets wrinkles; they keep our young selves alive long after those actual selves have vanished. In 1891, Oscar Wilde turned this idea into a fable of eternal friendship and homoerotic love via a portrait in his only novel, *The Picture of Dorian Gray*. In this tale, a painter infatuated by the young Dorian paints his portrait as he is in the full flower of his youth and beauty. As Dorian begins to age, he sells his soul to stay young and beautiful. Assured that his looks will never wither, he embarks on a life of increasing depravity, which does not mark his face, but only the face on the canvas, now hidden from sight, which depicts the true image of his soul, corrupted and blackened by sin. Dorian, by not ageing, is not really alive; his portrait, which does alter, is therefore not really an inanimate object.[26] Is one, or are both, a revenant, a ghost – a vampire, even, drawing on the vitality of others to stay 'alive'?

Fiction, from Mary Shelley's *Frankenstein* onwards, used monsters and vampires to explore the meaning of death, and the human urge to outrun it. When Frankenstein plans to create a new human who will not die, he begins by gathering the body parts of the dead. The Creature from which they are produced is not dead, but is also not really alive, and thus is 'my own vampire'. He is life literally made flesh: we are all the walking dead, made up of (future) corpse parts. In the 1847 penny-blood *Sweeney Todd*, which quickly became a popular melodrama, a pie-shop owner turns the bodies of those killed by her murderous neighbouring barber into dinner, the dead ingested by the living. This was a running theme in the nineteenth century, not just in fiction, but in everyday life: whether via miasma theory, whereby the living breathed in the 'dust' of the dead, which in turn made them sick and then killed them; or by the resurrectionists who physically brought the dead back to the land of the living to recycle their body parts.

These fictional characters, who were neither quite dead nor quite alive, appeared just as families and medical practitioners grew increasingly worried about the liminal state where patients might, or might not, be dead. The slow transmission of news could also create a situation where people were dead in one place and alive in another. In 1871, when the Prince of Wales was dangerously ill with typhoid, the Reverend Francis Kilvert, in Wales, fretted one Sunday: 'We do not know whether the Prince of Wales is alive or dead. Contradictory telegrams have been flying about, and we did not know whether to mention the Prince's name in the Litany or not ... [When the vicar] came to the petition in the Litany for the Royal Family he made a solemn pause and in a low voice prayed "that it may please Thee (if he still survive) to bless Albert Edward Prince of Wales." ... [T]his suspense between life and death is terribly sad.'[27] Sad, and frightening.

The most famous undead of all, the Transylvanian count who moves to England, appeared at the very end of the century, but he almost had a precursor. Dracula's ship ran aground at Whitby, in North Yorkshire. Half a century before him, also in Yorkshire, in Emily Brontë's *Wuthering Heights*, the servant Nelly Dean finds

Heathcliff lying dead: 'His eyes met mine, so keen and fierce . . . then, he seemed to smile. I could not think him dead . . . I tried to close his eyes . . . they seemed to sneer at my attempts, and his parted lips, and sharp, white teeth sneered too!'[28] How similar to the description of Dracula: 'The mouth . . . was fixed and rather cruel-looking, with peculiarly sharp white teeth . . .'[29] More importantly, the themes that interested Stoker, such as life and death being on a continuum, rather than opposite states of being, had other sources. As an Irishman, he may well have been thinking of the *sidhe* of folktales, the Irish people of the burial mounds, who were said to lure the young away from their families to live with them under-ground in a state of perpetual living death, as Dracula does with Lucy Westenra.[30] At the same time, Dracula, this ancient of days who cannot die, is also connected in Stoker's tale with modernity: Dr Seward first records his case notes onto a phonograph, which Mina types out for him. Once more we have the mysterious ability to hear the voices of those who are dead; and now they are also rendered into print without the intermediary of publisher or printer, but merely by the newfangled typewriter, which enables copies to be disseminated and the dead to speak even to those they do not know and whom they are not haunting.

The stark binary – living or dead – of the twentieth and twenty-first century was far from clear in the nineteenth. For many, the born, the unborn, the dead and the undead were always present. And it was not always easy to tell one from the other.

12

FROM THE BOY WHO NEVER GREW UP
TO THE WOMAN WHO LIVED
WITH THE DEAD

In 1904, a boy flew into a West End theatre, a child who embodied many of the ideas around death and dying that have been explored in this book. His name was Peter Pan, 'the boy who never grew up'. How we look at Peter Pan today, from his later incarnations and how he was understood by his contemporaries, is one way of understanding how our attitudes to death, and to life, have altered. For us, he is the epitome of childhood innocence and freedom, the incarnation of endless possibility as he spends his days playing and doing whatever he chooses in the moment. It is less certain that this was always the case.

J.M. Barrie (1860–1937) produced his first version of Peter Pan in 1902, in a novel called *The Little White Bird*. That Peter is a baby, only seven days old, who, 'like all infants', can fly. He flies out of his nursery and ends up in Kensington Gardens, where he decides to live with the fairies who come out at night after the gates are locked. In his next incarnation, in the theatre two years later, Barrie produced a Peter who was somewhat older, perhaps reaching pre-pubescence, although he gives no firm details. In his third outing, in a novel Barrie published in 1911, Peter still has all his milk teeth, and so must be around five or six years old. That Peter is described as wearing clothes made out of skeleton leaves, but all three Peters are bringers of death: like an epidemic, The Boy Who Never Grew Up scythes his way through the nursery of the Darling family. Peter's visits leave empty beds behind for devastated parents to find after their children have flown off to Neverland, the place where babies who fall out of their prams end up, together with those older children who wandered away while their nannies were not paying attention, none of them ever to be seen again. Clothes made from skeleton leaves, vanished children, empty beds and prams – the adventures in Neverland are adventures in the afterworld, because what is death, asks Peter, but 'an awfully big adventure'?

Peter Pan is death personified, because the only children who never grow up are children who are dead. There were tens, if not hundreds, of thousands who had experienced the death of a child who would have agreed that a dead child was a permanent child. J.M. Barrie knew this at first hand. When he was six, his fourteen-year-old brother died in a skating accident, a loss from which his mother never recovered. The child Barrie attempted to fill his brother's place for her by wearing his older brother's clothes and mimicking his voice in her hearing; she in turn found comfort that her dead son, like Peter, would never grow up, never lose his innocence, would always be a child in her mind.

By the time of Peter Pan's appearance in theatres, the public was well accustomed to thinking about eternal life. Apart from their individual concerns with death and its accompaniments, the arts had become obsessed with the dead and the undead. Every bit as popular as Dracula was the adventure-writer H. Rider Haggard's *She*, published in 1886/7. This was a wildly successful novel of jingoist imperial adventures in Africa, one that sold an average of a million copies a year for the next three-quarters of a century. In it, a trio of Englishmen follow a series of cryptic clues from Cambridge to Africa, where they are taken captive by a local tribe under the rule of a 2,000-year-old queen. This immortal ruler is Ayesha, the 'She' of the book's title, who lives in a tomb, sleeping beside the embalmed corpse of her one true love whom she murdered in a fit of jealousy 2,000 years before. When the Englishmen are brought into her presence she sees in one of them the reincarnation of this lost love.

Enchanted with his looks, and enchanting him in turn, she brings him to the Pillar of Fire that rendered her immortal, so that he can remain with her for all eternity. To allay his fears over this awful trial, she enters the fire first, but a second immersion destroys her, transforming her first into the 2,000-year-old woman she actually is, before she crumbles to dust.

So far, so far-fetched. But the modern reader might ask if Haggard drew on a person closer to home. By the time of publication Queen Victoria had reigned, if not for 2,000 years, for half a century, having ascended the throne two decades before Haggard's birth. Victoria, as is well known, mourned her lost husband from his early death at the age of forty-two, in 1861, until her own in 1901. She mourned ostentatiously, withdrawing from public life for five years, forever after dressing entirely in black and carrying out her duties grudgingly. 'She was their Queen, but she appeared very rarely, perhaps once in two or three years': is this a description of Ayesha or Victoria?[1]

The eternal, the immortal queen, in perpetual mourning. Victoria, like many in the nineteenth century that we have read about, found solace in thinking and reading about those she had lost. She also found the paraphernalia surrounding death to be a comfort. She and Albert had been the driving forces behind the elevation of the Duke of Wellington's funeral from a grand state occasion to the over-orchestrated orgy of pomp it became. Victoria herself had wanted the entire army to go into mourning. Not court mourning, nor complimentary mourning. Victoria wanted the army to be reclothed as if they had lost a member of their own family.[2] After the funeral she wrote to her uncle, Leopold I of the Belgians, 'how very touching' it had all been. '*What* a deep and *whemtühige* [a misspelling of *wehmütige*, poignant] impression it made on me! It was a beautiful sight! In the Cathedral it was more touching still!'[3] (That she was not present in the cathedral seems not to have dimmed her conviction, much less her enthusiasm.) It was not only funerals she enjoyed. Like many of her subjects, she was passionately interested in the medical details of her family's last days, asking in 1837 for the 'painfully interesting' details of the final illness of William IV.[4] In 1860, she and Albert visited Albert's childhood home in Coburg to view the mausoleum he and his brother had designed for their father in the 1840s. She found it 'cheerful', and commissioned a summerhouse that resembled the mausoleum for her mother, as well as planning a second one for her own family's use.[5]

After her mother's death in 1861, she and Albert read the Reverend William Branks' *Heaven Our Home* together. This very successful book had been published a few months before, and achieved great popularity with the reading public, promising as it did that all would ultimately meet in the '*eternal home of love*', where we would '*recognise*' our friends and family. Until then, Branks assured his readers that the dead kept up a '*deep* and *glowing* and *unquenchable* interest' in the activities of the living.[6] (The good clergyman appeared to enjoy italics as much as the queen did.) Certainly, her mother's death was not easy for Victoria. Mother and daughter had had periods of estrangement, and feelings of guilt provoked a deep depression in the already depressively inclined queen. She refused to join her family for meals, staying in her rooms alone. She went out only to attend ceremonies to mark events in her mother's life, such as a memorial birthday.[7]

Thus, when her own husband died nine months later, she was entirely overcome and unable to function. Albert had been ailing for at least two years, and was visibly ill to everyone except the queen, who steadfastly refused to believe in the seriousness of his chronic stomach trouble. In December 1861 he became bedridden, and the doctors pronounced typhoid fever. For much of his final illness, the queen continued to believe he would recover, and so his death, when it came on 14 December 1861, was not merely a great loss – it was also a great shock.

The depression she had suffered nine months before was nothing compared to her current state. She told her family and ministers that she was as good as dead. She required the deepest mourning for the court. She withdrew physically from all (except some of) her children, notably excluding Bertie, the Prince of Wales, for whom she had never felt much affection, repeating the Hanoverian pattern of terrible relations between monarch and heir. She decided that Bertie had caused his father's death, either through the (unlikely) possibility that Albert had caught typhoid on a trip to see Bertie to upbraid him for a recent escapade of lax, possibly immoral behaviour, or that that behaviour had caused Albert so much anxiety that he had been unable to rally from an otherwise survivable illness (even less likely). She disregarded all matters of state; she refused for years afterwards to perform the most basic of her duties, such as presiding at the state opening of parliament. For the first decade after Albert's death she was, at best, undergoing a major psychological breakdown. Her physician, William Jenner, as late as 1871 thought that what were referred to as her 'nerves' – which expressed themselves as bouts of hysterical weeping, fits of rage and intermittent panic – 'were a form of madness'.*[8]

Her religion became Albert worship. She began to use capital letters for pronouns when writing of him (Him). She had casts made of Albert's hands and face after his death, and referred to them as 'sacred relics'. She had post-mortem photographs taken and attached to the head of her bed in each of her bedrooms, so that she would lie beneath his image, almost as if it were a religious icon. One of the many portraits of him that she commissioned had the prince receiving a halo in place of his earthly crown (which, to her fury, he had never achieved, as she had never been able to talk the government into raising him from a prince consort to a king).[9] She

---

* It is notable that modern psychological checklists for a tendency to extreme, chronic and abnormal grieving include: being female; having a history of mood disorders; low perceived support from social equals; insecure attachment style, such as poor relationships with parents or children; pessimistic temperament; losing a parent in childhood; sudden death; the griever's own young age. Victoria ticked every one of these boxes, and she herself made the connection to the death of her own father when she was an infant: 'The poor fatherless baby of eight months is now the utterly broken-hearted and crushed widow of forty-two!'

began the construction of a mausoleum at Frogmore, in the grounds of Windsor Castle, and efficiently ordered an effigy of herself at the same time, so that on her own death the couple would be aligned in age and style, remaining a matched set.[10] When the mausoleum was complete, she used the verb 'translate' when talking about moving Albert's remains to it, a word more commonly used to refer to moving the relics of a saint.

Victoria also established a secular shrine, one that supposed that the definitely dead man continued to be alive. It is commonly said that the queen had ordered Albert's bedroom to be preserved exactly as it had been in his lifetime, with the clock and his watch kept wound, hot shaving water brought up daily, his clothes laid out several times a day for him to change into, his gloves set out on the table as if he had just stepped in from outdoors. However, Albert had not died in his own bedroom. In his final illness he had frequently been delirious and he wandered at night from room to room, happening on his final walk to end up in the room where both George IV and William IV had died. This suited the queen's need to mythologize, and, having been unable to persuade the country or her ministers to make Albert a king, she could present to the court the status she had desired for him by virtue of his dying in the room where past kings had died. Even so, the decor was given additional elements of homage: regularly refreshed mourning wreaths were laid out on the beds; a portrait bust of Albert was installed; his personal items were transferred from his dressing room and laid out as if for use, even as new washstand china was ordered for the dead man's ablutions.[11]

Today it is often assumed that Queen Victoria's prolonged grieving was characteristic of the age and was considered admirable by her contemporaries. Neither of these statements is true. Her adoption of perpetual mourning dress was a choice made by many widows, but certainly not by all. The wife of a textile manufacturer whose husband died in the year of Victoria's accession wore black for a number of years, as was customary, and then turned to fabrics that included 'white embroidered muslins . . . blue-and-white striped silk, [and] purple-checked cotton and gold damask': hardly our conception of a nineteenth-century widow.[12] Victoria was stubborn in her grief, however. Those concerned with matters of state thought that she was using her loss as an excuse to do exactly what she wanted to do, and to not do whatever she did not want to do. At least in part, the queen herself knew this, as the confused reasoning in a letter she wrote to Lord Russell, the prime minister, shows. Five years after Albert's death, she continued to refuse to attend the state opening of parliament. She wrote, referring to herself in the third person, as was her custom: 'That the public should wish to see her she fully understands, and has no wish to prevent – quite the contrary; but why this wish should be of so unreasonable and unfeeling a nature, as to long to witness the spectacle of a poor, broken-hearted widow . . . dragged in deep mourning, alone in State as a Show . . . to be gazed at without delicacy of feeling, is a thing that she can't understand.'[13] As far as it can be untangled, Victoria was saying she could entirely understand the reasonable desire of the people that she should attend to matters of state, even as she could not understand how they could be so unreasonable as to expect her to attend to matters of state.

Alexandra of Denmark, engaged to the Prince of Wales, arrived in Britain some fifteen months after Albert's death. Victoria felt that a festive greeting from a mourning populace would be unseemly, and so sent a coach for her entry into London that was so old and shabby her ministers were ashamed. (Another even less generous, but still plausible, interpretation of the gesture was that she did not want the arrival of the last royal fiancé, Albert himself more than two decades previously, to be overshadowed.) At the wedding, held at St George's Chapel, Windsor, instead of Westminster Abbey, to accommodate the queen's mourning, Victoria refused to doff her widow's weeds for the ceremony as custom and etiquette dictated, nor would she join the wedding party, but sequestered herself in the Royal Closet above the altar, like a ghost at the feast, faithfully replicated by the artist

The happy couple: the wedding portrait of the Prince of Wales and
Princess Alexandra, with Queen Victoria and a bust of Prince Albert.

William Powell Frith. (See plate section.) She also decreed that none
of her children should divest themselves of their mourning, also
against custom, and insisted that not only should they wear half-
mourning, but that they should wear it for another full year – three
years after their father's death – before extending that later to five
years for some of her daughters.

Even more gloom-laden was the official portrait taken of the sovereign with the newly wedded heir to the throne and his bride. Instead of a standard photograph of the happy couple, the queen drew on the tradition of mourning photographs where the bereaved hold pictures of their lost loved ones. Bertie and Alexandra stand, looking rather nonplussed, neither touching nor looking at each other, with the queen between them but ostentatiously turned away from both to stare grimly at a bust of the groom's dead father, her lost beloved. Jane Carlyle spoke for many of the population when she wrote that she sympathized with the new Princess of Wales 'in the prospect of the bother she will have by and by with that mean-natured, half distracted Queen'.[14]

Others who had undergone similar, or far worse, losses were no more sympathetic. Mrs Oliphant, who had seen her husband and all of her children die, wrote, some quarter-century after Albert's death: 'I doubt whether *nous autres* poor women who have had to fight with the world all alone without much sympathy from anybody, can quite enter into the "unprecedented" character of the Queen's sufferings. A woman is surely a poor creature if with a large, happy affectionate family of children around her she can't take heart to do her duty whether she likes it or not. *We* have to do it, with very little solace, and I don't see that there is anybody particularly sorry for us.'[15]

But Victoria could not 'take heart to do her duty'. Instead she channelled Albert, becoming the sole conduit for what he would have said, done or wanted. Before the marriage of the Prince of Wales, she took the couple to his tomb and said, 'He gives you his blessing', joining their hands over his grave.[16] She also participated in the contemporary pastimes of table-turning, rapping and other spiritualist practices.

But the currency of Albert worship was most visibly expressed through objects. Victoria had always had an intense connection to her own possessions, which became more extreme after she was widowed. Unlike most women of the time, she neither gave away her old clothes nor had them refashioned, but instead stored what ultimately turned out to be nearly seventy years' worth of items. She kept her childhood china, and her children's childhood china. She kept her children's baby teeth, which she had turned into jewellery. (The infant Beatrice's milk teeth make the stamens of earrings and a pendant designed to look like fuchsia, see plate section.)

More than that, she ordered that 'Every piece of plate and china, every picture, chair, table ornament and articles of the most trivial description' be photographed from multiple angles, the photographs then bound up in ledgers which she liked to look over several times a week. Notes were made of the date each object was acquired, how and by whom, and where it was located. Once something was in place, it was not allowed to be moved: that was where it belonged for evermore, as if by cataloguing and freezing her possessions in time, she could control the world around her. All the rooms in her residences had small cards at the thresholds, noting that everything in that particular room had been selected and arranged by Albert. Hangings, curtains, carpets and other textiles were copied, so that when they wore out or faded, they could be replaced without any discernible change.[17]

As many people did, the queen had numerous pieces of her husband's hair made into jewellery, of which nearly a dozen pieces are known. She also commissioned portraits for lockets and other jewellery, as well as copies of the casts of Albert's face and arm, and portrait busts, to be given away to friends, family and government ministers. Initially Victoria had had an ambivalent relationship with some of the objects, refusing to look at the death mask made immediately after Albert's death, even as she would not 'allow the sacred cast . . . to go out of the house'.[18] She wore other pieces, such as the bracelet containing Albert's portrait and his hair, every day. More than thirty years after his death the bracelet one day snapped, and despite a jeweller being summoned immediately, in the few hours before it was repaired and back on her wrist, recorded one observer, she remained in a heightened state of 'unhappiness and anxiety'.[19]

These memorial lockets and jewels were a continuation of the virtual shrines that were her own suites of rooms in each of her residences. An anonymous member of the royal household described them in the 1890s. The queen's Windsor sitting room contained a life-sized portrait of Albert by one of her favourite painters, Franz Xaver Winterhalter; another by sentimental favourite Sir Edwin Landseer, with the prince dressed in shooting costume; a 'little' picture of him with his brother, and a portrait of him in historical costume for a fancy-dress ball. In her bedroom there were two portraits of the dead prince as a child, a sketch of the queen 'garbed as a nun' receiving a vision of Albert, a portrait of Victoria's mother, as well as 'a pictorial recollection of her [mother's] room, and the sofa on which she died'. There were, says this report, 231 portraits in the queen's private rooms, none of which depicted her daughters-in-law, her sons-in-law or her grandchildren. Other residences contained life-sized statues of Albert before which fresh wreaths were laid ceremonially on the queen's orders, including one in the grounds of Balmoral, where 'her family and Court, her servants and tenantry' gathered on the prince's birthday every year. Victoria enjoyed marking commemorative days: Albert's birthday; his death day, which she spent in total seclusion; her mother's birthday and death day; and so on. Until her own death, she remained consumed by the minutiae of mourning: state papers were returned unsigned if the black border on them was not sufficiently wide, while as late as 1897 her maids of honour were forbidden to wear mauve, a very ordinary half-mourning colour, because she felt it was too close to pink, the cheerfulness of which she decreed to be unseemly.[20]

The queen's death fixation was not solely focused around Albert, her mother or even her own family. One of her ladies-in-waiting wrote that she took 'the keenest interest in death and all its horrors, our whole talk has been of coffins and winding sheets'. She enjoyed discussing the funeral of a servant ('overdone', remarked the lady-in-waiting, and 'very trying for the Household'). At Balmoral she went to lay a wreath on the tomb of her old dresser. It was not even necessary that she have any acquaintance with the dead. One holiday in France saw her attending the funeral of a soldier who had died of consumption while she was staying nearby. '[T]he Queen really enjoys these melancholy entertainments,' wrote a bystander.[21]

Victoria was eighty-one when she died. By dying in January 1901, she could be said to have seen the old 'Victorian' century die. She too lay in state, first in her bedroom at Osborne, on the Isle of Wight, where she was viewed by her family and servants. Her son, the new king, did not share her enjoyment of death and death rituals. When his own son had died at birth, thirty years earlier, he said, 'I think it is one's duty not to nurse one's sorrow, however much one may feel it.'[22] Now, on the death of the woman whom many had long called 'the old queen', sacred pictures and flowers were scattered around her coffin as it was moved from her bedroom to the dining room, from private to public, old style. The family and servants were joined by members of the community, now also with the addition of journalists into the mix.

The age of death, dying and mourning was itself dead. The age of celebrity had arrived, the age of silver-screen death. Now grief and mourning were less and less public, outward-facing community events. Twentieth-century death was to become mechanized – witness the mass slaughter of the killing fields of World War I – but it was also to become a personal, inward emotion, shared only with family or close friends. The 'old queen' and her forty years of ostentatious grieving were to be replaced by the twentieth century's byword, individualism.

Acknowledgements

Working in a world of Covid closures, I am grateful, and astonished, to be able to record a whole new level of scholarly cooperation, as offprints and downloads are traded like the precious commodities they are.

For assistance, information and advice, I am grateful to Karin J. Bohleke, Dagni Bredesen, Dr Richard Cruess and the late Dr Sylvia Cruess, Heather Fitzsimmons Frey, Tony Gee, Sean Grass, Christopher Guyver, Audrey Jaffe, Leslie Katz, Christine Maiocco, Daniel Monk, Sara E. Murphy, Heather Nelson, Lee O'Brien, Peter Orford, Carolyn Oulton, Samantha Perrin, Ruth Richardson and Sarah Ross.

Some of the above are virtual colleagues, members of the Victoria 19th-century British Culture & Society mailbase, and I would once again like to record my debt of gratitude both to the list members, and most especially to Patrick Leary, who as listmaster creates and maintains both the content and the atmosphere of this haven of scholarly collegiality.

I can be only one of the many who owe a particular debt of gratitude to the London Library, whose heroic efforts to keep members supplied with books during the Covid shutdowns made this book possible. I am grateful to [*name redacted to protect the guilty*], who gave me their sign-in to their institutional library so that I could read material online that had suddenly become entirely inaccessible in the non-virtual world. I also thank the British Library, the Wellcome Collection and the National Libraries of Scotland, whose collections I later accessed in a more legitimate fashion.

As always, I must thank my agent, Bill Hamilton of A.M. Heath, and my editor, Ravi Mirchandani, both of whom before this particular book found its feet dealt with my vacillations and what felt like weekly subject changes with remarkable good humour and equanimity. Georgina Morley, Rosie Shackles, Robina Pelham Burn and Nicholas Blake, Helen Hughes, Connor Hutchinson, Lindsay Nash and Stuart Wilson at Picador saw the book through the publication process with consummate professionalism and kindness, and have my gratitude.

I began work on this book on death and dying before Covid first emerged, and it only gained resonance as the full force of the pandemic became apparent. My mother devoted her life to the provision of palliative care for the dying, but neither I nor my sisters could ever have expected to find ourselves nursing her on her own deathbed as millions died around the world. To the three of them, this book is dedicated.

Bibliography

Owing to Covid and library closures, and the virtually samizdat sharing of material, online and off, some material may have been incompletely catalogued online and therefore may have a less than complete bibliographic entry here.

Primary sources

Anon., 'The Cemetery. A Brief Appeal to the Feelings of Society on Behalf of Extra-Mural Burial', 'Report from the Dissection Committee', *Monthly Magazine*, vol. 6, no. 34, pp. 337–46

—, *The Cemetery. A Brief Appeal to the Feelings of Society on Behalf of Extra-Mural Burial* (London, William Pickering, 1848)

—, 'The Derby Mourning & Funeral Warehouse' (Derby, Bemrose and Sons, printers, [*c*.1876])

—, 'Dialogues of the Dead. On Sepulchral Rites and Rights', *Fraser's Magazine*, vol. 6, no. 36, 1832, pp. 728–46

—, *Etiquette for Ladies and Gentlemen* (London, Frederick Warne, 1876)

—, *Etiquette for Ladies and Gentlemen, including the Etiquette of Weddings* (London, Frederick Warne, [n.d.])

—, 'Extramural Burial. The Three Schemes: I. The London Clergy Plan; II. The Board of Health or Erith Plan; III. The Woking Necropolis Plan' (London, Effingham Wilson, 1850)

—, *Fairburn's Edition of the Funeral of Admiral Lord Nelson* (London, John Fairburn, [1806])

—, *Manners and Rules of Good Society* (15th ed., London, Frederick Warne & Co., 1888)

—, *Mixing in Society: A Complete Manual of Manners*, 'by The Right Hon. the Countess of ***' (London, George Routledge and Sons, 1870)

—, 'Modes des Mantelets' nos. 247 & 249 (London, The London General Mourning Warehouse [Jay's], [*c*.1847])

—, *Monumenta, or, Designs for Tombs, Wall Monuments, Head-Stones, Grave-Crosses, &c.* (London, J. Hagger, 1868)

—, 'Notices Historical and Miscellaneous concerning Mourning Apparel &c. in England' ([London, n.p., *c*.1850])

—, 'Our Mourning Customs. Three Articles Reprinted from the "Inquirer"' (London, E.T. Whitfield, [1850?])

—, *The Private Life of the Queen*, by 'A Member of the Royal Household' (New York, D. Appleton, 1897)

—, 'Prospectus of a New Joint-Stock Company. The London Suicide Company', *Bentley's Miscellany*, vol. 1, no. 6, 1839, pp. 540–42, reprinted in *The Cambridge University Magazine* as 'The London Suicide Company', vol. 1, 1840, pp. 460–63; 'First Report of the London Suicide Company', ibid., pp. 463–69

—, *A Remedy for Self-Murder. Suggested in a Letter to a Friend* (London, Wilson, 1819)

—, 'Sanatory Progress: Being the Fifth Report of the National Philanthropic Association . . . for the Promotion of Social and Salutiferous Improvements' ([1842], 2nd ed., London, J. Hatchard and Son, 1850)

—, *The Whole Duty of Woman, or, A Guide to the Female Sex . . . Shewing Women . . . How to Behave themselves for Obtaining Not Only Present but Future Happiness*, 'By a Lady', (Stourbridge, Heming and Tallis, 1815)

Acorn, George, *One of the Multitude* (London, William Heinemann, 1911)

Andrews, William, *Curious Church Customs and Cognate Subjects* (Hull, William Andrews & Co., 1895)

Arbuthnot, Mrs, *The Journal of Mrs Arbuthnot*, eds. Francis Bamford and the Duke of Wellington (London, Macmillan & Co., 1950)

Atkinson, Rev. J.C., *Forty Years in a Moorland Parish: Reminiscences and Researches in Danby in Cleveland* (London, Macmillan and Co., 1891)

Bailey, James Blake, *The Diary of a Resurrectionist, 1811–1812* (London, Swan Sonnenschein & Co., 1896)

Barrie, J.M., *The Little White Bird* (London, Hodder and Stoughton, 1902)

—, *Peter Pan in Kensington Gardens* (London, Hodder and Stoughton, 1912)

[Basset, Josiah], *The Life of a Vagrant, or, The Testimony of an Outcast to the Value and Truth of the Gospel* (London, Charles Gilpin, [1850])

[Beckett, Charles], *My First Grief: or, Recollections of a Beloved Sister, by a Provincial Surgeon* (Bath, Binns and Goodwin, [1852])

Benham, Rev. William, *Catharine and Craufurd Tait . . . A Memoir* (London, Macmillan & Co., 1881)

Bennett, Alfred Rosling, *London and Londoners in the Eighteen-fifties and Sixties* (London, T. Fisher Unwin, 1924)

Blair, Robert, 'The Grave. A Poem' (3rd ed., London, J. Waugh, 1749)

Blakeborough, Richard, *Wit, Character, Folklore and Customs in the North Riding of Yorkshire* (London, Henry Frowde, 1898)

Blanchard, [Samuel] Laman, *The Cemetery at Kensal Green: The Grounds & Monuments* (London, Cunningham & Mortimer, [1843])

[Brontë, Charlotte], *Jane Eyre: An Autobiography*, 'edited by Currer Bell' (Leipzig, Bernhard Tauchnitz Jun., 1848)

Brontë, Emily, *Wuthering Heights*, 'edited by Ellis Bell', with Acton Bell [Anne Brontë], *Agnes Grey*, a new edition (London, Smith, Elder & Co., 1858)

Brooke, Rev J. Ingham, 'A Lecture of Burial Reform' (London, J. Masters, 1879)

Browning, Robert, 'Mr Sludge, "the Medium"', in *Dramatis Personae* (2nd ed., London, Chapman and Hall, 1864)

Burn, James Dawson, *The Autobiography of a Beggar Boy*, ed. David Vincent ([1855], London, Europa, 1978)

Burne, Charlotte Sophia, ed., from the Collections of Georgina F. Jackson, *Shropshire Folklore: A Sheaf of Gleanings* (London, Trübner & Co., 1883)

Butler, Samuel, *The Way of all Flesh* (1873–84, published 1903)

Campbell, Lady Colin, *Etiquette of Good Society* (London, Cassell, 1893)

Cansick, Frederick Teague, *A Collection of Curious and Interesting Epitaphs copied from the monuments of Distinguished and Noted Characters in the Ancient Church and Burial Grounds of Saint Pancras* (London, J. Russell Smith, 1869)

Carleton, William, *The Autobiography of William Carleton* ([1896], London, MacGibbon & Kee, 1968)

Carlyle, Thomas and Jane Welsh, *The Collected Letters of Thomas and Jane Welsh Carlyle*, ed. Charles Richard Sanders, 37 vols. (Durham, NC, Duke University Press, 1970), online at https://carlyleletters.dukeupress.edu/home

Cassell's Household Guide (London, Cassell, Petter and Galpin, 1869); ibid., 1877; ibid (London, Waverley Book Co., 1911)

Chadwick, Edwin, *A Supplementary Report on the Results of a Spiecal [sic] Inquiry into the Practice of Interment in Towns* (London, Poor Law Commissioners, 1843)

Clark, Benjamin, *Hand-book for Visitors to the Kensal Green Cemetery* (London, Joseph Masters, 1843)

Coates, James, *Photographing the Invisible: Practical Studies in Supernormal Photography, Script and Other Allied Phenomena* (London, L.N. Fowler, [1922])

Coleridge, Sara, *Memoirs and Letters of Sara Coleridge, edited by Her Daughter* (2nd ed., London, Henry S. King, 1873)

Collison, George, *Cemetery Interment* (London, Longman, Orme, Brown, Green and Longman, 1840)

Cooper, Bransby Blake, *The Life of Sir Astley Cooper, Bart., Interspersed with Sketches from His Note-Books of Distinguished Contemporary Characters* (London, John W. Parker, 1843)

Courtauld Family Letters, 1782–1900 (Cambridge, privately printed, 1916)

Croft, H.J., *Guide to Kensal Green Cemetery* (rev. ed., London, C. & E. Layton, [1867])

Davey, Richard, *A History of Mourning* (London, Jay's [Mourning Warehouse], [1889])

Davies, Rev. Edwin, *Children in Heaven; or, Comfort for Bereaved Parents* (Belfast, William M'Comb, 1854)

Dickens, Charles, *The Adventures of Oliver Twist* (Boston, Ticknor and Fields, 1866)

—, *Bleak House* (London, Bradbury and Evans, 1853)

—, *A Christmas Carol, in Prose, being, A Ghost Story of Christmas* ([1843], London, Bradbury and Evans, [n.d.])

—, *Dealings with the Firm of Dombey and Son, Wholesale, Retail and for Exportation* (London, Bradbury and Evans, 1848)

—, *Great Expectations* (Boston, Estes and Lauriat, 1881)

—, *Little Dorrit* (London, Chapman and Hall, 1892)

—, *The Old Curiosity Shop* (London, Chapman and Hall, 1841)

—, *Our Mutual Friend* (London, Chapman and Hall, 1865)

—, *The Personal History and Experience of David Copperfield the Younger* (Leipzig, Bernhard Tauchnitz, 1849–50)

—, *The Posthumous Papers of the Pickwick Club* (London, Chapman and Hall, 1837)

—, *The Uncommercial Traveller* (2nd ed., London, Chapman and Hall, 1861)

—, 'Down with the Tide', *Household Words*, no. 150, 5 February 1853, pp. 481–5

—, 'From the Raven in the Happy Family', Part II, *Household Words*, no. 11, 8 June 1850, pp. 241–3

—, 'Trading in Death', *Household Words*, no. 140, 27 November 1852, pp. 241–5

—, 'The Uncommercial Traveller' [City Churchyards], *All the Year Round*, 18 July 1863, pp. 493–5

—, 'Wapping Workhouse', *All the Year Round*, 18 February 1860, pp. 392–3

—, and W.H. Wills, 'The Doom of English Wills', *Household Words*, Part I: no. 27, 28 September 1850, pp. 1–4; Part II: no. 28, 5 October 1850, pp. 25–9; Part III: W.H. Wills only: no. 32, 2 November 1850, pp. 125–8; Part IV: W.H. Wills only, no. 35, 23 November 1850, pp. 203–5

D'Israeli, Isaac, *A Second Series of Curiosities of Literature*: vol. 2: 'The History of the Skeleton of Death', 'The Book of Death' (London, John Murray, 1823)

Douglas, Mrs [Fanny], *The Gentlewoman's Book of Dress* (London, Henry and Co., [1895])

Dyer, Rev. T.F. Thistelton, *Domestic Folk-lore* (London, Cassell, Petter, Galpin & Co., [1881])

[East, Timothy], *Death Bed Scenes; or, The Christian's Companion; On Entering the Dark Valley* (London, Francis Westley, 1825)

Edwards, James, 'The Health of Towns. An Examination of the Report and Evidence of the Select Committee; of Mr MacKinnon's Bill and of the Acts for Establishing Cemeteries around the Metropolis' (London, House of Commons, 1843)

Ellis, Mrs [Sarah Stickney], *The Women of England, Their Social Duties and Domestic Habits* (London, Fisher, Son & Co., [1845])

Epps, John, *Diary of the Late John Epps, M.D. Edin.*, ed. 'by Mrs. Epps' (London, Kent & Co., [1875])

Fleming, Marjory, *The Complete Marjory Fleming: Her Journals, Letters & Verses*, ed. Frank Sidgwick (London, Sidgwick and Jackson, 1934)

Forster, John, *The Life of Charles Dickens* (London, Chapman and Hall, 1874)

Foster, D.B., 'Leeds Slumdon' (Leeds, C.H. Halliday, 1897)

Fox, W.J., 'On Suicide', in *Letters Addressed Chiefly to the Working Classes: Published from the Reporter's Notes* (London, 4 vols., C. Fox, 1844–6)

French, James Branwhite, *Walks in Abney Park* (London, James Clarke & Co., 1883)

'Fritz', *Where are the Dead?, or, Spiritualism Explained* (Manchester, A. Ireland, 1873)

Frost, Thomas, *Reminiscences of a Country Journalist* (London, Ward and Downey, 1886)

Furniss, Rev. J, *The House of Death*, Books for Children and Young Persons, no. VII (Dublin, James Duffy, 1860); *The Terrible Judgment and the Bad Child*, ibid., no. IX (Dublin, James Duffy, 1861); *The Sight of Hell*, no. X (Dublin, James Duffy, 1861)

Gaskell, Mrs [Elizabeth], *Ruth* (London, Chapman and Hall, 1853)

[Geering, Thomas], *Our Sussex Parish. A Medley. By One Who has Never Lived Out of It* (Lewes, 'Sussex Advertiser' Office, 1884)

Glendinning, Andrew, ed., *The Veil Lifted: Modern Developments in Spirit Photography* (London, Whittaker & Co., 1894)

Godwin, William, 'Essay on Sepulchres: or, A Proposal for Erecting Some Memorial of the Illustrious Dead in All Ages on the Spot Where their Remains Have been Interred' (London, W. Miller, 1809)

Gosse, Philip Henry, *A Memorial of the Last Days on Earth of Emily Gosse*, 'by her husband' (London, James Nisbet & Co., 1857)

Haggard, H. Rider, *She: A History of Adventure* (Leipzig, Bernhard Tauchnitz, 1887)

Hamley, Edward Bruce, *Lady Lee's Widowhood* (Edinburgh, William Blackwood and Sons, 1854)

[Hannay, James], 'Graves and Epitaphs', *Household Words*, no. 134, 16 October 1852, pp. 105–9

Hare, Augustus J.C., *Memorials of a Quiet Life* (2nd ed., London, Strahan & Co., 1872–6)

Hart, W., *Anti-Suicide, A Poem, (Sentimental and Argumentative) in Four Books; Tending to Display the Folly and Unlawfulness of Self-Murder* (London, Galabin, 1809)

Hartshorne, Albert, *Hanging in Chains* (London, T. Fisher Unwin, 1891)

Haweis, Rev. H.R., *Ashes to Ashes: A Cremation Prelude* (London, Daldy, Isbiter & Co., 1875)

Holmes, Mrs Basil, *The London Burial Grounds: Notes on their History from the Earliest Times to the Present Day* (London, T. Fisher Unwin, 1896)

Hood, Thomas, 'The House of Mourning: A Farce', *Hood's Magazine and Comic Miscellany*, vol. 1, Jan–June 1844, pp. 190–4

—, 'Jack Hall', in *The Complete Poetical Works of Thomas Hood* (New York, G. Putnam and Sons, 1869), vol. 3, pp. 270–9

Hopkinson, James, *Victorian Cabinet Maker. The Memoirs of James Hopkinson, 1819–1894*, ed. Jocelyne Baty Goodman (London, Routledge & Kegan Paul, 1968)

Houghton, Miss [Georgiana], *Chronicles of the Photographs of Spiritual Beings and Phenomena Invisible to the Material Eye, Interblended with Personal Narratives* (London, E.W. Allen 1882)

Hume-Rothery, Mrs [Mary Catherine], 'Anti-mourning. A Lecture against the Unchristian Custom of Wearing Mourning for the Dead' (revised ed., London, James Speirs, 1876)

Humphry, Mrs, '("Madge" of "Truth")', *Manners for Women* (London, Ward, Lock & Co., [1897])

Hunt, Leigh, 'Deaths of Little Children' (1820), in *Essays of Leigh Hunt*, ed. Reginald Brimley Johnson (London, J.M. Dent and Co., 1891)

James, Alice, *The Diary of Alice James*, ed. Leon Edel (New York, Dodd, Mead, 1964)

Kaines, Joseph, *Last Words of Eminent Persons, Comprising . . . a Brief Account of their Last Hours* (London, George Routledge & Sons, 1866)

Kelley, Philip, and Betty A. Coley, eds., *The Browning Collections: A Reconstruction with Other Memorabilia* (London, Mansell, 1984)

Kilvert, Rev. Francis, *Kilvert's Diary: Selections from the Diary of the Rev. Francis Kilvert*, ed. William Plomer (London, Jonathan Cape, 1938)

[Lamb, Thomas], 'Moriturus', 'On Burial Societies; and the Character of an Undertaker', *The Reflector: A Quarterly Magazine, on Subjects of Philosophy, Politics, and the Liberal Arts*, vol. 2 (London, John Hunt, 1811), pp. 140–44

Latham, Charlotte, 'Some West Sussex Superstitions Lingering in 1868', *The Folk-Lore Record*, vol. 1, 1878, pp. 160–75

Law, L.A., and W. Crooke, 'Death and Burial Customs in Wiltshire', *Folklore*, vol. 11, no. 3, 1900, pp. 344–7

Levy, Amy, *The Romance of a Shop* (London, T. Fisher Unwin, 1888)

[Leigh, Percival], 'Address from an Undertaker to the Trade', *Household Words*, no. 13, 22 June 1850, pp. 301–4

Logan, William, ed., *Words of Comfort for Parents Bereaved of Little Children* (5th ed., London, James Nisbet, 1868)

Loudon, J.C., *On the Laying Out, Planting and Managing of Cemeteries; and on the Improvement of Churchyards* (London, Longman, Brown, Green, and Longmans, 1843)

'Luigi', *Sweet Songs for Mourning Mothers* (London, J. Masters and Co., 1884)

Machen, Arthur, *The Great God Pan* (London, John Lane, 1894)

Mackenzie, William, 'An Appeal to the Public and to the Legislature, on the Necessity of Affording Dead Bodies to the Schools of Anatomy by Legislative Enactment' (Glasgow, Robertson & Atkinson, &c., 1824)

McQueen, William, 'Scotch Funerals', *Macmillan's Magazine*, vol. 46, May to October 1882, pp. 161–5

Mallet, Marie, *Life with Queen Victoria: Marie Mallet's Letters from Court, 1887–1901*, ed. Victor Mallet (London, John Murray, 1968)

Mantell, Gideon, *The Journal of Gideon Mantell, Surgeon and Geologist*, ed. E. Cecil Curwen (London, Oxford University Press, 1940)

[Martineau, Harriet], *Deerbrook* (London, Smith, Elder and Co., 1859)

—, *Life in the Sick-room: Essays. By an Invalid* (London, Edward Moxon, 1844)

Maurice, Priscilla, *Help and Comfort for the Sick Poor* (London, Rivington's, 1881)

[—], *Sickness, its Trials and Blessings* (London, Francis & John Rivington, 1850); new edition (London, Rivingtons, 1885)

[—], 'Suggestions to Persons in Attendance on the Sick and Dying; Being, An Appendix to *Sickness: Its Trials and Blessings*' (London, Francis & John Rivington, 1851)

'M.G.', *Comforting Words for Widows and Others who Mourn* (London, Elliot Stock, 1905)

[Millard, Ann], *An Account of the Circumstances Attending the Imprisonment and Death of the Late William Millard . . . and of the Barter and Sale of the Patients' Dead Bodies for the Purposes of Dissection* (London, Ann Millard, 1825)

Mogridge, G[eorge], *The Churchyard Lyrist: Consisting of Five Hundred Original Inscriptions to Commemorate the Dead* (London, Houlston and Son, 1832)

Moore, Charles, *A Full Inquiry into the Subject of Suicide* (2 vols., London, J.F. and C. Rivington, 1790)

[Morley, Henry], 'Between the Cradle and the Grave', *All the Year Round*, no. 145, 1 February 1862, pp. 454–6

—, 'Burning and Burying', *Household Words*, no. 389, 5 September 1857, pp. 226–7

—, 'An Enemy's Charge', *Household Words*, no. 291, 20 October 1855, pp. 265–70

—, 'Life and Death in St Giles', *Household Words*, no. 451, 13 November 1858, pp. 524–8

—, 'Use and Abuse of the Dead', *Household Words*, no. 419, 3 April 1858, pp. 361–5

Mudford, William, 'Cemeteries and Churchyards – A Visit to Kensal Green', *Bentley's Miscellany*, vol. 9 (London, Richard Bentley, 1841), pp. 92–7

Oliphant, Margaret, *The Autobiography of Margaret Oliphant: The Complete Text*, ed. Elisabeth Jay (Oxford, Oxford University Press, 1990)

Payn, James, 'Among the Tombs', *Household Words*, no. 419, 3 April 1858, pp. 372–5

Peacock, Florence, 'Traditions and Customs relating to Death and Burial in Lincolnshire', *The Antiquary*, no. 71, new series, November 1895, pp. 330–35

Polidori, John, *The Vampyre, and Other Tales of the Macabre*, ed. Robert Morrison and Chris Baldick (Oxford, Oxford University Press, 2008)

Post, Frederick James, *Extracts from the Diary and Other Manuscripts of the Late Frederick James Post, of Islington* (London, privately printed, 1838)

Punch, 'The Bermondsey Horror. The Commodity of Murder', vol. 17, 1 September 1849, p. 83

—, 'Fashions for the Old Bailey Ladies', vol. 17, 1 September 1849, p. 186

—, 'Performers in 'The Grave Scene',' 17 October 1857, p. 163

Reeve, Clara, *The Old English Baron*, ed. James Trainer, introduction by James Watt ([1778], Oxford, Oxford University Press, 2003)

Report from the Select Committee on Anatomy (London, House of Commons, 1828)

Reynolds, G.M.W., *The Mysteries of London*, foreword by Louis James, annotated by Dick Collins ([1844–6], Kansas City, Valancourt, 2013, 2 vols.)

Ritchie, James, 'An Account of the Watch-houses, Mortsafes and Public Vaults in Aberdeenshire Churchyards, formerly used for the Protection of the Dead from the Resurrectionists', *Proceedings of the Society of Antiquaries of Scotland*, 4th series, vol. 10, 1911–12, pp. 285–326

—, 'Relics of the Body-Snatchers: Supplementary Notes on Mortsafe Tackle, Mortsafes, Watch-houses and Public Vaults, mostly in Aberdeenshire', *Proceedings of the Society of Antiquaries of Scotland*, 5th series, vol. 7, 1921, pp. 221–30

Ross, Alex, *Hints on Dress, and on the Arrangement of the Hair* (London, Ross and Co., [1861])

Rossetti, William Michael, *Some Reminiscences of William Michael Rossetti* (London, Brown Langham & Co., 1906)

[Rymer, James Malcolm, or Thomas Peckett Prest], *Varney the Vampyre, or, The Feast of Blood* (1847), online at https://archive.org/details/VarneyTheVampyre/page/n5/mode/2up

Sewell, Rev. W.H., *On Christian Care of the Dying and the Dead: A Few Hints Designed for the Use of Friendly Readers*, 'By a Clergyman of the Church of England' (London, J.T. Hayes, 1870)

[—], *Practical Papers on Funeral Reform, Mourning Dress and Obituary Memorials* ([no place of publication, privately printed, 1883])

Shelley, Mrs [Mary], *Frankenstein, or, The Modern Prometheus* (London, George Routledge and Sons, 1891)

Sherwood, Mrs [Mary Martha], *The History of the Fairchild Family; or, The Child's Manual* (London, F. Houlston, 1818)

Shonfield, Zuzanna, *The Precariously Privileged: A Professional Family in Victorian London* (Oxford, Oxford University Press, 1987)

Shore, Emily, *Journal of Emily Shore* (London, Kegan Paul, Trench, Trübner & Co., 1891)

[Smith, Thomas Southward], 'Use of the Dead to the Living', *Westminster Review*, vol. 2, no. 3, 1824, pp. 59–97

Southey, Robert, 'The Surgeon's Warning' (1799), in *Robert Southey: Poetical Works, 1793–1810*, ed. Lynda Pratt; vol. 5: *Selected Shorter Poems, c.1793–1810* (Abingdon, Routledge, 2016)

Stanley, Arthur Penrhyn, *Historical Memorials of Westminster Abbey* (7th ed., London, John Murray, 1890)

Steele, Richard, *The Funeral: or, Grief A-la-mode. A Comedy* ([1701/2], 6th ed., London, J. Tonson, 1730)

Stephen, Leslie, *Sir Leslie Stephen's Mausoleum Book*, intro. Alan Bell (Oxford, Clarendon Press, 1977)

Stephen, Mrs Leslie, *Notes from Sick Rooms* ([London, Smith, Elder, 1883])

Stevenson, *Strange Case of Dr Jekyll and Mr Hyde* (London, Longman, Green and Co., 1886)

Stoker, Bram, *Dracula* (London, Archibald Constable & Co., 1899)

Stone, Mrs [Elizabeth], *God's Acre, or, Historical Notices Relating to Churchyards* (London, John W. Parker and Son, 1858)

Strang, John, *Necropolis Glasguensis, with Observations on Ancient and Modern Tombs and Sepulture* (Glasgow, Atkinson and Co., 1831)

Taylor, Shephard T., *The Diary of a Medical Student during the Mid-Victorian Period, 1860–1864* (Norwich, Jarrold and Sons, 1927)

[Tennyson, Hallam], *Alfred Lord Tennyson: A Memoir by His Son* (London, Macmillan, 1897)

[—], *Lionel Tennyson* (London, Macmillan, 1891)

Theobald, Morell, 'Spiritualism at Home. Read before the London Spiritualist Alliance, June 10th, 1884' (London, E.W. Allen, [1884])

—, *Spirit Workers in the Home Circle: An Autobiographic Narrative of Psychic Phenomena in Family Daily Life, Extending over a Period of Twenty Years* (London, T. Fisher Unwin, 1887)

Thomas, E. Lewis, *Baker's Law Relating to Burials* (London, Sweet and Maxwell, 1898)

Thornbury, George Walter, 'Old Stories Re-Told: Resurrection Men. Burke and Hare', *All the Year Round*, 16 March 1867, no. 412, pp. 282–8

Trollope, Anthony, *Can You Forgive Her?* (London, Chapman and Hall, 1864)

—, *The Prime Minister* (Leipzig, Bernhard Tauchnitz, 1876)

—, *The Small House at Allington* (London, Smith, Elder & Co., 1865)

Trollope, Frances, *Mabel's Progress* (London, Chapman and Hall, 1867)

Walker, G.A., *Burial-Ground Incendiarism: The Last Fire at the Bone-House in the Spa-Fields Golgotha* (London, Longman, Brown, Green and Longmans, 1846)

—, *Gatherings from Graveyards; Particularly those of London* (London, Longman and Co., 1839)

—, *On the Past and Present State of Intramural Burying Places, with Practical Suggestions* (London, Longman, Brown, Green and Longmans, 1851)

[Walton, Mrs O.F.], *Little Dot* (London, Religious Tract Society, [1873])

[Warren, Samuel], *Passages from the Diary of a Late Physician* (Edinburgh, William Blackwood, 1834)

Wilde, Oscar, *The Picture of Dorian Gray* (London, Ward, Lock and Co., 1891)

[Wills, W.H.], 'A Coroner's Inquest', *Household Words*, no. 5, 27 April 1850, pp. 109–13

Winslow, Rev. Geo. Erving, 'A Plain and Practical Description of Asiatic Cholera, Containing Rules and Directions for its Prevention and Treatment' (London, J. Hatchard, 1848)

'W.J.', *The Illustrated Guide to Kensal Green Cemetery* (London, Petter and Galpin, [1861])

Wood, Mrs Henry, *East Lynne* (London, Richard Bentley, 1862)

Yonge, Charlotte M., *The Young Step-Mother; or, A Chronicle of Mistakes* (London, Macmillan and Co., 1874)

Secondary sources

Adburgham, Alison, *Shops and Shopping, 1800–1914: Where, and in What Manner, the Well-dressed Englishwoman Bought her Clothes* (2nd ed., London, George Allen and Unwin, 1981)

Alexander, Kaelin B.C., 'Turning Mourning: Trollope's Ambivalent Widows', *Victorian Literature and Culture*, vol. 43, 2015, pp. 607–20

Anderson, Michael, 'The Social Position of Spinsters in Mid-Victorian Britain', *Journal of Family History*, vol. 9, no. 4, 1984, pp. 377–93

Anderson, Olive, *Suicide in Victorian and Edwardian England* (Oxford, Clarendon Press, 1987)

Ariès, Philippe, *The Hour of Our Death*, trs. Helen Weaver (London, Allen Lane, 1981)

—, *Images of Man and Death*, trs. Janet Lloyd (Cambridge, MA, Harvard University Press, 1985)

—, *Western Attitudes toward Death: From the Middle Ages to the Present*, trs. Patricia Ranum (Baltimore, Johns Hopkins University Press, 1974)

Armstrong, David, 'The Invention of Infant Mortality', *Sociology of Health and Illness*, vol. 8, no. 3, 1986, pp. 211–32

Arnold, A.J., and J.M. Bidmead, 'Going to Paradise by Way of Kensal Green: A Most Unfit Subject for Trading Profit?', *Business History*, vol. 50, no. 3, 2008, pp. 328–50

Arnold, Catharine, *Necropolis: London and its Dead* (London, Simon & Schuster, 2006)

Auerbach, Nina, 'Ghosts of Ghosts', *Victorian Literature and Culture*, vol. 32, no. 1, 2004, 277–284.

Avery, Gillian, and Kimberley Reynolds, eds., *Representations of Childhood Death* (Basingstoke, Macmillan, 2000)

Bailey, Brian, *The Resurrection Men: A History of the Trade in Corpses* (London, Macdonald, 1991)

Bailey, Victor, *This Rash Act: Suicide Across the Life Cycle of the Victorian City* (Stanford, CA, Stanford University Press, 1998)

Bailin, Miriam, *The Sickroom in Victorian Fiction: The Art of Being Ill* (Cambridge, Cambridge University Press, 1994)

Bann, Jennifer, 'Ghostly Hands and Ghostly Agency: The Changing Figure of the Nineteenth-century Specter', *Victorian Studies*, vol. 51, no. 4, 2009, pp. 663–85

Barnard, Sylvia, *To Prove I'm not Forgot: Living and Dying in a Victorian City* (Manchester, Manchester University Press, 1990)

Barreca, Regina, ed., *Sex and Death in Victorian Literature* (Basingstoke, Macmillan, 1990)

Batchen, Geoffrey, *Forget Me Not: Photography and Remembrance* (New York, Princeton Architectural Press, 2004)

—, 'Ere the Substance Fade: Photography and Hair Jewellery', in Elizabeth Edwards and Janice Hart, eds., *Photographs Objects Histories: On the Materiality of Images* (London, Routledge, 2004)

Beardmore, Carol, Cara Dobbing, Steven King, eds., *Family Life in Britain, 1650–1910* (Cham, Palgrave Macmillan, 2019)

Bebbington, David W., *The Evangelical Quadrilateral*, vol. 1: *Characterizing the British Gospel Movement* (Waco, TX, Baylor University Press, 2021)

—, *Evangelicalism in Modern Britain: A History from the 1730s to the 1980s* (London, Unwin Hyman, 1989)

Behlmer, George K., 'Deadly Motherhood: Infanticide and Medical Opinion in Mid-Victorian England', *Journal of the History of Medicine*, vol. 34, 1979, pp. 403–27

—, 'Grave Doubts: Victorian Medicine, Moral Panic, and the Signs of Death', *Journal of British Studies*, vol. 42, no. 2, 2003, pp. 206–35

Behrendt, Stephen C., *Royal Mourning and Regency Culture: Elegies and Memorials of Princess Charlotte* (Basingstoke, Macmillan, 1997)

Bell, Richard J., 'Our People Die Well: Deathbed Scenes in John Wesley's *Arminian* Magazine', *Mortality*, vol. 10, no. 3, 2005, pp. 210–23

Belsey, Catherine, *Tales of the Troubled Dead: Ghost Stories in Cultural History* (Edinburgh, Edinburgh University Press, 2019)

Bending, Lucy, *The Representation of Bodily Pain in Late Nineteenth-century English Culture* (Oxford, Clarendon Press, 2000)

Bennett, Gillian, and Steve Roud, 'Death in Folklore: A Selective Listing from the Journal of the Folklore Society', *Mortality*, vol. 2, no. 3, 1997, pp. 221–38

Berridge, Virginia, and Griffith Edwards, *Opium and the People: Opiate Use in Nineteenth-century England* (London, Allen Lane, 1981)

Blount, Trevor, 'The Graveyard Satire of *Bleak House* in the Context of 1850', *The Review of English Studies*, vol. 14, no. 1963, pp. 370–78

Bohleke, Karin J., 'Identifying Stages of Grief in Nineteenth-century Images', *The Daguerreian Annual 2015: Official Yearbook of the Daguerreian Society* (Pittsburgh, 2015), pp. 166–91

Bown, Nicola, 'Empty Hands and Precious Pictures: Post-mortem Portrait Photographs of Children', *Australasian Journal of Victorian Studies*, vol. 14, no. 2, 2009, pp. 8–24

—, ed., 'Rethinking Victorian Sentimentality', Special Issue, *Interdisciplinary Studies in the Long Nineteenth Century*, issue 4, 2007, 'Crying Over Little Nell', pp. 1–13

Brandon, Ruth, *The Spiritualists: The Passion for the Occult in the Nineteenth and Twentieth Centuries* (London, Weidenfeld and Nicolson, 1983)

Bratton, Jackie, *The Victorian Popular Ballad* (London, 1975)

Bredesen, Dagni, 'At the Drop of the Veil: Widowhood and Victorian Fictions of (dis)Coverture', in Lyndsay Mills Campbell, et al., *Inter/National Intersections: Law's Changing Territories* (Vancouver, University of British Columbia Press, 1998)

—, 'An Emblem of All the Rest: Wearing the Widow's Cap in Victorian Literature', in Cristina Giorcelli and Paula Rabinowitz, eds., *Fashioning the Nineteenth Century* (Minneapolis, University of Minnesota Press, 2014)

—, '"What's a Woman to Do?": Managing Money and Manipulating Fictions in Trollope's *Can You Forgive Her?* and *The Eustace Diamonds*', *Victorian Review*, vol. 31, no. 2, 2005, pp. 99–122

—, 'The "Widdy's" Empire: Queen Victoria as Widow in Kipling's Soldier Stories and in the *Barrack-Room Ballads*', in Margaret Homans and

Adrienne Munich, eds., *Remaking Queen Victoria* (Cambridge, Cambridge University Press, 1997)

Bremmer, Jan N., and Lourens van den Bosch, eds., *Between Poverty and the Pyre: Moments in the History of Widowhood* (London, Routledge, 1995)

Brewster, Scott, and Luke Thurston, *The Routledge Handbook to the Ghost Story* (New York, Routledge, 2018)

Briefel, Aviva, '"Freaks of Furniture": The Useless Energy of Haunted Things', *Victorian Studies*, vol. 59, no. 2, 2017, pp. 209–34

Brightfield, Myron, 'The Medical Profession in Early Victorian England, as Depicted in the Novels of the Period (1840–1870)', *Bulletin of the History of Medicine*, vol. 35, 1961, pp. 238–56

Bronfen, Elisabeth, *Over Her Dead Body: Death, Femininity and the Aesthetic* (Manchester, Manchester University Press, 1992)

—, and Beate Neumeier, eds., *Gothic Renaissance: A Reassessment* (Manchester, Manchester University Press, 2014)

Brooks-Gordon, Belinda, Fatemeh Ebtehaj, Jonathan Herring, Martin H. Johnson, Martin Richards, eds., *Death Rites and Rights* (Oxford and Portland, OR, Hart, 2007)

Brown, Michael, 'From Foetid Air to Filth: The Cultural Transformation of British Epidemiological Thought, ca.1780–1848', *Bulletin of the History of Medicine*, vol. 82, no. 3, 2008, pp. 515–44

Browne, Ray B., ed., *Objects of Special Devotion: Fetishism in Popular Culture* (Bowling Green, OH, Bowling Green University Press, [1982?])

Buck, Anne, 'The Trap Re-baited: Mourning Dress[,] 1860–90', *High Victorian Costume, 1860–1890: Proceedings of the Second Annual Conference of the Costume Society, March 1968* (London, 'published for the Society', 1969)

Buckham, Susan, 'Commemoration as an Expression of Personal Relationships and Group Identities: A Case Study of York Cemetery', *Mortality*, vol. 8, no. 2, 2003, pp. 160–75

Budge, Gavin, *Romanticism, Medicine and the Natural Supernatural: Transcendent Vision and Bodily Spectres, 1789–1852* (Basingstoke, Palgrave Macmillan, 2012)

Bullen, J.B., Rosalind White and Lenore A. Beaky, eds., *Pre-Raphaelites in the Spirit World: The Séance Diary of William Michael Rossetti* (Oxford, Peter Lang, 2022)

Bury, Shirley, *An Introduction to Sentimental Jewellery* (London, HMSO, 1985)

Cadwallader, Jen, 'Spirit Photography and the Victorian Culture of Mourning', *Modern Language Studies*, vol. 37, no. 2, 2008, pp. 8–31

Carlton, William J., 'When the Cholera Raged at Chatham', *Dickensian*, June 1953, pp. 113–18

Carpenter, Edward, ed., *A House of Kings: The History of Westminster Abbey* (London, John Baker, 1966)

Carpenter, Mary Wilson, *Health, Medicine and Society in Victorian England* (Santa Barbara, ABC Clio, 2010)

Carvalho, Luís Mendonça de, Francisca Maria Fernandes, Maria de Fátima Nunes and João Brigola, 'Whitby Jet Jewels in the Victorian Age', *Harvard Papers in Botany*, vol. 18, no. 2, 2013, pp. 133–6

Casteras, Susan P., *Images of Victorian Womanhood in English Art* (London, Associated University Presses, 1987)

Cecil, Robert, *Masks of Death: Changing Attitudes in the Nineteenth Century* (Lewes, Book Guild, 1991)

Chamberlain, Mary, *Old Wives' Tales: The History of Remedies, Charms and Spells* (Stroud, Tempus, 1981, 2006)

Chandler, Roy A., and Louise Macniven, 'The Unusual Tale of an Auditing Spiritualist', *Accounting History*, vol. 19, no. 3, 2014, pp. 333–49

Chaudhary, Zahid R., *Afterimage of Empire: Photography in Nineteenth-century India* (Minneapolis, University of Minnesota Press, 2012)

—, 'Phantasmagoric Aesthetics: Colonial Violence and the Management of Perception', *Cultural Critique*, vol. 59, 2005, pp. 63–119

Chéroux, Clément, et. al., *The Perfect Medium: Photography and the Occult*, trs. Trista Selous (New Haven, Yale University Press, 2005)

Clarke, John M., *The Brookwood Necropolis Railway* (Usk, Oakwood, 2006; rev. ed.)

Clymer, Lorna, 'Cromwell's Head and Milton's Hair: Corpse Theory in Spectacular Bodies of the Interregnum', *The Eighteenth Century*, vol. 40, no. 2, 1999, pp. 91–112

Cockshut, A.O.J., *Truth to Life: The Art of Biography in the Nineteenth Century* (London, Collins, 1974)

Cohen, Emily Jane, 'Museums of the Mind: The Gothic and the Art of Memory', *ELH*, vol. 62, no. 4, 1995, pp. 883–905

Colls, Robert, *This Sporting Life: Sports and Liberty in England, 1760–1960* (Oxford, Oxford University Press, 2020)

Connell, Philip, 'Death and the Author: Westminster Abbey and the Meanings of the Literary Monument', *Eighteenth-century Studies*, vol. 38, no. 4, 2005, pp. 557–85

Cooper, Diana, and Norman Battershill, *Victorian Sentimental Jewellery* (Newton Abbot, David and Charles, 1972)

Cortés-Rocca, Paola, 'Ghosts in the Machine: Photographs of Specters in the Nineteenth Century', *Mosaic*, vol. 38, no. 1, 2005 [unpaginated]

Courtney, Julia, and Clemence Schultze, eds., *The Charlotte M. Yonge Fellowship Journal*, Special issue, 'Illness and Death in Yonge's Novels', vol. 15, 2022

Cowdell, Paul, 'Cannibal Ballads: Not Just a Question of Taste', *Folk Music Journal*, vol. 9, no. 5, 2010, pp. 723–47

Cox, Margaret, *Life and Death in Spitalfields, 1700 to 1850* (York, Council for British Archaeology, 1996)

—, ed., *Grave Concerns: Death and Burial in England, 1700 to 1850* (York, Council for British Archaeology, 1998)

Craik, Jennifer, *Fashion: The Key Concepts* (Oxford, Berg, 2009)

Cressy, David, *Birth, Marriage and Death: Ritual, Religion and the Life-cycle in Tudor and Stuart England* (Oxford, Oxford University Press, 1997)

Crone, Rosalind, 'Mrs and Mrs Punch in Nineteenth-century England', *The Historical Journal*, vol. 49, no. 4, 2006, pp. 1055–82

—, *Violent Victorians: Popular Entertainment in Nineteenth-century London* (Manchester, Manchester University Press, 2012)

Cunnington, Phillis, and Catherine Lucas, *Costume for Births, Marriages and Deaths* (London, Adam and Charles Black, 1972)

—, *Occupational Costume in England from the Eleventh Century to 1914* (London, Adam & Charles Black, 1967)

Curl, James Stevens, *The Victorian Celebration of Death* (Newton Abbot, David & Charles, 1972)

Curran, Cynthia, 'Private Women, Public Needs: Middle-class Widows in Victorian England', *Albion*, vol. 25, no. 2, 1993, pp. 217–36

—, *When I First Began My Life Anew: Middle-class Widows in Nineteenth-century Britain* (Bristol, IN, Wyndham Hall Press, [2000])

Cutt, M. Nancy, *Ministering Angels: A Study of Nineteenth-century Evangelical Writing for Children* (Wormley, Herts, Five Owls Press, 1979)

—, *Mrs Sherwood and Her Books for Children* (London, Oxford University Press, 1974)

Darby, Elizabeth, and Nicola Smith, *The Cult of the Prince Consort* (New Haven, Yale University Press, 1983)

Davidoff, Leonore, *The Best Circles: Society, Etiquette and the Season* (London, Croom Helm, 1973)

—, and Megan Doolittle, Janet Fink, Katherine Holden, *The Family Story: Blood, Contract and Intimacy, 1830–1960* (London, Longman, 1999)

Davies, Douglas, *Death, Ritual and Belief: The Rhetoric of Funerary Rites* (London, Bloomsbury, 2017, 3rd ed.)

—, and Alastair Shaw, *Reusing Old Graves: A Report on Popular British Attitudes* (Crayford, Shaw and Sons, 1995)

Davies, Owen, *The Haunted: A Social History of Ghosts* (Basingstoke, Palgrave Macmillan, 2007)

—, ed., *Ghosts: A Social History*, vol. 3: *1820–1848: Religion vs Science – The Debate Updated*; vol. 4: *1848–1914: Spiritualism and Hauntings* (5 vols., London, Pickering and Chatto, 2010)

—, and Francesca Matteoni, *Executing Magic in the Modern Era: Criminal*

Bodies and the Gallows in Popular Medicine (Cham, Switzerland, Palgrave Macmillan, 2017)

Davison, Carol Margaret, ed., *The Gothic and Death* (Manchester, Manchester University Press, 2017)

—, ed., with the participation of Paul Simpson-Housley, *Bram Stoker's Dracula: Sucking through the Century, 1897–1997* (Toronto, Dundurn Press, 1997)

Denney, Peter, Bruce Buchan, David Ellison and Karen Crawley, eds., *Sound, Space and Civility in the British World, 1700–1850* (London, Routledge, 2019)

Derrida, Jacques, *The Work of Mourning*, trs. Pascale-Anne Brault and Michael Naas (Chicago, Chicago University Press, 2001)

Dickerson, Vanessa, *Victorian Ghosts in the Noontide: Women Writers and the Supernatural* (Columbia, University of Missouri Press, 1996)

Dijkstra, Bram, *Idols of Perversity: Fantasies of Feminine Evil in Fin-de-siècle Culture* (New York, Oxford University Press, 1986)

Doherty, Ruth, '"Blest" or "t'othered": Alternative Graveyards in *Bleak House*, Reynolds, and Walker', *Victoriographies*, vol. 8, no. 3, 2018, pp. 267–89

Douglas, Gillian, Hilary Woodward, Alun Humphrey, Lisa Mills and Gareth Morrell, 'Enduring Love? Attitudes to Family and Inheritance Law in England and Wales', *Journal of Law and Society*, vol. 38, no. 2, 2011, pp. 245–71

Dryden, Linda, *The Modern Gothic and Literary Doubles: Stevenson, Wilde and Wells* (Basingstoke, Palgrave Macmillan, 2003)

Durey, M.J., 'Bodysnatchers and Benthamites: The Implications of the Dead Body Bill for the London Schools of Anatomy, 1820–42', *The London Journal*, vol. 2, no. 2, 1976, pp. 200–225

Edmond, Rod, 'Death Sequences: Patmore, Hardy and the New Domestic Elegy', *Victorian Poetry*, vol. 19, no. 2, 1981, pp. 151–65

Egan, Joseph J., 'Grave Sites and Moral Death: A Reëxamination of Stevenson's "The Body-Snatcher"', *English Literature in Transition, 1880–1920*, vol. 13, no. 1, 1970, pp. 9–15

Eubanks, Elizabeth Babson Bittle, 'Illness and the Asiatic Cholera in the Lives and Works of the Brontë Family', *Brontë Studies*, vol. 46, no. 2, 2021, pp. 118–31

Fido, Martin, *Bodysnatchers: A History of the Resurrectionists, 1742–1832* (London, Weidenfeld & Nicolson, 1988)

Field, David, Jenny Hockey, and Neil Small, eds., *Death, Gender and Ethnicity* (London, Routledge, 1997)

Firenze, Paul, 'Spirit Photography: How Early Spiritualists Tried to Save Religion by Using Science', *Skeptic*, vol. 11, no. 2, 2004, pp. 70–78

Fisher, Pam, 'Houses for the Dead: The Provision of Mortuaries in London, 1843–1889', *The London Journal*, vol. 34, no. 1, 2009, pp. 1–15

Fletcher, Ronald, *The Akenham Burial Case* (London, Wildwood House, 1974)

Fowler, Louise, and Natasha Powers, *Doctors, Dissection and Resurrection Men: Excavations in the 19th-century Burial Ground of the London Hospital, 2006* (London, Museum of London Archaeology, 2012)

Fraser, John, 'Beato's Photograph of the Interior of the Sikandarbagh at Lucknow', *Journal of the Society for Army Historical Research*, vol. 59, no. 237, 1981, pp. 51–5

Frawley, Maria H., *Invalidism and Identity in Nineteenth-century Britain* (Chicago, University of Chicago Press, 2004)

Frayling, Christopher, *Vampyres: Genesis and Resurrection from* Count Dracula *to* Vampirella (London, Thames and Hudson, 2016)

Freud, Sigmund, 'The Uncanny', *The Standard Edition of the Complete Psychological Works of Sigmund Freud*; vol. 17: *An Infantile Neurosis and Other Works (1917–1919)*, trs. and ed. James Strachey, with Anna Freud; assisted by Alix Strachey and Alan Tyson (London, Vintage/Hogarth Press, 2001)

Friedman, Alan W., 'Narrative is to Death as Death is to the Dying: Funerals and Stories', *Mosaic*, vol. 15, no. 1, 1982, pp. 65–76

Frisby, Helen, 'Drawing the Pillow, Laying Out and Port Wine: The Moral Economy of Death, Dying and Bereavement in England, c.1840–1930', *Mortality*, vol. 20, no. 2, 2015, pp. 103–27

—, '"Them Owls Know": Portending Death in Later Nineteenth- and Early Twentieth-century England', *Folklore*, vol. 126, no. 2, 2015, pp. 196–214

Fritz, Paul S., 'The Undertaking Trade in England: Its Origins and Early Development, 1660–1830', *Eighteenth-century Studies*, vol. 28, no. 2, 1994/5, pp. 241–53

Fuss, Diana, 'Last Words', *ELH*, vol. 76, no. 4, 2009, pp. 877–910

Gallagher, Catherine, *The Body Economic: Life, Death and Sensation in Political Economy and the Victorian Novel* (Princeton, Princeton University Press, 2006)

Galvan, Jill, *The Sympathetic Medium: Feminine Channeling, the Occult and Communication Technologies, 1859–1919* (Ithaca, New York, Cornell University Press, 2010)

Gammon, Vic, *Desire, Drink and Death in English Folk and Vernacular Song, 1600–1900* (London, Routledge, 2016)

Garlick, Harry, 'The Staging of Death: Iconography and the State Funeral of the Duke of Wellington', *Australian Journal of Art*, vol. 9, no. 1, 1991, pp. 58–77

Garrigan, Kristine Ottesen, ed., *Victorian Scandals: Representations of Gender and Class* (Athens, Ohio University Press, 1992)

Garton, Stephen, 'The Scales of Suffering: Love, Death and Victorian
    Masculinity', *Social History*, vol. 27, no. 1, 2002, pp. 40–58
Gasperini, Anna, *Nineteenth-century Popular Fiction, Medicine and Anatomy:
    The Victorian Penny Blood and the 1832 Anatomy Act* (Cham, Palgrave
    Macmillan/Springer Verlag, 2019)
Gates, Amy L., 'Fixing Memory: The Effigial Forms of Felicia Hemans and
    Jeremy Bentham', *Women's Writing*, vol. 21, no. 1, 2014, pp. 58–73
Gates, Barbara T., *Victorian Suicide: Mad Crimes and Sad Histories* (Princeton,
    Princeton University Press, 1988)
Gennep, Arnold van, *The Rites of Passage*, trs. Monika B. Vizedom and
    Gabrielle L. Caffe (London, Routledge and Kegan Paul, 1960)
Georgas, Marilyn, 'Little Nell and the Art of Holy Dying: Dickens and Jeremy
    Taylor', *Dickens Studies Annual*, vol. 20, 1991, pp. 35–56
Gilbert, Pamela K., *Cholera and the Nation: Doctoring the Social Body in
    Victorian England* (Albany, State University of New York Press, 2008)
—, *The Citizen's Body: Desire, Health and the Social in Victorian England*
    (Columbus, The Ohio State University Press, 2007)
—, *Mapping the Victorian Social Body* (Albany, State University of New York
    Press, 2004)
Gitter, Elisabeth G., 'The Power of Women's Hair in the Victorian
    Imagination', *PMLA*, vol. 99, no. 5, 1984, pp. 936–54
Gittings, Clare, *Death, Burial and the Individual in Early Modern England*
    (London, Croom Helm, 1984)
Glasgow, Gordon H.H., 'The Campaign for Medical Coroners in Nineteenth-
    century England and its Aftermath: A Lancashire Focus on Failure', Parts
    I and II, *Mortality*, vol. 9, no. 2, 2004, pp. 150–67, and vol. 9, no. 3,
    2004, pp. 223–34
Goggin, Maureen Daly, and Beth Fowkes Tobin, eds., *Women and Things,
    1750–1950: Gendered Material Strategies* (Farnham, Ashgate, 2009)
Goodwin, Sarah Webster, *Kitsch and Culture: The Dance of Death in
    Nineteenth-century Literature and Graphic Arts* (New York, Garland, 1988)
—, and Elisabeth Bronfen, eds., *Death and Representation* (Baltimore, Johns
    Hopkins University Press, 1993)
Grainger, Hilary, *Death Redesigned: British Crematoria History, Architecture and
    Landscape* (Reading, Spire Books, 2005)
Groth, Helen, *Victorian Photography and Literary Nostalgia* (Oxford, Oxford
    University Press, 2003)
Guerrini, Anita, 'Anatomists and Entrepreneurs in Early Eighteenth-century
    London', *Journal of the History of Medicine and Allied Sciences*, vol. 59, no.
    2, 2004, pp. 219–39
Gunning, Tom, 'Phantom Images and Modern Manifestations: Spirit
    Photography, Magic Theater, Trick Films and Photography's Uncanny', in

Patrice Petro, ed., *Fugitive Images: From Photography to Video* (Bloomington, Indiana University Press, 1995)

Guthke, Karl S., *Last Words: Variations on a Theme in Cultural History*, rev. and trs. by the author (Princeton, Princeton University Press, 1992)

Hackenberg, Sara, 'Vampires and Resurrection Men: The Perils and Pleasures of the Embodied Past in 1840s Sensational Fiction', *Victorian Studies*, vol. 52, no. 1, 2009, pp. 63–75

Hacker, Daphna, 'Disappointed "Heirs" as a Socio-Legal Phenomenon', *Oñati Socio-Legal Series*, vol. 4, no. 2, 2014, pp. 243–63

Hallam, Elizabeth, and Jenny Hockey, *Death, Memory and Material Culture* (Oxford, Berg, 2001)

Halttunen, Karen, *Confidence Men and Painted Women: A Study of Middle-class Culture in America, 1830–1870* (New Haven, Yale University Press, 1982)

Hamlett, Jane, *Material Relations: Domestic Interiors and Middle-class Families in England, 1850–1910* (Manchester, Manchester University Press, 2010)

Harrison, Robert Pogue, *The Dominion of the Dead* (Chicago, University of Chicago Press, 2003)

Hartland, E. Sidney, 'The Sin-Eater', *Folklore*, vol. 3, no. 2, 1892, pp. 145–7

Hartog, Hendrik, *Someday All This will be Yours: A History of Inheritance and Old Age* (Cambridge, MA, Harvard University Press, 2012)

Hay, Daisy, 'Hair in the Disraeli Papers: A Victorian Harvest', *Journal of Victorian Culture*, vol. 19, no. 3, 2014, pp. 332–45

Hay, Douglas, Peter Linebaugh, John G. Rule, E.P. Thompson and Cal Winslow, *Albion's Fatal Tree: Crime and Society in Eighteenth-century England* (London, Verso, 2011)

Hay, Simon, *The History of the Modern British Ghost Story* (Basingstoke, Palgrave Macmillan, 2011)

Hayter, Alethea, *A Sultry Month: Scenes of London Literary Life in 1846* (London, Faber, 1965)

Heath, Kay, *Aging by the Book: The Emergence of Mid-Life in Victorian Britain* (Albany, State University of New York Press, 2009)

Henry, Wanda S., 'Women Searchers of the Dead in Eighteenth- and Nineteenth-century London', *Social History of Medicine*, vol. 29, no. 3, 2015, pp. 445–56

Hepburn, Allan, 'The Irish Way of Dying: *Ulysses* and Funeral Processions', *The Canadian Journal of Irish Studies*, vol. 38, nos. 1/2, 2014, pp. 184–207

Herman, Agatha, 'Death has a Touch of Class: Society and Space in Brookwood Cemetery, 1853–1903', *Journal of Historical Geography*, vol. 36, 2010, pp. 305–14

Hibbard, Andrea, 'Cannibalism and the Late-Victorian Adventure Novel: *The Queen v. Dudley and Stephens*', *English Literature in Transition, 1880–1920*, vol. 62, no. 3, 2019, pp. 305–27

Hind, Heather, '"I Twisted the Two, and Enclosed Them Together": Hairwork, Touch and Emily Brontë's *Wuthering Heights*', *Victorian Review*, vol. 46, no. 1, 2020, pp. 31–47

Hodgson, Pat, *Early War Photographs* (Reading, Osprey, 1974)

Hoeveler, Diane Long, *Gothic Riffs: Secularizing the Uncanny in the European Popular Imaginary, 1780–1820* (Columbus, Ohio State University Press, 2010)

Holm, Christiane, 'Sentimental Cuts: Eighteenth-century Mourning Jewelry with Hair', *Eighteenth-century Studies*, vol. 38, no. 1, 2004, pp. 139–43

Holubetz, Margarete, 'Death-bed Scenes in Victorian Fiction', *English Studies*, vol. 67, no. 1, 1986, pp. 14–34

Hotz, Mary Elizabeth, *Literary Remains: Representations of Death and Burial in Victorian England* (Albany, State University of New York Press, 2009)

—, 'Down among the Dead: Edwin Chadwick's Burial Reform Discourse in Mid-nineteenth-century England', *Victorian Literature and Culture*, vol. 29, no. 1, 2001, pp. 21–38

Houlbrooke, Ralph, ed., *Death, Ritual and Bereavement* (London, Routledge, 1989)

—, 'Public and Private in the Funerals of the Later Stuart Gentry: Some Somerset Examples', *Mortality*, vol. 1, no. 2, 1996, pp. 163–76

Houston, R. A., *Punishing the Dead? Suicide, Lordship, and Community in Britain, 1500–1830* (Oxford, Oxford University Press, 2010)

Howarth, Glennys, and Oliver Leaman, eds., *Encyclopedia of Death and Dying* (London, Routledge, 2001)

Huggins, Mike, 'Reading the Funeral Rite: A Cultural Analysis of the Funeral Ceremonials and Burial of Selected Leading Sportsmen in Victorian England, 1864–1888', *Journal of Sport History*, vol. 38, no. 3, 2011, pp. 407–24

Humphreys, Clare, 'Waiting for the Last Summons: The Establishment of the First Hospices in England, 1878–1914', *Mortality*, vol. 6, no. 2, 2001, pp. 146–66

Hurren, Elizabeth T., *Dissecting the Criminal Corpse: Staging Post-Execution Punishment in Early Modern England* (London, Palgrave Macmillan, 2016)

—, *Dying for Victorian Medicine: English Anatomy and its Trade in the Dead Poor, c.1834–1929* (Basingstoke, Palgrave Macmillan, 2012)

—, 'A Pauper Dead-House: The Expansion of the Cambridge Anatomical Teaching School under the late-Victorian Poor Law, 1870–1914', *Medical History*, vol. 48, no. 1, 2004, pp. 69–94

—, 'Whose Body is it Anyway? Trading the Dead Poor, Coroner's Disputes and the Business of Anatomy at Oxford University, 1885–1929', *Bulletin of the History of Medicine*, vol. 82, no. 4, 2008, pp. 775–819

—, and Steve King, '"Begging for a Burial": Form, Function and Conflict in

Nineteenth-century Pauper Burial', *Social History*, vol. 30, no. 3, 2005, pp. 321–41

Hutter, Albert D., 'Dismemberment and Articulation in *Our Mutual Friend*', *Dickens Studies Annual*, vol. 11, 1983, pp. 135–75

—, 'The Novelist as Resurrectionist: Dickens and the Dilemma of Death', *Dickens Studies Annual*, vol. 12, 1983, pp. 1–39

Hwang, Haewon, *London's Underground Spaces: Representing the Victorian City, 1840–1915* (Edinburgh, Edinburgh University Press, 2013)

Jackson, Mark, ed., *Infanticide: Historical Perspectives on Child Murder and Concealment, 1550–2000* (Farnham, Ashgate, 2002)

Jalland, Pat, *Death in the Victorian Family* (Oxford, Oxford University Press, 1996)

—, and John Hooper, *Women from Birth to Death: The Female Life Cycle in Britain, 1830–1914* (Brighton, Harvester Press, 1986)

Jenks, Timothy, 'Contesting the Hero: The Funeral of Admiral Lord Nelson', *Journal of British Studies*, vol. 39, no. 4, 2000, pp. 422–53

Jupp, Peter C., *From Dust to Ashes: Cremation and the British Way of Death* (Basingstoke, Palgrave Macmillan, 2006)

—, and Clare Gittings, *Death in England: An Illustrated History* (Manchester, Manchester University Press, 1999)

—, and Glennys Howarth, *The Changing Face of Death: Historical Accounts of Death and Disposal* (Basingstoke, Macmillan, 1997)

Kammen, Michael, *Digging up the Dead: A History of Notable American Reburials* (Chicago, University of Chicago Press, 2010)

Kaplan, Louis, *The Strange Case of William Mumler, Spirit Photographer* (Minneapolis, University of Minnesota Press, 2008)

Kellehear, Allan, ed., *A Social History of Dying* (Cambridge, Cambridge University Press, 2007)

—, *The Study of Dying: From Autonomy to Transformation* (Cambridge, Cambridge University Press, 2009)

Kent, David A., 'Christina Rossetti's Dying', *Journal of Pre-Raphaelite Studies*, vol. 5, 1996, pp. 83–99

Killeen, Jarlath, *History of the Gothic: Gothic Literature, 1825–1914* (Cardiff, University of Wales Press, 2009)

Kingstone, Helen, and Kate Lister, eds., *Paraphernalia! Victorian Objects* (New York, Routledge, 2018)

Knott, John, 'Popular Attitudes to Death and Dissection in Early Nineteenth-Century Britain: The Anatomy Act and the Poor', *Labour History*, vol. 49, 1985, pp. 1–18

Kontou, Tatiana, and Sarah Willburn, eds., *The Ashgate Research Companion to Nineteenth-century Spiritualism and the Occult* (Farnham, Ashgate, 2012)

Krauss, Rolf H., *Beyond Light and Shadow: The Role of Photography in Certain Paranormal Phenomena: A Historical Survey* (Munich, Nazraeli Press, 1995)

Kucich, John, 'Death Worship among the Victorians: *The Old Curiosity Shop*', *PMLA*, vol. 95, no. 1, 1980, pp. 58–72

Kwint, Marius, Christopher Breward and Jeremy Aynsley, eds., *Material Memories* (Oxford, Berg, 1999)

Landers, John, *Death and the Metropolis: Studies in the Demographic History of London, 1670–1830* (Cambridge, Cambridge University Press, 1993)

Laqueur, Thomas W., *The Work of the Dead: A Cultural History of Mortal Remains* (Princeton, Princeton University Press, 2015)

—, 'Cemeteries, Religion and the Culture of Capitalism', in John A. James and Mark Thomas, eds., *Capitalism in Context: Essays on Economic Development and Cultural Change in Honour of R.M. Hartwell* (Chicago, University of Chicago Press, 1994)

—, 'Crowds, Carnival and the State in English Executions, 1604–1868', in A.L. Beier, David Cannadine and James M. Rosenheim, eds., *The First Modern Society: Essays in Honour of Lawrence Stone* (Cambridge, Cambridge University Press, 1989)

—, 'Bodies, Death and Pauper Funerals', *Representations*, vol. 1, 1983, pp. 109–31

—, 'The Deep Time of the Dead', *Social Research*, vol. 78, no. 3, 2011, pp. 799–820

Ledger, Sally, 'Don't be So Melodramatic! Dickens and the Affective Mode', *Interdisciplinary Studies in the Long Nineteenth Century*, vol. 4, 2007

—, 'From Queen Caroline to Lady Dedlock: Dickens and the Popular Radical Imagination', *Victorian Literature and Culture*, vol. 32, no. 2, 2004, pp. 575–600

Lee, Daryl, *The History of Suicide in England, 1650–1850*; vol. 7: *1800–1850: Legal Contexts, Religious Writings and Medical Writers*; vol. 8: *1800–1850: Medical Writers (continued), Statistical Inquiries, Social Criticism, Poetic and Popular Representations and Cases* (London, Pickering and Chatto, 2013)

Lerner, Laurence, *Angels and Absences: Child Deaths in the Nineteenth Century* (Nashville, Vanderbilt University Press, 1997)

Lévi-Strauss, Claude, *A World on the Wane* (*Tristes Tropiques*), trs. John Russell (London, Hutchinson, 1961)

Liggins, Emma, *Odd Women?: Spinsters, Lesbians and Widows in British Women's Fiction, 1850s–1930s* (Manchester, Manchester University Press, 2014)

Linkman, Audrey, *Photography and Death* (London, Reaktion, 2011)

Litten, Julian, *The English Way of Death: The Common Funeral Since 1450* (London, Robert Hale, 1991)

Llewellyn, Nigel, *The Art of Death: Visual Culture in the English Death Ritual,*
    c.1500–c.1800 (London, Reaktion, 1991)
Luciano, Dana, *Arranging Grief: Sacred Time and the Body in Nineteenth-century*
    America (New York, New York University Press, 2007)
Luthi, Anne Louise, *Sentimental Jewellery* (Princes Risborough, Shire, 2001)
Lutz, Deborah, *Relics of Death in Victorian Literature and Culture* (Cambridge,
    Cambridge University Press, 2015)
—, 'The Dead Still Among Us: Victorian Secular Relics, Hair Jewelry, and
    Death Culture', *Victorian Literature and Culture*, vol. 39,
    no. 1, 2011, pp. 127–42
—, 'Relics and Death Culture in *Wuthering Heights*', *NOVEL: A Forum on*
    Fiction, vol. 45, no. 3, 2012, pp. 389–408
Lynch, Linda G., 'Death and Burial in the Poor Law Union Workhouses in
    Ireland', *Journal of Irish Archaeology*, vol. 23, 2014, pp. 189–203
Lysaght, Patricia, 'Hospitality at Wakes and Funerals in Ireland from
    the Seventeenth to the Nineteenth Century: Some Evidence from the
    Written Record', *Folklore*, vol. 114, no. 3, 2003, pp. 403–26
McAllister, David, *Imagining the Dead in British Literature and Culture,*
    1790–1848 (Cham, Switzerland, Palgrave Macmillan, 2018)
McCarthy, Patrick, 'Lydgate, "The New, Young Surgeon" of Middlemarch',
    Studies in English Literature, 1500–1900, vol. 10, no. 4, 1970, pp. 805–16
McCorristine, Shane, *Spectres of the Self: Thinking about Ghosts and Ghost-seeing*
    in England, 1750–1920 (Cambridge, Cambridge University Press, 2010)
—, *William Corder and the Red Barn Murder: Journeys of the Criminal Body*
    (Basingstoke, Palgrave Macmillan, 2014)
—, ed., *Interdisciplinary Perspectives on Mortality and its Timings: When is*
    Death? (London, Palgrave Macmillan, 2017)
McDannell, Colleen, and Bernhard Lang, *Heaven: A History* (New Haven,
    Yale University Press, 1988)
McDonagh, Josephine, *Child Murder and British Culture, 1720–1900*
    (Cambridge, Cambridge University Press, 2003)
—, 'Child-murder Narratives in George Eliot's *Adam Bede*: Embedded
    Histories and Fictional Representation', *Nineteenth-century Literature*,
    vol. 56, no. 2, 2001, pp. 228–59
Macdonald, Helen, *Human Remains: Dissection and its Histories* (London, Yale
    University Press, 2006)
—, 'Legal Bodies: Dissecting Murderers at the Royal College of Surgeons,
    London, 1800–1832', *Traffic, An Interdisciplinary Postgraduate Journal*,
    vol. 2, 2003, pp. 9–32
MacDonald, Michael, and Terence R. Murphy, *Sleepless Souls: Suicide in Early*
    Modern England (Oxford, Clarendon Press, 1990)

McGavran, James Holt, Jr, ed., *Romanticism and Children's Literature in Nineteenth-century England* (Athens, University of Georgia Press, 1991)

Mack, Douglas S., 'The Body in the Opened Grave: Robert Burns and Robert Wringhim', *Studies in Hogg and his World*, vol. 7, 1996, pp. 70–79

Makala, Melissa Edmundson, *Women's Ghost Literature in Nineteenth-century Britain* (Cardiff, University of Wales Press, 2013)

Mangham, Andrew, ed., *The Cambridge Companion to Sensation Fiction* (Cambridge, Cambridge University Press, 2013)

Marshall, Gail, 'Popular Sentiments and Public Executions', *19: Interdisciplinary Studies in the Long Nineteenth Century*, vol. 14, 2012, online at http://19.bbk.ac.uk

Marshall, Nancy Rose, 'A Fully Consummated Sacrifice upon Her Altar: Victorian Cremation as Metamorphosis', *Victorian Studies*, vol. 56, no. 3, 2014, pp. 458–69

Marshall, Peter, *Beliefs and the Dead in Reformation England* (Oxford, Oxford University Press, 2002)

Marshall, Tim, *Murdering to Dissect: Grave-robbing, Frankenstein and the Anatomy Literature* (Manchester, Manchester University Press, 1995)

Mason, Laura, ed., *Food and the Rites of Passage*, Leeds Symposium on Food History, 'Food and Society' series (London, Prospect, 2002)

Matteoni, Francesca, 'The Criminal Corpse in Pieces', *Mortality*, vol. 21, no. 3, 2016, pp. 198–209

Matthews, Samantha, *Poetical Remains: Poets' Graves, Bodies and Books in the Nineteenth Century* (Oxford, Oxford University Press, 2004)

—, 'Burying Tennyson: The Victorian Laureate Immortalized', *Mortality*, vol. 7, no. 3, 2002, pp. 247–68

Maunder, Andrew, and Grace Moore, eds., *Victorian Crime, Madness and Sensation* (London, Routledge, 2016)

May, Trevor, *The Victorian Undertaker* (Princes Risborough, Shire, 1996)

Mays, Sas, and Neil Matheson, eds., *The Machine and the Ghost: Technology and Spiritualism in Nineteenth- to Twenty-first-century Art and Culture* (Manchester, Manchester University Press, 2013)

Menefee, Samuel Pyeatt, and Allen D.C. Simpson, 'The West Port Murders and the Miniature Coffins from Arthur's Seat', *The Book of the Old Edinburgh Club*, new series, vol. 3, 1994, pp. 63–81

Metcalf, Peter, and Richard Huntington, *Celebrations of Death: The Anthropology of Mortuary Ritual* (Cambridge, Cambridge University Press, 1991)

Miller, Ian, 'Representations of Suicide in Urban North-west England *c.*1870–1910: The Formative Role of Respectability, Class, Gender and Morality', *Mortality*, vol. 15, no. 3, 2010, pp. 191–204

Millward, Robert, and Frances Bell, 'Infant Mortality in Victorian Britain: The

Mother as Medium', *Economic History Review*, vol. 54, no. 4, 2001, pp. 699–733

Mitchell, Piers, ed., *Anatomical Dissection in Enlightenment England and Beyond: Autopsy, Pathology and Display* (Farnham, Ashgate, 2012)

Mitchell, Rebecca N., 'Death Becomes Her: On the Progressive Potential of Victorian Mourning', *Victorian Literature and Culture*, vol. 41, no. 4, 2013, pp. 595–620

—, ed., *Fashioning the Victorians: A Critical Sourcebook* (London, Bloomsbury Visual Arts, 2018)

Mogensen, Jannie Uhre, 'Fading into Innocence: Death, Sexuality and Moral Restoration in Henry Peach Robinson's "Fading Away"', *Victorian Review*, vol. 32, no. 1, 2006, pp. 1–17

Monk, Daniel, 'Wealth, Families and Death: Socio-Legal Perspectives on Wills and Inheritance: Introduction', *Oñati Socio-Legal Series*, vol. 4, no. 2, 2014, pp. 170–75

Morley, John, *Death, Heaven and the Victorians* (London, Studio Vista, 1971)

Morris, R.J., *Cholera, 1832: The Social Response to an Epidemic* (London, Croom Helm, 1976)

Munich, Adrienne, *Queen Victoria's Secrets* (New York, Columbia University Press, 1996)

Munn, Geoffrey C., *The Triumph of Love: Jewellery, 1530–1930* (London, Thames & Hudson, 1993)

Murdoch, Lydia, '"Suppressed Grief": Mourning the Death of British Children and the Memory of the 1857 Indian Rebellion', *Journal of British Studies*, vol. 51, 2012, pp. 364–92

Mytum, Harold, 'Public Health and Private Sentiment: The Development of Cemetery Architecture and Funerary Monuments from the Eighteenth Century Onwards', *World Archaeology*, vol. 21, no. 2, 1989, pp. 283–97

Natale, Simone, *Supernatural Entertainments: Victorian Spiritualism and the Rise of Modern Media Culture* (University Park, The Pennsylvania State University Press, 2016)

Nelson, Claudia, Julie-Marie Strange, Susan B. Egenolf, eds., *British Family Life, 1780–1914* (5 vols., London: Pickering & Chatto, 2012)

Nelson, Heather, 'Case Study: Widowhood: "It's a Great Shame she has to Part with Anything"', in *I Do?: Women, Consent, and Marriage in Nineteenth-Century England* (forthcoming)

Nicoletti, Lisa J., 'Resuscitating Ophelia: Images of Suicide and Suicidal Insanity in Nineteenth-century England', Ph.D. thesis, 1999

Nikolajeva, Maria, ed., *Aspects and Issues in the History of Children's Literature* (Westport, CT, Greenwood Press, 1995)

Nisbet, Jeff, 'We're Not Dead! The Arthur's Seat Coffins Rise Again', April

2017, online at https://www.academia.edu/36453451/Were_Not_Dead_
The_Arthurs_Seat_Coffins_Rise_Again

Nutt, Alfred, 'Tommy on the Tub's Grave', *Folklore*, vol. 5, no. 4, 1894,
pp. 290–92

O'Briain, Helen Conrad, and Julie Anne Stevens, eds., *The Ghost Story from the
Middle Ages to the Twentieth Century: A Ghostly Genre* (Dublin, Four
Courts Press, 2010)

O'Brien, Ellen L., *Crime in Verse: The Poetics of Murder in the Victorian Era*
(Columbus, Ohio State University Press, 2008)

Ofek, Galia, *Representations of Hair in Victorian Literature and Culture*
(Farnham, Shire, 2009)

Oppenheim, Janet, *The Other World: Spiritualism and Psychical Research in
England, 1850–1914* (Cambridge, Cambridge University Press, 1985)

Oulton, Carolyn W. de la L., *Below the Fairy City: A Life of Jerome K. Jerome*
(Brighton, Victorian Secrets, 2012)

Owen, Alex, *The Darkened Room: Women, Power and Spiritualism in Late
Nineteenth-century England* (London, Virago, 1989)

Packard, Jerrold M., *Farewell in Splendour: The Death of Queen Victoria and
Her Age* (Stroud, Sutton, 2000)

Parsons, Brian, *Committed to the Cleansing Flame: The Development of
Cremation in Nineteenth-century England* (Reading, Spire, 2005)

Parvaresh, Vahid, and Alessandro Capone, eds., *The Pragmeme of
Accommodation: The Case of Interaction around the Event of Death* (Cham,
Switzerland, Springer, 2017)

Pascoe, Judith, *The Hummingbird Cabinet: A Rare and Curious History of
Romantic Collectors* (Ithaca, NY, Cornell University Press, 2006)

Peacock, Mabel, 'Executed Criminals and Folk-Medicine', *Folklore*, vol. 7,
no. 3, 1896, pp. 268–83

Pearsall, Cornelia, 'Burying the Duke: Victorian Mourning and the Funeral of
the Duke of Wellington', *Victorian Literature and Culture*, vol. 27, 1999,
pp. 365–93

Pelling, Margaret, *Cholera, Fever and English Medicine, 1825–1865* (Oxford,
Oxford University Press, 1978)

Penny, N.B., 'The Commercial Garden Necropolis of the Early Nineteenth
Century and its Critics', *Garden History*, vol. 2, no. 3, 1974, pp. 61–76

Pionke, Albert D., and Denise Tischler Millstein, eds., *Victorian Secrecy:
Economies of Knowledge and Concealment* (Farnham, Ashgate, 2010)

Pointon, Marcia, *Brilliant Effects: A Cultural History of Gem Stones and Jewellery*
(New Haven, Yale University Press, 2009)

—, 'Wearing Memory: Mourning, Jewellery and the Body', in Gisela Ecker,
ed., *Trauer tragen – Trauer zeigen: Inszenierungen der Geschlechter*
(Munich, Wilhelm Fink Verlag, 1999)

Pollock, Linda, *A Lasting Relationship: Parents and Children over Three Centuries* (London, Fourth Estate, 1987)

Porter, Roy, 'The Hour of Philippe Ariès', *Mortality*, vol. 4, no. 1, 1999, pp. 83–90

Punter, David, ed., *A New Companion to the Gothic* (Chichester, Wiley-Blackwell, 2012)

Quigley, Christine, *Dissection on Display: Cadavers, Anatomists and Public Spectacle* (Jefferson, NC, McFarland & Co., 2012)

Rack, Henry D., 'Evangelical Endings: Death-beds in Evangelical Biography', *Bulletin of the John Rylands University Library of Manchester*, vol. 74, 1992, pp. 39–56

Ragon, Michel, *The Space of Death: A Study of Funerary Architecture, Decoration and Urbanism*, trs. Alan Sheridan (Charlottesville, University Press of Virginia, 1983)

Ramchandani, Dilip, 'Pathological Grief: Two Victorian Case Studies', *Psychiatric Quarterly*, vol. 67, no. 1, 1996

Rappaport, Helen, *Magnificent Obsession: Victoria, Albert and the Death that Changed the Monarchy* (London, Hutchinson, 2011)

Reed, John R., *Victorian Conventions* ([Athens], Ohio University Press, 1975)

Reeve, Jez, and Max Adams, *The Spitalfields Project*, vol. 1: *The Archaeology: Across the Styx* (York, Council for British Archaeology, 1993)

Reich, Noa, 'Victorian Inheritance, Speculation and *Middlemarch*'s "Dead Hand"', *Law and Literature*, 2021, pp. 1–28

Rennell, Tony, *Last Days of Glory: The Death of Queen Victoria* (London, Viking, 2000)

Retford, Kate, 'A Death in the Family: Posthumous Portraiture in Eighteenth-century England', *Art History*, vol. 22, no. 1, 2010, pp. 74–97

Richards, Thomas, *The Commodity Culture of Victorian England: Advertising and Spectacle, 1851–1914* (London, Verso, 1991)

Richardson, Ruth, *Death, Dissection and the Destitute* (London, Routledge and Kegan Paul, 1987)

—, '"Trading Assassins" and the Licensing of Anatomy', in Roger French and Andrew Wear, eds., *British Medicine in the Age of Reform* (Abingdon, Routledge, 1991)

Ridley, Jane, 'Bertie Prince of Wales: Prince Hal and the Widow of Windsor', in Frank Lorenz Müller, Heidi Mehrkens, eds., *Royal Heirs and the Uses of Soft Power in Nineteenth-century Europe* (London, Palgrave Macmillan, 2016)

Riso, Mary, *The Narrative of the Good Death: The Evangelical Deathbed in Victorian England* (Farnham, Ashgate, 2015)

Rosner, Lisa, *The Anatomy Murders: Being the True and Spectacular History of Edinburgh's Notorious Burke and Hare and the Men of Science who Abetted them in the Commission of their Most Heinous Crimes* (Philadelphia, University of Pennsylvania Press, 2010)

Rugg, Julie, 'Lawn Cemeteries: The Emergence of a New Landscape of Death', *Urban History*, vol. 33, no. 2, 2006, pp. 213–33

—, Fiona Stirling and Andy Clayden, 'Churchyard and Cemetery in an English Industrial City: Sheffield, 1740–1900', *Urban History*, vol. 41, no. 4, 2014, pp. 627–46

Rutherford, Sarah, *The Victorian Cemetery* (Oxford, Shire, 2008)

Sabatos, Terri R., 'Images of Death and Domesticity in Victorian Britain', D.Phil. thesis, Indiana University (2001)

Saglia, Diego, '"The Frightened Stage": The Sensational Proliferation of Ghost Melodrama in the 1820s', *Studies in Romanticism*, vol. 54, no. 2, 2015, pp. 269–93

Sánchez-Eppler, Karen, 'Decomposing: Wordsworth's Poetry of Epitaph and English Burial Reform', *Nineteenth-century Literature*, vol. 42, no. 4, 1988, pp. 415–31

Sanders, Andrew, *Charles Dickens, Resurrectionist* (London, Macmillan, 1982)

Sayer, Duncan, 'Death and the Dissenter: Group Identity and Stylistic Simplicity as Witnessed in Nineteenth-century Nonconformist Graves', *Historical Archaeology*, vol. 45, no. 4, 2011, pp. 115–34

Scandura, Jani, 'Deadly Professionals: *Dracula*, Undertakers and the Embalmed Corpse', *Victorian Studies*, vol. 40, no. 1, 1996, pp. 1–30

Schor, Esther, *Bearing the Dead: The British Culture of Mourning from the Enlightenment to Victoria* (Princeton, Princeton University Press, 1994)

Scoggin, Daniel P., 'A Speculative Resurrection: Death, Money and the Vampiric Economy of *Our Mutual Friend*', *Victorian Literature and Culture*, vol. 30, no. 1, 2002, pp. 99–125

Scott, Patrick, 'Anatomizing Professionalism: Medicine, Authorship and R.L. Stevenson's "The Body-Snatcher"', *Victorians Institute Journal*, vol. 27, 1999, pp. 91–130

Semmel, Stuart, 'Reading the Tangible Past: British Tourism, Collecting and Memory after Waterloo', *Representations*, no. 69, 2000, special issue: 'Grounds for Remembering', pp. 9–37

Sheumaker, Helen, *Love Entwined: The Curious History of Hairwork in America* (Philadelphia, University of Pennsylvania Press, 2007)

—, '"This Lock You See": Nineteenth-century Hair Work as the Commodified Self', *Fashion Theory*, vol. 1, no. 4, 1997, pp. 421–45

Shorter, Edward, 'The History of the Doctor–Patient Relationship', in W.F. Bynum and Roy Porter, eds., *Companion Encyclopedia of the History of Medicine* (Abingdon, Routledge, 1993)

Sigsworth, Michael, and Michael Warboys, 'The Public's View of Public Health in Mid-Victorian Britain', *Urban History*, vol. 21, no. 2, 1994, pp. 237–50

Sinnema, Peter W., *The Wake of Wellington: Englishness in 1852* (Athens, Ohio University Press, 2006)

—, 'Anxiously Managing Mourning: Wellington's Funeral and the Press', *Victorian Review*, vol. 25, no. 2, 2000, pp. 30–60

Smith, Andrew, *The Ghost Story, 1840–1920: A Cultural History* (Manchester, Manchester University Press, 2010)

—, *Gothic Death, 1740–1914: A Literary History* (Manchester, Manchester University Press, 2016)

—, *Victorian Demons: Medicine, Masculinity and the Gothic at the* Fin-de-siècle (Manchester, Manchester University Press, 2004)

Smith, Michael, *The Secularization of Death in Scotland, 1815–1900: How the Funeral Industry Displaced the Church as Custodians of the Dead* (Lewiston, NY, Edwin Mellen, 2014)

—, 'The Church of Scotland and the Funeral Industry in Nineteenth-century Edinburgh', *The Scottish Historical Review*, vol. 88, no. 225, part 1, 2009

Snell, K.D.M., 'Gravestones, Belonging and Local Attachment in England, 1700–2000', *Past and Present*, vol. 179, 2003, pp. 97–134

Solicari, Sonia, 'Selling Sentiment: The Commodification of Emotion in Victorian Visual Culture', *Interdisciplinary Studies in the Long Nineteenth Century*, vol. 4, 2007

Sparks, Tabitha, *The Doctor in the Victorian Novel: Family Practices* (Farnham, Ashgate, 2009)

Stannard, David E., *The Puritan Way of Death: A Study in Religion, Culture and Social Change* (Oxford, Oxford University Press, 1977)

Stauffer, Andrew M., 'Ruins of Paper: Dickens and the Necropolitan Library', *Romanticism and Victorianism on the Net*, no. 47, August 2007, online at http://id.erudit.org/iderudit/016700ar.

Stearns, Peter N., *American Cool: Constructing a Twentieth-century Emotional Style* (New York, New York University Press, 1994)

Stone, Harry, *The Night Side of Dickens: Cannibalism, Passion, Necessity* (Columbus, Ohio State University Press, 1994)

Strachey, Lytton, *Queen Victoria* (New York, Harcourt, Brace & Co., 1921)

Strange, Julie-Marie, *Death, Grief and Poverty in Britain, 1870–1914* (Cambridge, Cambridge University Press, 2005)

—, 'Tho' Lost to Sight, to Memory Dear': Pragmatism, Sentimentality and Working-class Attitudes towards the Grave, c.1875–1914', *Mortality*, vol. 8, no. 2, 2003

Strasdin, Kate, *The Dress Diary of Mrs Anne Sykes: Secrets from a Victorian Woman's Wardrobe* (London, Chatto & Windus, 2023)

—, *Inside the Royal Wardrobe: A Dress History of Queen Alexandra* (London, Bloomsbury Academic, 2017)

Strasser, Susan, ed., *Commodifying Everything: Relationships of the Market* (London, Routledge, 2003)

Staves, Susan, *Married Women's Separate Property in England, 1660–1833* (Cambridge, MA, Harvard University Press, 1990)

Summers, Anne, 'The Mysterious Demise of Sarah Gamp: The Domiciliary Nurse and Her Detractors, *c.*1830–1860', *Victorian Studies*, vol. 32, no. 3, 1989

Tarlow, Sarah, *The Golden and Ghoulish Age of the Gibbet in Britain* (London, Palgrave Macmillan, 2017)

—, 'Curious Afterlives: The Enduring Appeal of the Criminal Corpse', *Mortality*, vol. 21, no. 3, 2016, pp. 210–28

—, 'Landscapes of Memory: The Nineteenth-century Garden Cemetery', *European Journal of Archaeology*, vol. 3, no. 2, 2000, pp. 217–39

—, and Emma Battell Lowman, *Harnessing the Power of the Criminal Corpse* (Cham, Switzerland, Palgrave Macmillan, 2018)

—, and Zoe Dyndor, 'The Landscape of the Gibbet', *Landscape History*, vol. 36, no. 1, 2015, pp. 71–88

—, and Susie West, eds., *The Familiar Past? Archaeologies of Later Historical Britain* (London, Routledge, 1999)

Taylor, Lou, *Mourning Dress: A Costume and Social History* (London, George Allen and Unwin, 1983)

Thane, Pat, *Old Age in English History: Past Experiences, Present Issues* (Oxford, Oxford University Press, 2000)

Thompson, F.M.L., ed., *The Cambridge Social History of Britain, 1750–1950*, vol. 3: *Social Agencies and Institutions* (Cambridge, Cambridge University Press, 1990)

Thorsheim, Peter, 'The Corpse in the Garden: Burial, Health and the Environment in Nineteenth-century London', *Environmental History*, vol. 16, no. 1, 2011, pp. 38–68

Thurschwell, Pamela, *Literature, Technology and Magical Thinking, 1880–1920* (Cambridge, Cambridge University Press, 2001)

Toewe, Anne M., 'Widowers' Weeds: Men's Victorian Mourning Fashion, 1837–1901', *The Journal of Dress History*, vol. 4, no. 2, 2020, pp. 162–94

Tomes, Nancy, 'A "Torrent of Abuse": Crimes of Violence Between Working-class Men and Women in London, 1840–1875', *Journal of Social History*, vol. 11, no. 3, 1978, pp. 328–45

Torgerson, Beth, 'Representing Illness: Competing Religious and Scientific Discourses in Harriet Martineau's *Life in the Sick-Room* and *Autobiography*', *Victorians: A Journal of Culture and Literature*, no. 135, 2019, pp. 13–27

Tromp, Marlene, *Altered States: Sex, Nation, Drugs and Self-Transformation in Victorian Spiritualism* (Albany, State University of New York Press, 2006)

Tucker, Herbert F., ed., *A Companion to Victorian Literature and Culture* (Malden, MA, Blackwell, 1999)

Twitchell, James B., *The Living Dead: A Study of the Vampire in Romantic Literature* (Durham, NC, Duke University Press, 1981)

Vincent, David, 'Love and Death and the Nineteenth-century Working Class', *Social History*, vol. 5, no. 2, 1980, pp. 223–47

Vita, Paul, 'In Keeping with Modern Views: Publishing Epitaphs in the Nineteenth Century', *Victorian Review*, vol. 25, no. 1, 1999, pp. 14–34

Vovelle, Michel, *Ideologies and Mentalities*, trs. Eamon O'Flaherty (Cambridge, Polity, 1990)

—, *La Mort et l'occident: de 1300 à nos jours* (Paris, Gallimard, 1983)

Walvin, James, 'Dust to Dust: Celebrations of Death in Victorian England', *Historical Reflections / Réflexions Historiques*, vol. 9, no. 3, 1982, pp. 353–71

Ward, Richard, ed., *A Global History of Execution and the Criminal Corpse* (Basingstoke, Palgrave Macmillan, 2015)

Waters, Catherine, 'Materializing Mourning: Dickens, Funerals and Epitaphs', *19: Interdisciplinary Studies in the Long Nineteenth Century*, vol. 14, 2012

—, 'Trading in Death: Contested Commodities in *Household Words*', *Victorian Periodicals Review*, vol. 36, no. 4, 2003, pp. 313–30

Wheeler, Michael, *Death and the Future Life in Victorian Literature and Theology* (Cambridge, Cambridge University Press, 1990)

White, Stephen, 'A Burial Ahead of its Time? The Crookenden Burial Case and the Sanctioning of Cremation in England and Wales', *Mortality*, vol. 7, no. 2, 2002, pp. 171–90

Whyte, Nicola, 'The Deviant Dead in the Norfolk Landscape', *Landscapes*, vol. 4, no. 1, 2003, pp. 24–39

Wiener, Martin, 'Alice Arden to Bill Sikes: Changing Nightmares of Intimate Violence in England, 1558–1869', *Journal of British Studies*, vol. 40, 2001, pp. 184–212

Wildgoose, Jane, 'Beyond All Price: Victorian Hair Jewelry, Commemoration and Story-telling', *Fashion Theory*, vol. 22, no. 6, 2018, pp. 699–726

Williams, Jacob Steere, 'The Perfect Food and the Filth Disease: Milk-borne Typhoid and Epidemiological Practice in Late Victorian Britain', *Journal of the History of Medicine and Allied Sciences*, vol. 65, no. 4, 2010, pp. 514–45

Willis, Martin, '"The Invisible Giant", *Dracula* and Disease', *Studies in the Novel*, vol. 39, no. 3, 2007, pp. 301–25

Wise, Sarah, *The Italian Boy: Murder and Grave-robbery in 1830s London* (London, Jonathan Cape, 2004)

Wolffe, John, *Great Deaths: Grieving, Religion and Nationhood in Victorian and Edwardian Britain* (Oxford, British Academy/Oxford University Press, 2000)

—, 'Responding to National Grief: Memorial Sermons on the Famous in
    Britain, 1800–1914', *Mortality*, vol. 1, no. 3, 1996, pp. 283–96
Wolfreys, Julian, *Victorian Hauntings: Spectrality, Gothic, the Uncanny and
    Literature* (Basingstoke, Palgrave, 2002)
Wood, Christopher, *Victorian Painting* (London, Weidenfeld and Nicolson,
    1999)
Wood, Claire, *Dickens and the Business of Death* (Cambridge, Cambridge
    University Press, 2015)
Woods, Robert, and P.R. Andrew Hinde, 'Mortality in Victorian England:
    Models and Patterns', *The Journal of Interdisciplinary History*, vol. 18,
    no. 1, 1987, pp. 27–54
Wooffitt, Robin, and Hannah Gilbert, 'Discourse, Rhetoric and the
    Accomplishment of Mediumship in Stage Demonstrations', *Mortality*,
    vol. 13, no. 3, 2008, pp. 222–40
Wright, David, 'The Certification of Insanity in Nineteenth-century England
    and Wales', *History of Psychiatry*, vol. 9, 1998, pp. 267–89
Zemka, Sue, 'The Death of Nancy "Sikes", 1838–1912', *Representations*, vol. 110,
    no. 1, 2010, pp. 29–57

Notes

INTRODUCTION

1 Contemporary newspaper reports appeared in, amongst others: *The Scotsman*, 16 July 1836; *Caledonian Mercury*, 25 August 1836; *Edinburgh Witness*, 31 August 1842. *The Scotsman* returned to the story, 16 May 1906, to report on the donation to the museum; and in 1956, Robert Chapman, *Edinburgh Evening Dispatch* (and reprinted widely, e.g. *Leicester Evening Mail*, 5 December 1956), revived and elaborated the episode. The main modern source on these figures and their coffins is Samuel Pyeatt Menefee and Allen D.C. Simpson, 'The West Port Murders and the Miniature Coffins from Arthur's Seat', *The Book of the Old Edinburgh Club*, new series, vol. 3, 1994, pp. 63–81. As can be seen from the title, they are adherents of the Burke and Hare story explored on pp. 224–5. Another theory, by Jeff Nisbet, 'We're Not Dead! The Arthur's Seat Coffins Rise Again', April 2017, https://www.academia.edu/36453451/ Were_Not_Dead_The_Arthurs_Seat_Coffins_Rise_Again, accessed 21 September 2021, connects these figures to the Radical War of 1820, when unemployed artisans called for a national strike to improve working conditions. Nineteen men were transported, and Nisbet, not unpersuasively, suggests that the figurines are representations of them.
2 Robert Blair, 'The Grave. A Poem' (3rd ed., London, J. Waugh, 1749), p. 30.
3 Cited in David McAllister, *Imagining the Dead in British Literature and Culture, 1790–1848* (Cham, Switzerland, Palgrave Macmillan, 2018), pp. 6–7.
4 Charles Dickens, 'Night Walks', *The Uncommercial Traveller* (London, Chapman and Hall, 1866), p. 93.
5 Charles Dickens, *Bleak House* (London, Bradbury and Evans, 1853), p. 459.
6 See Sarah Webster Goodwin, *Kitsch and Culture: The Dance of Death in Nineteenth-century Literature and Graphic Arts* (New York, Garland, 1988), pp. 13, 23ff.

I THE SICKROOM

1 Even during the early days of the global Covid pandemic in 2020, when those badly afflicted with this novel virus were desperately ill on ventilators in ICU units, it was still likely that three out of every four patients would survive to go home, in the first, and at this writing the most deadly, wave of the pandemic. Sara C. Auld, et al., 'ICU and ventilator mortality among critically ill adults with COVID-19', *Crit. Care Med.*, preprint, https://www.ncbi.nlm.nih.gov/pmc/articles/PMC7276026/, accessed 11 February 2022.

2 Allan Kellehear, ed., *The Study of Dying: From Autonomy to Transformation* (Cambridge, Cambridge University Press, 2009), p. 2.

3 My thanks to Dr Richard Cruess for this information. He points out that the economist John Maynard Keynes died after a series of heart attacks in 1942 that were almost certainly engendered by an earlier bout of scarlet fever.

4 These types of fevers are itemized by a doctor in Albany Fonblanque's novel *Cut Adrift* (London, Richard Bentley, 1869), vol. 2, p. 46, who adds that he cannot say which, as he is 'not a conjuror'.

5 The paragraphs outlining the story of the Taits are drawn from Rev. William Benham, *Catharine and Craufurd Tait . . . A Memoir* (London, Macmillan & Co., 1881), passim; and Pat Jalland, *Death in the Victorian Family* (Oxford, Oxford University Press, 1996), pp. 124ff.

6 John Epps, *Diary of the Late John Epps, M.D. Edin.*, ed. 'by Mrs. Epps' (London, Kent & Co., [1875]), pp. 151–2. Footnote: This particular advertisement appeared in Mme Tussaud's catalogue of 1870, John Johnson Collection, Bodleian Library, Waxworks 5 (16).

7 Ruth Bernard Yeazell, ed., *The Death and Letters of Alice James* (Berkeley, University of California Press, 1981), pp. 10–12.

8 Alice James, *The Diary of Alice James*, ed. Leon Edel (New York, Dodd, Mead, 1964), p. 6.

9 Florence Nightingale, 'Cassandra', printed in Ray Strachey, *The Cause: A Short History of the Women's Movement in Great Britain* (London, Virago, 1978), pp. 406–8.

10 Monica E. Baly and H.C.G. Matthew, 'Florence Nightingale', *The Oxford Dictionary of National Biography*, https://doi-org.lonlib.idm.oclc.org/10.1093/ref:odnb/35241, accessed 16 February 2022.

11 Elizabeth Gaskell, *Ruth* (London, Chapman and Hall, 1853), vol. 3, p. 170.

12 Mrs Leslie [Julia] Stephen, *Notes from Sick Rooms* (London, privately printed, Smith, Elder, 1883).

13 [Priscilla Maurice], 'Suggestions to Persons in Attendance on the Sick

and Dying; Being, An Appendix to *Sickness: Its Trials and Blessings'* (London, Francis & John Rivington, 1851), pp. 4–5, 41ff., 51ff., 65, 75.

14 William Thackeray, *The History of Pendennis: His Fortunes and Misfortunes, His Friends and His Greatest Enemy* (London, Bradbury and Evans, 1850), p. 661.

15 Menella B. Smedley, *A Mere Story* (London, Sampson Low, 1865), cited in Roy Porter, 'The Hour of Philippe Ariès', *Mortality*, vol. 4, no. 1, 1999, p. 87.

16 Olive Anderson, *Suicide in Victorian and Edwardian England* (Oxford, Clarendon Press, 1987), p. 159.

17 Cited in Edward Shorter, 'The History of the Doctor–Patient Relationship', in W.F. Bynum and Roy Porter, eds., *Companion Encyclopedia of the History of Medicine* (Abingdon, Routledge, 1993), p. 785. Unfortunately, this advertisement is not geographically located beyond 'England', nor is it dated.

18 [James Malcolm Rymer or Thomas Peckett Prest], *Varney the Vampire, or, The Feast of Blood* (1847), Chapter 88, https://archive.org/details/VarneyTheVampyre/page/n5/mode/2up, accessed 21 February 2022.

19 *Courtauld Family Letters, 1782–1900* (Cambridge, privately printed, 1916), 8 ?October 1840, vol. 6, p. 2851.

20 Katherine Ott, *Fevered Lives, Tuberculosis in American Culture since 1870* (Cambridge, MA, Harvard University Press, 1996), p. 88.

21 Maria H. Frawley, *Invalidism and Identity in Nineteenth-century Britain* (Chicago, University of Chicago Press, 2004), pp. 13–14; the hydrostatic bed belonged to Emily Shore, *Journal of Emily Shore* (London, Kegan Paul, Trench, Trübner & Co., 1891), p. 35.

22 Virginia Berridge and Griffith Edwards, *Opium and the People: Opiate Use in Nineteenth-century England* (London, Allen Lane, 1981), pp. 98–104.

23 Cited in Jalland, *Death in the Victorian Family*, p. 98.

24 Shore, *Journal*, passim.

25 Miriam Bailin, *The Sickroom in Victorian Fiction: The Art of Being Ill* (Cambridge, Cambridge University Press, 1994), p. 31.

26 Stephen, *Notes*, pp. 3–4.

27 Jalland, *Death in the Victorian Family*, p. 99, citing Charlotte Madden in an essay on nursing.

28 Charlotte M. Yonge, *The Young Step-Mother; or, A Chronicle of Mistakes* (London, Macmillan and Co., 1874), p. 304.

29 Benham, *Catharine and Craufurd Tait*, pp. 179, 230, 233, 234, 244.

30 Zuzanna Shonfield, *The Precariously Privileged: A Professional Family in Victorian London* (Oxford, Oxford University Press, 1987), pp. 26–7, 34.

31 *Courtauld Letters*, 6 January 1824, vol. 3, p. 1145ff; vol. 6, p. 2663.

32   Anne Summers, 'The Mysterious Demise of Sarah Gamp: The
     Domiciliary Nurse and Her Detractors, *c.*1830–1860', *Victorian Studies*,
     vol. 32, no. 3, 1989, pp. 367, 374–7.
33   Elizabeth Babson Bittle Eubanks, 'Illness and the Asiatic Cholera in the
     Lives and Works of the Brontë Family', *Brontë Studies*, vol. 46, no. 2,
     2021, pp. 119–20, 125.
34   These deaths summarized from [Margaret Oliphant], *The Autobiography
     of Margaret Oliphant: The Complete Text*, ed. Elisabeth Jay (Oxford,
     Oxford University Press, 1990), passim.
35   Ibid., p. 84.
36   Jalland, *Death in the Victorian Family*, pp. 99, 147.
37   The progress of her illness was recorded by her brother, William Michael
     Rossetti; David A. Kent, 'Christina Rossetti's Dying', *Journal of
     Pre-Raphaelite Studies* 5, 1996, pp. 85–6.
38   Alice Lovell, 'Death at the Beginning of Life', in David Field, Jenny
     Hockey and Neil Small, eds., *Death, Gender and Ethnicity* (London,
     Routledge, 1997), p. 36; David Armstrong, 'The Invention of Infant
     Mortality', *Sociology of Health and Illness*, vol. 8, no. 3, 1986, p. 214.
39   These figures are collated from A.J. Arnold and J.M. Bidmead, 'Going
     to Paradise by Way of Kensal Green: A Most Unfit Subject for
     Trading Profit?', *Business History*, vol. 50, no. 3, 2008, pp. 329–30;
     Jalland, *Death in the Victorian Family*, p. 144; and Teresa Mangum,
     'Growing Old: Age', in Herbert F. Tucker, ed., *A Companion to
     Victorian Literature and Culture* (Malden, MA, Blackwell, 1999),
     pp. 100–101.
40   Robert Millward and Frances Bell, 'Infant Mortality in Victorian Britain:
     The Mother as Medium', *Economic History Review*, 54, 4, 2001,
     pp. 707–10.
41   Pat Thane, *Old Age in English History: Past Experiences, Present Issues*
     (Oxford, Oxford University Press, 2000), p. 20; 'Population Dynamics',
     World Population Prospects, United Nations, Department of Economic
     and Social Affairs, https://population.un.org/wpp/Download/Standard/
     Population/, accessed 14 February 2022.
42   John Landers, *Death and the Metropolis: Studies in the Demographic
     History of London, 1670–1830* (Cambridge, Cambridge University Press,
     1993), p. 95.
43   Alfred Nutt, 'Tommy on the Tub's Grave', *Folklore*, vol. 5, no. 4, 1894,
     pp. 290–92; update, letter, ibid., vol. 7, no. 1, 1896, pp. 79–80, where an
     alternate name of Tommy on the Tub is recorded.
44   Evelyn Carrington, 'Singing Games', *The Folk-Lore Record*, vol. 3, no. 2,
     1880, pp. 169–73. It is worth noting that many middle-class reports and
     some fictional accounts tell of seeing working-class children 'playing at

funerals'. The sole contemporaneous record I have seen that comes close is Epps, p. 18, where a doll is given a funeral. I am not saying it did not happen; I have just so far been unable to find any first-hand reports.

45 Margaret Pelling, *Cholera, Fever and English Medicine, 1825–1865* (Oxford, Oxford University Press, 1978), p. 2.

46 Michael Durey, *The Return of the Plague: British Society and the Cholera, 1831–2* (Dublin, Gill and Macmillan, 1979), p. 125.

47 Eubanks, 'Illness', pp. 127–8.

48 R.J. Morris, *Cholera, 1832: The Social Response to an Epidemic* (London, Croom Helm, 1976), p. 33.

49 Rev. Geo. Erving Winslow, 'A Plain and Practical Description of Asiatic Cholera, Containing Rules and Directions for its Prevention and Treatment' (London, J. Hatchard, 1848), pp. 23–4.

50 Cited in Pamela K. Gilbert, *Mapping the Victorian Social Body* (Albany, State University of New York Press, 2004), p. 95.

51 Francis Kilvert, *Kilvert's Diary: Selections from the Diary of the Rev. Francis Kilvert*, ed. William Plomer (London, Jonathan Cape, 1938), vol. 1, pp. 261–2.

52 Primitive Methodism conversion: Mary Riso, *The Narrative of the Good Death: The Evangelical Deathbed in Victorian England* (Farnham, Ashgate, 2015), p. 16.

53 Cited in Gilbert, *Cholera*, p. 22.

54 Anon., 'Sanatory [sic] Progress: Being the Fifth Report of the National Philanthropic Association . . . for the Promotion of Social and Salutiferous Improvements' ([1842], 2nd ed., London, J. Hatchard and Son, 1850), p. 175.

55 Morris, *Cholera, 1832*, pp. 97–8, cites both *Cobbett's Weekly Political Register* and *The Times*, a wide spectrum indeed.

56 Cited in Peter C. Jupp, *From Dust to Ashes: Cremation and the British Way of Death* (Basingstoke, Palgrave Macmillan, 2006), p. 41.

57 *Courtauld Letters*, 2 August 1832, vol. 5, pp. 1999–2000.

58 Shore, *Journal*, pp. 180–81.

59 See the Carlyle Letters Online project, carlyleletters.dukeupress.edu/home, in particular Carlyle to John A. Carlyle, 10 January 1832; to Margaret A. Carlyle, 18 February 1832; to John A. Carlyle, 17 October 1832; to Jean Carlyle Aitken, 8 December 1848. For the decipherment of Southwood Smith's prescription in the footnote, I am grateful to Drs Sylvia and Richard Cruess.

60 Harriet Martineau, *Deerbrook* (London, Smith, Elder and Co., 1859), see particularly Chapters 41–4.

2 THE DEATHBED

1　Jeremy Taylor, *The Rule and Exercises of Holy Dying* (London, R. Royston, 2nd ed., 1652), pp. 5–6, 48.

2　Cited in Riso, *Narrative*, p. 190.

3　Cited in Jalland, *Death in the Victorian Family*, p. 23.

4　Suffering, wrote Harriet Martineau, was 'instrumental to good'; it was a route to redemption. Harriet Martineau, *Harriet Martineau's Autobiography* (3rd ed., London, Smith, Elder, 1877), vol. 2, p. 148.

5　Diana Fuss, 'Last Words', *ELH*, vol. 76, no. 4, 2009, pp. 878–81.

6　Benham, *Tait*, p. 18.

7　William Hett, *Miscellanies on Several Subjects, in Prose and Verse* (London, C. & J. Rivington, 1823), pp. 21–2, cited in Andrew Sanders, *Charles Dickens, Resurrectionist* (London, Macmillan, 1982), p. 24.

8　This was the Evangelical writer Hannah More, who thought Bishop Home's deathbed could not have been more 'delightful or edifying'. Cited in Jalland, *Death in the Victorian Family*, p. 30.

9　Samuel Butler, *The Way of All Flesh* (New York, E.P. Dutton, 1917), pp. 74, 76, 436.

10　All three of these deathbeds are described by Jalland, the first two in *Death in the Victorian Family*, pp. 165–6, 168–70, the final one in Pat Jalland and John Hooper, *Women from Birth to Death: The Female Life Cycle in Britain, 1830–1914* (Brighton, Harvester Press, 1986), pp. 314–5.

11　Peter W. Sinnema, *The Wake of Wellington: Englishness in 1852* (Athens, Ohio University Press, 2006), pp. 36–7.

12　J.G. Lockhart, *The Life of Sir Walter Scott, Bart* (abridged ed., Edinburgh, Adam and Charles Black, 1879), p. 779; letter: Karl S. Guthke, *Last Words: Variations on a Theme in Cultural History*, rev. and trs. by the author (Princeton, Princeton University Press, 1992), p. 75.

13　M.H., *Death-Bed Thoughts* (London, Hatchard, 1838), pp. iii–iv.

14　Hallam Tennyson, *Alfred Lord Tennyson: A Memoir by His Son* (London, Macmillan, 1897), pp. 425ff.

15　William Aldis Wright, ed., *The Letters and Literary Remains of Edward FitzGerald* (London, Macmillan and Co., 1889), vol. 1, p. 220.

16　Cited in Jalland, *Death in the Victorian Family*, p. 185.

17　Mrs [Catherine] Gore, *The Dean's Daughter, or, The Days We Live In* (Leipzig, Bernhard Tauchnitz, 1853), vol. 2, p. 315.

18　Cited in Jalland, *Death in the Victorian Family*, p. 91.

19　The figures on the middle classes who earned between £150 and £400 a year are found in Anthony Mandal, 'The Ghost Story and the Victorian Literary Marketplace', in Scott Brewster and Luke Thurston, *The Routledge Handbook to the Ghost Story* (New York, Routledge, 2018), p. 229.

20   David Vincent, 'Love and Death and the Nineteenth-century Working Class', *Social History*, vol. 5, no. 2, 1980, p. 245.

21   Julie-Marie Strange, *Death, Grief and Poverty in Britain, 1870–1914* (Cambridge, Cambridge University Press, 2005), fills many of the gaps that have existed regarding working-class death and emotion; for the repeated use of names, p. 259.

22   Kilvert, *Diary*, vol. 3, pp. 175–6.

23   Kilvert, *Diary*, vol. 3, p. 242.

24   Cited in Linda Pollock, *A Lasting Relationship: Parents and Children over Three Centuries* (London, Fourth Estate, 1987), p. 118.

25   *Courtauld Letters*, 6 November 1838, vol. 6, p. 2704.

26   Benham, *Tait*, pp. 155–6.

27   Rev. Edwin Davies, *Children in Heaven; or, Comfort for Bereaved Parents* (Belfast, William M'Comb, 1854), pp. 79–81.

28   'The Weeping Angel' cited in Gillian Avery and Kimberley Reynolds, eds., *Representations of Childhood Death* (Basingstoke, Macmillan, 2000), pp. 171–2; 'Their wings' is in 'Luigi', *Sweet Songs for Mourning Mothers* (London, J. Masters and Co., 1884), p. 3. Despite the pseudonym, from the preface 'Luigi' appears to have been a woman.

29   There is not a lot of scholarly work on death in nineteenth-century art when compared to the amount of exploration of the subject in literature; the excellent Terri R. Sabatos, 'Images of Death and Domesticity in Victorian Britain', D.Phil. thesis, Indiana University (2001), goes a long way to filling in many gaps, e.g. pp. 212, 243–4.

30   Cited in Laurence Lerner, *Angels and Absences: Child Deaths in the Nineteenth Century* (Nashville, Vanderbilt University Press, 1997), pp. 24–5.

31   This parenthesis is filled with doubt because the figures in the census have been historically very difficult to interpret. Not only is there some doubt about their accuracy, but the way the counting was structured makes assessments difficult, counting as it did the number of attendees at all services – those who went to two, or even three, services on a Sunday, a not entirely unusual practice, were counted two, or three, times. Even allowing for these difficulties, the census showed quite clearly that the majority of the population were non-churchgoers. For questions about the census and methodology, W.S.F. Pickering, 'The 1851 Religious Census – A Useless Experiment?', *The British Journal of Sociology*, vol. 18, 1967, pp. 382–407, continues to be a useful summary.

32   Roy Porter, 'The Hour of Philippe Ariès', *Mortality*, vol. 4, no. 1, 1999, p. 88.

33   Cited in Jalland, *Death in the Victorian Family*, p. 109.

34   Oliphant, *Autobiography*, pp. 37, 65, 80.

35   This newspaper was the liberal Belfast newspaper, the *Northern Whig*,

reprinted in Joseph Kaines, *Last Words of Eminent Persons, Comprising . . . A Brief Account of their Last Hours* (London, George Routledge & Sons, 1866), p. 3; 'save him for me' cited in Stanley Weintraub, *Uncrowned King: The Life of Prince Albert* (New York, Free Press, 1997), p. 427.

36   Taylor, *Holy Dying*, p. 88.

37   Cited in Hesketh Pearson, *Oscar Wilde: His Life and Wit* (New York, Harper and Row, 1946), p. 208.

38   Cited in Avery and Reynolds, *Representations*, p. 149.

39   Charles Dickens, *The Old Curiosity Shop*: (London, Chapman and Hall, 1841), p. 209; Forster: cited in Lerner, *Angels*, p. 105; William Wordsworth, *The Poetical Works of William Wordsworth*, ed. Henry Reed (Philadelphia, Hays and Zell, 1854), p. 76.

40   The idea of Dickens modelling Nell on Taylor is that of Marilyn Georgas, 'Little Nell and the Art of Holy Dying: Dickens and Jeremy Taylor', *Dickens Studies Annual*, vol. 20, 1991, pp. 41, 46–7. Dickens owned a volume entitled *The Beauties of Jeremy Taylor, D.D.*, selected by 'B.S. Esq., Barrister at Law' (London, T.C. Newby, 1845); http://www.dickenslibraryonline.org/library/all, accessed 3 March 2022. My thanks to Sean Grass for supplying me with this information.

41   Cited in Jalland, *Death in the Victorian Family*, pp. 48–9, 181.

42   Frances Trollope, *Mabel's Progress* (London, Chapman and Hall, 1867), vol. 3, p. 269.

43   These examples all appear in the *Children's Friend*, cited in Diana Dixon, 'The Two Faces of Death: Children's Magazines and their Treatment of Death in the Nineteenth Century', in Ralph Houlbrooke, ed., *Death, Ritual and Bereavement* (London, Routledge, 1989), p. 144.

44   Mrs [Mary Martha] Sherwood, *The History of the Fairchild Family; or, The Child's Manual* (London, F. Houlston, 1818), pp. 293–301. Footnote: Charles Dickens, *Dealings with the Firm of Dombey and Son, Wholesale, Retail and for Exportation* (London, Bradbury and Evans, 1848), p. 75; 'Col. D. Streamer' [Harry Graham], *Ruthless Rhymes for Heartless Homes* (New York, R.H. Russell, 1902), p. 15.

45   Cited in A.O.J. Cockshut, *Truth to Life: The Art of Biography in the Nineteenth Century* (London, Collins, 1974), pp. 43–4.

46   Charles Dickens, *The Personal History and Experience of David Copperfield the Younger* (Leipzig, Berhard Tauchnitz, 1849–50), vol. 3, pp. 339, 383.

47   Cited in Jalland, *Death in the Victorian Family*, p. 128.

48   Augustus J.C. Hare, *Memorials of a Quiet Life* (2nd ed., London, Strahan & Co., 1872–6), vol. 1, p. 56. Footnote: ibid., p. 51.

49   [Philip Henry Gosse], *A Memorial of the Last Days on Earth of Emily Gosse*, 'by her husband' (London, James Nisbet & Co., 1857), passim. I have discussed this memoir, and the attendant medical horrors, in more

detail in my *The Victorian House: Domestic Life from Childbirth to Deathbed* (London, HarperCollins, 2003), pp. 310–15.

50 Cited in Thomas W. Laqueur, *The Work of the Dead: A Cultural History of Mortal Remains* (Princeton, Princeton University Press, 2015), p. 409.

51 Leslie Stephen, *Sir Leslie Stephen's Mausoleum Book*, intro. Alan Bell (Oxford, Clarendon Press, 1977), pp. 3, 22, 96.

52 James, *The Diary of Alice James*, pp. 229–32.

53 *The Times*, 2 July 1830, p. 3.

54 These reports over the three days, from 29 June 1850 to his death on 2 July, were reprinted in a vast number of newspapers. From them, it is possible to see that as well as bulletins on 30 June and 1 July, on the day of his death alone there were reports handed out at 8.30 a.m., 2 p.m., 4 p.m. and 6.30 p.m., before his death at 11.05.

55 Disraeli: John Wolffe, *Great Deaths: Grieving, Religion and Nationhood in Victorian and Edwardian Britain* (Oxford, British Academy/Oxford University Press, 2000), p. 19, 158; Tennyson: Samantha Matthews, *Poetical Remains: Poets' Graves, Bodies and Books in the Nineteenth Century* (Oxford, Oxford University Press, 2004), p. 269.

3 FROM CHURCHYARD TO CEMETERY

1 Dickens, *Old Curiosity Shop* p. 92.

2 Philippe Ariès, *Western Attitudes toward Death: From the Middle Ages to the Present*, trs. Patricia Ranum (Baltimore, Johns Hopkins University Press, 1974), pp. 46–7. As always with Ariès, what he presents as universal is often confined to the Catholic elites of France, but this particular statement seems to apply more generally to a wider European Christian population.

3 Ariès, *Western Attitudes*, pp. 23–4 cites edicts between 1231 and 1657.

4 K.D.M. Snell, 'Gravestones, Belonging and Local Attachment in England, 1700–2000', *Past and Present*, vol. 179, 2003, p. 103.

5 Sarah Tarlow, 'Wormie Clay and Blessed Sleep: Death and Disgust in Later Historic Britain', in Sarah Tarlow and Susie West, eds., *The Familiar Past? Archaeologies of Later Historical Britain* (London, Routledge, 1999), pp. 187–8.

6 Tarlow, 'Wormie', in Tarlow and West, *Familiar Past*, p. 189.

7 William Godwin, 'Essay on Sepulchres: or, a Proposal for Erecting Some Memorial of the Illustrious Dead in All Ages on the Spot Where their Remains Have been Interred' (London, R. Miller, 1809), pp. 40, 49.

8 Thomas E. Lewis, *Baker's Law Relating to Burials* (London, Sweet and Maxwell, 1898), p. 302.

9 Margaret Cox, *Life and Death in Spitalfields, 1700 to 1850* (York, Council for British Archaeology, 1996), pp. 5, 98.

10   Pepys, *Diary*, 18 March 1664. Owing to the Covid pandemic, I have been
     unable to access the standard Pepys printed edition, edited by Robert
     Latham and William Matthews, and published by Bell & Hyman in the
     1980s. I have instead turned to the very useful www.pepysdiary.com, run
     by Phil Gyford using text from Project Gutenberg. All entries can be
     found using either the date or a word search.

11   Allan Cunningham, 'The Master of Logan', in *The Vampyre, and Other
     Tales of the Macabre*, ed. Robert Morrison and Chris Baldick (Oxford,
     Oxford University Press, 2008), p. 63. The story uses a narrative framing
     device, setting it in the times of 'James Stuart', most likely from the
     detail James VI and I, but the incidental nature of this introduction does
     not appear to be part of any historic scene-setting.

12   Julie Rugg, 'A New Burial Form and its Meanings: Cemetery
     Establishment in the First Half of the 19th Century', in Margaret Cox,
     Grave Concerns: Death and Burial in England, 1700 to 1850 (York, Council
     for British Archaeology, 1998), p. 44.

13   Harold Mytum, 'Public Health and Private Sentiment: The Development
     of Cemetery Architecture and Funerary Monuments from the Eighteenth
     Century Onwards', *World Archaeology*, vol. 21, no. 2, 1989, pp. 287–91.

14   It is Laqueur, *Work*, who makes this connection, and expands it to other
     garden cemeteries, pp. 247ff.

15   Cited in Mary Elizabeth Hotz, *Literary Remains: Representations of Death
     and Burial in Victorian England* (Albany, State University of New York
     Press, 2009), pp. 30–32.

16   Laqueur, *Work*, p. 156.

17   This Act is 6 & 7 Will. IV. c.136 local.

18   17 February 1837, carlyleletters.dukeupress.edu, accessed 27 January 2021.

19   Cited in Ruth Richardson, *Death, Dissection and the Destitute* (London,
     Routledge and Kegan Paul, 1987), pp. 224–8.

20   G.A. Walker, *Gatherings from Graveyards; Particularly those of London*
     (London, Longman and Co., 1839), pp. 149–51.

21   G.A. Walker, *On the Past and Present State of Intramural Burying Places,
     with Practical Suggestions* (London, Longman, Brown, Green and
     Longmans, 1851), appendix, p. i.

22   This is the view of Laqueur, *Work*, p. 222.

23   G.A. Walker, *Burial-Ground Incendiarism: The Last Fire at the Bone-House
     in the Spa-Fields Golgotha* (London, Longman, Brown, Green and
     Longmans, 1846), pp. 21–2.

24   Walker, *Gatherings*, pp. 154–8; idem., *Spa-Fields*, pp. 32ff. Footnote:
     The historian is Peter C. Jupp, 'Enon Chapel: No Way for the Dead', in
     Peter C. Jupp and Glennys Howarth, *The Changing Face of Death: Historical
     Accounts of Death and Disposal* (Basingstoke, Macmillan, 1997), p. 103.

25 G.W.M. Reynolds, *The Mysteries of London*, foreword by Louis James, annotated by Dick Collins ([1844–6], Kansas City, Valancourt, 2013), vol. 1, p. 913.

26 [James Hannay], 'Graves and Epitaphs', *Household Words*, no. 134, 16 October 1852, p. 105.

27 [Samuel] Laman Blanchard, *The Cemetery at Kensal Green: The Grounds & Monuments* (London, Cunningham & Mortimer, [1843]), p. 26 and passim.

28 G.K. Chesterton, cited in the *Oxford English Dictionary*, 'Kensal Green'.

4 BEFORE THE FUNERAL

1 Armstrong, 'Invention', pp. 211, 220, although a typo there ascribes the Act to 1834. The Act is formally entitled An Act for registering Births, Deaths and Marriages in England, [17 August 1836], 6 & 7 Will. IV. c.86, and it came into force the following year.

2 [Rev. W.H. Sewell], *On Christian Care of the Dying and the Dead: A Few Hints Designed for the Use of Friendly Readers*, 'by a Clergyman of the Church of England' (London, J.T. Hayes, 1870), pp. 29–30.

3 Wanda S. Henry, 'Women Searchers of the Dead in Eighteenth- and Nineteenth-century London', *Social History of Medicine*, vol. 29, no. 3, 2015, pp. 445–56.

4 Registrars: Henry, 'Women Searchers', p. 461; causes of death: Alexander Watt, *Glasgow Bills of Mortality for 1841 & 1842* (Glasgow, Edward Khull, 1844), and the London bills, passim.

5 Sewell, *On Christian Care*, p. 6.

6 Helen Frisby, 'Drawing the Pillow, Laying Out and Port Wine: The Moral Economy of Death, Dying and Bereavement in England, c.1840–1930', *Mortality*, vol. 20, no. 2, 2015, p. 110.

7 Sewell, *On Christian Care*, pp. 6–15 passim.

8 Stephen, *Notes*, p. 52.

9 Florence Peacock, 'Traditions and Customs relating to Death and Burial in Lincolnshire', *The Antiquary*, no. 71, new series. November 1895, p. 333.

10 Robert Janaway, 'An Introductory Guide to Textiles from 18th and 19th Century Burials', in Cox, *Grave Concerns*, pp. 17–18, 32.

11 Janaway, 'Introductory Guide' in Cox, *Grave Concerns*, pp. 26–7.

12 The 1666 Act for Burial in Wool is 18 & 19 Car. II c.4; its repeal in 1814 is 54 Geo. III c.78.

13 Only two copies of John Dickenson, *Greene in Conceipt* have survived, although the text is now available online: https://www.proquest.com/docview/2138574993/Z000026486/B5179CBADEE345A9PQ/5?accountid=25070. For information on the work's history, I am indebted to Shirley Stacey, 'John Dickenson's "Greene in Conceipt" (1598): A Critical Edition with Commentary',

(MA thesis, Memorial University of Newfoundland, 1991), https://research.library.
mun.ca/5444/2/Stacey_Shirley.pdf.

14   M. Mission, *M. Mission's Memoirs and Observations in His Travels over
England*, 'translated by Mr. Ozell' (London, D. Browne, 1719), pp. 88–9.

15   Sewell, *On Christian Care*, pp. 14–15. Footnote: Ruth Richardson, *Death,
Dissection*, p. 303n. She is not here discussing the crossed arms of the
body specifically, although the inference is there. She notes that Eric
Partridge, the slang lexicographer, and Iona and Peter Opie, historians of
childhood play, all date the expression to at least the nineteenth century.

16   Sara Coleridge, *Memoirs and Letters of Sara Coleridge*, 'edited by Her
Daughter' (2nd ed., London, Henry S. King, 1873), vol. 2, p. 211.

17   Customs in these paragraphs are from a wide range of sources. See:
Atkinson, Rev. J.C., *Forty Years in a Moorland Parish: Reminiscences and
Researches in Danby in Cleveland* (London, Macmillan and Co., 1891),
pp. 214–15; Richard Blakeborough, *Wit, Character, Folklore and Customs in
the North Riding of Yorkshire* (London, Henry Frowde, 1898), pp. 79–81;
Peter Brears, 'Arvals, Wakes and Month's Minds: Food for Funerals', in
Laura Mason, ed., *Food and the Rites of Passage*, Leeds Symposium on Food
History 'Food and Society' Series (London, Prospect, 2002), pp. 87–114;
Charlotte Sophia Burne, ed., from the Collections of Georgina F. Jackson,
Shropshire Folklore: A Sheaf of Gleanings (London, Trübner & Co., 1883),
p. 301; Davies, *Haunted*, pp. 18–19; Rev. T.F. Thistelton Dyer, *Domestic
Folk-lore* (London, Cassell, Petter, Galpin & Co., [1881]), pp. 51–61; Helen
Frisby, 'Drawing the Pillow', pp. 103–27; Charlotte Latham, 'Some West
Sussex Superstitions Lingering in 1868', *The Folk-Lore Record*, vol. 1, 1878,
pp. 160–75; Kilvert, *Diary*, vol. 3, pp. 211–12; L.A. Law and W. Crooke,
'Death and Burial Customs in Wiltshire', *Folklore*, vol. 11, no. 3, 1900,
pp. 344–7; Dolly MacKinnon, '"The Bell, Like a Speedy Messenger, Runs
from House to House, and Ear to Ear": The Auditory Markers of Gender,
Politics and Identity in England, 1500–1700', in Peter Denney, Bruce
Buchan, David Ellison and Karen Crawley, eds., *Sound, Space and Civility
in the British World, 1700–1850* (London, Routledge, 2019), pp. 66–71;
Peacock, 'Traditions and Customs', pp. 333–4; Richardson, *Death,
Dissection*, pp. 7–8, 15, 17–18; Regina Sexton, 'Food and Drink at Irish
Weddings and Wakes', in Mason, *Food and Rites*, pp. 115–42; Mrs
[Elizabeth] Stone, *God's Acre, or, Historical Notices Relating to Churchyards*
(London, John W. Parker and Son, 1858), pp. 379–80.

18   The Barrett caul: Philip Kelley and Betty A. Coley, eds., *The Browning
Collections: A Reconstruction with Other Memorabilia* (London, Mansell,
1984), p. 514.

19   Edwin Chadwick, *A Supplementary Report on the Results of a Spiecal [sic] Inquiry
into the Practice of Interment in Towns* (London, W. Clowes, 1843), p. 154.

20 Jalland and Hooper, *Women from Birth to Death*, pp. 308–9.
21 Shonfield, *Precariously*, p. 28.
22 Reported in the *London Evening Standard*, 10 June 1858.
23 Cited in Jalland, *Death in the Victorian Family*, p. 213.
24 Anon., 'The Derby Mourning & Funeral Warehouse' (Derby, Bemrose and Sons, printers, [c.1876]), p. 5.
25 Janaway, 'Introductory Guide', in Cox, *Grave Concerns*, p. 23. It is Clare Gittings, *Death, Burial and the Individual in Early Modern England* (London, Croom Helm, 1984), p. 115, who suggests the functional purpose of these items.
26 Oliphant, *Autobiography*, p. 83.
27 Shonfield, *Precariously*, pp. 28, 185.

5 THE GREAT FUNERAL

1 Gittings, *Death, Burial*, pp. 23–4, 31.
2 Gittings, *Death, Burial*, p. 192.
3 Julian Litten, *The English Way of Death: The Common Funeral Since 1450* (London, Robert Hale, 1991), p. 127; David Cressy, *Birth, Marriage and Death: Ritual, Religion and the Life-cycle in Tudor and Stuart England* (Oxford, Oxford University Press, 1997), p. 432.
4 Brent W. Tharp, '"Preserving their Form and Features": The Commodification of Coffins in the American Understanding of Death', in Susan Strasser, ed., *Commodifying Everything: Relationships of the Market* (London, Routledge, 2003), pp. 209–10, 221.
5 Sewell, *On Christian Care*, p. 19. Footnote: The advertisement for the casket appears in Tharp, 'Preserving their Form', in Strasser, *Commodifying*, p. 232.
6 Michael Smith, 'The Church of Scotland and the Funeral Industry in Nineteenth-century Edinburgh', *The Scottish Historical Review*, vol. 88, no. 225, part 1, 2009, pp. 111–12.
7 Kilvert, *Diary*, vol. 2, p. 189.
8 Illustrated in Lou Taylor, *Mourning Dress: A Costume and Social History* (London, George Allen and Unwin, 1983), p. 44.
9 The procession is itemized in Laqueur, *Work*, p. 319.
10 Paul S. Fritz, 'The Undertaking Trade in England: Its Origins and Early Development, 1660–1830', *Eighteenth-century Studies*, vol. 28, no. 2, 1994/5, p. 245.
11 Cited in Timothy Jenks, 'Contesting the Hero: The Funeral of Admiral Lord Nelson', *Journal of British Studies*, vol. 39, no. 4, 2000, p. 426. The historian cited in the following paragraph is also Jenks, ibid.
12 Jenks, 'Contesting', p. 428. Funeral details, passim, from Jenks, and from

Fairburn's Edition of the Funeral of Admiral Lord Nelson (London, John Fairburn, [1806]).

13 Wolffe, *Great Deaths*, p. 19.

14 Mrs Arbuthnot, *The Journal of Mrs Arbuthnot*, Frances Bamford and the Duke of Wellington, eds. (London, Macmillan & Co., 1950), vol. 2, p. 73.

15 Coffin: Mrs Arbuthnot, *Journal*, vol. 2, p. 371; heralds: Charles Greville, cited in Wolffe, *Great Deaths*, pp. 24–5.

16 *Courtauld Letters*, [no day] November 1817, vol. 1, pp. 291–2.

17 Esther Schor, *Bearing the Dead: The British Culture of Mourning from the Enlightenment to Victoria* (Princeton, Princeton University Press, 1994), pp. 197, 270n.

18 Stephen C. Behrendt, *Royal Mourning and Regency Culture: Elegies and Memorials of Princess Charlotte* (Basingstoke, Macmillan, 1997), pp. 213–14. See also among the very many newspaper reports, e.g. *Cheltenham Chronicle*, 20 November 1817, p. 2; *St James's Chronicle*, 20 November 1817, p. 3; *Commercial Chronicle*, 20 November 1817, p. 4; *London Courier and Evening Gazette*, 20 November 1817, p. 4.

19 Schor, *Bearing the Dead*, p. 210.

20 *Courtauld Letters*, 8 November 1817, vol. 1, pp. 302–3.

21 *Courtauld Letters*, [no day] December 1817, vol. 1, p. 314. In actuality, Leopold was not at this stage a 'Royal', but merely a 'Serene' Highness by virtue of his German title as the son of the Duke of Saxe-Coburg-Saalfeld. It was 1818 before he was given the title of Royal Highness by order of the Prince Regent. I am grateful to Christopher Guyver, biographer of Leopold, for this information.

22 Lord Holland, *The Journal of the Hon. Edward Henry Fox (afterwards fourth and last Lord Holland), 1818–1830*, the Earl of Ilchester, ed. (London, Thornton, Butterworth, 1923), p. 81.

23 The London servant told the story to Kilvert, *Diary*, vol. 3, p. 418; the funeral route and schedule: Wolffe, *Great Deaths*, pp. 21–2.

24 Thomas W. Laqueur, 'Bodies, Death and Pauper Funerals', *Representations*, vol. 1, 1983, pp. 117–19. Footnote: Laqueur, *Work*, p. 330.

25 Cited in Mary Elizabeth Hotz, 'Down among the Dead: Edwin Chadwick's Burial Reform Discourse in Mid-nineteenth-century England', *Victorian Literature and Culture*, vol. 29, no. 1, 2001, p. 31.

26 Hotz, *Literary Remains*, p. 24.

27 Laqueur, *Work*, pp. 332–3.

28 Playbills in the John Johnson Collection, Bodleian Library, Oxford. *Romeo and Juliet*, Theatre Royal, Norwich company, at Colchester, 1800; *Antony and Cleopatra*, Theatre Royal, Covent Garden, 1811.

29 Kilvert, *Diary*, vol. 3, p. 121.

30 The description of Sayers' funeral is derived from Mike Huggins,

'Reading the Funeral Rite: A Cultural Analysis of the Funeral Ceremonials and Burial of Selected Leading Sportsmen in Victorian England, 1864–1888', *Journal of Sport History*, vol. 38, no. 3, 2011, pp. 408, 412, 417, 420; Robert Colls, *This Sporting Life: Sports and Liberty in England, 1760–1960* (Oxford, Oxford University Press, 2020), p. 92; and reports, passim, in *Bell's Life in London, and Sporting Chronicle*, *Pall Mall Gazette*, and *Illustrated Sporting News*. I am grateful to the historian of pugilism Tony Gee for directing me to many of these sources.

31 Footnote: Edward Carpenter, ed., *A House of Kings: The History of Westminster Abbey* (London, John Baker, 1966), p. 249, which notes that when Samuel Johnson was buried there in 1784, charges were made for both music and lamps, despite no music being performed, and the service being held at lunchtime on a 'sun shiney [sic] day', p. 250.

32 Wolffe, *Great Deaths*, pp. 138ff.

33 I have written in detail about the duke's funeral. See my *The Victorian City: Everyday Life in Dickens' London* (London, Atlantic Books, 2012), pp. 335–46.

34 All cited in Wolffe, *Great Deaths*, pp. 28–9.

35 *Illustrated London News*, 6 November 1852, passim.

36 Cornelia Pearsall, 'Burying the Duke: Victorian Mourning and the Funeral of the Duke of Wellington', *Victorian Literature and Culture*, vol. 27, 1999, pp. 365, 374, 388.

37 Cited in Jen Cadwallader, 'Spirit Photography and the Victorian Culture of Mourning', *Modern Language Studies*, vol. 37, no. 2, 2008, pp. 11–12.

38 *Household Words*, November 1852, p. 469. Footnote: Pearsall, 'Burying', p. 384.

39 *The Morning Herald*, 20 November 1852, p. 7.

40 These figures come from Laqueur, *Work*, p. 334, and Wolffe, *Great Deaths*, p. 34.

41 Laqueur, *Bodies, Death*, p. 120.

42 Funeral car cost: Claire Wood, *Dickens and the Business of Death* (Cambridge, Cambridge University Press, 2015), p. 13; clergymen's seats: Charles Dickens, 'Trading in Death', *Household Words*, no. 140, 27 November 1852, p. 317; post-funeral sales: Pearsall, 'Burying', p. 389.

43 James Anthony Froude, *Thomas Carlyle: A History of his Life in London, 1834–1881* (New York, Charles Scribner's Sons, 1884), vol. 2, p. 107.

44 Carlyle, *Letters*, 15 November 1852, and 16 November 1852, at carlyleletters.dukepress.edu/home, accessed 19 April 2022.

6 THE FAMILY FUNERAL

1 Thomas Carlyle was the friend, and recorded the details in Carlyle, *Letters*, 5 July 1867, carlyleletters.dukepress.edu, accessed 27 June 2021.

2 The full episode can be found in Kilvert, *Diary*, vol. 1, pp. 266–75.

3   An advertisement placed by The Original London and Worcester General Mourning and Funeral Warehouse in the *Worcester Journal*, 26 October 1867, p. 1. Despite the company's name, only a Worcester address is given.

4   All these possibilities appear passim in Cox, *Life and Death*, especially pp. 11, 99, 102, 105; and Cox, *Grave Concerns*, pp. 22–3.

5   Richard Steele, *The Funeral: or, Grief A-la-mode. A Comedy* ([1701/2], 6th ed., London, J. Tonson, 1730), preface, n.p., p. 13.

6   Charles Lamb, cited in 'Fritz', *Where are the Dead?, or, Spiritualism Explained* (Manchester, A. Ireland, 1873), p. 250.

7   'Performers in "The Grave Scene"', *Punch*, 17 October 1857, p. 163.

8   House of Commons, 'Select Committee Report on the Improvement of the Health of Towns: Effect of Interment of Bodies in Towns', 1842.

9   Reynolds, *Mysteries*, vol. 1, pp. 914–15.

10   Examples of bidding appear in both memoirs and fiction. See Atkinson, *Forty Years*, p. 226; Sherwood, *The Fairchild Family*, p. 296. It is also discussed in Frisby, 'Drawing the Pillow', p. 115.

11   *Cassell's Household Guide* (London, Cassell, Petter and Galpin, 1869), pp. 314–15; Anon., *Etiquette for Ladies and Gentlemen, including the Etiquette of Weddings* (London, Frederick Warne, [n.d.]), p. 102; Sewell, *Christian Care*, pp. 128–9.

12   Carlyle, *Letters*, 27 December 1853 and 28 August 1854, carlyleletters. dukeupress.edu, accessed 27 January 2021.

13   Carlyle, *Letters*, 29 April 1862, carlyleletters.dukeupress.edu, accessed 27 January 2021.

14   Atkinson, *Forty Years in a Moorland Parish*, p. 217.

15   Pepys, *Diary*, 18 March 1663/4.

16   Many memoirists and writers on folklore describe funeral biscuits. A good outline can be found in Brears, 'Arvals, Wakes', in Mason, *Food and Rites*, pp. 103–5. The examples here are also drawn from: Atkinson, *Forty Years*, p. 217; Burne, *Shropshire Folktales*, p. 304; William Andrews, *Curious Church Customs and Cognate Subjects* (Hull, William Andrews & Co., 1895), p. 146.

17   [Charles Dickens], 'From the Raven in the Happy Family', Part II, *Household Words*, no. 11, 8 June 1850, pp. 241–2.

18   Shonfield, *Precariously*, p. 82.

19   Funerals of girls: Peacock, 'Traditions and Customs', p. 332; garlands: Andrews, *Curious Church Customs*, p. 142; Portsmouth 'wedding': Taylor, *Mourning Dress*, p. 184.

20   'Derby Mourning & Funeral Warehouse' (Derby, Bemrose and Sons, printers, [c.1876]), passim.

21   Kilvert, *Diary*, vol. 2, p. 180.

22 *Cassell's Household Guide*, 1869 ed., vol. 3, pp. 292ff.

23 Frisby, *Folklore Customs*, pp. 119–20.

24 Footnote: Dickens, *Bleak House*, p. 505; card from undertaker: this wording is suggested in *Cassell's Household Guide*, 1869 ed., p. 315.

25 Epps, *Diary*, p. 534.

26 Funeral of Mr E. Drummond, reported in the *Illustrated London News*, 4 February 1843.

27 Litten, *English Way*, p. 138.

28 Scotland: William McQueen, 'Scotch Funerals', *Macmillan's Magazine*, vol. 46, May to October 1882, p. 164; Yorkshire: Atkinson, *Forty Years*, p. 231.

29 Disraeli: Wolffe, *Great Deaths*, p. 152; Gladstone: Litten, *English Way*, p. 138.

30 'Derby Mourning & Funeral Warehouse', pp. 4–5.

31 Cited in Jalland, *Death in the Victorian Family*, p. 202.

32 John M. Clarke, *The Brookwood Necropolis Railway* (Usk, Oakwood, 2006; rev. ed.), p. 15.

33 One report of many can be found in the *London Evening Standard*, 24 December 1887.

34 [Charles Beckett], *My First Grief: or, Recollections of a Beloved Sister*, 'by a Provincial Surgeon' (Bath, Binns and Goodwin, [1852]), p. 42.

35 Funerals and singing: Vic Gammon, *Desire, Drink and Death in English Folk and Vernacular Song, 1600–1900* (London, Routledge, 2016), pp. 196ff. For the two Sussex villages, p. 204.

36 Atkinson, *Forty Years*, pp. 231–2.

37 Frederick James Post, *Extracts from the Diary and Other Manuscripts of the Late Frederick James Post, of Islington* (London, privately printed, 1838), pp. 129–30.

38 McQueen, 'Scotch Funerals', pp. 161, 163.

39 Atkinson, *Forty Years*, p. 305.

40 Brears, 'Arvals, Wakes', in Mason, *Food and Rites*, p. 99. I have estimated the number from their purchase of '100 cards', which I suggest are cards bidding the mourners.

41 Patricia Lysaght, 'Hospitality at Wakes and Funerals in Ireland from the Seventeenth to the Nineteenth Century: Some Evidence from the Written Record', *Folklore*, vol. 114, no. 3, 2003, pp. 409–13.

42 George Acorn, *One of the Multitude* (London, William Heinemann, 1911), pp. 40–5.

43 *Courtauld Letters*, 13 June 1832, vol. 5, pp. 1985–6.

44 Fees are discussed in Louise Fowler and Natasha Powers, *Doctors, Dissection and Resurrection Men: Excavations in the 19th-century Burial Ground of the London Hospital, 2006* (London, Museum of London Archaeology, 2012), p. 24; Elizabeth T. Hurren, *Dying for Victorian Medicine: English Anatomy and its Trade in the Dead Poor, c.1834–1929*

(Basingstoke, Palgrave Macmillan, 2012), pp. 123–4.

45   Elizabeth T. Hurren and Steve King, '"Begging for a Burial": Form, Function and Conflict in Nineteenth-century Pauper Burial', *Social History*, vol. 30, no. 3, 2005, p. 330.

46   Strange, *Death, Grief*, p. 238ff.

47   Hurren and King, 'Begging', p. 329.

48   Strange, *Death, Grief*, pp. 148–51.

49   Cited in Hotz, *Literary Remains*, p. 25.

50   Strange, *Death, Grief*, pp. 138–43.

51   Charles Dickens, *The Posthumous Papers of the Pickwick Club* (London, Chapman and Hall, 1837), vol. 1, pp. 217, 223.

52   *Cassell's Household Guide*, 1869 ed., vol. 3, p. 344.

53   Yonge, *Young Step-mother*, p. 398.

54   Anon., *Manners and Rules of Good Society* (15th ed., London, Frederick Warne & Co., 1888), p. 228.

55   Oliphant, *Autobiography*, p. 83.

56   Shonfield, *Precariously*, pp. 29, 184–5.

57   Margaret Cox, 'Eschatology, Burial Practice and Continuity: A Retrospection from Christ Church, Spitalfields', in Cox, *Grave Concerns*, p. 112.

58   Rev. W.H. Sewell, *Practical Papers on Funeral Reform, Mourning Dress and Obituary Memorials* ([no place of publication, privately printed, 1883]), pp. 1–2.

59   Kilvert, *Diary*, vol. 1, pp. 92ff., 99; vol. 2, p. 166. Stone, *God's Acre*, p. 275, also notes this was a Welsh custom, although there the interest is primarily antiquarian.

60   Cited in John Forster, *The Life of Charles Dickens* (London, Chapman and Hall, 1874), vol. 3, p. 517.

61   Cited in Sanders, *Charles Dickens*, p. 39.

7 MOURNING DRESS

1   Instructions and details of condolence calls can be found in: Isabella Beeton, *The Book of Household Management* (London, S.O. Beeton, 1861), pp. 10–11; Anon., *Etiquette for Ladies and Gentlemen, including the Etiquette of Weddings* (London, Frederick Warne, [n.d.]), pp. 17, 66, 102, 117–18; *Manners and Rules of Good Society*, p. 227. Jane Carlyle: Carlyle Letters, 18 May 1857, carlyleletters.dukeupress.edu/home, accessed 20 January 2021; Yonge, *Young Step-mother*, p. 84.

2   Cited in John Morley, *Death, Heaven and the Victorians* (London, Studio Vista, 1971) , pp. 71–2.

3   Mrs Henry Wood, *East Lynne* (London, Richard Bentley, 1862), vol. 1, p. 142.

4   Morley, *Death*, has an excellent summary on crape, pp. 64–5. I have

amended his date of the creation of Albert crape, which he suggests was the 1870s; *Cassell's Household Guide* of 1869 was already praising it, vol. 3, p. 335.

5   Taylor, *Mourning Dress*, pp. 130ff.

6   One such recipe is cited in Karin J. Bohleke, 'Identifying Stages of Grief in Nineteenth-century Images', *The Daguerreian Annual 2015: Official Yearbook of the Daguerreian Society* (Pittsburgh, 2015), p. 178.

7   *Girl's Own Paper*, 5 February 1881, p. 393.

8   These were the recommendations of Jay's Mourning Warehouse, cited in Alison Adburgham, *Shops and Shopping, 1800–1914. Where, and in What Manner, the Well-dressed Englishwoman Bought her Clothes* (2nd ed., London, George Allen and Unwin, 1981), p. 66.

9   'On the Etiquette of Mourning', *Englishwoman's Domestic Magazine*, June 1876, p. 66.

10   Edward Bruce Hamley, *Lady Lee's Widowhood* (Edinburgh, William Blackwood and Sons, 1854), vol. 1, pp. 4–5.

11   Mrs [Fanny] Douglas, *The Gentlewoman's Book of Dress* (London, Henry and Co., [1895]), pp. 110–15.

12   Thomas Hood, 'The House of Mourning: A Farce', *Hood's Magazine and Comic Miscellany*, vol. 1, Jan–June 1844, pp. 190–94.

13   Cited in Jalland, *Death in the Victorian Family*, p. 257.

14   *Cassell's Household Guide*, vol. 3, pp. 344–5.

15   *Manners and Rules of Good Society*, p. 94.

16   Yonge, *Young Step-mother*, p. 387.

17   *Courtauld Letters*, 28 November 1853, vol. 8, p. 3603.

18   Kilvert, *Diary*, vol. 3, p. 156.

19   Carlyle, *Letters*, 14 November 1852, carlyleletters.dukeupress.edu, accessed 26 January 2021.

20   Cited in Morley, *Death*, p. 63.

21   Seventeenth century: Cressy, *Birth, Marriage and Death*, p. 441; Pepys: Pepys, *Diary*, 18 March 1663/4.

22   Pepys, *Diary*, 29 May 1667.

23   As with the Carlyle letters, the open access availability online of all 48 volumes of Horace Walpole, *The Yale Edition of the Correspondence of Horace Walpole*, ed. W.S. Lewis (New Haven, Yale University Press, 1937–83), has been a godsend during Covid, and can be found at https://libsvcs-1.its.yale.edu/hwcorrespondence/. As with Pepys and Carlyle, I will cite by date. Here, 29 June 1770.

24   *Courtauld Letters*, 4 November 1831, vol. 4, p. 1884.

25   Cited in Morley, *Death*, pp. 69–70.

26   Kate Strasdin, *Inside the Royal Wardrobe: A Dress History of Queen Alexandra* (London, Bloomsbury Academic, 2017), pp. 116, 119–21.

27 Anthony Trollope, *The Prime Minister* (Leipzig, Bernhard Tauchnitz, 1876), vol. 4, p. 134.

28 Cited in Taylor, *Mourning Dress*, pp. 31, 258.

29 Carlyle, *Letters*, 17 July 1843, www.carlyleletters.dukeupress.edu, accessed 26 January 2021.

30 Taylor, *Mourning Dress*, p. 179. Footnote: Victoria and mourning: Taylor, *Mourning Dress*, p. 179; advice books: Anne Buck, 'The Trap Re-baited: Mourning Dress[,] 1860–90', *High Victorian Costume, 1860–1890: Proceedings of the Second Annual Conference of the Costume Society, March 1968* (London, 'published for the Society', 1969), p. 35.

31 Sewell, *Funeral Reform*, p. 2.

32 Cited in Phillis Cunnington and Catherine Lucas, *Costume for Births, Marriages and Deaths* (London, Adam and Charles Black, 1972), p. 250.

33 Kate Strasdin, *The Dress Diary of Mrs Anne Sykes* (London, Chatto and Windus, 2023), p. 187. This excellent volume, based on the author's remarkable find and subsequent sleuthing to discover its author, sheds much light on the differences between actual lived choices for middle-class women and advice book and upper-class dictates.

34 Shonfield, *Precariously*, p. 85. Footnote: ibid., p. 82.

35 *Illustrated London News*, 6 May 1843, p. 300.

36 *Illustrated London News*, 4 January 1862, p. 7.

37 Carlyle, *Letters*, 2 May 1866, carlyleletters.dukeupress.edu, accessed 26 January 2021; the reformer: W.H. Sewell, *Christian Care*, p. 129.

38 Dress prices: *Myra's Threepenny Journal*, 4 July 1862, p. 128.

39 For example, *Courtauld Letters*, 25 October 1825, where Mrs P.A. Courtauld 'rummage[s] up some old mourning for a poor girl's friends', vol. 3, p. 1392.

8 MOURNING CUSTOMS

1 *Illustrated London News*, 28 December 1861, p. 11.

2 Ralph Houlbrooke, 'Public and Private in the Funerals of the Later Stuart Gentry: Some Somerset Examples', *Mortality*, vol. 1, no. 2, 1996, p. 173.

3 Cited in Jalland, *Death in the Victorian Family*, pp. 298–9.

4 Diana Cooper and Norman Battershill, *Victorian Sentimental Jewellery* (Newton Abbot, David and Charles, 1972), pp. 19, 26; Luís Mendonça de Carvalho, Francisca Maria Fernandes, Maria de Fátima Nunes and João Brigola, 'Whitby Jet Jewels in the Victorian Age', *Harvard Papers in Botany*, vol. 18, no. 2, 2013, pp. 133–6; Shirley Bury, *An Introduction to Sentimental Jewellery* (London, HMSO, 1985), pp. 29, 31. There is no single satisfactory academic overview of mourning jewellery in Britain; I have drawn on these works, together with Geoffrey Batchen, 'Ere the Substance Fade:

Photography and Hair Jewellery', in Elizabeth Edwards and Janice Hart, eds., *Photographs Objects Histories: On the Materiality of Images* (London, Routledge, 2004); Christiane Holm, 'Sentimental Cuts: Eighteenth-century Mourning Jewelry with Hair', *Eighteenth-century Studies*, vol. 38, no. 1, 2004, pp. 139–43; Pamela Miller, 'Hair Jewelry as Fetish' in Ray B. Browne, ed., *Objects of Special Devotion: Fetishism in Popular Culture* (Bowling Green, OH, Bowling Green University Press, [1982?]); Marcia Pointon, 'Wearing Memory: Mourning, Jewellery and the Body', in Gisela Ecker, ed., *Trauer tragen – Trauer zeigen: Inszenierungen der Geschlechter* (Munich, Wilhelm Fink Verlag, 1999); Helen Sheumaker, '"This Lock You See": Nineteenth-century Hair Work as the Commodified Self', *Fashion Theory*, vol. 1, no. 4, 1997, pp. 421–45; ibid., *Love Entwined: The Curious History of Hairwork in America* (Philadelphia, University of Pennsylvania Press, 2007); and Jane Wildgoose, 'Beyond All Price: Victorian Hair Jewelry, Commemoration and Story-telling', *Fashion Theory*, vol. 22, no. 6, 2018, pp. 699–726.

5   Matthews, *Poetical Remains*, pp. 47–8; Lorna Clymer, 'Cromwell's Head and Milton's Hair: Corpse Theory in Spectacular Bodies of the Interregnum', *The Eighteenth Century*, vol. 40, no. 2, 1999, p. 104.

6   Cited in Matthews, *Poetical Remains*, pp. 158–9.

7   Matthews, *Poetical Remains*, p. 249.

8   Dickens, *David Copperfield*, vol. 2, p. 42.

9   Robert Browning and Elizabeth Barrett Browning, *The Letters of Robert Browning and Elizabeth Barrett Browning, 1845–6* (London, Smith, Elder & Co., 1899), vol. 1, pp. 296–8. Footnote: Wilkie Collins, *No Name* (New York, Harper & Brothers, 1863), vol. 1, p. 91.

10 Shore, *Journal*, p. 351.

11 *The Lady's Treasury*, 1 October 1868, pp. 53–4.

12 This is the thought-provoking idea of Deborah Lutz, 'The Dead Still Among Us: Victorian Secular Relics, Hair Jewelry, and Death Culture', *Victorian Literature and Culture*, vol. 39, no. 1, 2011, p. 135.

13 Charles Dickens, *Great Expectations* (Boston, Estes and Lauriat, 1881), p. 196.

14 The full extent of the Brownings' memorial treasures can be known because their son, Pen, died intestate and with no children, leading to his possessions being catalogued for sale. Kelley and Coley, *The Browning Collections*, have used the sale catalogues to give a remarkably complete overview. For these items, pp. 508–12, 515–16.

15 Godwin, 'Essay on Sepulchres', pp. 6–7.

16 Jalland, *Death in the Victorian Family*, pp. 295–6.

17 Cited in Jane Hamlett, *Material Relations: Domestic Interiors and Middle-class Families in England, 1850–1910* (Manchester, Manchester University Press, 2010), pp. 191, 193–4.

18 Gosse, *Memorial*, p. 72. Footnote: Audrey Linkman, *Photography and*

Death (London, Reaktion, 2011), pp. 46–51 surveys techniques and requirements.

19   Cited in Pat Jalland, 'Victorian Death and its Decline, 1850–1918', in Peter Jupp and Clare Gittings, *Death in England: An Illustrated History* (Manchester, Manchester University Press, 1999), pp. 246–7.

20   Cited in Linkman, *Photography and Death*, p. 18.

21   Strange, *Death, Grief*, p. 215.

22   These figures are based on a search of the online catalogue of the Brontë Parsonage Museum: http://bronte.adlibsoft.com/brief.aspx, accessed 6 August 2022.

23   Linkman, *Photography and Death*, p. 160.

24   Roger Taylor, 'Roger Fenton', *Oxford Dictionary of National Biography*, https://doi-org.lonlib.idm.oclc.org/10.1093/ref:odnb/37412, accessed 8 August 2022; Pat Hodgson, *Early War Photographs* (Reading, Osprey, 1974), p. 11.

25   Michael G. Wilson, 'Felice Beato', *Oxford Dictionary of National Biography*, https://doi-org.lonlib.idm.oclc.org/10.1093/ref:odnb/41130, accessed 8 August 2022; Zahid R. Chaudhary, *Afterimage of Empire: Photography in Nineteenth-century India* (Minneapolis, University of Minnesota Press, 2012), p. 77; John Fraser, 'Beato's Photograph of the Interior of the Sikandarbagh at Lucknow', *Journal of the Society for Army Historical Research*, vol. 59, no. 237, 1981, pp. 51–3; Tytler: Chaudhary, op. cit., p. 39.

26   Heather Nelson, 'Case Study: Widowhood: "It's a Great Shame she has to Part with Anything"', in *I Do?: Women, Consent, and Marriage in Nineteenth-Century England* (forthcoming).

27   Nelson, 'Case Study'; Susan Staves, *Married Women's Separate Property in England, 1660–1833* (Cambridge, MA, Harvard University Press, 1990), pp. 27ff., 205, gives a far more cynical, feminist reading, which I find entirely persuasive. I am grateful to Professor Daniel Monk for exploring the topic with me, and also for his assistance in explicating the mysteries of legal terminology.

28   Cynthia Curran, 'Private Women, Public Needs: Middle-class Widows in Victorian England', *Albion*, vol. 25, no. 2, 1993, pp. 225–6.

29   'By a Lady', *The Whole Duty of Woman, or, A Guide to the Female Sex . . . Shewing Women . . . How to Behave themselves for Obtaining Not Only Present but Future Happiness* (Stourbridge, Heming and Tallis, 1815), p. 81.

30   Trollope, *Can You Forgive Her?* (London, Chapman and Hall, 1864), vol. 1, p. 42.

31   I owe this reading to Dagni Bredesen, '"What's a Woman to Do?": Managing Money and Manipulating Fictions in Trollope's *Can You Forgive Her?* and *The Eustace Diamonds*', *Victorian Review*, vol. 31, no. 2, 2005, pp. 111–14.

32   Cited in Jalland, *Death in the Victorian Family*, p. 259.

33   Hamley, *Lady Lee*, vol. 1, pp. 248–9.

34   Colleen McDannell and Bernhard Lang, *Heaven: A History* (New Haven, Yale University Press, 1988), p. 262.

35   Anthony Trollope, *The Small House at Allington* (London, Smith, Elder & Co., 1865), pp. 565–6.

36   Stephen Collins, '"A Kind of Lawful Adultery": English Attitudes to the Remarriage of Widows, 1550–1800', in Jupp and Howarth, *Changing Face*, pp. 37–45.

37   Sabatos, 'Images of Death and Domesticity', pp. 114–16.

38   These women are itemized in Sabatos, 'Images of Death and Domesticity', in Hicks, 'Dividend Day at the Bank'; Frith, 'Ramsgate Sands'; Lefevre Cranston, 'Waiting at the Station'; and others, pp. 82–7.

39   Richard J. Bell, 'Our People Die Well: Deathbed Scenes in John Wesley's *Arminian* Magazine', *Mortality*, vol. 10, no. 3, 2005, p. 200.

40   Kim Price, 'Victorian Professions: The Galvanising (and Shaping) Force of Death on Families', in Carol Beardmore, Cara Dobbing and Steven King, eds., *Family Life in Britain, 1650–1910* (Cham, Palgrave Macmillan, 2019), pp. 55–6.

41   Oliphant, *Autobiography*, pp. 6–7.

42   Branks: Jalland, 'Victorian Death', in Jupp and Gittings, p. 237; Bishop of Ripon and Macleod: Lerner, *Angels*, p. 50.

43   William Michael Rossetti, *Some Reminiscences of William Michael Rossetti* (London, Brown Langham & Co., 1906) , vol. 2, p. 538.

44   Cited in Richardson, *Death, Dissection*, p. 4.

45   Henry Crabb Robinson, *Diary, Reminiscences and Correspondence of Henry Crabb Robinson*, Thomas Sadler, ed. (London, Macmillan & Co, 1872), vol. 1, p. 267.

46   The guidebooks were Galignani's, Murray's and Baedeker's. Hardy: Sanders, *Dickens*, pp. 46–8.

47   Matthews, *Poetical Remains*, pp. 38–42.

48   Arthur Penrhyn Stanley, *Historical Memorials of Westminster Abbey* (7th ed., London, John Murray, 1890), pp. 249ff; Edward Carpenter, ed., *A House of Kings: The History of Westminster Abbey* (London, John Baker, 1966), pp. 250–51; Philip Connell, 'Death and the Author: Westminster Abbey and the Meanings of the Literary Monument', *Eighteenth-century Studies*, vol. 38, no. 4, 2005, p. 559; Matthews, *Poetical Remains*, pp. 222–37; Wolffe, *Great Deaths*, pp. 71–2.

9 UNNATURAL DEATH

1   Josephine McDonagh, *Child Murder and British Culture, 1720–1900* (Cambridge, Cambridge University Press, 2003), pp. 3–4. The two Acts are 1624: 21 Jac. I c.27; 1803: 45 Geo. III c.58.

2   *Telegraph*: cited in Mark Jackson, ed., *Infanticide: Historical Perspectives on Child Murder and Concealment, 1550–2000* (Farnham, Ashgate, 2002), p. 253; clergyman: cited in McDonagh, *Child Murder*, p. 123.

3   Ann R. Higginbotham, '"Sin of the Age": Infanticide and Illegitimacy in Victorian London', in Kristine Ottesen Garrigan, ed., *Victorian Scandals: Representations of Gender and Class* (Athens, Ohio University Press, 1992), pp. 274–5.

4   Michael MacDonald and Terence R. Murphy, *Sleepless Souls: Suicide in Early Modern England* (Oxford, Clarendon Press, 1990), p. 44.

5   Percy Bysshe Shelley, *The Masque of Anarchy* (London, Edward Moxon, 1832), p. 2.

6   Cited in George Jacob Holyoake, *The Life and Character of Richard Carlile* (London, J. Watson, 1849), p. 37.

7   Daryl Lee, *The History of Suicide in England, 1650–1850*; vol. 7: *1800–1850: Legal Contexts, Religious Writings and Medical Writers* (London, Pickering and Chatto, 2013), p. 301.

8   There are a number of excellent works on suicide and its history in Britain. These paragraphs have been drawn from: Olive Anderson, *Suicide in Victorian and Edwardian England* (Oxford, Clarendon Press, 1987), pp. 22, 219–40; Margaret Cox: 'Eschatology, Burial Practice and Continuity: A Retrospection from Christ Church, Spitalfields', pp. 112–125, in Margaret Cox, ed., *Life and Death*, pp. 4–6; R.A. Houston, *Punishing the Dead? Suicide, Lordship, and Community in Britain, 1500–1830* (Oxford, Oxford University Press, 2010), pp. 189–215; Daryl Lee, *The History of Suicide in England, 1650–1850*; vol. 7: *1800–1850: Legal Contexts, Religious Writings and Medical Writers*; vol. 8: *1800–1850: Medical Writers (continued), Statistical Inquiries, Social Criticism, Poetic and Popular Representations and Cases* (London, Pickering and Chatto, 2013), passim; MacDonald and Murphy, *Sleepless Souls*, pp. 15–16, 109ff.; Sarah Tarlow, *The Golden and Ghoulish Age of the Gibbet in Britain* (London, Palgrave Macmillan, 2017), pp. 17–18.

9   Cited in Lisa J. Nicoletti, 'Resuscitating Ophelia: Images of Suicide and Suicidal Insanity in Nineteenth-century England', Ph.D. thesis, 1999, p. 44.

10   Trollope: Lopez in *The Prime Minister*; Dickens: Ralph Nickleby, Jonas Chuzzlewit, Carker, Mr Merdle, Deedles (in *The Chimes*); Reade: James Little in *Put Yourself in His Place*, to name only the best known.

11   The 'tortured, shameful death' is from Arthur Machen, *The Great God Pan* (London, John Lane, 1894), p. 73.

12   Reynolds, *Mysteries of London*, in volume 3 alone, see chapters 14, 18, 40, 47, 56, 69, 77, 79, 80 and 109.

13   [Rymer or Prest], *Varney the Vampyre*, chapter 83, https://archive.org/

details/VarneyTheVampyre/page/n5/mode/2up, accessed 21 February 2022.
14 Anderson, *Suicide*, pp. 117–19.
15 See, for example, Harriet Martineau, 'Self-Murder', *Once a Week*, 17 December 1859, pp. 510–14.
16 *Oliver Twist*: p. 373; [Charles Dickens], 'Wapping Workhouse', *All the Year Round*, 18 February 1860, vol. 43, pp. 392–3.
17 The following account is drawn from Alethea Hayter, *A Sultry Month: Scenes of London Literary Life in 1846* (London, Faber, 1965), pp. 68–113, passim.
18 Shakespeare, *Hamlet*, V.i.24–6.
19 Laqueur, *Work*, p. 150.
20 Anon., 'Extramural Burial. Three Schemes: I. The London Clergy Plan; II. The Board of Health or Erith Plan; III. The Woking Necropolis Plan' (London, Effingham Wilson, 1850), pp. 3–6.
21 Every step of the Akenham burial case can be found in exhausting detail in Ronald Fletcher, *The Akenham Burial Case* (London, Wildwood House, 1974); it is also summarized in Duncan Sayer, 'Death and the Dissenter: Group Identity and Stylistic Simplicity as Witnessed in Nineteenth-century Nonconformist Graves', *Historical Archaeology*, vol. 45, no. 4, 2011, p. 119; and Hotz, *Literary Remains*, pp. 101–8. It is in the latter that the story of the twins can be found, and she who writes 'to go out of their way . . .'
22 This is the suggestion of Sayer, 'Death and the Dissenter', although he queries why a journalist was at the funeral of a labouring man's child, apparently not knowing, or possibly not believing, that Tozer wrote the initial report.
23 Matthews, *Poetical Remains*, pp. 127–44.
24 *The Lancet*, 22 August 1857, pp. 199–200.
25 Cited in Jalland, *Death in the Victorian Family*, p. 205.
26 Jennifer Leaney, 'Ashes to Ashes: Cremation and the Celebration of Death in Nineteenth-century Britain', in Houlbrooke, *Death, Ritual*, pp. 120–23.
27 Brian Parsons, *Committed to the Cleansing Flame: The Development of Cremation in Nineteenth-century England* (Reading, Spire, 2005), p. 30.
28 The story of William Price can be found in, inter alia, Laqueur, *Work*, pp. 540–41; Parsons, *Flame*, p. 101; James Gregory, 'William Price', *Oxford Dictionary of National Biography*.
29 Brian Parsons, 'Premature Burial and the Undertakers', in Shane McCorristine, ed., *Interdisciplinary Perspectives on Mortality and its Timings: When is Death?* (London, Palgrave Macmillan, 2017), p. 70.
30 Sewell, *Funeral Reform*, p. 2.
31 The paragraphs on premature burial are drawn from: George K. Behlmer,

'Grave Doubts: Victorian Medicine, Moral Panic, and the Signs of Death', *Journal of British Studies*, vol. 42, no. 2, 2003, pp. 207–18; Laqueur, *Work*, pp. 507–8; Parsons, 'Premature Burial', pp. 69ff; Hood: 'The Death-Bed', *Poems of Thomas Hood* (New York, G.P. Putnam and Son, 1872), p. 206. Cholera and death: Richardson, *Death, Dissection*, p. 227. Hogg: 'Some Terrible Letters from Scotland', 1832, reprinted in John Polidori, *The Vampyre, and Other Tales of the Macabre*, ed. Robert Morrison and Chris Baldick (Oxford, Oxford University Press, 2008), p. 101ff. Charles Dickens, *Our Mutual Friend* (London, Chapman and Hall, 1865), vol. 1, p. 12.

32   Reynolds, *Mysteries*, vol. 1, p. 945.

10 CRIMINAL DEATH

1   The 1788 case was R. v. Lynn; the 1744 case concerned the theft of the body of a Dr Sacheverell, cited in Martin Fido, *Bodysnatchers: A History of the Resurrectionists, 1742–1832* (London, Weidenfeld & Nicolson, 1988), pp. 10–11. 'In flagrante dissecto', Ruth Richardson, private communication. I am grateful to Professor Daniel Monk for his thoughts on who, exactly, was the ultimate owner of the grave-clothes for the theft of which resurrectionists were being tried, and for his suggestion of the Crown.

2   1822 case: R. v. Cuddock, cited in Laqueur, *Work*, p. 350; Dickens, *Our Mutual Friend*, vol. 1, p. 4. Footnote: The Scottish law is outlined in Houston, *Punishing the Dead?*, p. 246.

3   Matthews, *Poetical Remains*, pp. 66–75.

4   Clymer, 'Cromwell's Head', pp. 91–103. Pepys, 13 October 1664, repeats contemporary doubts on even the likelihood of the 1660s head on the post being Cromwell's, crediting this story to the French writer Samuel Sorbière, who lived in the Netherlands in the 1650s, when the exiled Charles II was staying in the Hague. The rumours may well have begun there. Sorbière did not travel to Britain until after the Restoration.

5   The Home Secretary had only been assigned this power a few years before, in 1857, under the 1857 Burial Act (20 & 21 Vict. c.81), which regulated exhumation.

6   These seances were recorded by Rossetti's brother, William Michael Rossetti, in his diary, in J.B. Bullen, Rosalind White and Lenore A. Beaky, eds., *Pre-Raphaelites in the Spirit World: The Séance Diary of William Michael Rossetti* (Oxford, Peter Lang, 2022), passim.

7   Stoker, 'The Secret of Growing Gold' cited in Galia Ofek, *Representations of Hair in Victorian Literature and Culture* (Farnham, Shire, 2009), p. 82.

8   The Murder Act is, more formally, 25 Geo. II c.37 5.

9 Elizabeth T. Hurren, *Dissecting the Criminal Corpse: Staging Post-Execution Punishment in Early Modern England* (London, Palgrave Macmillan, 2016), p. 38.

10 Hurren, *Dissecting*, pp. 36–7, 52–3.

11 Helen Macdonald, 'Legal Bodies: Dissecting Murderers at the Royal College of Surgeons, London, 1800–1832', *Traffic, An Interdisciplinary Postgraduate Journal*, vol. 2, 2003, p. 11. I am grateful to Dr Lee O'Brien for locating a copy of this journal for me. The surgeon here was Astley Cooper.

12 This is the estimate of Laqueur, *Work*, p. 354.

13 Cox, *Grave Concerns*, p. 48.

14 Dentists: Bransby Blake Cooper, *The Life of Sir Astley Cooper, Bart., Interspersed with Sketches from His Note-Books of Distinguished Contemporary Characters* (London, John W. Parker, 1843), vol. 1, pp. 148, 401–2.

15 'Thing' is the word used by the resurrectionist who kept a brief diary, who may (or may not) have been Joseph Naples. One entry reads: 'Met together me & Butler went to Newington, thing bad' – that is, the body was too far decomposed to be sold. James Blake Bailey, *The Diary of a Resurrectionist, 1811–1812* (London, Swan Sonnenschein & Co., 1896), p. 152.

16 Richardson, *Death, Dissection*, pp. 81–3.

17 Cox, *Life and Death*, p. 107.

18 Cited in Matthews, *Poetical Remains*, p. 51.

19 Helen Macdonald, *Human Remains: Dissection and its Histories* (London, Yale University Press, 2006), pp. 11, 28.

20 Cooper, *Life*, vol. 1, pp. 395–6.

21 Ibid., pp. 341–4.

22 Ibid., p. 348.

23 Ibid., pp. 388–90.

24 Ibid., pp. 363–6, 368.

25 Brian Bailey, *The Resurrection Men: A History of the Trade in Corpses* (London, Macdonald, 1991), p. 88.

26 The resurrectionist who told parliament he raised a hundred bodies a year in a good year was identified as 'A.B.' Many think this was Ben Crouch, e.g. Bailey, *Resurrection Men*, p. 95. Sarah Wise, however, thinks A.B. might have been John Bishop, who gives the second set of figures here. Sarah Wise, *The Italian Boy: Murder and Grave-robbery in 1830s London* (London, Jonathan Cape, 2004), p. 36.

27 Anna Gasperini, *Nineteenth-century Popular Fiction, Medicine and Anatomy: The Victorian Penny Blood and the 1832 Anatomy Act* (Cham, Palgrave Macmillan/Springer Verlag, 2019), p. 11.

28 Richardson, *Death, Dissection*, pp. 197, 245–55, 271. The entire book needs to be read for its formidable range of research and analysis, and for its barely restrained fury at this act (and Act) of savagery against the weakest members of society by the most powerful. The Anatomy Act is, formally, 1832, Wm. IV c.75 2&3.

29 Robert Southey, 'The Surgeon's Warning' (1799), in *Robert Southey: Poetical Works, 1793–1810*, ed. Lynda Pratt; vol. 5: *Selected Shorter Poems, c.1793–1810* (Abingdon, Routledge, 2016).

30 Laqueur, *Work*, pp. 351–3.

31 Ford's diary, 13 March 1856, cited in Shonfield, *Precariously*, p. 5.

32 Macdonald, *Human*, pp. 14–15, 18.

33 Mary Shelley, *Frankenstein, or, The Modern Prometheus* (London, George Routledge and Sons, 1891), p. 74.

34 *Varney the Vampyre*, https://archive.org/details/VarneyTheVampyre/page/n5/mode/2up, chapter 77; Reynolds, *Mysteries*, vol. 3, p. 54.

35 A piece of Burke's skin was given to an assistant after his dissection; another was used to bind a book, owned by the Edinburgh Royal College of Surgeons; other criminals, like William Corder, also had their skin used to bind books. Laqueur, *Work*, p. 356; Menefee and Simpson, 'The West Port Murders', p. 78; see also the catalogues of the Wellcome Collection, which contains remains of both Jeremy Bentham and William Burke; and the Science Museum, inv. A667469.

36 Cited in Isabel Raphael, 'Southwood Smith: His Extraordinary Life and Family', *Camden History Review*, vol. 33, 2009, p. 6.

37 Thomas Hardy, for one, aged nine in 1856, cited in Beth Kalikoff, 'The Execution of Tess d'Urberville at Wintoncester', in William B. Thesing, ed., *Executions and the British Experience from the 17th to the 20th Century: A Collection of Essays* (Jefferson, NC, McFarland, 1990), p. 111; see also James Dawson Burn, *The Autobiography of a Beggar Boy*, ed. David Vincent ([1855], London, Europa, 1978), pp. 40–41; James Hopkinson, *Victorian Cabinet Maker. The Memoirs of James Hopkinson, 1819–1894*, ed. Jocelyne Baty Goodman (London, Routledge & Kegan Paul, 1968), p. 9.

38 Marjory Fleming, *The Complete Marjory Fleming: Her Journals, Letters & Verses*, ed. Frank Sidgwick (London, Sidgwick and Jackson, 1934), pp. 3, 87–8.

39 Owen Davies and Francesca Matteoni, *Executing Magic in the Modern Era: Criminal Bodies and the Gallows in Popular Medicine* (Cham, Switzerland, Palgrave Macmillan, 2017), pp. 65–6; Richardson, *Death, Dissection*, p. 53. Warts and growths: Mabel Peacock, 'Executed Criminals and Folk-Medicine', *Folklore*, vol. 7, no. 3, 1896, pp. 268–9; teeth: Francesca Matteoni, 'The Criminal Corpse in Pieces', *Mortality*, vol. 21, no. 3, 2016, p. 201.

40   Tarlow, *Golden,* pp. 104–12; Steve Pool, '"For the Benefit of Example":
     Crime Scene Executions in England, 1720–1830', in Richard Ward, ed., *A
     Global History of Execution and the Criminal Corpse* (Basingstoke, Palgrave
     Macmillan, 2015), pp. 78–83.

41   Sarah Tarlow and Zoe Dyndor, 'The Landscape of the Gibbet', *Landscape
     History,* vol. 36, no. 1, 2015, pp. 59–60.

42   Albert Hartshorne, *Hanging in Chains* (London, T. Fisher Unwin,
     1891), p. 73; Tarlow and Dyndor, 'Landscape', p. 76; Tarlow, *Golden,*
     pp. 34–5.

43   Tarlow and Dyndor, 'Landscape', pp. 74–8; Tarlow, *Golden,* p. 90.

44   William Carleton, *The Autobiography of William Carleton* ([1896],
     London, MacGibbon & Kee, 1968), pp. 114, 117. It is he who reports a
     man gibbeted 'within a couple of hundred yards of his own mother's
     door', the executed man being the local schoolmaster, parish clerk,
     Sunday school teacher and the perpetrator of a Ribbonman massacre.

45   Tarlow and Dyndor, 'Landscape', p. 83; Davies, *Haunted,* p. 53.

46   Wordsworth, *The Prelude, or, Growth of a Poet's Mind* (London, Edward
     Moxon, 1850), p. 327.

11 THE NON-DEAD AND THE UNDEAD

1   Reynolds, *Mysteries,* vol. 1, p. 11.

2   Clara Reeve, *The Old English Baron,* ed. James Trainer, intro. James Watt
     ([1778], Oxford, Oxford University Press, 2003).

3   Sigmund Freud, 'The Uncanny', *The Standard Edition of the Complete
     Psychological Works of Sigmund Freud;* vol. 17: *An Infantile Neurosis and
     Other Works (1917–1919),* trs. and ed. James Strachey, with Anna Freud;
     assisted by Alix Strachey and Alan Tyson (London, Vintage/Hogarth
     Press, 2001), pp. 222–5.

4   Charles Dickens, *A Christmas Carol, in Prose, being, A Ghost Story of
     Christmas* (London, Bradbury and Evans, [n.d.]), p. 1.

5   Dickens, *Our Mutual Friend* (London, Chapman and Hall, 1865) vol. 1,
     p. 38.

6   Davies, *Haunted,* p. 126.

7   Dickens, *A Christmas Carol,* p. 27.

8   Shane McCorristine, *Spectres of the Self: Thinking about Ghosts and
     Ghost-seeing in England, 1750–1920* (Cambridge, Cambridge University
     Press, 2010), p. 35.

9   [Charlotte Brontë], *Jane Eyre: An Autobiography,* 'edited by Currer Bell'
     (Leipzig, Bernhard Tauchnitz Jun., 1848), vol. 2, p. 1.

10   Cited in Davies, *Haunted,* p. 122.

11   Cited in Melissa Edmundson Makala, *Women's Ghost Literature in*

Nineteenth-century Britain (Cardiff, University of Wales Press, 2013), p. 73.

12   The story of Morell Theobald is told by himself in *Spirit Workers in the Home Circle: An Autobiographic Narrative of Psychic Phenomena in Family Daily Life, Extending over a Period of Twenty Years* (London, T. Fisher Unwin, 1887) and in 'Spiritualism at Home. Read before the London Spiritualist Alliance, June 10th, 1884' (London, E.W. Allen, [1884]). A modern account can be found in Alex Owen, *The Darkened Room: Women, Power and Spiritualism in Late Nineteenth-century England* (London, Virago, 1989), pp. 76ff.; and the business side of Theobald's life: Roy A. Chandler and Louise Macniven, 'The Unusual Tale of an Auditing Spiritualist', *Accounting History*, vol. 19, no. 3, 2014, pp. 333–49.

13   Cited in Janet Oppenheim, *The Other World: Spiritualism and Psychical Research in England, 1850–1914* (Cambridge, Cambridge University Press, 1985), p. 39.

14   Anthony Enns, 'The Undead Author: Spiritualism, Technology and Authorship', in Tatiana Kontou and Sarah Willburn, eds., *The Ashgate Research Companion to Nineteenth-century Spiritualism and the Occult* (Farnham, Ashgate, 2012), pp. 60–61.

15   McCorristine, *Spectres*, pp. 2, 147ff.

16   Matthews, *Poetical Remains*, pp. 254–5.

17   Cited in Owen, *Darkened*, p. 53.

18   Enns, 'Undead Author', in Kontou and Willburn, *Ashgate*, p. 63.

19   Kate Retford, 'A Death in the Family: Posthumous Portraiture in Eighteenth-century England', *Art History*, vol. 22, no. 1, 2010, pp. 75–6; Michael Benton, 'Hogarth's Children: Images of Temporality and Transience', *The Journal of Aesthetic Education*, vol. 52, no. 3, p. 13.

20   Cited in Helen Groth, *Victorian Photography and Literary Nostalgia* (Oxford, Oxford University Press, 2003), p. 1. Honoré de Balzac, *Cousin Pons* (Boston, Roberts Brothers, 1886), p. 156.

21   Louis Kaplan, *The Strange Case of William Mumler, Spirit Photographer* (Minneapolis, University of Minnesota Press, 2008), p. 24.

22   Clément Chéroux, et al., *The Perfect Medium: Photography and the Occult*, trs. Trista Selous (New Haven, Yale University Press, 2005), pp. 20–1, 34, 63.

23   Miss [Georgiana] Houghton, *Chronicles of the Photographs of Spiritual Beings and Phenomena Invisible to the Material Eye, Interblended with Personal Narratives* (London, E.W. Allen, 1882), pp. 4, 9.

24   The story of Florence Cook has been thoroughly researched. See: Jill Galvan, *The Sympathetic Medium: Feminine Channeling, the Occult and Communication Technologies, 1859–1919* (Ithaca, New York, Cornell University Press, 2010), p. 10; Rolf H. Krauss, *Beyond Light and Shadow: The Role of Photography in Certain Paranormal Phenomena: A Historical*

Survey (Munich, Nazraeli Press, 1995), pp. 117–20; Owen, *Darkened Room*, p. 55, 170–73; Marlene Tromp, *Altered States: Sex, Nation, Drugs and Self-Transformation in Victorian Spiritualism* (Albany, State University of New York Press, 2006), pp. 36–46. Haweis: Andrew Glendinning, ed., *The Veil Lifted: Modern Developments in Spirit Photography* (London, Whittaker & Co., 1894), pp. 76–7.

25 Samuel Johnson, *The Idler*, 24 February 1759, p. 45.

26 Andreas Höfele, 'The Rage of Caliban: Dorian Gray and the Gothic Body', in Elisabeth Bronfen and Beate Neumeier, eds., *Gothic Renaissance: A Reassessment* (Manchester, Manchester University Press, 2014), p. 249.

27 Kilvert, *Diary*, vol. 2, p. 95.

28 Ellis Bell [Emily Brontë], *Wuthering Heights*, and Acton Bell [Anne Brontë], *Agnes Grey*, a new edition (London, Smith, Elder & Co., 1858), p. 280.

29 Bram Stoker, *Dracula* (London, Archibald Constable & Co., 1899), p. 18.

30 Robert Tracy: 'Loving You All Ways: Vamps, Vampires, Necrophiles and Necrofilles in Nineteenth-century Fiction', in Regina Barreca, *Sex and Death in Victorian Literature* (Basingstoke, Macmillan, 1990), p. 38.

12 FROM THE BOY WHO NEVER GREW UP TO THE WOMAN WHO LIVED WITH THE DEAD

1 It is Ayesha. H. Rider Haggard, *She: A History of Adventure* (London, Longmans, Green and Co., 1911), p. 90.

2 This was reported by Lord Derby to Lord Hardinge: Wolffe, *Great Deaths*, pp. 30–31.

3 Cited in Sinnema, *Wake*, p. 69.

4 Cited in Elizabeth Longford, *Queen Victoria: Born to Succeed* (New York, Pyramid, 1966), p. 310.

5 Adrienne Munich, *Queen Victoria's Secrets* (New York, Columbia University Press, 1996), pp. 88–9.

6 Cited in Elizabeth Darby and Nicola Smith, *The Cult of the Prince Consort* (New Haven, Yale University Press, 1983), p. 4.

7 Munich, *Secrets*, p. 81.

8 Jenner cited in Jalland, *Death in the Victorian Family*, p. 320. Footnote: Most of this checklist can be found in M. Katherine Shear, et al., 'Complicated Grief and Related Bereavement Issues for DSM-t', *Depression and Anxiety*, vol. 28, no. 2, 2011, pp. 103–17, https://www.ncbi. nlm.nih.gov/pmc/articles/PMC3075805/, accessed 15 June 2022; poor fatherless baby: Victoria's journal, cited by Jane Ridley, 'Bertie Prince of Wales: Prince Hal and the Widow of Windsor', in Frank Lorenz Müller

and Heidi Mehrkens, eds., *Royal Heirs and the Uses of Soft Power in Nineteenth-century Europe* (London, Palgrave Macmillan, 2016), p. 125.

9   Darby and Smith, *Cult*, p. 20.

10   Ibid., p. 81.

11   Ibid., pp. 83, 86–7.

12   Strasdin, *Dress Diary*, p. 33.

13   Cited in Munich, *Secrets*, p. 82.

14   Jane Carlyle, *Carlyle Letters*, 17 March 1863, carlyleletters.dukeupress.edu/home, accessed 26 January 2021.

15   Cited in Munich, *Secrets*, p. 99.

16   Ibid., p. 90.

17   'A Member of the Royal Household', *The Private Life of the Queen* (New York, D. Appleton, 1897), p. 114.

18   Weintraub, *Uncrowned*, epilogue.

19   *Private Life*, p. 117.

20   Ibid., p. 60.

21   Marie Mallet, *Life with Queen Victoria: Marie Mallet's Letters from Court, 1887–1901*, ed. Victor Mallet (London, John Murray, 1968), pp. 44, 50, 52, 122, 166 for a range of examples.

22   Cited in Ridley, 'Bertie Prince of Wales', in Müller and Mehrkens, *Royal Heirs*, p. 127.

Index

Numbers in **bold** refer to pages with illustrations.